Encyclopedia of Place Names in the United States

HENRY GANNETT

JUERGEN BECK

Encyclopedia of Place Names in the US, H. Gannett, J. Beck

Jazzybee Verlag Jürgen Beck

86450 Altenmünster, Loschberg 9

Deutschland

ISBN: 9783849675103

www.jazzybee-verlag.de

admin@jazzybee-verlag.de

Printed by Createspace, North Charleston, SC, USA

CONTENTS:

INTRODUCTION.

ACKNOWLEDGMENTS.

During the compilation of this work, a large correspondence was carried on with State and local historical societies, State, county, and township officers, and individuals in all parts of the country for the purposes of obtaining information concerning the subject in hand.

The greatest interest was shown and much work done by correspondents, who have thus contributed very largely to the work. Much valuable material was collected in this way which otherwise would have been unavailable.

Among my correspondents, special thanks are due to the following persons and organizations: Thomas M. Owen, Department of Archives and History, Montgomery, Alabama, for valuable references.

C. M. Drake, of Eureka, California, for information concerning names in Monterey and Humboldt counties.

The Bureau of American Ethnology, to which I am especially indebted, not only for much information concerning Indian names, but for guidance, advice, and suggestions in obtaining sources of information. Indeed, most of the information concerning the meaning of Indian names is derived, either directby or indirectly, from this source.

William N. Bvers, of Denver, Colorado, for additions and corrections to county names.

Otis Ashmore, Georgia Historical Society, Savannah, Georgia, for revising list of counties.

C. J. Bassett, Secretaiy of State, Boise, Idaho, for revising and adding to list of counties.

J. P. Dunn, Indiana Historical Society, Indianapolis, Indiana, for additions and corrections to list of counties.

George W. Martin, Kansas State Historical Society, for much valuable material concerning the place names of his State. In addition to the list of counties he also sent a great deal of material concerning town names, in which was included information furnished by Mrs. N. R. Calver, of Hagerstown, Maryland.

Charles Evans, Chicago Historical Society, who sent a comprehensive list embracing most of the important names in his State.

M. W. Davis, State Historical Society, Iowa City, Iowa, for much valuable information about his State. All of the information concerning town names in this State was received from him.

Mrs. Jennie C. Morton, Kentucky Historical Society, Frankfort, Kentucky, for additions to and revisions of names of counties.

William Beer, Howard Memorial Library, New Orleans, Louisiana, for helpful references and suggestions.

Grace King, Louisiana Historical Society, New Orleans, Louisiana, for additions and corrections to parish names.

Francis E. Sparks, Maryland Historical Society, Baltimore, Maryland, for valuable information regarding names of counties.

Samuel A. Green, Massachusetts Historical Society, Boston, Massachusetts, for references which proved of great assistance in compiling information concerning the State.

C. M. Burton, Michigan Historical Society, Detroit, Michigan, for assistance in collecting information. Mr. Burton went to much trouble to get information concerning the names of towns in his State, which resulted in adding much material to that branch of the work.

Franklin L. Riley, Mississippi Historical Society, University, Mississippi, for information concerning town names in his State.

Marjory Dawson, Missouri Historical Society, St. Louis, Missouri, for nearly all of the information here presented concerning her State.

Mrs. Laura E. Howey, Montana Historical Library, Helena, Montana, for data concerning county and town names in the State.

Eugene Howell, by A. W. Morris, Deputy, Department of State, Carson City, Nevada, for correcting list of names of counties.

William Nelson, New Jersey Historical Society, Paterson, New Jersey, for references, for revision of names of counties and a valuable list of town names.

E. Tuttle, Long Island Historical Society, Brooklyn, New York, for list of town names.

Julius Schoonmaker, Kingston, New York, great assistance concerning town names.

F. J. H. Merrill, Historical and Art Society, Albany, New York, for names of towns in the State.

Robert H. Kelly, New York Historical Society, for additions and corrections to list of counties.

J. W. Raynolds, Secretary of New Mexico, for corrections and additions to list of counties.

N. F. Carter, New Hampshire Historical Society, for valuable references.

Kemp P. Battle, Department of History, Chapel Hill, North Carolina, for complete list of town names.

E. F. Porter, Secretary of State, Bismarck, North Dakota, for many additions to list of counties. Nearly all the information concerning county names in this State was furnished by him.

John W. Jordan, Historical Society of Pennsylvania, Philadelphia, Pennsylvania, for much valuable aid. Names of counties, town, and natural features were sent by him.

Clarence S. Brigham, Rhode Island Historical Society, for numerous references concerning names in his State.

A. S. Salley, South Carolina Historical Society, Charleston, South Carolina, for much material of value in connection with the State names. Complete lists of county and town names were sent by him, and information not otherwise available was added to that concerning his State.

Doane Robinson, Department of History, Sioux Falls, South Dakota, for names of counties and many town names.

Charles P. Garrison, Texas Historical Society, Austin, Texas, for list of town names.

Joseph A. De Boer, Vermont Historical Society, Montpelier, Vermont, for list of county and town names.

John M. Comstock, Chelsea, Vermont, list of town names in Orange County.

Virginia Historical Society, corrected list of names of counties.

Edward N. Fuller, Washington Historical Society, Tacoma, Washington, for references and other assistance.

J. P. Hale, Historical and Antiquarian Society, Charleston, West Virginia, for material in the shape of county and town lists.

R. G. Thwaites, State Historical Society of Wisconsin, Madison, Wisconsin, for much material, valuable suggestions, and references, especially in the way of putting me into communication with other sources of information.

Mrs. E. W. Parker, for county names in Texas. Through her courtesy and kindness were obtained the origins of nearly all the county names of that State.

In addition to the above, many courteous and useful letters have been received from county clerks, treasurers, and other State and county officials, all of whom have shown interest and have furnished all the material in their power.

A large amount of material has been drawn from manuscript books compiled by Mr. Watkins, of Beaver, Pennsylvania.

AUTHORITIES.

Information was obtained from the following books, two and three authorities being quoted in cases where differing opinions exist concerning origins:

INDIAN NAMES.

The Aboriginal Races of North America, by Samuel G. Drake; fifteenth edition, revised by Prof. H. L. Williams.

The American Indian, by Elijah M. Haines, 1888.

League of the Iroquois, by L. H. Morgan, 1857.

Indian Local Names, with their Interpretations, by S. G. Boyd, 1885.

Algonquin Series, by W. W. Tooker.

The Story of the Indian, by George Bird Grinnell.

The Siouan Tribes of the East, by James Mooney: Bureau of American Ethnology, Bulletin 22.

Indian Linguistic Families of America North of Mexico, by J. W. Powell: Seventh Annual Report Bureau of American Ethnology, pp. 1-142.

The Ghost-dance Religion and the Sioux Outbreak of 1890, by James Mooney: Fourteenth Annual Report Bureau of American Ethnology, pp. 641-1110.

Calendar History of the Kiowa Indians, by James Mooney: Seventeenth Annual Report Bureau of American Ethnology, pp. 129-445.

Tribes of the Extreme Northwest, by W. H. Dall: Contributions to North American Ethnology, Vol. I.

Vocabularies of Tribes of the Extreme Northwest, by W. H. Dall: Contributions to North American Ethnology, Vol. I, pp. 121-153.

Cherokee Nation of Indians, by Charles C. Royce: Fifth Annual Report of the Bureau of American Ethnology, pp. 121-378.

The Menomini Indians, by W. J. Hoffman: Fourteenth Annual Report Bureau of American Ethnology, pp. 3-328.

Klamath Indians of Southwestern Oregon, by Albert Samuel Gatschet: Contributions to North American Ethnology, Vol. H, 1890.

The Seminole Indians of Florida, by Clay MacCauley: Fifth Annual Report Bureau of Ethnology, pp. 469-531.

Tribes of California, by Stephen Powers: Contributions to American Ethnology, Vol. III.

Dakota-English Dictionary, by Stephen R. Riggs: Contributions to American Ethnology, Vol. II.

Pamunkey Indians of Virginia, by John Garland Pollard: Bureau of American Ethnology, Bulletin 17.

Tribes of Western Washington, by George Gibbs: Contributions to North American Ethnology, Vol. I, pp. 157-241.

INDIVIDUAL STATES.

ALABAMA.

History of Alabama, Georgia, and Mississippi, by Albert James Pickett.

ARKANSAS.

A Journal of Travels into the Arkansas Territory, by Thomas Nuttall, 1821.

Some Old French Place Names in the State of Arkansas, by John C. Brauner.

CALIFORNIA.

History of the State of California, by John Frost.

History of the State of California, by Miguel Venegas.

Report of Exploring Expedition to Oregon and California, 1843-44, by John Charles Fremont: Senate Doc, Twenty-eighth Congress, second session.

History of Oregon and California, by Robert Greenhow, 1845.

CONNECTICUT.

Gazetteer of Connecticut and Rhode Island. by J. C. Pease and J. M. Niles, 1819.

Indian Names of Places in Connecticut, by J. H. Trumbull.

Connecticut Historical Collections, by J. W. Barber, 1849.

FLORIDA.

Gazetteer of Florida, by Adiel Sherwood.

Handbook of Florida, by Charles Ledyard Norton, 1890.

GEORGIA.

Gazetteer of Georgia, by Adiel Sherwood, 1829.

History of Georgia, by William Bacon Stevens.

History of Alabama, Georgia, and Mississippi, by Albert James Pickett.

INDIANA.

Indiana Gazetteer or Topographical Dictionary, published by E. Chamberlain, 1849.

History of Indiana to 1856, by John B. Dillon, 1859.

Indiana, by J. P. Dunn.

KENTUCKY.

Historical Sketches of Kentucky, by Lewis Collins, 1848.

LOUISIANA.

A description of Louisiana, by Father Louis Hennepin, translated from the edition of 1683, and compiled with Nouvelle Decouverte, the La Salle Documents, and other contemporaneous papers, by John Gilmary Shea, 1880.

MAINE.

History of Maine to 1842, by George J. Varney, 1873.

Gazetteer of Maine, by N. E. Hayward.

History of Maine, 1602-1820, by W. D. Williamson, 1832.

Collections of the Maine Historical Society, 1847-1859. (In seven volumes.)

MASSACHUSETTS.

Gazetteer of the State of Massachusetts, by Rev. Elias Nason, 1874.

Historical Collections relating to every town in Massachusetts, by John Warner Barber, 1846.

Gazetteer of Massachusetts, by J. Hayward, 1847.

The Indian Names of Boston and Their Meaning, by Eben Norton Hosford: New England Historical and Genealogical Register, Vol. XL, 1886, pp. 94-103.

Massachusetts Historical Society Proceedings, Vol. XH, 1873.

MICHIGAN.

Gazetteer of Michigan, by John T. Blois, 1840.

Memorials of a Half Century in Michigan and the Lake Region, by Bela Hubbard.

MISSISSIPPI.

A history of Mississippi from the Discovery of the Great River by Hernando de Soto, including the Earliest Settlements made by the French under Iberville to the Death of Jefferson, by Robert Lowry and William H. McCardle.

Mississippi River, by Henry R. Schoolcraft.

History of Alabama, Georgia, and Mississippi, by Albert James Pickett.

NEW JERSEY.

Gazetteer of New Jersey, by Thomas F. Gordon, 1834.

Historical Collections of New Jersey, by J. W. Barber and H. Howe.

Indian Names in New Jersey, by T. Gordon: Historical Collections of the State of New Jersey, 1844, p. 512.

NEW HAMPSHIRE.

Gazetteer of New Hampshire, by Alonzo J. Fogg.

New Hampshire State Papers.

New Hampshire Town Papers.

Manual of the Court of New Hampshire.

Gazetteer of New Hampshire, by J. Hayward, 1849.

Gazetteer of New Hampshire, by J. Farmer and J. B. Moore, 1823.

NEW MEXICO.

Historical Sketches of New Mexico, by Le Baron Bradford Prince, 1883.

Doniphan's Expedition, by John T. Hughes, 1849.

NEW YORK.

History of the State of New York, 1609-1664, by John Romeyn Brodhead.

Gazetteer of New York, by Thomas F. Gordon, 1836.

Gazetteer of New York, by Horatio Gates Spafford, 1813.

New York State Register, by Orville Luther Holley, 1843.

History of Lewis County, 1860.

History of St. Lawrence and Franklin counties, by Franklin B. Hough.

New York State Register, by John Disturnell, 1858.

Historical Collections of New York, 1524-1845, by J. W. Barber and H. Howe, 1845.

History of the Late Province of New York to 1732, by W. Smith, 1757.

OHIO.

Gazetteer of Ohio, by John Kilbourn, 1821.

Pioneer History of Ohio, by S. P. Hildreth.

Biographical and Historical Memoirs of the Early Pioneer Settlers of Ohio, by S. P. Hildreth.

Historical Collections of Ohio, by Henry Howe. 3 volumes in 2. 1889, 1891.

Ohio Gazetteer, by Warren Jenkins, 1837.

OREGON.

History of Oregon, by Hubert Howe Bancroft, 1886.

Report of the Exploring Expedition to Oregon and North California, 1843-44, by John Charles Fremont: Senate Doc, Twenty-eighth Congress, second session.

History of Oregon and California, by Robert Greenhow, 1845.

Oregon; the Struggle for Possession, by William Barrows, 1884.

Mountains of Oregon, by W. G. Steel.

Tribes of Western Washington and Northwestern Oregon, by George Gibbs: Contributions to American Ethnology", Vol. I, 1877, pp. 157-241.

PENNSYLVANIA.

Historical Collections of Pennsylvania (1680-1778). by S. Day, 1843.

History of Pennsylvania to 1776, by Thomas F. Gordon, 1829.

RHODE ISLAND.

Gazetteer of Rhode Island, by Pease and Niles.

Rhode Island Historical Society Proceedings, 1886-87, pp. 42-51.

Indian Names of Places in Rhode Island, by U. Parsons, 1861.

Gazetteer of Connecticut and Rhode Island, by J. C. Pease and J. M. Niles, 1819.

SOUTH CAROLINA.

Historical Collections of South Carolina, by B. R. Carroll, 1836.

Documents Connected with the History of South Carolina, by P. C. J. Weston.

Collections of the South Carolina Historical Society, Vols. I-V, 1857-1897.

VERMONT.

Vermont Historical Gazetteer, by A. B. Hemenway, 1867-1871.

VIRGINIA.

Historical Collections of Virginia (Virginia Historical Society publications).

History of Virginia to 1754, by W. II. Brockenbrough. (In History of Virginia, by Joseph Martin, 1835.)

TENNESSEE.

History of Tennessee; the Making of a State, by James Phelan.

UTAH.

Exploration and Survey of the Valley of the Great Salt Lake of Utah, by Howard Stansbury: Senate Ex. Doc. No. 3, special session, March, 1851.

WASHINGTON.

Tribes of Western Washington and Northwestern Oregon, by George Gibbs: Contribution to American Ethnology, Vol. I, 1877, pp. 157-241.

History of Washington, by Elwood Evans.

MISCELLANEOUS.

Canoe Voyage up the Minnay Sotor, by George William Featherstonehaugh.

Astoria, by Washington Irving.

Henry-Thompson Journals, by Elliot Coues.

The Expeditions of Zebulon Montgomery Pike, by Elliot Coues. 3 volumes. 1895.

History of the Expedition under Lewis and Clarke, by Elliot Coues (Philadelphia American Philosophical Society, pp. 17-33), 1893.

Account of an Expedition from Pittsburg to the Rocky Mountains under the Command of Maj. Stephen H. Long. Compiled by Edwin James, 3 volumes, 1823.

Narrative of an Expedition to the Source of St. Peters River, Lake Winnepeek, Lake of the Woods, etc., under the Command of Stephen H. Long, by William H. Keating, 2 volumes, 1825.

The Adventures of Captain Bonneville, or Scenes beyond the Rocky Mountains and the Far West, by Washington Irving, 1850.

Yellowstone Park, by H. M. Chittenden.

Geographic Names as Monuments of History: Transactions of the Oneida Historical Society, No. 5, 1889-1892.

Report of Reconnaissance of Northwestern Wyoming, including the Yellowstone Park, in 1873, by William A. Jones, 1875.

Exploration of the Colorado River of the West, by J. W. Powell, 1875.

Report upon the Colorado River of the West, by Joseph C. Ives: Thirty-sixth Congress, Senate document.

Excursion to the Grand Canyon of the Colorado, by W. M. Davis.

Colorado Exploring Expedition, by Joseph C. Ives: War Department, Office Explorations and Surveys, pp. 31-42, 1859.

THE NAMES AND THEIR ORIGIN.

A

Aaronsburg; town in Center County, Pennsylvania, named for Aaron Levy, who laid it out in 1786.

Abahtacook; creek in Maine, branch of the Matamiscontis River. An Indian word, meaning " a stream that runs parallel with a big river." Abajo; mountains in Utah. A Spanish word, meaning "low."

Abauaka; village in Van Wert County, Ohio, named from an Indian tribe. The word means "the east land."

Abaquage; pond near the source of Little River, Connecticut. An Indian word, meaning "flaggy meadow."

Abbeville; county and town in same county, South Carolina, settled and named by immigrants from France, for the French town of that name.

Abbot; town in Piscataquis County, Maine, named for Prof. John Abbot, treasurer of Bowdoin College.

Abbotsford; village in St. Clair County, Michigan, named from the home of Sir Walter Scott.

Abbott; village in Arapahoe County, Colorado, named for Albert F. Abbott, who platted it.

Abbottstown; town in Adams County, Pennsylvania, named for John Abbott, who laid it out in 1753.

Aberdeen; town in Moore County, North Carolina, city in Monroe County, Mississippi, and numerous other places, named from the city in Scotland.

Abert; lake in Oregon, named for Col. J. J. Abert, of the topographical engineers, United States Army.

Abiathar; peak in Yellowstone Park, named for Charles Abiathar White, of the United States Geological Survey.

Abilene; city in Dickinson County, Kansas, and village in Charlotte County, Virginia, named from the province of ancient Syria. The word means " a grassy plain."

Abilene; city in Taylor County, Texas, named from the city in Kansas.

Abingdon; city in Knox County, Illinois, town in Washington County, Virginia, and several other places, named from a borough in Berkshire, England.

Abington; town in Plymouth County, Massachusetts, and several other places, named from a parish of Cambridgeshire, England.

Ableman; village in Sauk County, Wisconsin, named for Col. S. V. R. Ableman, who settled there in 1851.

Abocadneticook; creek in Maine, branch of the Penobscot River. An Indian word, meaning "a stream narrowed by the mountains."

Aboljackarmegas; creek in Maine, branch of the Penobscot River, at the foot of Mount Katahdin. An Indian word, meaning "bare or bold."

Abrigada; hill in Waterbury, Connecticut, having on its side a deep cavern-like cliff called the "Indian House," whence the name, which is an Indian word, meaning "shelter or hiding place."

Absaroka; range of mountains in Wyoming, named from the native name of the Crow Indians. Grinnell says the word refers to some kind of a bird, possibly crows.

Absecon; bay and town in Atlantic County, New Jersey. The name is derived from the Indian words wabisse, "swan," and ong, "a place," and was given because of the numbers of swans which resorted there.

Acabonack; harbor in Long Island. An Indian word, meaning "root place," applied to the harbor from the meadows near, where the Indians found roots which they prized.

Acadia; parish in Louisiana, and villages in Aroostook County, Maine, and Lee County, Virginia, named from the original name of Nova Scotia. Acadians emigrated to Louisiana and gave the name to the parish. The word is the French form of the Indian word kadi, meaning "the region," "the land."

Acampo; village in San Joaquin County, California. A Spanish word, meaning "a portion of common given to herds for pasture."

Accomac; county and village in same county, in Virginia. An Indian word, the meaning of which is given by some authorities as "on the other side," by others, "the limit of the woodland."

Acequia; village in Douglas County, Colorado. A Spanish word, meaning "canal or channel."

Aceyedan; creek in Iowa. An Indian word, meaning "the place of weeping." The name was given by the Indians upon the occasion of the death of some relatives.

Achor; village in Columbiana County, Ohio, named from the valley of the Scriptures.

Ackerman; town in Choctaw County, Mississippi, named for a landowner.

Ackley; town in Hardin County, Iowa, laid out in 1857 by J. W. Ackley.

Acme; village in Grand Traverse County, Michigan. A Greek word, meaning "a point."

Acquackanonk; township in Passaic County, New Jersey. An Indian word, meaning "where gum blocks were made, or procured, for pounding corn."

Acquehadongonock; point in Maine. Indian word, said to mean "Smoked Fish Point."

Acton; town in York County, Maine, named from Acton, Massachusetts, in honor of the citizens of that town, originally a part of Concord, who took part in the battle of Concord.

Acton; town in Middlesex County, Massachusetts, named from the town in Middlesex County, England.

Acton; town in Meeker County, Minnesota. An Indian word, meaning "more than."

Acushnet; town and river in Bristol County, Massachusetts. The name of the Indian village which stood upon the spot where New Bedford now stands.

Acworth; town in Sullivan County, New Hampshire, named in honor of Lord Ac worth.

Ada; county in Idaho, named for the eldest daughter of H. C. Riggs.

Ada; town in Kent County, Michigan, named for the daughter of Sidney Smith.

Adair; counties in Iowa, Kentucky, and Missouri; Adairville; town in Logan County, Kentucky. Named for Gen. John Adair, governor of Kentucky.

Adams; counties in Iowa, Ohio, Pennsylvania, Mississippi, and Washington, peak of the White Mountains in New Hampshire, mountain in Washington, and point at the mouth of the Columbia River in Oregon, village in Herkimer County and town in Jefferson County, New York, named for President John Adams.

Adams; counties in Illinois, Indiana, and Wisconsin, named for President John Quincy Adams.

Adams; town in Berkshire County, Massachusetts, named for Samuel Adams.

Adams; village in Gage County, Nebraska, named for an early settler, J. O. Adams.

Adams; town in Robertson County, Tennessee, named for the owner of the town site, Reuben Adams.

Adams, J. Q.; peak in New Hampshire, named for President John Quincy Adams.

Adamsboro; village in Cass County, Indiana, named for George E. Adams, its founder.

Adamsburg; borough in Westmoreland County, Pennsylvania; Adamstown; borough in Lancaster County, Pennsylvania. Said to have been named for President John Adams.

Addison; town in Steuben County, New York, county and town in Vermont, town in Washington County, Maine, and township in Somerset County, Pennsylvania, named for the celebrated English writer, Joseph Addison.

Addison; town in Webster County, West Virginia, named for Addison McLaughlin, a prominent lawyer.

Adel; town in Dallas County, Iowa. So named from its situation on a dell of North Raccoon River; formerly written Adell.

Adena; town in Jefferson County, Ohio, named for the home or country seat of the late Governor Worthington, of Ohio, which was in Ross County. The word means "paradise."

Adirondack; mountains in New York and village in Warren County, of the same State. Indian word compounded from doran, "a people who eat bark," and dak, "trees," with the French particle la prefixed.

Admiralty; inlet in Washington named by Vancouver, the English explorer, for incumbent in the Admiralty.

Adrian; city in Lenawee County, Michigan, named for the Roman Emperor Hadrian or Adrian.

Advance; village in Boone County, Indiana, so named because located in anticipation of the Midland Railroad.

Afton; town in Union County, Iowa, laid out in 1854 and named by Mrs. Baker, wife of one of the proprietors, from the little river in Scotland immortalized by Burns. Many other places bear the same name.

Agamenticus; mountain in York County, Maine. An Indian word meaning "on the other side of the river." Agassiz; mountains in New Hampshire and Arizona, named for Prof. Louis Agassiz.

Agate; bay in Lake Superior, Michigan, and creek in Yellowstone Park, so named from the agates found in them.

Agawam; river and town of Hampden County, Massachusetts. An Indian word meaning "lowland, marsh, or meadow."

Agency; town in Wapello County, Iowa, and village in Buchanan County, Missouri, named so because formerly Indian agencies.

Agua Caliente; villages in Maricopa County, Arizona, and Sonoma County, California, so named from warm springs in the vicinity. A Spanish name meaning "hot water."

Agua Dulce; creek in Texas. A Spanish name meaning "sweet water."

Agua Fria; valley in Yavapai County, Arizona. A Spanish name, meaning "cold water."

Agua Fria; peak and village in New Mexico. A Spanish name meaning " cold water." Ahiki; eastern tributary of the Chattahoochee River, Georgia. An Indian word, ahi-iki, meaning "sweet potato mother."

Aiken; county and town in South Carolina, named for William Aiken, governor of the State in 1844-1846.

Aikin; landing and swamp in Chesterfield County, Virginia, named for the late owner, Albert Aikin.

Ainsworth; town in Washington County, Iowa, named for D. H. Ainsworth, civil engineer.

Ainsworth; station on the Union Pacific Railroad in Franklin County, Washington, named for J. C. Ainsworth, a prominent western railroad man.

Aitkin; county and village in Minnesota, named for Samuel Aiken or Aitken, an old trapper and fur dealer.

Akron; village in Erie County, New York, named from the city in Ohio.

Akron; city in Summit County, Ohio, which occupies the highest ground in the northern part of the State, and several other places named for the same reason. A Greek word meaning "the summit or peak."

Alabama; State of the Union and a river of that State, named from an Indian tribe. There are several explanations of the meaning of the word. Gatchet gives "burnt clearing." Others say it means "here we rest." Haines, in his American Indian, gives "thicket clearers."

Alabaster; mount in Arkansas which has an eminence composed of alabaster.

Alabaster; post-office in Iosco County, Michigan, so named from its quarry of gypsum and manufactory of calcined plaster.

Alachua; county and town in Florida. An Indian word, the meaning of which is variously interpreted as Alachua savanna, "grassy, marshy plain," referring to a feature of this description in the county north of Lake Orange; or "place where water goes down," the "big jug."

Alamance; county and creek in North Carolina. The word is said to have been given by Germans, from Allamanca, who settled in the valley of the creek, which received the name first. Some authorities say it is of Indian origin.

Alameda; county and city in California, town in Bernalillo County, New Mexico, and post-office in Clarke County, Alabama, named from the Cottonwood trees growing in the vicinity. A Spanish word meaning "grove of poplar trees."

Alamo; post-office in Contra Costa County, California, and many other places named from the old fort in Texas, which was so called from a grove of cottonwood trees. A Spanish word meaning "poplar or cottonwood."

Alamogordo; city in Otero County, New Mexico. A Spanish word meaning "large poplar or cottonwood."

Alamooscok: pond in Hancock County, Maine, near Orland. An Indian word meaning "great dog place."

Alamosa; town of Conejos County and stream in Colorado. The stream was named by the early Spanish explorers, the town taking its name from the stream. A Spanish word meaning "shaded with elms," though cottonwood is the actual growth.

Alaqua; river and town of Walton County, Florida. An Indian word meaning "sweet gum."

Alaska; Territory of the United States. An Indian word meaning "great country," "continent," or "great land."

Albany; county and city in New York, named for the Duke of York, whose Scotch title was "Duke of Albany," afterwards James H of England. Many places named from the city.

Albemarle; county in Virginia, sound in North Carolina, and town in Stanly County, North Carolina, named for Gen. George Monk, Earl of Albemarle, one of the original proprietors.

Alberhill; railroad station and coal mine in Riverside County, California, named for the two owners of the mine, Messrs. Albers and Hill.

Albert Lea; city in Freeborn County, Minnesota, between two lakes, from one of which it derives its name. The lake was named for Lieut. Albert M. Lea, who explored the " Blackhawk purchase" and published an account of his explorations in 1836.

Albertville; town in Marshall County, Alabama, named for the first settler.

Albina; village, now a part of Portland, Oregon, named for the wife of Judge Page, of Portland.

Albion; town in Kennebec County, Maine, and many other places named from the ancient name of England.

Albuquerque; city in Bernalillo County, New Mexico, named for the Spanish Duke of Albuquerque, who visited this spot in 1703-1710.

Alburg; town in Grand Isle County, Vermont, named for Gen. Ira Allen, one of the original grantees.

Alcatraz; island and post-office in San Francisco County, California. A Spanish word, meaning "pelican."

Alcona; county and post-office in Michigan. Indian word, meaning "unknown."

Alcorn; county in Mississippi, named for James L. Alcorn, governor of the State in 1870-71.

Alden; town in Hardin County, Iowa, named for Henry Alden, who settled there in 1854.

Alden; town in Erie County, New York, named by one of its citizens for his wife's mother.

Alderson; town in Monroe County, West Virginia, named for Rev. John Alderson, pioneer settler.

Aleutian; islands in the Pacific Ocean. A derivation of the Russian word aleaut, meaning "bald rock."

Alexander; county in Illinois, named for Dr. William M. Alexander, a pioneer.

Alexander; village in Genesee County, New York, named for Alexander Rea, first settler and State senator.

Alexander; county in North Carolina. named for several prominent citizens: William J. Alexander, State solicitor; Gov. Nathaniel Alexander, and J. McNitt Alexander, secretary of the Mecklenburg Congress.

Alexander Lake; lake in Connecticut, named for Nell Alexander, who was owner of a large tract in the town of Killingly, Connecticut.

Alexandria; village in Thayer County, Nebraska, named for S. J. Alexander, secretary of state.

Alexandria; town in Jefferson County, New York; named for Alexander Le Ray, son of J. D. Le Ray, who fell in a duel in 1836.

Alexandria; county and city in Virginia, named for a prominent family of early settlers, of which Dr. Archibald Alexander was a distinguished member.

Alexandria Bay; bay and village in Jefferson County, New York; named for Alexander Le Ray.

Alford; town in Berkshire County, Massachusetts, named for Hon. John Alford, of Charlestown.

Alfordsville; village in Daviess County, Indiana, named for James Alford, who built the first house.

Alfred; town in York County, Maine, named for King Alfred of England.

Algansee: township and post-office in Branch County, Michigan; Indian word, meaning "the lake prairie, or the prairie resembling a lake."

Alger; county in Michigan and village in Hardin County, Ohio, named for Hon. Russell A. Alger, Secretary of War during McKinley's administration.

Algoma; city in Kewaunee County, Wisconsin, and places in several other States. Indian word formed from Algonquin and "maig," meaning "Algonquin waters."

Algona; city in Kossuth County, Iowa, and post-office in Jefferson County, New York. Indian word, meaning probably the same as "Algoma," "Algonquin waters." It is said to be the Indian name for Lake Superior.

Algonac; village in St. Clair County, Michigan. Indian word, by some said to mean "pertaining to the Algonquin language;" by others it is thought to be compounded for "Algonquin " and " auke," meaning " land of the Algons."

Algonquin; village in McHenry County, Illinois, post-offices in Franklin County, New York, and Carroll County, Ohio, named from the Indian tribe. The word means "people living on the other side of the stream."

Alhambra; village in Madison County, Illinois, post-office in Los Angeles County, California, and many other places named for the palace in Spain.

Aliquippa; borough in Beaver County, Pennsylvania, named for an Indian chief.

Alkali; creek in Montana, so named from the alkaline quality of the water.

Allagash; principal branch of St. Johns River, Maine, plantation and post-office in Aroostook County, Maine. An Indian word meaning "bark cabin lake." The Indians had a hunting camp near the headwaters of the river, hence the name.

Allamakee; county in Iowa. The Iowa Historical Society says it was named for Allen Makee, an Indian trader. Haines's "American Indian" gives allamakee, Algonquin Indian, meaning "thunder."

Allegan; county and village in Michigan, named from an Indian tribe. Haines says that this was the oldest tribe in the United States, and gives the derivation from sagiegan, "a lake."

Allegany; counties in Maryland and New York, and town in Cattaraugus County, of the latter State; post-office in Coos County, Oregon; Alleghany; counties in North Carolina and Virginia; "Allegheny; county, city, and river in Pennsylvania, and mountains in eastern United States. An Indian word variously spelled, the origin of which is in dispute. The most generally accepted derivation is from "welhikhanna," "the best, or "the fairest river."

Allemands; town in St. Charles Parish, Louisiana, situated on Bayou des Allemands, " bayou of the Germans." Allen; county in Indiana, named for Col. William Allen, of Kentucky.

Allen; county in Kansas, named for William Allen, United States Senator from Ohio, 1837-1849.

Allen; counties in Kentucky and Ohio, named for Col. John Allen, who fell at the battle of Raisin River, in the war of 1812.

Allendale; town in Barnwell County, South Carolina, named for the Allen family, prominent in that district.

Allenhill: post-office in Ontario County, New York, named for Nathaniel Allen, one of the first settlers.

Allenstown; town in Merrimack County, New Hampshire, named for Samuel Allen, to whose children the grant was made in 1722. He died while engaged in a lawsuit over the governorship.

Allentown; city in Lehigh County, Pennsylvania, and borough in Monmouth County, New Jersey, named for William Allen, of Pennsylvania, at one time chief justice of the province.

Alliance; town in Stark County, Ohio, because it was thought that two systems of railroads would form an alliance.

Alligator; river and swamp in North Carolina, so called from the number of alligators found there.

Alloway; township and creek in New Jersey, named for an Indian chief who resided upon it.

Allum; pond in Connecticut, named for a Quinebaug captain, called by the Pequot Indians "the fox." The Indian word allum means "fox, or fox pond."

Alma; town in Park County, Colorado, named by Mr. James, a merchant, for his wife.

Alma; city in Wabaunsee County, Kansas, named by Germans who settled it, from the city and battle of Alma, Germany.

Alma; city in Harlan County, Nebraska, named for the daughter of one of the first settlers.

Almaden; township in Santa Clara County, California, containing mines of mercury. These mines are named after the quicksilver mines in Spain.

Almont; village in Lapeer County, Michigan, named for the Mexican general, Almonte.

Alpena; county and city in Michigan, and village in Jerauld County, South Dakota. An Indian word, derived from penaise, "a bird."

Alpine; county in California, so named because of its mountainous surface, being traversed by the Sierra Nevada. Many places in the United States bear this name in reference to their elevation.

Alta; town in Buena Vista County, Iowa, situated upon the highest point between the Mississippi and Missouri rivers. A Latin word, meaning "high." Many other places bear this name in reference to their elevation.

Altamaha; river and post-office in Tattnall County, Georgia; Altamahaw; post-office in Alamance County, North Carolina. An Indian word, meaning "place of the village."

Altamont; town in Effingham County, Illinois, situated on the highest point between St. Louis and Terre Haute.

Altamont; post-office in Garrett County, Maryland, on the extreme summit of the Alleghenies. A Spanish word meaning "high mountains." Many other places bear the same name.

Alta Vista; village in Wabaunsee County, Kansas, so named by Rock Island Railroad officials because that road crosses the watershed between the Kansas and Neosho rivers at this point.

Alton; village in Humboldt County, California, named from the city in Illinois. Many other places are named from the same.

Alton; city in Madison County, Illinois, named by Rufus Easton, the founder, for his son.

Alton; town in Belknap County, New Hampshire, named from a place in England.

Altoona; city in Wilson County, Kansas, named from the city in Pennsylvania.

Altoona; city in Blair County, Pennsylvania, so named because of its high situation in the Allegheny Mountains, and town in Polk County, Iowa, situated on the highest point between the Des Moines and Mississippi rivers. A derivative of the Latin word altus, "high."

Alturas; town in Modoc County, California, so named from its mountains. A Spanish word, meaning "summits of mountains."

Alum; creek in Yellowstone Park. Characteristic, as the water is a strong solution of alum.

Alvarado; town in Alameda County, California, named for Juan B. Alvarado, Mexican governor of California.

Alvord; lake in Oregon, named for Gen. Benjamin Franklin Alvord, who was stationed there at one time.

Amador; county, town, and valley in California, named for Jose M. Amador, formerly manager of the property of the mission of San Jose.

Amakalli, tributary of Flint River, Mississippi. An Indian word, meaning "tumbling water."

Amalthea; village in Franklin County, Ohio, named for the nurse of Jupiter.

Amargosa; river in California. A Spanish word, meaning "bitter water."

Ambajeejus; lake, and falls in the Penobscot River, Maine. An Indian word, referring to the two large, round rocks in the lake, one on top of the other.

Ambajemackomas; fall in the Penobscot River, Maine. An Indian word, meaning "little cross pond."

Ambler; borough in Montgomery County, Pennsylvania, named for the Ambler family, of which Joseph Ambler, who settled there in 1723, was a member.

Amboy; towns in Lee County, Illinois, and Miami County, Indiana, and many other places. Indian word, meaning "hollow inside, like a bowl."

Amelia; county and town in Virginia, named for the Princess Amelia, youngest daughter of George H of England.

Amenia; town in Dutchess County, New York, named by an early scholar of the State, who also named the State of Vermont. A Latin word, meaning "pleasant, delightful, lovely."

America; the Western Hemisphere, named for Amerigo Vespucci, sometimes spelled Americus Vespucius, who touched the South American coast somewhere near

Surinam in 1499. The name was first used in 1509, and first appeared on a map made in Frankfort, Germany, in 1520.

American; river in California, so called by the Spanish, Rio de los Americanos, because most of the Americans entering California at the time the Spaniards ruled there, came down that river.

Ames; city in Story County, Iowa, named for Oakes Ames.

Ames; post-office in Montgomery County, New York, named for Fisher Ames.

Amesbury; town in Essex County, Massachusetts, named from an English town.

Amethyst; mountain in Yellowstone Park, so named by United States Geological Survey, from the crystalline amethysts formerly abundant on its broad summit.

Amethyst; creek in Yellowstone Park, so named by the United States Geological Survey because it flows from Amethyst Mountain.

Amherst; town in Hancock County, Maine, named from the town in New Hampshire.

Amherst; county in Virginia, and towns in Hillsboro County, New Hampshire, and Hampshire County, Massachusetts, named for Lord Jeffrey Amherst.

Amicalola; town in Dawson County, Georgia. An Indian word, meaning "tumbling or rolling water."

Amite; town in Tangipahoa Parish, Louisiana, named from a neighboring stream.

Amite; county and river in Mississippi. The French named the river in commemoration of the friendly manner in which they were received by the Indians.

Amity; town in Yamhill County, Oregon, so named as a result of the settlement of a neighborhood contention regarding the location of a schoolhouse in 1849. The schoolhouse was named first and the town took its name from the former.

Ammonoosuc; river in New Hampshire. An Indian word, interpreted by some to mean " stony fish place;" by others, " fish story river." Amo; towns in Hendricks County, Indiana, El Paso County, Colorado, and Cottonwood County, Minnesota. An Indian word, meaning "bee."

Amphitheater; creek in Yellowstone Park, named by the United States Geological Survey, from the form of a valley near its mouth.

Amsterdam; city in Montgomery County, New York, named by Emanuel E. De Graff, a Hollander and early settler, from the city in Holland. Several places in the United States are named from the city in New York.

Anacostia; village in the District of Columbia, named from an Indian tribe called Nacostines.

Anamosa; city in Jones County, Iowa. Some authorities say it was named for the daughter of Nasinus, an Indian chief. Haines gives the meaning "you walk from me." Another theory derives it from anamoosh, "dog," or "species of fox."

Anastasia; island off the coast of Florida, named by tha early Spanish explorers, St. Anastasia, for one of the numerous saints in the Catholic Church.

Ancona; town in Livingston County, Illinois, named from the city in Italy.

Andalusia; town in Covington County, Alabama; village in Rock Island County, Illinois, and post-offices in Bucks County, Pennsylvania, and Randolph County, Georgia, named from the ancient name of a province in Spain.

Anderson; city in Madison County, Indiana, named for the English name of a Delaware chief.

Anderson; county in Kansas, named for Joseph C. Anderson, member of the first Territorial legislature of Kansas.

Anderson; county in Kentucky, named for Richard C. Anderson, a former member of Congress.

Anderson; county and city in South Carolina, named for Col. Robert Anderson, Revolutionary soldier.

Anderson; county in Texas, named for Kenneth L. Anderson, vice-president of the Republic of Texas.

Anderson; island in Puget Sound, Washington, named for the surgeon of the ship Resolution, who died just before its discovery.

Andersonburg; village in Perry County, Pennsylvania, named for the original owner.

Andersonville; village in Sumter County, Georgia, named for the original proprietor.

Andes; town in Delaware County, New York, named from the mountains of South America, because of its mountainous character.

Andover; towns in Essex County, Massachusetts, and Windsor County, Vermont, named from the town in England.

Andrew; county in Missouri, named for Andrew S. Hughes, of Clay County, who first publicly proposed the "Platte purchase."

Andrews; county in Texas, named for the only man killed in a two days' skirmish with the*Mexicans near San Antonio, in 1835.

Androscoggin; river in Maine and New Hampshire, and county in Maine. An Indian word first given to the river, from the tribe Amasagunticook, that formerly lived on its banks. The authorities give the meaning "a fishing place for alewives," or "fish spearing."

Angel; island in San Francisco Bay, California, named for a pioneer miner.

Angelica; town in Allegany County, New York, named for Mrs. Angelica Church, daughter of Gen. Philip Schuyler.

Angel Island; post-office in Marin County, California, named from the island on which it is situated.

Angels; town in Calaveras County, California, named for Henry Angel, who discovered gold in that vicinity in 1848.

Anglesea; borough in Cape May County, New Jersey, named from the town in Wales.

Aniwa; village in Shawano County, Wisconsin. Corruption of an Indian word, aniwi, meaning " those," a Chippewa prefix signifying superiority.

Ann; cape, eastern extremity of Essex County, Massachusetts, named for Queen Anne, wife of James I of England.

Anna; city in Union County, Illinois, named for Mrs. Anna Davis, wife of the owner of the land.

Annapolis; city in Anne Arundel County, Maryland, named in honor of Queen Anne, wife of James 1 of England.

Ann Arbor; city in Washtenaw County, Michigan. The first part of the name was given in honor of the wives of the two early settlers, Allen and Rumsey; the latter part refers to the grove-like appearance of the site.

Annawan; town in Henry County, Illinois, named from the Indian; probably from awan, "fog."

Anne Arundel; county in Maryland, named in honor of Lady Anne Arundel, wife of Cecilius Calvert, second Lord Baltimore.

Annisquam; lake, bay, and river in New Hampshire, and village in Essex County, Massachusetts. Indian word, meaning "rock summit," or "point of rock."

Annsville; town in Oneida County, New York, named for the wife of J. W. Bloomfield, first settler.

Anoka; county and city in Minnesota, and villages in Cass County, Indiana, and Broome County, New York. An Indian word, meaning "on both sides."

Anson; county in North Carolina, named for Admiral Anson, British navy, who purchased land in the State.

Anson; town in Jones County, Texas, named for Anson Jones, first president of the Texas Republic.

Ansonia; city in New Haven County, Connecticut, named for Anson G. Phelps, senior partner of the firm of Phelps, Dodge & Co., which established the place.

Ansonville; town in Anson County, North Carolina, named for Admiral Anson of the British navy, who built the town.

Ansted; town in Fayette County, West Virginia, named for Professor Ansted, the English geologist, who reported on a tract of coal land there and had an interest in it.

Antelope; county in Nebraska, named at the suggestion of Mr. Leander Gerrard, in commemoration of the killing and eating of an antelope during the pursuit of some Indians. There are many places in various parts of the country which bear this name, generally in reference to the former presence of that animal.

Antero; mount in the Sawatch Range, Colorado, named for a prominent Ute Indian.

Anthony; city in Harper County, Kansas, named for Governor George T. Anthony.

Anthony's Nose; promontory on the Hudson River, New York, said by Irving to have been named so in reference to Anthony Van Corlear's nose; Lossing says, "Anthony de Hooges, secretary of Rensselaerwick, had an enormous nose, and the promontory was named in honor of that feature."

Antioch; town in Contra Costa County, California, village in Lake County, Illinois, as well as many other places, named from the city in Syria.

Antrim; county in Michigan, and town in Guernsey. County, Ohio, named by early Irish settlers from the town in Ireland. Many other places are named from the same.

Antwerp; town in Jefferson County, New York, built by a company which was formed in Holland, who named the new place from the city in Belgium. Village in Paulding County, Ohio, named from the same.

Apache; county and pass in Arizona, town in Caddo County, Oklahoma, and village in Huerfano County, Colorado, named for a tribe of Indians. Some authorities give the meaning, "the men, the people." Grinnell interprets it as meaning "enemies."

Apalachee; river, and post-office in Morgan County, Georgia. Indian word, supposed to be derived from apalatchiokli, " those on the other side," or "the people on the other side."

Apalachicola; river, and city in Franklin County, Florida. An Indian word, variously interpreted. Gatchet translates it, "people on the other side." Brinton supposed the name to be derived from Apalache, "those by the sea," and the Choctaw suffix, okla, or uklah, "nation, or town." De Vere gives the meaning, "town of low cottages on the river."

Apex; village in Wake County, North Carolina, so named because it is the highest point between Raleigh and Deep rivers.

Apollo; borough in Armstrong County, Pennsylvania, named for the classical god.

Apopka; town in Orange County, Florida. Name derived from the Indian word tsalopopkohatchee, meaning "catfish eating creek."

Apostles; group of islands in Lake Superior, so called by the early Jesuits, under the impression that they numbered twelve.

Appalachia; village in Wise County, Virginia. Name derived from Appalachian.

Appalachian; general appellation of the mountain system in the southeastern part of North America, extending under various names from Maine southwestward to the northern part of Alabama. The name was given by the Spaniards under De Soto, who derived it from the neighboring Indians. Heckewelder supposed this name to be derived from the Carib word, apaliche, "man." Brinton holds its radical to be the Muscogee apala, "the great sea, or the great ocean," and that apalache is a compound of this word with the Muscogee personal participle "chi," and means "those by the sea."

Appanoose; county in Iowa, and a village of Douglas County, Kansas. An Indian word, meaning "a chief when a child." The name of a chief of the Sacs and Foxes.

Applebachville; village in Bucks County, Pennsylvania, named for Gen. Paul Applebach and his brother Henry.

Applegate; town in Jackson County, Oregon, named for an early settler.

Appleton; town in Knox County, Maine, named for Nathaniel Appleton, one of the original proprietors.

Appleton; village in Cape Girardeau County, Missouri, situated on Apple Creek; hence the name.

Appleton; city in Outagamie County, Wisconsin, named for Samuel Appleton, one of the founders of Lawrence University, located at that place.

Appling; county, and town in Columbia County, Georgia, named for Col. Dan Appling.

Appomattox; river, and county in Virginia. An Indian word, meaning "a tobacco plant country."

Aptakisic; village in Lake County, Illinois. An Indian word, meaning "half dry," or "sun at meridian."

Apukwa; lake in Wisconsin. An Indian word, meaning "rice."

Apulia; village in Onondaga County, New York, named from the ancient province of southern Italy.

Aquaschicola; creek, and village in Carbon County, Pennsylvania. An Indian word, meaning " where we fish with the bush net."

Aquebogue; village in Suffolk County, New York. An Indian word, meaning "at the end of a small pond."

Aransas; county in Texas, named from the river which flows into Aransas Harbor, through the county.

Arapahoe; county in Colorado, towns in Furnas County, Nebraska, and Custer County, Oklahoma, and post-office in Pamlico County, North Carolina. Named from an Indian tribe. The word means "pricked," or "tattooed."

Arbuckle; town in Colusa County, California. Named for the founder of the town.

Arbuckle; mountains in Chickasaw Nation, Indian Territory. Named from Fort Arbuckle, which was named for Brevet Brig. Gen. Matthew Arbuckle, who fought in the Mexican war.

Areata; town in Humboldt County, California. An Indian word, meaning "sunny spot."

Archdale; town in Randolph County, North Carolina, named for John Archdale, a lord proprietor and governor of Carolina.

Archer; county in Texas; Archer City; village in above county. Named for Dr. Branch T. Archer, prominent in the early days of the State.

Archuleta; county in Colorado, named for J. M. Archuleta, head of one of the old Spanish families of New Mexico.

Arden; town in Buncombe County, North Carolina, named from the Forest of Arden, in Shakespeare's play "As You Like It."

Arenac; county and village in Michigan. An Indian word, auke, "earth, or land," compounded with the Latin word, arena. The name was coined by Schoolcraft and a party of early explorers.

Arenzville; village in Cass County, Illinois, named for Francis A. Arenz, pioneer and founder.

Arequa; gulch in Colorado, named for a man named Requa.

Argenta; villages in Beaverhead County, Montana, and Salt Lake County, Utah, so named becauseof near-by silver mines. A Latin word, meaning "silver."

Argentine; city in Wyandotte County, Kansas, so named from "argenta," "silver," a smelter being the first industry there.

Argonia; city in Sumner County, Kansas, named from the ship Argo, in which Jason sailed to Colchis in quest of the "golden fleece."

Argos; town in Marshall County, Indiana, named from the town in Greece.

Argusville; village in Schoharie County, New York, named for its principal paper, the Albany Argus.

Argyle; towns in Walton County, Florida, and Winnebago County, Illinois, settled by Scotch, and named by them for the city in Scotland.

Argyle; town in Washington County, New York, named for the Duke of Argyle in 1786.

Arietta; town in Hamilton County, New York, named for the wife of Rensselaer Van Rennselaer.

Arikaree; river and village in Arapahoe County, Colorado. An Indian word, meaning "horn people."

Arizona; Territory of the United States. The word means arid zone, or desert, but Mowry claims that the name is Aztec, from Arizuma, signifying "silver bearing."

Arkadelphia; town in Clark County, Arkansas. The word is compounded of the abbreviation of Arkansas and the Greek word, adelphus, "brother."

Arkansas; river, State, county and town in said State, and city in Cowley County, Kansas. Marquette and other French explorers wrote the word Alkansas and Akamsca, from the Indian tribe. The usual etymology derives the name from the French arc, "a bow," and Kansas, "smoky water," while another theory makes the prefix a Dakota word meaning "people;" hence, "people of the smoky water." Schoolcraft says there is a species of acacia found in Arkansas from which the Indians made bows. This is thought to have been the origin of the name of the Arc or Bow Indians. A writer in the

Atlantic Monthly suggests the French arc-en-sang, " bloody bow," and supposes the likeness to Kansas to have been accidental.

Armagh; borough and town in Indiana County, Pennsylvania, named from the Irish town.

Armonk; village in Westchester County, New York. An Indian word, meaning "fishing place."

Armourdale; formerly a village, now a station in Kansas City, Kansas, named for the Armour brothers, bankers and pork packers.

Armstrong; county in Pennsylvania, named for Gen. John Armstrong, of Pennsylvania, who commanded the expedition against the Indians at Kittanning in 1756.

Armstrong; county in South Dakota, named for Moses K. Armstrong, Congressman and legislator, 1870.

Armstrong; county in Texas, named for a pioneer of the State.

Arnolds; creek in Ohio County, Indiana, named for Colonel Arnold, of the Revolutionary war.

Aroostook; river and county in Maine. An Indian word, meaning "good river," or "clear of obstruction."

Arrow; lake in Minnesota, so called from the name given by the early French explorers, Lac aux Fleches, "lake of the arrows."

Arrowhead; hot springs in southern California, named from a huge discoloration on the slopes of a mountain north of San Bernardino, which takes the form of an Indian arrowhead.

Arrow Rock; village in Saline County, Missouri, built upon a spot where the Indians formerly resorted for arrowheads, because of the suitability of the rock found there.

Arroyo; villages in Elk County, Pennsylvania, and Cameron County, Texas. A Spanish word, meaning "creek, brook, or rivulet."

Arroyo Grande; town in San Luis Obispo County, California. A Spanish name, meaning "great brook, or creek."

Arroyo Hondo; village in Taos County, New Mexico, which takes its name from a near-by creek. A Spanish name, meaning "deep creek."

Artesia; town in Lowndes County, Mississippi, so named from an artesian well near.

Asbury Park; borough and a city, a summer resort in Monmouth County, New Jersey, named for Francis Asbury, the pioneer bishop of Methodism in America.

Several towns in the Southern States bear his name.

Ascension; parish in Louisiana, named by the early French from the festival of the Ascension.

Ascutney; mountain in Vermont. An Indian word, meaning "fire mountain," from its having been burned over. It is also said to signify " the three brothers," and is supposed to refer to three singular valleys which run down the western slope of the mountain.

Ascutneyville; village in Windsor County, Vermont, named from the mountain of the same name.

Ashbee; harbor in Virginia, named for Solomon Ashbee.

Ashburnham; town in Worcester County, Massachusetts, named for John Ashburnham, second Earl of Ashburnham.

Ashbyburg; village in Hopkins County, Kentucky, named for Gen. Stephen Ashby.

Ashe; county in North Carolina; Asheboro; town in above county. Named for Samuel Ashe, governor of the State in 1795-1798.

Ashersville; village in Clay County, Indiana, named for John Asher, its founder.

Asheville; city in Buncombe County, North Carolina.

Ashflat; village in Sharp County, Arkansas, named from a prairie Upon which the town is situated, in early days surrounded by ash timber.

Ashford; village in Henry County, Alabama, named for Thomas Ashford, or his son, Frederick A. Ashford.

Ashkum; village in Iroquois County, Illinois. An Indian word, meaning "more and more."

Ashland; city in Boyd County, Kentucky, so named, according to Henry Clay, from the ash timber which abounded in the vicinity. His home there was called "Ashland."

Ashland; counties in Ohio and Wisconsin; cities in Clark County, Kansas, and Jackson County, Oregon; towns in Middlesex County, Massachusetts, Benton County, Mississippi, and Greene County, New York; borough in Schuylkill County, Pennsylvania, and villages in Saunders County, Nebraska, and Ashland County, Ohio; named for the home of Henry Clay. There are many other places named from the same, generally by the founders, who thus expressed their admiration for Henry Clay.

Ashley; county in Arkansas, named for Senator Chester Ashley.

Ashley; city in Washington County, Illinois, named for Colonel Ashley, of the Illinois Central Railroad.

Ashley; village in Gratiot County, Michigan, named for H. W. Ashley, general manager of the Ann Arbor Railroad, which passes through the village.

Ashley; town in Pike County, Missouri, named for General Ashley, of Arkansas.

Ashley; river in South Carolina which unites with the Cooper, both named for the Earl of Shaftesbury, Lord Anthony Ashley Cooper, one of the original proprietors.

Ashley; lake in Utah, named for its discoverer, W. H. Ashley, a St. Louis fur trader.

Ashowugh; island off the coast of Connecticut, near New London. An Indian word, meaning "halfway place," or "the place between."

Ashtabula; county, river, and city in Ohio, and village in Barnes County, North Dakota, An Indian word, meaning " fish river."

Ashuelot: river and village in Cheshire County, New Hampshire. An Indian word, meaning "collection of many waters."

Aspen; town in Pitkin County, Colorado, which takes its name from a near-by mountain, Quaking Asp.

Aspetuc; river and hill of New Milford, Connecticut. An Indian word, meaning "a height."

Asproom; mountain in Connecticut. An Indian word, meaning "high, lofty."

Assaria; city in Saline County, Kansas, named from a church which was, built by Swedish Lutherans previous to the incorporation of the place. The word means "In God is our help."

Assawa; lake near the sources of the Mississippi. An Indian word, meaning "perch lake."

Assawampset; pond in Middleboro, Massachusetts. An Indian word, meaning "a white stone."

Assawog; river in Connecticut. An Indian word, meaning "place between," or "the halfway place."

Assinniboine; fort and military reservation in Choteau County, Montana, named from a tribe of Indians. The name was given to them either on account of the stony nature of their country, or because of the singular manner they have of boiling their meat by dropping heated stones into the water in which the meat is placed until it is cooked. This custom is said to have given them the name, which means "stone roasters." In Lewis and Clarke's journal of their expedition it is said that the name was borrowed from the Chippewas, who called them Assinniboan, "stone Sioux," hence the name "stone Indian," which is sometimes applied to them.

Assiscunk; creek in Burlington County, New Jersey. An Indian word, meaning "muddy," or "dirty."

Assumption; parish in Louisiana, named in honor of the festival of the assumption of the Virgin Mary.

Astoria; town in Fulton County, Illinois; villages in Wright County, Missouri, Queens County, New York, and Deuel County, South Dakota, named for the Astor family, of New York.

Astoria; city in Clatsop County, Oregon, named for the founder, John Jacob Astor, who established a fur-trading station there in early days.

Aswaguscawadic; branch of the Mattawamkeag River, Maine. An Indian word, meaning "a place where one is compelled to drag his canoe through a stream."

Atacosa; county and village in Bexar County, Texas. Spanish word, meaning "boggy" or "miry."

Atalla; town in Etowah County, Alabama; named for Atala, the heroine of an Indian romance, by Chateaubriand.

Atchafalaya; bayou of Red River, Louisiana. An Indian word, meaning "long river." Atchison; county and city in Kansas, and county in Missouri, named for David R. Atchison, United States Senator from Missouri.

Aten; village in Cedar County, Nebraska, named for John Aten, a State senator.

Athens; county in Ohio, cities in Clarke County, Georgia, and Menard County, Illinois; villages in Claiborne County, Louisiana, Greene County, New York, and many other places, named for the celebrated city in Greece.

Athol; town in Worcester County, Massachusetts, said to have been named for James Murray, second Duke of Athol.

Atisowil; creek in Washington, emptying into Willapa Harbor. An Indian word, meaning " bear river."

Atkins; bay at the mouth of Kennebec River, Maine, named for an early landowner.

Atkins; peak in Yellowstone Park, named by the United States Geological Survey, for John D. C. Atkins, Indian commissioner.

Atkinson; town in Piscataquis County, Maine, named for Judge Atkinson, a prominent resident.

Atkinson; town in Rockingham County, New Hampshire, named for Theodore Atkinson, a large landholder.

Atkinsonville; village in Owen County, Indiana, named for Stephen Atkinson.

Atlanta; city in Georgia, so named to designate its relationship to the Atlantic Ocean, by means of a railway running to the coast.

Atlantic; ocean named from the Greek word, meaning "the sea beyond Mount Atlas."

Atlantic; county and city in New Jersey, named from the ocean.

Atlantic; creek in Yellowstone Park, named because it flows from Two-Ocean Pass down the slope toward the Atlantic Ocean.

Atlantic Highlands; borough in Monmouth County, New Jersey, so named from its situation, which overlooks the ocean.

Atoka; town in Choctaw Nation, Indian Territory. An Indian word, meaning "in another place," or "to another place."

Attala; county in Mississippi. Attalaville; village in above county. Named for Atala, the heroine of an Indian romance by Chateaubriand.

Attapulgus; village in Decatur County, Georgia. An Indian word, meaning "boring holes into wood to make a fire."

Attica; city in Fountain County, Indiana; village in Wyoming County, New York, and many other places, named for the ancient division in Greece.

Attitah; peak of the White Mountains in New Hampshire. An Indian word, meaning "blueberries."

Attleboro; town in Bristol County, Massachusetts, named from a town in England.

Atwater; village in Kandiyohi County, Minnesota, probably named for Isaac Atwater, early settler of St. Paul.

Atwater; town in Portage County, Ohio, named for Amzi Atwater, an early surveyor in the Western Reserve.

Atwood; city in Rawlins County, Kansas, named for Attwood Matheny, son of the founder, J. M. Matheny.

Aubrey; valley in Arizona, named for an army officer.

Auburn; this name occurs many times in the United States, given in reference to the village in Goldsmith's poem of The Deserted Village.

Audrain; county in Missouri, named for its first settler, Samuel Audrain.

Audubon; mount in Colorado, county in Iowa, and village in Becker County, Minnesota, named for the celebrated ornithologist, John James Audubon. Many other places bear his name.

Aughwick; tributary of the Juniata River, Pennsylvania. An Indian word, meaning "overgrown with brush."

Auglaize; river and county in Ohio, and river in Missouri. A French word, meaning "at the clay or loam," used descriptively.

Augusta; city in Richmond County, Georgia, named for one of the royal princesses.

Augusta; city in Butler County, Kansas, named for the wife of C. N. James, a trader.

Augusta; county in Virginia, and city in Kennebec County, Maine, named for Augusta of Saxe-Gotha, wife of Frederick, Prince of Wales.

Auraria; town in Lumpkin County, Georgia, surrounded by a hilly country containing valuable gold mines. A Latin word, meaning "gold town."

Aurelius; town in Cayuga County, New York, named for the Roman emperor.

Aurora; city in Dearborn County, Indiana, named for the association which laid it out.

Aurora; county in South Dakota, and many other places named from the Latin word, meaning "morning, dawn, east."

Ausable; river and town in Clinton County, New York. A French word, meaning "sandy," or "at the sand."

Austin; city in Mower county, Minnesota, named for Horace Austin, governor in 1870-1874.

Austin; town in Tunica County, Mississippi, named for Colonel Austin, on whose plantation the town was built.

Austin; county and city in Travis County, Texas, and town in Lonoke County, Arkansas, named for Stephen Fuller Austin, the first man to establish a permanent American colony in Texas.

Austinburg; town in Ashtabula County, Ohio, named for Judge Austin, early settler.

Autauga; county in Alabama.

Autaugaville; town in Autauga County, Alabama. From an Indian word said to mean "land of plenty."

Autryville; town in Sampson County, North Carolina, named for a member of the State legislature.

Auxvasse; village in Callaway County, Missouri, named from the French word vasseux, meaning "muddy."

Ava; town in Oneida County, New York, named from the city in Burma.

Avalon; town in Livingston County, Missouri, named from the town in France. Several other places bear this name.

Avery; gores in Essex and Franklin counties, Vermont, named for the original grantee, Samuel Avery.

Avoca; town in Steuben County, New York, named by Sophia White, a resident, in allusion to Thomas Moore's poem, "Sweet Vale of Avoca."

Avon; village in Livingston County, New York, also many other places, named from the river in England, upon which Shakespeare's home was situated.

Avoyelles; parish in Louisiana, named from an Indian tribe. The name was doubtless given to the tribe by the early French.

Axtell; city in Marshall County, Kansas, named for Dr. Jesse Axtell, an officer of the St. Joseph and Grand Island Railway.

Ayden; town in Pitt County, North Carolina, named from the place mentioned in Poe's "Raven," "In the distant Aideen."

Ayer; town in Middlesex County, Massachusetts, named for James C. Ayer, a manufacturer of Lowell.

Ayish; bayou in Texas, named from an Indian tribe.

Ayr; village in Adams County, Nebraska, named for Dr. Ayr, of Iowa, a railroad director.

Ayrshire; town in Palo Alto County, Iowa, named for the town in Scotland.

Azalia; village in Bartholomew County, Indiana, named for the flower.

Aztec; village in San Juan County, New Mexico, named for one of the native tribes of Mexico. The word is said to mean "place of the heron." Other interpretations give "white," or "shallow land where vapors arise." Humboldt gives "land of flamingoes." The word azcatl means "ant," but Buschmann says that this word has no connection with the name of the tribe.

Babruly; creek in Missouri. The word is a corruption of the French Bois Brule, "burning wood."

Babylon; village in Suffolk County, New York, named from the ancient city in Syria.

Baca; county in Colorado, named for a prominent Mexican family of Trinidad, Colorado. » Bache; mount in California, named for A. D. Bache, Superintendent of the Coast and Geodetic Survey.

Baconhill; village in Saratoga County, New York, named for Ebenezer Bacon, tavern keeper in early days.

Bad; river in Michigan, named by the Dakota Indians Wakpashicha, "bad river."

Badaxe; river in Wisconsin and village in Huron County, Michigan. Said to be a translation of the Indian name of the river, Trompeleau or Trempeleau.

Baden; borough in Beaver County, Pennsylvania, and several other places in the United States, named from the German baths.

Badger; creeks in Iowa, Yellowstone Park, and many other places, so named from the presence of that animal.

Bad Lands; term applied to a region in South Dakota. It is said that the old French voyageurs described the region as "mauvaise terres pour traverser," meaning that it was a difficult country to travel through; from this the term has been carelessly shortened and translated into the present misnomer.

Baggers; point on Indian River, Florida, named for the owner, John Baggers.

Bailey; county in Texas, named for one of the men who fell at the Alamo, March 6, 1836. His first name is worn away on the stone monument, which is the only record of him.

Baird; town in Sunflower County, Mississippi. named for the man who owned the land upon which it was built.

Baker; county in Georgia, named for Col. John Baker, an officer in the war of the Revolution.

Baker; county and city in Oregon, named for Edward Dickinson Baker, officer in the Union Army and Senator from Oregon.

Baker; mount in "Washington, named by the explorer Vancouver for a lieutenant in his party.

Bakers; river in Grafton County, New Hampshire, named for Captain Baker, a soldier of the Indian wars.

Bakersfield; town in Franklin County. Vermont, named for Joseph Baker, who owned the land in 1789.

Bakers Mills; village in Warren County, New York, named for the owner.

Bakersville; town in Mitchell County, North Carolina, named for a prominent resident.

Bakersville; town in Coshocton County, Ohio. named for John Baker, who laid it out in 1848.

Bald Eagle; valley, creek, and village in York County, Pennsylvania, named for the noted Seneca chief, Bald Eagle.

Baldwin; county in Alabama, and county and town in Georgia, named for Abraham Baldwin, United States Senator from Georgia.

Baldwin; town in Jackson County, Iowa, named for Judge Baldwin.

Baldwin; city in Douglas County, Kansas, named for John Baldwin, of Berea, Ohio.

Baldwin; town in Cumberland County, Maine, named for Loammi Baldwin, one of the proprietors.

Baldwin; village in Lake County, Michigan, named for Governor Baldwin, of Michigan.

Baldwin; town in Chemung County, New York, named from Baldwin Creek, which was named for Isaac, Walter, and Thomas Baldwin, early settlers at the mouth of the creek.

Baldwin; village in St. Croix County, Wisconsin, named for D. A. Baldwin, early settler.

Baldwinsville; village in Onondaga County, New York, named for Dr. Jonas C. Baldwin, its founder.

Baldwyn; town in Lee County, Mississippi, named for a landowner.

Balize; pilot town at the northeast pass at the mouth of the Mississippi in Plaquemines Parish, Louisiana, the name of which comes from the French word balize, "a stake," "a beacon," the most of the houses being built on piles.

Ballard; county in Kentucky, named for Capt. Bland Ballard, an officer in the war of 1812.

Ballena; town in San Diego County, California. A Spanish word, meaning "whale."

Ballston; town in Saratoga County, New York; Ballston Spa; village in Saratoga County, New York. Named for Rev. Eliphalet Ball, an early settler, the "spa" being added in reference to the medicinal springs, from the celebrated watering place in Belgium.

Baltimore; county and city in Maryland, and town in Windsor County, Vermont, named for the proprietor of a large tract of land in Maryland, Cecilius Calvert, Lord Baltimore, who settled the province in 1635.

Bamberg; county and town in South Carolina, named for a family prominent in recent history of the State.

Bandera; county in Texas, named from a pass in the State. The word is Spanish, meaning " flag." Bangor; city in Penobscot County, Maine, named by the Rev. Seth Noble, its representative in legislature, from an old psalm tune.

Bangor; borough in Northampton County, Pennsylvania, and village in La Crosse County, Wisconsin, named from the town in Wales because of the Welsh settlers in these places.

Bangs; mount in Arizona, named for James E. Bangs, clerk upon the King Survey.

Banks; county in Georgia; IBanksville; village in Banks County. Named for Dr. Richard Banks.

Banner; village in Wells County, Indiana, named for a newspaper, the Blufton Banner.

Banner; county in Nebraska, so named because it was considered the banner county of the State when named.

Bannock; county and peak in Idaho, peak in Yellowstone Park, and town in Beaverhead County, Montana, named for a tribe of Indians. This tribe inhabited the country southwest of Yellowstone Park, finally settling on a reservation in southern Idaho. Some authorities give the derivation from bannai' hti, "southern people." Haines and others say the word signifies "root diggers," because the Indians subsisted upon roots.

Bantam; river, and village in Litchfield County, Connecticut. Name derived from the Indian word peantum, "he prays, or is praying."

Baptist Hill; village in Ontario County, New York, named from a Baptist church erected there at an early date.

Baraboo; city in Sauk County, Wisconsin, named for Jean Baribault, a French settler.

Baraga; county and village in Michigan, named for Bishop Friedrich Baraga, a missionary among the Indians of the Lake Superior region.

Baranof; island in Alaska, named for the man who for a long time managed the affairs of the Russian-American Company.

Barataria; bay, and post-office in Jefferson Parish, Louisiana. The name is derived from an old French word, meaning "deceit."

Barber; creek in Humboldt County, California, named for a settler.

Barber; county in Kansas, named for Thomas W. Barber, Free State martyr.

Barbour; county in Alabama, named for James Barbour, governor of Virginia, and Secretary of War under John Quincy Adams.

Barbour; county in West Virginia; Barboursville; town in Cabell County, West Virginia, and several other towns in the Southern States. Named for Philip P. Barbour, early governor of Virginia.

Bardstown; city in Nelson County, Kentucky, named for David Baird, one of the original proprietors.

Bardwell; village in Hampshire County, Massachusetts, named for the Bardwell family, early and prominent residents.

Bargersville; village in Johnson County, Indiana, named for Jefferson Barger.

Bar Harbor; village in Hancock County, Mount Desert Island, Maine, so named from a sandy bar, visible only at low tide.

Baring; town in Washington County, Maine, said to be named for the Baring family, celebrated bankers of London, England.

Barker; town in Broome County, New York, named for John Barker, the first settler.

Barlow; town in Clackamas County, Oregon, named for John L. Barlow, early settler.

Barlow; peak in Yellowstone Park, named by the United States Geological Survey for Capt. J. W. Barlow, Engineer Corps, United States Army.

Barnard; town in Windsor County, Vermont, named for Francis Barnard, a grantee.

Barnegat; inlet, and village in Ocean County, New Jersey. A Dutch name, given by Henry Hudson, meaning "breaker's inlet."

Barnes; city in Washington County, Kansas, named for A. S. Barnes, publisher of the United States history.

Barnes; county in North Dakota, named for Hon. A. II. Barnes, early Territorial judge.

Barnesville; village in Belmont County, Ohio, named from a family of early settlers.

Barnet; town in Caledonia County, Vermont, said to be named from the place in England from which the ancestors of Enos Stevens, an early settler, emigrated.

Barnstable; county and town in Massachusetts, named from a seaport in England.

Barnum; town in Arapahoe County, Colorado, named for P. T. Barnum, who owned a large tract of land there.

Barnum; town in Carlton County, Minnesota, named for a paymaster on the St. Paul and Duluth Railroad.

Barnwell; county and town in South Carolina, named for a distinguished family of the State.

Baronette; peak in Yellowstone Park, named for "Yellowstone Jack," C. D. Baronette, a famous scout.

Barraque; township in Jefferson County, Arkansas, named for a Frenchman, Monsieur Barraque, who lived on the Arkansas River.

Barre; town in Worcester County, Massachusetts, named for Col. Isaac Barre, the friend of America in the British Parliament.

Barre; towns in Orleans County, New York, and Washington County, Vermont, named for the town in Massachusetts.

Barren; island in the Hudson River. The name is derived from the Dutch word beeren, "bears," which was applied to the island by the early Dutch settlers.

Barren; county in Kentucky, in the Carboniferous limestone region. The name is supposed to have been given in reference to this formation, though the soil is in reality fertile.

Barrington; town in Bristol County. Rhode Island. probably named for Sir John Barrington, dissenter, who died in 1784, though by some it is thought to have received its name from some of the early settlers who came from the parish of Barrington in Somersetshire, England.

Barron; county and city in Wisconsin, named for Judge Henry D. Barron, of that State.

Barry; county in Michigan, named for William T. Barry, Postmaster-General under President Jackson.

Barry; county in Missouri, named for Commodore John Barry.

Bartholomew; county in Indiana, named for Gen. Joseph Bartholomew, United States Senator from that State.

Bartlett; town in Carroll County, New Hampshire, named for Governor Josiah Bartlett, 1792-1794.

Barton; county in Kansas, named for Clara Barton, founder of the Red Cross Society in America.

Barton; county in Missouri, named for David Barton, member of Congress from Missouri.

Barton; town in Orleans County, Vermont, named for William Barton, a Revolutionary general and principal proprietor.

Bartow; county and town in Jefferson County, Georgia, named for Gen. F. S. Bartow, killed at the battle of Manassas.

Basalt; peak which gives name to a town in Eagle County, Colorado, named from the summit rock.

Bashes Kil; creek in Orange County, New York, named for Bashe, an Indian woman.

Baskahegan; river and lake in Maine. An Indian word meaning "a branch stream which turns down."

Baskingridge; village in Somerset County, New Jersey, where it is said animals resorted in chilly weather to bask in the milder air.

Basswood; island in Lake Superior, one of the Apostles, a translation of wigobiminiss, the Indian name for the island.

Bastrop; county and town in Texas, and town in Morehouse County, Louisiana, named for Baron de Bastrop, a Mexican, who was commissioner of Texas to extend land titles in 1823.

Batavia; town in Genesee County, New York, and many other places, named from the Dutch name for Holland.

Batchelders; grant in Oxford County, Maine, named for the original grantee, Josiah Batchelder.

Bates; county in Missouri, named for Edward Bates, member of Congress from that State.

Batesburg; town in Lexington County, South Carolina. named for a family of that State.

Batesville; city in Independence County, Arkansas, named for James Woodson Bates.

Batesville; village in Noble County, Ohio, named for Rev. Timothy Bates, Methodist preacher.

Bath; counties in Kentucky and Virginia, and village in Rensselaer County, New York, named so because of the medical springs present.

Bath; city of Maine, named from the city in England, by seafaring men on account of their association with that city.

Bath; town in Steuben County, New York, named for Lady Henrietta, Countess of Bath, daughter of Sir William Pultney.

Bath Alum Spring; town in Virginia, so called from the medicinal springs situated there.

Bath Springs; town in Decatur County, Tennessee, so named because of the medicinal springs within their limits.

Baton Rouge; city in East Baton Rouge Parish, Louisiana. It is a French name, neaning "red staff or stick," given because of a tall cypress tree which stood upon the spot where it was first settled. Some authorities say that the name is derived from the name of an Indian chief, whose name translated into French was Baton Rouge. Still another theory ascribes the name to the fact that a massacre by the Indians took place upon the spot upon the arrival of the first settlers.

Battenkill; creek, tributary to the Hudson River, called originally Bartholomew's Kill, for an early settler, Bartholomew Van Hogeboom, who was usually called Bart or Bat.

Battleboro; town in Nash County, North Carolina, named for James S. and Joseph Battle, railroad contractors. Battle Creek; city and creek in Calhoun County, Michigan, so called because a battle was fought upon the banks of the creek.

Battle Creek; village in Madison County, Nebraska, situated on Battle Creek.

Battle Ground; creek in Illinois, so called from a battle fought on its banks between the Cahokia and Kaskaskia Indians in 1782.

Battle Ground; town in Tippecanoe County, Indiana, named in commemoration of the battle of Tippecanoe.

Battlement; mesa in western Colorado, named by Harden because of its shape.

Bavaria; village in Saline County, Kansas, named for one of the divisions of Germany.

Baxter; county in Arkansas, named for Elisha Baxter, twice governor of the State.

Baxter Springs; city in Cherokee County, Kansas, named for A. Baxter, the first settler. There are also springs in the vicinity.

Bay; county in Michigan, named from its situation on Saginaw Bay.

Bayard; town in Grant County, West Virginia, named for Senator Bayard.

Bayboro; town in Pamlico County, North Carolina, so named from its situation on Pamlico Sound.

Bay City; city in Bay County, Michigan, so named from its situation on Saginaw Bay.

Bayfield; county and village in Wisconsin, named for Rear-Admiral H. D. Bayfield, who surveyed the Great Lakes.

Bayhead; borough in Ocean County, New Jersey. Name descriptive of its geographical position at the head of Barnegat Bay.

Baylor; county in Texas, named for Henry W. Baylor, who fell at Dawson's massacre in 1842.

Bay of Noquet; bay in Michigan, named from an Indian tribe. Their name was Noukek, the early French giving it the present orthography.

Bayou; village in Livingston County, Kentucky. The word is used frequently in the Southern States, being a French term to denote "a stream derived from some other stream."

Bayou Boeuf; creek in Louisiana. A French name meaning " Buffalo Creek." See "Bayou."

Bayou Chetimaches; creek in Louisiana, named for an Indian who dwelt in the vicinity.

Bayou des Buttes; creek of Louisiana, named by the French "Bayou of the Mounds," from the mounds found along its course.

Bayou Huffpower; creek in Louisiana, named for an old settler.

Bayou Sale; creek emptying into Cote Blanche Bay. A French name meaning "Salt bayou or creek."

Bay St. Louis; city in Hancock County, Mississippi, named for Louis XI of France, and situated on a bay, hence the prefix.

Bay Spring; town in Tishomingo County, Mississippi, named for the home of Robert Lowery in the same county.

Beacon; town in Mahaska County, Iowa, named for Lord Beaconsfield.

Beadle; county in South Dakota, named for W. H. Beadle, superintendent of public instruction in 1884.

Bear; creek in Missouri, sometimes called Loose Creek, probably from a careless corruption of the French, L'ourse, bear.

Bear; creek in Yellowstone Park, named from a hairless cub found there by a party of explorers. This name is applied to numerous places in the United States, from the presence of the animal at the time of naming.

Beardstown; city in Cass County, Illinois, named for Thomas Beard, the founder.

Bear Lake; county in Idaho, named from a lake.

Bear Lake; village in Manistee County, Michigan, so named because some surveyors thought the outline looked like a sleeping bear.

Beatrice; town in Humboldt County, California, named for a woman living there.

Beattie; city in Marshall County, Kansas, named for A. Beattie, mayor of St. Joseph, Missouri, in 1870.

Beattyville; town in Lee County, Kentucky, named for Samuel Beatty, one of the first settlers.

Beaufort; county and town in Carteret County, North Carolina, named for the Duke of Beaufort, a lord proprietor.

Beaufort; county and town in South Carolina, said by some authorities to be named for the Duke of Beaufort, but other authorities claim that the name was given by the French Protestants, who took refuge there from Lord Berkeley, giving the name of the town in Anjou, France.

Beauregard; town in Copiah County, Mississippi, named for Gen. Pierre Gustave Toutant Beauregard, Confederate army.

Beaver; counties in Oklahoma and Utah, county and borough in Pennsylvania, twenty post-offices, and numerous creeks, lakes, and other natural features in the United States. It was adopted by the Indians as a personal as well as tribal name, because of the widespread presence of the animal.

Beaver; lake in Indiana, called by the Indians, Sagayiganuhnickyug, "the lake of beavers." Beaverdam; city in Dodge County, Wisconsin, creek in Yellowstone Park, and numerous post-offices, so called from an obstacle placed in streams by beavers.

Beaverhead; county in Montana, named from a rock in the county shaped like a beaver's head.

Bechler; creek in Yellowstone Park, named by the United States Geological Survey for Gustavus R. Bechler, topographer, with the Hayden survey.

Bechtelsville; borough in Berks County, Pennsylvania, named for the family of which Judge O. P. Bechtel is a prominent member.

Becker; county and town in Minnesota. named for George L. Becker, who was one of the leading men of the State at the time.

Beckley; village in Raleigh County, West Virginia, named for Gen. Alfred Beckley, early settler.

Beckwith; butte and town in Plumas County, California, and mountain in Colorado, named for Lieutenant Beckwith, of the Pacific Railroad Exploring Expedition.

Bedford; town in Middlesex County, Massachusetts, named for Wriothesley Russell, Duke of Bedford.

Bedford; town in Westchester County, New York, named for Bedfordshire, England.

Bedford; county and borough in Pennsylvania, said by some to be named for the county in England; by others it is thought that the name was given in honor of the Dukes of Bedford.

Bedford; county in Tennessee, and village in county, named for Thomas Bedford.

Bedford; county and town in Virginia, named for Edward, Duke of Bedford.

Bedloe; island in New York Harbor, named for Isaac Bedlow, its first proprietor.

Bee; county in Texas, named for Bernard E. Bee, minister to Mexico in 1830.

Beebe; town in White County, Arkansas, said to have been named for Roswell Beebe, an early settler.

Beech; this word, with various suffixes, forms the name of numerous features. There are six post-offices named Beech in the country and thirty-six with various suffixes, the name being applied because of the occurrence of this tree in the vicinity.

Beech. Creek; creek and borough of Clinton County, Pennsylvania. A translation of the Indian name Schauweminsch-kanna.

Beecher City; village in Effingham County, Illinois, named for Charles A. Beecher, railway solicitor.

Beechy; cape in Alaska, named for Capt. F. W. Beechy, the navigator.

Beekman; village in Dutchess County, New York, named for Henry Beekman, who owned a grant there in 1703.

Beekmanton; town in Clinton County, New York, named for William Beekman, one of the original grantees.

Bekuennesee; rapids in the Menominee River, Wisconsin. An Indian word, meaning "smoky falls."

Belair; town in Harford County, Maryland, and post-offices in Richmond County, Georgia, Plaquemines Parish, Louisiana, and Lancaster County, South Carolina. A French name meaning " fine air, good climate."

Belchertown; town in Hampshire County, Massachusetts, named for Jonathan Belcher, one of the original grantees and one time governor of Massachusetts.

Belen; town in Quitman County, Mississippi, named from the battle ground upon which Col. John A. Quitman fought during the Mexican war.

Belew; town in Jefferson County, Missouri, named for Silas Belew, who owned property in the vicinity.

Belfast; city in Waldo County, Maine, named by James Miller, early settler, for his native city in Ireland. Numerous other places in the country bear this name.

Belknap; county in New Hampshire. The origin of this name is in doubt, but by some the county is thought to have been named for Jeremy Belknap, who wrote a history of the State.

Belknap; mount in Utah, named for the Secretary of War under President Grant, William Worth Belknap.

Bell; county in Kentucky, named for Josh Bell.

Bell; county in Texas, named for P. H. Bell, governor of the State in 1849-1857.

Belle; a French word meaning "beautiful," of frequent occurrence in the country with various suffixes, there being seventy-eight post-offices which have this name in combination with descriptive suffixes.

Belleville; city in Republic County, Kansas, named for Arabelle, wife of A. B. Tutton, president of the town-site company.

Belleville; village in Dane County, Wisconsin, named by the first settler, John Frederick, for his native village in Canada; a village in Jefferson County, New York, named for the same.

Bellingham; town in Norfolk County, Massachusetts, named for Governor Richard Bellingham.

Bellingham; bay in Washington, named by Vancouver, the explorer, probably for Sir Henry Bellingham, who was knighted in 1796.

Bellmont; village in Franklin County, New York, named for William Bell, an early proprietor.

Bellows Falls; village in Windham County, Vermont, named for Col. Benjamin Bellows, an early settler and founder of Walpole.

Bell Spring; mountain in Humboldt County, California, so named by an early explorer, who found a cow bell in a spring on the mountain.

Bellwood; village in Butler County, Nebraska, named for D. J. Bell, its proprietor and patron.

Belmont; town in Mississippi County, Missouri, and town in Belknap County, New Hampshire, named for August Belmont, of New York.

Belmont; county and village in Ohio, named for an early settler. Howe says it is named in reference to its hilly surface; French, "fine mountain."

Belmont; village in Lafayette County, Wisconsin, named for three mounds within its limits which the early French travelers called "Belles Montes."

Beloit; city in Rock County, Wisconsin. A coined name, selected by a committee, to whom it was suggested by the name Detroit.

Beloit; city in Mitchell County, Kansas, named for the above.

Belpre; town in Washington County, Ohio, named from the French, meaning "beautiful prairie," from its situation on a prairie.

Belton; town in Anderson County, South Carolina, named for a prominent family.

Belton; city in Bell County, Texas, named for Governor P. H. Bell.

Beltrami; county and village in same county, Minnesota, named for Count C. C. Beltrami, an Italian, with Major Long's exploring expedition into the Northwest country.

Belvidere; town in Boone County, Illinois, and village in Allegany County, New York, as well as many other places, named for the Italian word, meaning "beautiful sight."

Belzoni; town in Washington County, Mississippi, named for an Italian, Giambattuta Belzoni, a celebrated archaeologist.

Bemis Heights; village in Saratoga County, New York, named for Jonathan Bemis, innkeeper there during the Revolution.

Benedicta; town in Aroostook County, Maine, named for Bishop Benedicta Fenwick, who was an early proprietor.

Benicia; city in Solano County, California, named by General Vallejo for his wife.

Ben Lomond; post-offices in Sevier County, Arkansas; Santa Cruz County, California; Issaquena County, Mississippi, and Mason County, West Virginia; named for the beautiful lake in Scotland.

Bennett; town in Cedar County, Iowa, named for diet Bennett, a railroad man.

Bennett; point in Maryland, named for Richard Bennett.

Bennett; town in Lancaster County, Nebraska, named for a resident.

Bennett Creek; village in Nansemond County, Virginia, named for Richard Bennett, governor in 1652-1656.

Bennettsville; town in Marlboro County, South Carolina, named for a family prominent in the State.

Bennetts Wells; two shallow dug wells in Death Valley, Inyo County, California, named for the survivor of an emigrant party which entered the valley in 1850.

Bennington; town in Hillsboro County, New Hampshire, and county, township, and town in Vermont, named for Governor Benning Wentworth, of New Hampshire.

Benson; town in Johnston County, North Carolina, named for a prominent citizen.

Benson; county in North Dakota, named for Hon. B. W. Benson, member of the State legislature and banker, of Valley City, North Dakota.

Benson; town in Rutland County, Vermont, said by some to have been named for Judge Egbert Benson, one of the original proprietors. The Vermont Historical Society says that it was named by James Meacham, a proprietor, for a Revolutionary officer.

Bent; county in Colorado, named for William Bent, first United States governor of New Mexico.

Benton; counties in Arkansas, Indiana, Iowa, Minnesota, Mississippi, Missouri, Oregon, Tennessee; village in Marshall County, Kentucky; town in Bossier Parish, Louisiana; village in Minnesota; town in Grafton County, New Hampshire; named for Senator Thomas H. Benton, of Missouri. Thirty-one other places in the country bear this name; almost all of them were named for the same man.

Benton; town in Yates County, New York, named for Levi Benton, the first settler.

Bentonia; town in Yazoo County, Mississippi, named for the Christian name of Mrs. Hal Green, a resident.

Benwood; city in Marshall County, West Virginia, named for Benjamin Latrobe, engineer on the Baltimore and Ohio Railroad.

Benzie; county in Michigan. Probably named from the town of Benzonia, which was founded and named before the county. There are some, however, who think the name a corruption from Betsie River and Point, which were originally called Aux Bees Scies, meaning "at the snout of the sawfish."

Benzonia; village in Benzie County, Michigan, named from the Hebrew, meaning "sons of light," by the Rev. J. B. Walker, member of a company formed to found a college where poor students could be educated, which was built upon the spot where the village now stands.

Beowawe; post-office in Eureka County, Nevada, so named from the peculiar shape of the hills at this point, which gives the effect of an open gateway up the valley to the canyon beyond. An Indian word meaning "gate."

Berea; towns in Adair County, Iowa; Madison County, Kentucky, and Cuyahoga County, Ohio, named from the ancient city in Macedonia.

Berenda; town in Madera County, California. A Spanish word meaning "antelope," given in this case because the country in the vicinity of the town was covered with antelope in early days.

Beresford; lake in Florida, named for an early English proprietor.

Bergen; county in New Jersey, which received its name from Bergen Point, which in turn was named by colonists from Bergen, Norway.

Bergholtz; village in Niagara County, New York, named for the town in Prussia.

Bering; several geographical points between Asia and America, named for the celebrated Dutch navigator, Vitus Bering.

Berkeley; county in South Carolina, named for John, Lord Berkeley, one of the original proprietors.

Berkeley; county in West Virginia; Berkeley Springs; town in Morgan County, West Virginia. Named for William Berkeley, governor of Virginia in 1642.

Berkley; town in Bristol County, Massachusetts, probably named for Dean Berkley, Bishop of Cloyne, though some authorities say for James and William Berkley, members of the Privy Council.

Berkley; town in Norfolk County, Virginia, named for Norborne Berkeley, Lord Botetourt.

Berks; county in Pennsylvania, named for the county of Berks in England.

Berkshire; county in Massachusetts, named for Berkshire, England. Several towns in the country are named from the same.

Berlin; thirty-seven post offices in the United States bear the name of the city in Germany.

Bermuda; villages in Conecuh County, Alabama; Gwinnett County, Georgia; Natchitoches Parish, Louisiana; Marion County, South Carolina, and Knox County, Tennessee; named from the group of islands in the Atlantic Ocean, which were named for the Spanish discoverer, Juan Bermudez.

Bern; towns in Adams County, Indiana, and Albany County, New York; Bernville; borough in Berks County, Pennsylvania. Named for the town of Bern 'in Switzerland.

Bernardstown; town in Franklin County, Massachusetts, named for the British governor, Sir Francis Bernard.

Berrien; county and town in Georgia and county and town in Michigan, named for John McPherson Berrien, Attorney-General of the United States in 1829.

Berry; creek in Idaho, named by Captain Clarke, the explorer, because he subsisted entirely on berries at that place.

Berry; village in Harrison County, Kentucky, named for a man who had a station there called Berry's station.

Berryville; town in Carroll County, Arkansas, named for James H. Berry, governor of the State.

Berthoud; village in Larimer County, Colorado, named for E. L. Berthoud, chief engineer of the Union Pacific Railroad.

Bertie; county in North Carolina, named for James and Henry Bertie, in whom the proprietary rights of the Earl of Clarendon rested.

Berwick; town in York County, Maine, named from the city in England, Berwick-upon-Tweed.

Bessemer; town in Jefferson County, Alabama; city in Gogebic County, Michigan; town in Gaston County, North Carolina, and several other places; named for Sir Henry Bessemer, who invented the process of reducing iron ore.

Bethany; seventeen post-offices in the country, named from the village in Palestine.

Bethel; thirty-two post-offices in the United States, named for the town in Palestine.

Bethesda; several places in the country, named for the pool of Jerusalem.

Bethlehem; thirteen post-offices bear the name of the town in Palestine.

Betsie; river, point, and town in Michigan, named for the corruption of a French name given to the river in early days, Aux Bees Scies, meaning "at the snout of the sawfish."

Beulah; twenty-two post-offices in the United States bear this Scriptural name.

Beverly; the name of nineteen places in the United States, probably derived from the Yorkshire Beverley.

Beverly; town in Randolph County, West Virginia, doubtless named for William Beverly, the original grantee of Beverly Manor.

Bevier; village in Muhlenberg County, Kentucky, and city in Macon County, Missouri, named for Col. Robert Bevier, of Kentucky.

Bexar; county and village in Texas, and villages in Marion County, Alabama; Fulton County, Arkansas, and Lauderdale County, Tennessee; named for the Duke of Bexar, a Spanish nobleman.

Bibb; counties in Alabama and Georgia, named for Dr. William Wyatt Bibb, member of Congress from Georgia.

Bicknell; village in Knox County, Indiana, named for John Bicknell.

Biddeford; city in York County, Maine, named from the place in England whence some of the early settlers emigrated.

Bienville; parish and town in Louisiana, named for Governor Jean Baptiste Lemoine Bienville, son of the French explorer who accompanied La Salle on his expedition.

Big Blackfoot; river in the Rocky Mountains, Montana, the name of which is derived from the Blackfeet Indian tribe.

Big Blue; creek in Missouri, which was formerly called Bluewater Creek, the name being derived from its French name, Riviere de l'Eau Bleue.

Bigbone; village in Boone County, Kentucky, so named from the numbers of bones of mastodons discovered in the vicinity.

Big Dry; creek in Montana, so named by Lewis and Clarke, because it was dry when they reached it.

Big Gravois; creek in Missouri, a French name, meaning "rubbish."

Bighorn; river in Montana, tributary to the Yellowstone River, so named from the Rocky Mountain sheep, frequently called "big horn." Its Indian (Dakota) name was Papatunkau, meaning "big head."

Bighorn; county in Wyoming, named from the range of mountains, which took their name from the sheep which were found in them. The Indian (Absaroka) name of the mountains was Ahsahta, meaning "big head."

Bigler; lake in California, named for John Bigler, governor of the State.

Big Muddy; creek in Missouri, the name derived from that given it by the early French, Grande Riviere Vaseuse, "great muddy river."

Big Rapids; city in Mecosta County, Michigan, so named from rapids in the Muskegon River.

Big Sioux; river in Minnesota and South Dakota, named from the Indian tribe.

Big Spring"; town in Meade County, Kentucky, so named from a spring which rises near the middle of the town. There are fifteen other places in the country that bear this name because of the presence of springs.

Bigstone; county in Minnesota, which takes its name from a river, which was doubtless named descriptively.

Bigtooth; creek in Center County, Pennsylvania, named from the Indian name of the creek, Mangipisink, "the place where big teeth are found."

Big Tree; village in Erie County, New York, so called from the Indian village which formerly occupied the site, Deonundaga, "a big tree."

Big Trees; village in Calaveras County, California, so named from a grove of about ninety enormous trees of the genus Sequoia.

Bigwood; river in Idaho, the name of which is derived from the name given by the early French traders, Boise or Boisee, "woody;" so called because of its wooded banks.

Bijou; hills in South Dakota, named for an early French hunter.

Bijou Hills; village in Brule County, South Dakota, named from the hills.

Billerica; town in Middlesex County, Massachusetts, named from a town in Essex, England.

Billings; county in North Dakota, and city in Yellowstone County, Montana, named for Frederick Billings, at one-time president of the Northern Pacific Railroad.

Billingsport; town in Gloucester County, New Jersey, named for an English merchant, Edward Bylling.

Billington Sea; pond in Plymouth, Massachusetts, named for the discoverer, Billington, one of the Mayflower passengers, who reported it is an inland sea.

Bill Williams; mountain in Arizona, named for a guide and trapper.

Biloxi; hay, and city in Harrison County, Mississippi. An Indian tribe of this name inhabited this part of the country. Mooney says the word B'luksi signifies "trifling or worthless," while other authorities give the meaning, "turtle," the B referring to the catch of turtles.

Biltmore; town in Buncombe County, North Carolina, named by George Vanderhilt from the last part of his name.

Bingham; county in Idaho, named by Governor Bunn for his friend, Perry Bingham, Congressman from Pennsylvania.

Bingham; town in Somerset County, Maine, named for William Bingham, a large landowner in early days.

Binghamton; city in Broome County, New York, named for William Bingham, of Philadelphia. a benefactor of the town.

Birch; nineteen post-offices, besides many natural features, bear this name, either alone or with suffixes, generally indicating the presence of the tree.

Bird; city in Cheyenne County, Kansas, named for its founder, Benjamin Bird.

Birdsall; town in Allegany County, New York, named for Judge John Birdsall.

Birdsboro; borough in Berks County, Pennsylvania, named for William Bird, who in 1740 bought the tract on which the town now stands.

Birmingham; twelve places in the country, named from the manufacturing town in England.

Bismarck; city in St. Francois County, Missouri, city in Burleigh County, North Dakota (capital of State), and many other places, named for Prince Otto von Bismarck of Germany.

Bison; peaks in Colorado, and Yellowstone Park, named for their shape.

Bitterwater; branch of Grand River, Utah, so named from the character of the water.

Blackbird; town in Holt County, Nebraska, named for the great warrior and chief of the Omaha Indians, Washingasahba, "Blackbird."

Black Creek; town in Wilson County, North Carolina, named from a creek of dark water.

Black Diamond; town in Contra Costa County, California, so named from its coal mines.

Blackfeet; Indian agency ill Montana, named from an Indian tribe. According to tradition, the name originated in this way: A nameless chief was unsuccessful in the chase until his father blackened his feet with charcoal and named him Satsiaqua, "blackfeet."

Blackfoot; peak, and village in Bingham County, Idaho, named from the Blackfeet Indian tribe.

Blackford; county and village in Jasper County, Indiana, named for Isaac Blackford, judge of the supreme court of Indiana.

Blackhawk; town in Gilpin County, Colorado, named from one of the earliest mining companies.

Blackhawk; county and village in Davis County, Iowa, named for a noted chief of the Sac and Fox Indians.

Blackhawk; town in Carroll County, Mississippi, named for a Choctaw Indian chief.

Black Hills; mountain range in South Dakota, called by the early French traders Cote-Noire, "black hills." from the character of the timber which grows on them, giving a dark appearance.

Blackiston; village in Kent County, Delaware, named for one of the original proprietors of large tracts of land in the county.

Blacklick; creek in Pennsylvania. called by the Indians Naeskahoni, "a lick of blackish color."

Black Mingo; river in South Carolina, named from an Indian tribe.

Blackmore; mount in Montana, named for the English ethnologist, William Blackmore, of London.

Black Mountain; range in North Carolina, so named from the dark green foliage of the balsam fir which covers its tops and sides.

Black Mountain; town in Buncombe County, North Carolina, named from the mountain towering above it.

Black River; village in Jefferson County, New York, named from a river the waters of which are the color of sherry.

Black River Falls; city in Jackson County, Wisconsin, named from the falls of Black River, near which it is situated.

Blacksburg; town in Cherokee County, South Carolina, named for a prominent family in the neighborhood.

Blackstone; river, and town in Worcester County, Massachusetts, named for William Blackstone, the first settler in Boston.

Black Warrior; river in Alabama, translation of the Indian word Tuscaloosa.

Blackwells; island in East River, New York, named for the Blackwell family, who owned it for one hundred years.

Bladen; county in North Carolina; Bladenboro; town in above county. Named for Martin Bladen, one of the lord commissioners of trades and plantations.

Blain; borough in Perry County, Pennsylvania, named for James Blain, the warrantee of the land upon which it was built.

Blaine; counties in Idaho, Oklahoma, and Nebraska, mountain in Colorado, and town in Aroostook County, Maine, and many post-offices in the country, named for James G. Blaine.

Blair; county, Pennsylvania, named for John Blair.

Blair; city in Washington County, Nebraska; Blairstown; town in Benton County, Iowa; Blairstown; town in Warren County, New Jersey. Named for John I. Blair, of New Jersey.

Blairsville; borough and town in Indiana County, Pennsylvania, named for John Blair, a prominent resident of Blairs Gap.

Blakely; town in Early County, Georgia, named for Captain Blakely, naval officer.

Blakiston; island in Potomac River, named for Nehemiah Blakiston, collector of customs.

Blalock; village in Gilliam County, Oregon, named for Dr. Blalock, an early settler.

Blanca; peak in the Sierra Blanca, Colorado, so named from the white rocks on its summit.

Blanchard; town in Piscataquis County, Maine, named for one of the early proprietors, Charles Blanchard.

Blanco; cape on the coast of Oregon, discovered by Martin de Aguilar, the Spanish explorer, who named it. Spanish word, meaning "white."

Blanco; county in Texas, named from the Rio Blanco, "white river."

Bland; county in Virginia, said to have been named for John Bland, a London merchant.

Blandford; town in Hampden County, Massachusetts, named for the Duke of Marlborough, whose second title was Marquis of Blandford.

Blandville; town in Ballard County, Kentucky, named for Capt. Bland Ballard.

Bledsoe; county in Tennessee, named for Jesse Bledsoe, United States Senator.

Bleecker; village in Fulton County, New York, named for Rutger Bleecker, an early patentee.

Blennerhassett; island in the Ohio River, named for Herman Blennerhassett, who was accused of complicity with Aaron Burr.

Blissfield; village in Lenawee County, Michigan, named for Henry Bliss, an early settler, upon whose homestead the village is built.

Block; island off the coast of Rhode Island, named for Adrien Block, the Dutch discoverer.

Blocksburg; town in Humboldt County, California, named for Ben Blockburger, the founder.

Bloods; village in Steuben County, New York, named for Calvin Blood.

Bloomer; village in Chippewa County, Wisconsin, named probably for a Galena merchant.

Bloomfield; city in Stoddard County, Missouri, named from the field of flowers which grew there when the place was founded.

Bloomfield; town in Essex County, New Jersey, named for Governor Joseph Bloomfield of that State.

Blossburg; borough in Tioga County, Pennsylvania, named for Aaron Bloss, who settled there in 1806.

Blount; county in Alabama, named for Willie Blount, governor of Tennessee in 1809-1815.

Blount; county in Tennessee, named for William Blount, governor in 1790-1796.

Blountsville; village in Henry County, Indiana, named for Andrew Blount, its founder.

Blowing Rock; town in Watauga County, North Carolina, named from a cliff where the wind blows upward.

Blue Earth; county, city, and river in Minnesota, so named because of the bluish color of the earth, due to the presence of copper.

Bluefield; city in Mercer County, West Virginia, named from the bluegrass valley in which it is situated.

Blue Grass; villages in Fulton County, Indiana; Scott County, Iowa; Knox County, Tennessee; and Russell County, Virginia, named from a variety of grass which grows in Kentucky.

Blue Hill; town in Hancock County, Maine, named from a mountain.

Blue Hills; range of hills in Massachusetts, which are said to have given name to the State, the Indian name having been Massachusetts, "great hills."

Blue Mounds; village in Dane County, Wisconsin, named from mounds appearing blue in the distance.

Blue Mountain; town in Tippah County, Mississippi, named from a large bluish hill near the site.

Blue Ridge; the most eastern of the principal ridges of the Appalachian chain of mountains, so called from the hue which frequently envelopes its distant summits.

Blue Springs; town in Union County, Mississippi, named from springs with water of bluish hue.

Bluffton; city in Wells County, Indiana, so named on account of the high bluffs which once surrounded the town.

Blunts; reef on the coast of California, named for Captain Blunt, of the Hudson Bay Company.

Blyville; village in Knox County, Nebraska, named for George W. Bly, early settler.

Boardman; mountain in Franklin County, Maine, named for Herbert Boardman, who settled at its base in 1795.

Boardman; town in Columbus County, North Carolina, named for a pioneer Baptist preacher.

Boardman; township and village in Mahoning County, Ohio, named for the original proprietor, Frederick Boardman.

Boca; post-office in Nevada County, California, at the mouth of the Truckee River. A Spanish word, meaning "mouth."

Bodie; island in North Carolina, named for Hon. N. W. Boddie, of Nashville, North Carolina.

Bodock; creek in Arkansas, corrupted from the French, hois d'arc, a species of wood.

Boerne; village in Kendall County, Texas, named for the German writer, Louis Boerne.

Bogota; borough in Bergen County, New Jersey, named for the South American city.

Bogue Chitto; town and creek in Lincoln County, Mississippi. An Indian name, meaning "big creek."

Bohemia; villages in Escambia County, Florida; Suffolk County, New York; and Douglas County, Oregon, named from the province in Austria-Hungary.

Bois Brule; township in Perry County, Missouri. A French name, meaning "burnt wood."

Bois d'Arc; village in Greene County, Missouri, named from a tree from which the Indians procured wood for their bows. A French name, meaning "bow wood."

Bois des Sioux; tributary of the Red River, North Dakota. A French name, meaning "the wood of the Sioux."

Boise; county and city in Idaho, situated on Boise River. A French word, meaning "woody," given by the early French traders because of the trees upon the banks of the river.

Bolinas; bay, and town in Marin County, California. A Spanish word, meaning "whale."

Bolivar; county and village in Mississippi; city in Polk County, Missouri; town in Allegany County, New York; town in Hardeman County, Tennessee; and five other places, named for Gen. Simon Bolivar.

Bollinger; county in Missouri, named for Maj. George F. Bollinger, an early settler.

Bolton; town in Worcester County, Massachusetts, named for Charles Powlet, third Duke of Bolton.

Bolton; town in Hinds County, Mississippi, named for a man interested in building a railroad from Vicksburg to Jackson.

Bombay; town in Franklin County, New York, named by Mr. Hogan, an early settler, whose wife had lived in Bombay, India.

Bonair; towns in Howard County, Iowa, White County, Tennessee, and village in Chesterfield County, Virginia. A French word, meaning "good air."

Bonanza; village in Klamath County, Oregon, and seven other places in the country. A Spanish word meaning "prosperity."

Bonaparte; town in Van Buren County, Iowa, and village in Lewis County, New York, named for Napoleon Bonaparte.

Bonaqua; town in Hickman County, Tennessee, so called because it is situated near mineral springs. Latin name, meaning "good water."

Bond; county in Illinois, named for Shadrack Bond, first governor of the State, 1818-1822.

Bondurant; town in Polk County, Iowa, named for A. C. Bondurant.

Bonham: town in Fannin County, Texas, named for Col. J. B. Bonham, who died in the Alamo in 1836.

Bonhomme; county in South Dakota, named for Jacques Bon Homme, the Frenchman's "Uncle Sam." This name was given by the early French traders to an island in the Missouri River, in the above State, and afterwards the name was transferred to the county.

Bonita; point in California, and a village in Ottertail County, Minnesota. A Spanish word, meaning "pretty, graceful."

Bonner Springs; city in Wyandotte County, Kansas, named for Robert Bonner, horseman, and editor of the New York Ledger.

Bonneterre; town in St. Francois county, Missouri. A French word, meaning "good earth," having been given by early French settlers to a mine which contained lead.

Bonneville; mounts in Nevada and Wyoming, and a village in Multnomah County, Oregon, named for Capt. B. L. E. Bonneville, early explorer in the Northwest.

Bonpas; creek and town in Richland County, Illinois, named from the prairie which is now called Bompare, but which was named by the early French, Bon Pas, meaning "good walk."

Bonpland; mount in Nevada and lake in California, named for Aime Bonpland, the French botanist.

Bon Secours; triangular projection on the east side of Mobile Bay, and post-office in Baldwin County, Alabama. A French name, meaning "good succor."

Book; plateau in Colorado; so named from its shape.

Boon; town in Wexford County, Michigan; Boone; counties in Arkansas, Illinois, Indiana, Kentucky, Missouri, Nebraska, and West Virginia, and town in Wautauga County, North Carolina. Named for Daniel Boone. His name appears in combination with different suffixes, such as "boro," "lake," etc., in many parts of the United States.

Boone; county, city, and creek in Iowa, named for Captain Boone, United States dragoons, who captured Des Moines Valley above Coon Forks.

Boone; creek in Yellowstone Park, named for Robert Withrow, who called himself "Daniel Boone the second."

Boone Station; village in Fayette County. Kentucky, named for Daniel Boone.

Booneville; town in Prentiss County, Mississippi, named for an early settler, Colonel Boone.

Boonton; town in Morris County, New Jersey, named for Thomas Boone, its colonial governor in 1760.

Boonville; town in Warrick County, Indiana. Some authorities say that it received its name in honor of Daniel Boone, while Conklin says it was named for Ratliffe Boone, second governor of the State, who laid it out.

Boonville; village in Oneida County, New York, named for Gerrit Boon, agent of the Holland Land Company, who made the first settlement.

Boonville; town in Yadkin County, North Carolina, named for Daniel Boone.

Boothbay; town in Lincoln County, Maine, named for the town in England.

Borax; lake in California, the waters of which are a solution of borax.

Bordeaux; town in Abbeville County, South Carolina, named from the city in France.

Borden; county and village in Colorado County, Texas, named for Gail Borden, member of the consultation of 1833, collector of customs at Galveston in 1837, editor and financier.

Bordentown; city in Burlington County, New Jersey, named for Joseph Borden, its founder.

Borgne; lake in Louisiana. A French word, meaning "one-eyed," hence something "defective," given to the lake by the French because they did not consider it a lake, but rather a bay, as it had the appearance of being separated from the main body of the sea by numerous islands.

Borodino; village in Onondaga County, New York, named from the town in Russia.

Boscawen; town in Merrimac County, New Hampshire, named for Admiral Edward Boscawen.

Boscobel; city in Grant County, Wisconsin, named for a place in Shropshire, England.

Bosque; county and river in Texas. A French and Portuguese word, meaning "a wood, a forest," applied to the country because of the forests of live oak, oak, and cedar.

Bosqueville; village in McLennan County, Texas; so named because near Bosque River.

Bossier; parish and village in Louisiana, named for General Bossier, a celebrated duelist.

Bostic; town in Rutherford County, North Carolina, named for George T. Bostic.

Boston; city in Massachusetts. By some authorities the name is said to have been given in honor of John Cotton, vicar of St. Bodolph's church in Boston, Lincolnshire, England, and one of the first clergymen in the American Boston. Others say it was named before the arrival of John Cotton, for three prominent colonists from Boston, England. Sixteen places in the country have taken their names from the Massachusetts city.

Botetourt; county in Virginia, named for Norborne Berkeley, Lord de Botetourt, royal governor of Virginia in 1768.

Bottineau; county and town in North Dakota, named for Pierre Bottineau, one of the early settlers of the Red River Valley.

Bouckville; village in Madison County, New York, named for Governor William C. Bouck.

Bouff; creek in Chicot County, Arkansas. Corruption of the French Bayou aux Boeufs, "bayou of cattle."

Boulder; county and city in Colorado, named from the huge boulders found in the county.

Boundbrook; borough in Somerset County, New Jersey, named from a creek emptying into the Raritan River, which was the northern boundary of the grant made to Governor Carteret. It is now part of the boundary between Middlesex and Somerset counties.

Bouquet; river in Essex County, New York; said to be named from the flowers upon its banks. Some authorities think it is derived from the French baquet, "a trough."

Bourbeuse; river in Missouri. A French name applied to the river by the early French traders, meaning "muddy."

Bourbon; counties in Kansas and Kentucky, and town in Marshall County, Indiana, besides several small places, named for the royal family of France.

Bovina; town in Delaware County, New York; from the Latin. because of its fitness for grazing.

Bow; creek in Nebraska, named by the early French, Petit Arc, "little bow."

Bow; town in Merrimack County, New Hampshire, so named from a bend in the river within the town limits.

Bowdoinham; town in Sagadahoc County, Maine. Some authorities say it was named for James Bowdoin, governor of Massachusetts in 1785-86, while Varney claims that it was named for William Bowdoin, of Boston.

Bowen; town in Jones County, Iowa, named for Hugh Bowen.

Bowerbank; plantation in Piscataquis County, Maine, a London merchant, first owner.

Bowie; town in Prince George County, Maryland, named for Governor Oden Bowie.

Bowie; county and village in Montague County, Texas, named for James Bowie, Indian and Mexican lighter, the inventor of the bowie knife, who was killed at the Alamo.

Bowling Green; the name of seven places in the country. The word is said to be derived from a term denoting ornamental gardening, a plat of turf for bowling. This game was played at a point at the lower end of Broadway, still called Bowling Green. The name is found in Yorkshire, England.

Bowman; village in Fleming County, Kentucky, named for Col. Abram Bowman, first settler.

Bowman; town in Orangeburg County, South Carolina, named for the Fleming family, of Orangeburg.

Boxbutte; county and town in Nebraska, named from a butte in the county.

Boxelder; county in Utah and creek in Montana, also six other places in the country, named from the tree.

Boxford; town in Essex County, Massachusetts, probably named from a town in Suffolk, England.

Boyd; county and village in Harrison County, Kentucky, named for Linn Boyd, statesman of Tennessee, one-time lieutenant-governor of Kentucky.

Boyd; county in Nebraska, named for James E. Boyd, governor of the State in 1891-93.

Boyd Tavern; village in Albemarle County, Virginia, named for a family who kept a tavern there many years ago.

Boyerton; borough in Berks County, Pennsylvania, named for the Boyer family, early settlers.

Boyle; county in Kentucky, named for John Boyle, chief justice of the State.

Boylston; town in Worcester County, Massachusetts, named for a family, residents of Boston.

Boylston; town in Oswego County, New York, named for Thomas Boylston.

Bozeman; city in Gallatin County, Montana, named for J. M. Bozeman, an early colored trapper.

Bozrahville; town in New London County, Connecticut, named from the ancient town in Syria.

Bracken; county in Kentucky, named for two creeks, Big and Little Bracken, which were named for William Bracken, a pioneer hunter.

Bracks; butte in California, named for an old settler.

Braddock; borough in Allegheny County, Pennsylvania, named for the battlefield where General Braddock was defeated by the French and Indians.

Braddys; pond in Portage County, Ohio, named for Capt. Samuel Brady.

Bradford; county in Florida, named for Captain Bradford, who was killed in battle on an island in western Florida.

Bradford; village, now a part of Haverhill, Essex County, Massachusetts, named from a town in Yorkshire, England.

Bradford; town in Merrimack County, New Hampshire, and village in Orange County, Vermont, named for the above.

Bradford; town in Steuben County, New York, named for General Bradford.

Bradford; county and city in McKean County, Pennsylvania, named for William Bradford, Attorney-General of the United States.

Bradfordsville; town in Marion County, Kentucky, named for Peter Bradford, the first settler.

Bradley; county in Arkansas, named for Capt. Hugh Bradley.

Bradley; town in Greenwood County, South Carolina, named for a family of the State.

Bradley; county in Tennessee. The origin of the name is in doubt. Judge P. B. Mayfield, of Cleveland, Tennessee, says it was probably named for a schoolteacher.

Bradley Beach; borough in Monmouth County, New Jersey, named for the original owner, James A. Bradley.

Bradys Bend; town in Armstrong County, Pennsylvania, named for Capt. Samuel Brady, the noted Indian fighter.

Brainerd; city in Butler County, Kansas, named for E. B. Brainerd, who owned the farm upon which part of the city was built.

Brainerd; city in Crow Wing County, Minnesota, named for David Brainerd, celebrated missionary to the Indians.

Braintree; town in Norfolk County, Massachusetts, named for a town in Essex, England.

Braintree; town in Orange County, Vermont, named for the above, where many of the early grantees resided.

Bramwell; town in Mercer County, West Virginia, named for an English engineer and coal operator there.

Branch; county and township in Mason County, Michigan, named for John Branch, Secretary of the Navy under Jackson.

Branchport; town in Yates County, New York, which derives its name from its position on one of the branches of Crooked Lake.

Branchville; borough in Sussex County, New Jersey, named for the branch or river known as Long Branch.

Branchville; town in Orangeburg County, South Carolina, named from the forks of the two branches of the South Carolina Railroad.

Brandenburg; town in Meade County, Kentucky, named for a province in Prussia.

Brandon; town in Rankin County, Mississippi, named for Gerard C. Brandon, governor in 1828-32.

Brandt; lake and town in Erie County, New York, named for Col. Joseph Brandt, Mohawk chief.

Brandy wine; creek in Pennsylvania. According to a tradition, the name is derived from the occasion of a vessel laden with brantewein (brandy), which was lost in its waters. Other authorities derive it from Andrew Braindwine, who owned lands near its mouth in early days. A third theory is that the slough near Downington discharged its muddy waters into the creek, tinging it the color of brandy. A celebrated battle was fought there, which accounts for the name being given to eight places in the country.

Branford; town in New Haven County, Connecticut, named from the town of Brentford, England.

Brasher; town in St. Lawrence County, New York, named for Philip Brasher, part owner.

Brassua; lake of Moose River, Maine, said to be named from an Indian chief. The word is said to signify "frank."

Brattleboro; town in Windham County, Vermont, named for Col. William Brattle, a citizen of Boston.

Braxton; county in West Virginia, named for Carter Braxton, one of the signers of the Declaration of Independence.

Braysville; village in Owen County, Indiana, named for its founder.

Brazil; city in Clay County, Indiana, named for the country in South America.

Brazoria; county and town in Texas. The old municipality of Brazoria, founded under the Mexican rule, was named from the Brazos River.

Brazos; river and county in Texas. A Franciscan monk named the neighboring stream—now the Colorado—Brazos del Dio, "arms of God." The Mexicans confused the two rivers and called the Colorado the Brazos, and vice versa, and so the names stand to-day.

Breakabeen; village in Schoharie County, New York, named from the German word for the rushes which grew upon the banks of the creek at this point.

Breathitt; county in Kentucky, named for John Breathitt, former governor of the State.

Breckenridge; town in Summit County, Colorado, and city in Caldwell County, Missouri, named for John C. Breckenridge, Vice-President of the United States.

Breckenridge; county in Kentucky, named for John Breckenridge, a Kentucky statesman.

Breedsville; village in Van Buren County, Michigan, named for Silas Breed, an early settler.

Breese; village in Clinton County, Illinois, named for Lieutenant-Governor Sidney Breese.

Bremer; county in Iowa, named for Fredrika Bremer, the Swedish authoress, who spent some time in this region in 1850.

Brentwood; town in Rockingham County, New Hampshire, incorporated as Brintwood; probably named from a place in England.

Brevard; county in Florida, named for Dr. Brevard, author of the Mecklenburg Declaration of Independence.

Brevard; town in Transylvania County, North Carolina, named for Ephraim J. Brevard, a Revolutionary patriot.

Brewer; mount in California, named for Prof. W. H. Brewer.

Brewer; city in Penobscot County, Maine, named for Col. John Brewer, first settler.

Brewer; strait of Staten Island, New York, discovered by Brewer in 1643.

Brewster; a town in Barnstable County, Massachusetts, named for Elder William Brewster, one of the first settlers in Plymouth colony.

Brewster; village in Putnam County, New York, probably named after James and Walter F. Brewster, who at one time owned the tract of land comprising the village.

Brewster; county in Texas, named for H. P. Brewster, private secretary to Samuel Houston.

Briceland; village in Humboldt County, California, named for a resident.

Bridal Veil; falls in Yosemite Valley, California, and falls on a branch of the Columbia River, Oregon. A descriptive name.

Bridal Veil; village in Multnomah County, Oregon, named for falls.

Bridge; creek in Yellowstone Park, named from a natural bridge of trachyte over it.

Bridgeport; city in Connecticut, also of numerous other places, usually so called from abridge in or near the place. The suffixes "ton," "town," "water," and "ville" are also used frequently.

Bridger; peak, village in Carbon County, and river in Montana, lake in Yellowstone Park, and pass in the Rocky Mountains, named for Maj. James Bridger, a noted guide.

Bridgewater; town in Plymouth County, Massachusetts, named for the Duke of Bridgewater. Nason says the name was derived from a town in Somersetshire, England.

Bridgton; town in Cumberland County, Maine, named for an early settler, Moody Bridges.

Briensburg; village in Marshall County, Kentucky, named for James Brien, member of the legislature.

Brigham; city in Boxelder County, Utah, named for Brigham Young.

Bright Angel; creek in Arizona, so named because of the clearness of its waters.

Brighton; twenty-five places in the country named either, directly or indirectly, from the English town.

Briscoe; county in Texas, named for Andrew Briscoe, San Jacinto veteran.

Bristol; town in Lincoln County, Maine, named from the English town, whence two
[of the original proprietors came. Counties of Massachusetts and Rhode Island, t town

in Rhode Island, village in Bucks County, Pennsylvania, city in Virginia, and town in Ontario County, New York, all derive their name from the Englishtown.

Bristol; town in Kenosha County, Wisconsin, named for Rev. Ira Bristol, an early; settler. i Broad; descriptive word used with various suffixes. A mountain ridge in Pennsylvania which has a broad tableland almost destitute of trees.

Broadalbin; town in Fulton County, New York, named for a place in Scotland.

Broadhead; town in Rockcastle County, Kentucky, named for a resident.

Broadtop; mountain in Bedford and Huntingdon counties, Pennsylvania; descriptive name.

Broadwater; county in Montana, named for Col. Charles Broadwater.

Brock; village in Nemaha County, Nebraska, named for a resident.

Brockport; village in Monroe County, New York, named for Hiel Brockway, early settler.

Brokenstraw; village in Chautauqua County, New York, and creek in Warren County, Pennsylvania. A translation of the Indian name degasysnohdyahgah.

Bronson; village in Bourbon County, Kansas, named for Ira D. Bronson, of Fort Scott.

Bronx; river in Westchester County, New York;

Bronxdale; village in Westchester County, New York;

Bronxville; village in Westchester County, New York. Named for Jonas or Jacob Bronck, an early settler.

Brooke; county in West Virginia, named for Robert Brooke, governor of the State of Virginia in 1794-1796.

Brookfield; town in Orange County, Vermont, so called, according to tradition, because of the number of brooks there in early days.

Brookings; county in South Dakota, named for Wilmot W. Brookings, legislator.

Brookland; town in South Carolina, crossed by several small streams.

Brookline; part of Boston, Massachusetts. The name is said to be a modification of Brooklyn. Some authorities say, however, that the name was given because of a small creek running through the place.

Brooklyn; city in New York, corruption of the Dutch name Breuckelen, from a village in the province of Utrecht, Holland. The name signifies broken up land, or marshy land.

Brooklyn; villages in Jackson County, Michigan, and Perry County, Mississippi, named for the above.

Brooks; county in Georgia, named for Preston L. Brooks.

Brooks; town in Waldo County, Maine, named for Governor Brooks, of Massachusetts.

Brooksville; town in Noxubee County, Mississippi, named for a resident family.

Brookville; town in Franklin County, Indiana, named for Jesse Brook Thomas, the original proprietor.

Brookville; town in Bracken County, Kentucky, named for David Brooks.

Brookville; many places in the country bear this name, mostly given descriptive of the situation upon some stream. The word is used with various suffixes, such as "vale," "view," and "wood."

Broome; county in New York; Broome Center; village in Schoharie County, New York. Named for Lieutenant Governor John Broome.

Brown; counties in Illinois, Indiana, Ohio, and Wisconsin, named for Maj. Gen. Jacob Brown.

Brown; county in Kansas, named for O. H. Browne, member of the first Territorial legislature.

Brown; county in Minnesota, named for J. R. Brown, member of the council in 1855.

Brown; county in Nebraska, named for two members of the committee who reported the bill for the organization of the county.

Brown; county in South Dakota, named for Alfred Brown, legislator in 1870.

Brown; county in Texas, named for Henry S. Brown, an old settler.

Brownfield; town in Oxford County, Maine, named for Capt. Henry Young Brown, to whom the site was granted.

Brownington; town in Orleans County, Vermont, named for Timothy and Daniel Brown, to whom part of it was originally granted.

Brownstown; town in Jackson County, Indiana;

Brownsville; town in Edmonson County, Kentucky. Named for Gen. Jacob Brown.

Brownsville; borough in Fayette County, Pennsylvania, named for the Brown brothers. Thomas and Basil, early settlers.

Brownsville; city in Cameron County, Texas, named for Major Brown, who was killed there at the beginning of the war with Mexico.

Browntown; village in Green County, Wisconsin, named for William G. Brown, an early settler.

Brownville; town in Piscataquis County, Maine, named for Deacon Francis Brown, early resident.

Brownville; city in Nemaha County, Nebraska, named for the first settler, Richard Brown, who came there from Holt County, Missouri.

Brownville; town in Jefferson County, New York, named for John Brown, an early settler, father of General Brown.

Brownwood; city in Texas, named for Henry S. Brown, an old settler.

Bruceton Mills; town in Preston County, West Virginia, named for an early prominent settler.

Bruceville; village in Knox County, Indiana, named for William Bruce, its former owner.

Brule; county in South Dakota, towns in Keith County, Nebraska, and Douglas County, Wisconsin, and several other places, named for a tribe of Indians. The word "brule" means "burnt," and the tribe, the Bride Sioux, were said to have acquired the name from being caught in a prairie fire and being badly burned about the thighs.

Brunson; town in Hampton County, South Carolina, named for a prominent family.

Brunswick; town in Cumberland County, Maine, named for the house of Brunswick, to which the reigning King of Great Britain, William III, belonged.

Brunswick; city in Chariton County, Missouri, named for Brunswick Terrace in England, the former home of the founder, James Keyte.

Brunswick; counties in North Carolina and Virginia, named for the duchy in Germany.

Brush; creek in Pennsylvania. From the Indian name, Achweek, "bushy or overgrown with brush."

Brushland; village in Delaware County, New York, named for Alexander Brush, first settler and proprietor.

Brushton; village in Franklin County, New York, named for Henry N. Brush, extensive property owner.

Brutus; town in Cayuga County, New York, named by the State land board of New York, which gave names of celebrated Romans to townships in the military tract in central New York. Town in Emmett County, Michigan, villages in Clay County, Kentucky, and Pittsylvania County, Virginia, also bear this name.

Bryan; county in Georgia, named for Jonathan Bryan, one of the founders of the State.

Bryan; village in Williams County, Ohio, named for John A. Bryan, a former auditor of the State.

Bryn Mawr; village in Montgomery County, Pennsylvania, named for a town in Wales.

Bryson; town in Swain County, North Carolina, named for T. D. Bryson, member of the legislature, and owner of the town site.

Buchanan; counties in Iowa, Missouri, and Virginia, and several places in the country, named for President James Buchanan.

Buchanan; town in Botetourt County, Virginia. named for Col. John Buchanan, pioneer and Indian fighter of Augusta County.

Buck Creek; village in Greene County, Indiana, so named because a buck appeared each returning season on the banks of a near-by creek.

Buckeye; fourteen places in the country bear this name. The word is applied to a species of horse chestnut which grows on river banks in western Pennsylvania, Ohio, and Michigan, the fruit resembling the eye of a buck.

Buckfield; town in Oxford County, Maine, named for Abijah Bucks, one of the first settlers.

Buckhannon; river and town in Upshur County, West Virginia. An Indian name, said to mean "brick river."

Buckingham; county in Virginia;

Bucks; county in Pennsylvania. Named from Buckinghamshire, England.

Bucks Bridge; village in St. Lawrence County, New York, named for Isaac Buck, early settler.

Buckskin; village in Park County, Colorado, named for Joseph Higginbottom, "Buckskin Joe."

Bucksport; town in Humboldt County, California, named for David Buck, who laid it out in 1851.

Bucksport; town in Hancock County, Maine, named for Col. Jonathan Bucks, of Haverhill, who settled it.

Bucoda; village in Thurston County, Washington, named by taking the first part of the names of three men, Buckley, Collier, and Davis.

Bucyrus; city in Crawford County, Ohio, named by Col. James Kilbourne. The daughters of Samuel Norton, who live there, say that Colonel Kilbourne's favorite character was Cyrus, to which "bu" was prefixed, referring to the beautiful country. An old citizen, F. Adams, says that it was named by Colonel Kilbourne from Busiris in ancient Egypt.

Buel; village in Montgomery County, New York, named for Jesse Buel, of Albany.

Buena Vista; county in Iowa, city in Rockbridge County, Virginia, and twenty other places in the country. The name of the field upon which General Taylor won his victory, and doubtless given in some cases for patriotic reasons, but the majority of places named descriptively, it being a Spanish word meaning " beautiful view."

Buffalo; counties in Nebraska, South Dakota, and Wisconsin, city in New York, numerous creeks, rivers, towns, and villages, named because of the former presence of that animal.

Bullards Bar; town in Yuba County, California, named for an old settler.

Bullitt; county in Kentucky; Bullittsville; town in Boone County, Kentucky. Named for Alexander Scott Bullitt.

Bulloch; county in Georgia; Bullochville; village in Meriwether County, Georgia, named for Archibald Bull loch, one of the most eminent men of his time.

Bullock; county and village in Crenshaw County, Alabama. Named for E. C. Bullock, of that State.

Bunceton; city in Cooper County, Missouri, named for Harvey Bunce, of the county.

Buncombe; county in North Carolina and several places in the Southern States, named for Col. Edward Buncombe, of the Continental Army.

Bunker Hill; city in Macoupin County, Illinois, and eleven other places, named for the famous battle of the Revolution.

Bunsen; peak in Yellowstone Park, named by the United States Geological Survey for the eminent chemist and physicist, Robert Wilhelm Bunsen.

Burden; city in Cowley County, Kansas, named for Robert F. Burden, leading member of the town company.

Bureau; county and town in Illinois, named for a French trader, Pierre de Beuro, who established a trading post upon a creek which first bore his name.

Burgaw; village in Pender County, North Carolina, named for a resident family.

Burke; county in Georgia, town in Franklin County, New York, and town in Caledonia County, Vermont, named for Edmund Burke, the English statesman.

Burke; county in North Carolina, named for Thomas Burke, governor of North Carolina in 1781-82.

Burleigh; county and creek in North Dakota, named for Walter A. Burleigh, early settler, and Delegate to Congress.

Burleson; county and village in Johnson County, Texas, named for Edward Burleson, Indian fighter, and vice-president under Houston in 1841.

Burlingame; city in Osage County, Kansas, named for Anson Burlingame, minister to China.

Burlington; town in Coffey County, Kansas, city in Des Moines County, Iowa, and village in Calhoun County, Michigan, named from the city in Vermont.

Burlington; county and city in New Jersey, named from Brilington, commonly pronounced Burlington, England.

Burlington; city in Chittenden County, Vermont, named for the Burling family, of New York.

Burnet; county and town in Texas, named for David G. Burnet, twice governor of the State.

Burnett; town in Antelope County, Nebraska, named for the first superintendent of the Sioux City and Pacific Railroad.

Burnett; county in Wisconsin, named for Thomas P. Burnett, an early legislator of the State.

Burnside; river and island in Georgia, named for an early settler.

Burnsville; village in Bartholomew County, Indiana, named for Brice Burns, its founder.

Burnsville; town in Yancey County, North Carolina, named for Otway Burns, captain of the privateer Snapdragon.

Burr; creek in Humboldt County, California, named for early settlers.

Burrillville; town in Providence County, Rhode Island, named for Hon. James Burrill, jr., attorney-general of the State.

Burr Oak; village in St. Joseph County, Michigan, and city in Jewel County, Kansas, on a creek of the same name, so named from the species of trees growing there.

Burrs Mills; village in Jefferson County, New York, named for John Burr and sons, mill owners.

Burrton; city in Harvey County, Kansas, named for I. T. Burr, vice-president of the Atchison, Topeka and Santa Fe Railroad.

Burt; town in Kossuth County, Iowa, named for the president of the Union Pacific Railroad.

Burt; county in Nebraska, named for Francis Burt, governor of the Territory in 1854.

Bushkill; two creeks, and a village in Pike County, Pennsylvania. A Dutch word, meaning "bushy stream."

Bushy; creek in western Pennsylvania. A translation of the Indian name Achemek.

Buskirk Bridge; village in Washington County, New York, named for Martin Van Buskirk.

Busti; town in Chautauqua County, New York, named for Paul Busti, of the Holland Land Company.

Butler; county in Alabama, named for Capt. William Butler, of that State.

Butler; county in Iowa, and city in Bates County, Missouri, named for William O. Butler, of Kentucky, general in the Mexican war.

Butler; county in Kansas, named for Andrew P. Butler, United States Senator from South Carolina in 1846-1857.

Butler; counties in Kentucky, Ohio, and Pennsylvania, named for Gen. Richard Butler, who fell at St. Clair's defeat.

Butler; county in Nebraska, named for David Butler.

Butte; county in California, named from Marysville Buttes. French, meaning "a small knoll or hill."

Butte; city in Silverbow County, Montana, named from a bare butte overlooking the place.

Butte; county in South Dakota, so named from buttes, prominent features in the county.

Butte des Morts; town in "Winnebago County, Wisconsin. A French name, meaning "hill of the dead," so called by the early explorers from the native graves found there.

Butter Hill; an eminence on the Hudson River, so called from its resemblance to a huge lump of batter.

Butts; county in Georgia, named in honor of Capt. Samuel Butts, an officer in the war of 1812.

Buttzville; town in Ransom County, North Dakota, named for a resident.

Buxton; town in York County, Maine, named for the native place of Rev. Paul Coffin, the first minister.

Buxton; village in Washington County, Oregon, named for Henry Buxton, early settler.

Buzzards Bay; village in Barnstable County, Massachusetts, named for a small hawk which was very abundant on the coast.

Byers; town in Arapahoe County and mount in Colorado, named for W. N. Byers, of Denver.

Byhalia; town in Marshall County, Mississippi. Indian word, meaning "standing white oaks."

Bynumville; town in Chariton County, Missouri, named for Dr. Joseph Bynum, an early settler.

Byron; town in Houston County, Georgia, and Genesee County, New York, named for Lord Byron. Eighteen other places bear this name, all of which were probably named for the English poet.

C

Cabarrus; county in North Carolina, named for Stephen Cabarrus, speaker of the house of commons in that State.

Cabell; county in West Virginia, named for William Caboil, governor of Virginia in 1805-1808.' Cable; village in Mercer County, Illinois, named for Ransom R. Cable, railway manager.

Cabot; town in Washington County, Vermont, named for Miss Cabot, a descendant of Sebastian Cabot.

Cache; many streams, county, village, and valley in northeastern Utah. A French word, meaning "hiding place," probably applied because of certain things having been hidden there by early explorers and travelers.

Cache la Poudre; creek in Colorado, named from the French, meaning "powder hiding place."

Caddo; town in Choctaw Nation, Indian Territory; parish and lake in Louisiana; village in Stephens County, Texas, and several small places named from the Indian tribe who called themselves Ascena, "timber Indians," probably because of their residence in a wooded country. The name is derived from ka-ede, "chief."

Cadillac; city in Wexford County, Michigan, named for La Motte (or La Mothe) Cadillac, who established a fort on the Detroit River in 1701.

Cadiz; town in Harrison County, Ohio, named from the city in Spain. Six other small places in the country are so called.

Cadott; village in Chippewa County, Wisconsin, named for a half-breed Indian, Baptiste Cadotte, who lived near the falls which first bore his name.

Caernarvon; townships in Pennsylvania, named from the town in Wales.

Cahokia; creek and town in Illinois, named from an extinct Indian tribe. The name was spelled Kahokia or Kohokia, meaning "he is extremely lean."

Cahto; creek, and village in Mendocino County, California. Indian word, meaning "fish."

Cahuilla; valley, and village in Riverside County, California, named from an Indian tribe. The word means "master."

Caillou; lake and bayou in Louisiana. A French word, meaning "pebble or flint."

Ca Ira; town in Cumberland County, Virginia. A French expression used in a famous revolutionary song, meaning "it shall go on."

Cairo; fourteen places in the country bear the name of the capital of Egypt.

Calais; city in Washington County, Maine, and town in Washington County, Vermont, named for the French city.

Calamine; town in Sharp County, Arkansas, named from the zinc mines, calamina meaning the native siliceous oxide of zinc.

Calapooya; mountains in Oregon, named from an Indian tribe.

Calaveras; river and county in California, so called from the numbers of skulls found there, supposed to be the remains of a bloody battle among the Indians. The word is Spanish, meaning "skull."

Calcasieu; parish and village in Louisiana, named from an Indian tribe Kalkousiouk.

Calcutta; villages in Columbiana County, Ohio, and Pleasants County, West Virginia, named from the city in India.

Caldwell; city in Sumner County, Kansas, named for Alexander Caldwell, of Leavenworth, United States Senator.

Caldwell; counties in Kentucky and Missouri, named for Gen. John Caldwell, formerly lieutenant-governor of Kentucky.

Caldwell; parish in Louisiana, named for Matthew Caldwell, of North Carolina, a noted frontiersman.

Caldwell; borough in Essex County, New Jersey, named for Rev. James Caldwell, a patriotic clergyman of the Revolution.

Caldwell; town in Warren County, New York, named for Gen. James Caldwell, patentee.

Caldwell; county in North Carolina, named for Dr. Joseph Caldwell, first president of the State University.

Caldwell; village in Noble County, Ohio, named for Joseph and Samuel Caldwell, to whom the land belonged.

Caldwell; county and town in Burleson County, Texas, named for Matthew Caldwell, old settler and colonel of Texas regiment in 1841.

Caledonia; county in Vermont, village in Livingston County, New York, and 16 other places in the country, named from the ancient name of Scotland.

Calfee; creek in Yellowstone Park, named for H. B. Calfee, a photographer of note.

Calhoun; counties in Arkansas, Alabama, Florida, Georgia, Illinois, Iowa, Michigan, Mississippi, Texas, and West Virginia, also many small places, named for John C. Calhoun, of South Carolina, Vice-President in 1825-1833.

Calhoun; town in McLean County, Kentucky, named for Judge John Calhoun.

Calhoun; village in Washington County, Nebraska, so named because situated on the site of Fort Calhoun.

Calhoun Falls; town in Abbeville County, South Carolina, named from a prominent family.

California; one of the States of the Union. This name was applied by Cortez to the bay and country, which he supposed to be an island. The name is that of an island in an old Spanish romance, where a great abundance of precious stones were found. Eight post-offices bear this name.

Callahan; county in Texas; named for James M. Callahan, survivor of the massacre of 1836.

Callaway; county and village in Missouri, and several other places; named for Capt. James Callaway, grandson of Daniel Boone.

Callensburg; borough in Clarion County, Pennsylvania; named for Hugh Callen, its founder.

Callicoon; town in Sullivan County, New York. The word is said to signify "turkey" in both Dutch and Indian languages. The Dutch word for "turkey," however, is spelled kalkoen.

Calloway; county in Kentucky; named for Col. Richard Calloway.

Caloosa; river, and village in Lee County, Florida; named for an Indian tribe. The word means "village cruel."

Calumet; river in Illinois and Indiana, county and village in Wisconsin, and seven other places in the country. A Canadian corruption of the French, chalemel, which literally means "little reed," but which, in its corrupted form, refers to the "pipe of peace," used by the Indians to ratify treaties. Haines derives the word from calamo, "honey wood."

Calvary; town in Fond du Lac County, Wisconsin, and seven other places in the country, named from the hill near Jerusalem.

Calvert; county, and post village in Cecil County, Maryland, named for Cecil Calvert, Lord Baltimore. Eight other places are so named, doubtless, directly or indirectly from the same.

Camano; island in Puget Sound, Washington, which takes its name from a canal named for Don Jacinto Camano.

Camas; villages in Fremont County, Idaho, Missoula County, Montana, and Clarke County, Washington; Camas Valley; village in Douglas County, Oregon. The Indian name of a small onion which grows in those States.

Cambria; county in Pennsylvania, named for the ancient name of Wales.

Cambria; village in Columbia County, Wisconsin, probably so named because of the Welsh settlers.

Cambridge; city in Middlesex County, Massachusetts, so named for the English university town, after the general court decided to establish a college there. Twenty-two other places bear the name of the English town, two having the suffix "port" and one "springs."

Camden; county in Georgia, county and city in New Jersey, county and village in North Carolina, town in Knox County, Maine, and village in Oneida County, New York, named for Chief Justice Pratt, Earl of Camden, a friend of the colonies during the Revolution.

Camden; county in Missouri, named from Camden County, North Carolina.

Camels Hump; peak in the Green Mountains, Vermont, so named from its resemblance to the hump of a camel.

Cameron; county and town in Louisiana, county and village in Pennsylvania, and town in Marshall County, West Virginia, named for Simon Cameron.

Cameron; town in Steuben County, New York, named for Dugald Cameron, agent for the Pultney estate.

Cameron; town in Monroe County, North Carolina, named for a prominent family in the county.

Cameron; town in Orangeburg County, South Carolina, named for J. Don Cameron, United States Senator from Pennsylvania.

Cameron; county, and city in Milam County, Texas, named for Ervin or Erving Cameron, who fell in the expedition against Meir.

Camillus; village in Onondaga County, New York, built within the State Land Board limits, and named by members of the board for the Roman magistrate.

Camp; county in Texas, named for J. L. Camp, prominent lawyer.

Campbell; county in Georgia, named for Col. Duncan G. Campbell, of the State legislature.

Campbell; county in Kentucky, named for John Campbell of the State senate.

Campbell; town in Steuben County, New York, named for the Campbell family, early settlers.

Campbell; county and village in South Dakota, named for Gen. C. T. Campbell, pioneer.

Campbell; county in Tennessee, named for Col. Arthur Campbell.

Campbell; county in Virginia, named for Gen. William Campbell, an officer of the American Revolution.

Campbellsville; city in Taylor County, Kentucky, named for Adam Campbell, first settler.

Camp Hill; borough in Cumberland County, Pennsylvania, so named because the seat of a soldiers' orphan school.

Camp Knox; village in Green County, Kentucky, named from a camp of Col. James Knox and 22 men, in 1770.

Campo Seco; town in Calaveras County, California, so named from the general character of its surroundings. A Spanish name, meaning "dry plain."

Campton; town in Grafton County, New Hampshire, so called because the first surveyors of the site built a camp on the present town site.

Canaan; fifteen places in the country bear the name of the promised land of the Israelites.

Canada; villages in Marion County, Kansas; Pike County, Kentucky, and Muskegon County, Michigan, named from the Dominion of Canada. Authorities differ as to the derivation of this name. Father Hennepin says the Spaniards were the original discoverers of the country, but upon landing they were disappointed in the general appearance and expressed their feelings by saying, "Il capa di nada," "Cape nothing." Sir John Barlow says the Portuguese, who first ascended the St. Lawrence, believing it to be a passage to the Indian sea, expressed their disappointment when they discovered their mistake by saying "Canada," "Nothing here." This the natives are said to have remembered and repeated to the Europeans who arrived later, who thought it must be the name of the country. Dr. Shea says the Spanish derivation is fictitious. Some think it was named for the first man to plant a colony of French in the country, Monsieur Cana. Charlevoix says the word originated with the Iroquois Indians, Kanata, or Kanada, "a collection of huts, a village, a town," which the early explorers mistook for the name of the country. Other etymologies propose the two Indian words, Kan, "a mouth," and ada, "a country," hence "the mouth of the country," originally applied to the mouth of the St. Lawrence. There is a respectable authority that the name was first applied to the river. Lescarbot tells us that the Gasperians and Indians who dwelt on the borders of the bay of Chaleur called themselves Canadaquea; that the word meant " province or country." Sweetser says that the word came from the Indian Caughnawaugh, "the village of the rapids." Brant, the Indian chieftain, who translated the gospel into his own language, used the word Canada for "village."

Canadawa; creek in Chautauqua County, New York. An Indian word, meaning "running through the hemlocks."

Canadian; river in Indian Territory and Oklahoma, county in Oklahoma, town in Choctaw Nation, Indian Territory, and village in Hemphill County, Texas. A Spanish word, diminutive of canyon, "a steep-sided gorge."

Canajoharie; town in Montgomery County, New York. This name was originally given to a deep hole of foaming water at the foot of one of the falls in Canajoharie Creek. Indian, meaning "the pot or kettle that washes itself," or " a kettle-shaped hole in a rock." Morgan says the meaning is " washing the basin."

Canal; town in Venango County, Pennsylvania, so named because traversed by the Franklin canal.

Canal de Haro; canal in Washington, named for the Spanish explorer, Lopez de Haro.

Canal Lewisville; town in Coshocton County, Ohio, named for T. B. Lewis, who founded it.

Canandaigua; lake, town in Ontario County, New York, and village in Lenawee County, Michigan. An Indian word, the derivation of which is in dispute. Morgan gives canandargua, "a place selected for settlement, a chosen spot;" Haines, "a town set off." Others have thought the word to be derived from Cahnandahgwah, "sleeping beauty," while another theory is that it is corrupted from the Seneca Indian, Genundewahguah, "great hill people," so called from a large hill near the lake.

Canaseraga; village in Allegany County, New York. From an Indian word, kanasawaga, "several strings of beads with a string lying across."

Canastota; villages in Madison County, New York, and McCook County, South Dakota. An Indian word, Kniste, or Kanetota, "pine tree standing alone." The New York village took its name from a cluster of pines that united their branches over the creek which passes through the town.

Canavaral; cape, and village in Brevard County, Florida. A Spanish word, meaning "a cane plantation."

Canby; city in Clackamas County, Oregon, named for Gen. Edwara Canby, who was killed by the Modoc Indians in northern California.

Candelaria; post-offices in Esmeralda County, Nevada, and Presidio County, Texas. A Spanish word, meaning "tallow and wax chandler's shop."

Candia; town in Rockingham County, New Hampshire, named from the island in the Mediterranean where Governor Wentworth was once a prisoner.

Caneadea; town in Allegany County, New York. An Indian word, meaning "where the heavens rest upon the earth."

Caney; city in Montgomery County, Kansas, villages in Morgan County, Kentucky, Vernon Parish, Louisiana, and Matagorda County, Texas, besides several other small places. This word is frequently used alone and with the suffixes "branch," "spring," and "ville," in the Southern States, and refers to the cane which covers vast tracts of country in the alluvial bottoms.

Canfield; village in Mahoning County, Ohio, named for one of the original proprietors, Jonathan Canfield.

Canisteo; river, and town in Steuben County, New York. An Indian word, meaning "board on, or in, the water."

Cankapoja; lake at the head of Vermilion River, South Dakota. An Indian word, meaning "light wood."

Cannelburg; town in Daviess County, Indiana, named for the Buckeye Cannel Coal Company.

Cannelton; city in Perry County, Indiana, village in Beaver County, Pennsylvania, and town in Kanawha County, West Virginia, named from the beds of cannel coal in the vicinity.

Cannon; river in Minnesota. The name is a corruption of the name given by the early French, Riviere aux Canots, river of the "canoes."

Cannon; county in Tennessee, named for Newton Cannon, governor of the State in 1835-39.

Cannonball; river in North Dakota, translation of the French name, Le Boulet.

Cannon Falls; village in Goodhue County, Minnesota, named from the river.

Cannonsburg; town in Kent County, Michigan, named for Le Grand Cannon, of Troy, New York.

Cannonsville; village in Delaware County, New York, named for Benjamin Cannon, early owner.

Canoeridge; village in Indiana County, Pennsylvania, so named because it is situated on the highest point on the west branch of the Susquehanna to which a canoe could be pushed.

Canoga; village in Seneca County, New York, named from a large spring which affords permanent motive power for two mills. An Indian word meaning "oil floating on the water."

Canon; a name given by the Spaniards to narrow mountain gorges or deep ravines. Sometimes spelled canon, others canyon, from their proximity to gorges; such as Canyonville, Oregon, and Canon City, Colorado. A Spanish word meaning "a tube, a funnel."

Canon de Ugalde; pass in Texas named for a Mexican general.

Canonicut; island in Narragansett Bay, Rhode Island, named for Canonicus, an Indian chief of the Narragansett tribe, a friend of Roger Williams.

Canonsburg; town in Washington County, Pennsylvania, laid out by and named for Col. John Cannon.

Canoochee; river, and village in Emanuel County, Georgia. An Indian word, said to be derived from Ikanodshi, "the graves are there."

Canterbury; town in Windham County, Connecticut, and villages in Kent county, Delaware, Merrimack County, New Hampshire, and Mingo County, West Virginia, named from the English town.

Canton; numerous places in the country, which derive their name, either directly or indirectly, from the city in China.

Capac; town in St. Clair County, Michigan, named for Manco Capac, the first emperor or chief of the Peruvian empire. The word, manco, is said to mean "chief."

Cape Elizabeth; town in Cumberland County, Maine, named from the cape, which was named for Queen Elizabeth of England.

Cape Girardeau; county and city in Missouri, named for Sieur Girardot, of Kaskaskia.

Capell; mountain and fort in California, named for an officer.

Cape May; county and city in New Jersey, named from the cape named for Cornelis Jacobse May, a navigator in the employ of the Dutch West Indian Company.

Cape Vincent; town in Jefferson County, New York, named for Vincent, son of Le Ray de Chaumont.

Capitol; peak in Colorado, so named from its form.

Carancahua; village in Jackson County, Texas; named for an Indian tribe.

Carbon; a name of frequent occurrence in the country, given to indicate the presence of coal deposits. Counties in Montana, Pennsylvania, Utah, and Wyoming are so called. Various suffixes, such as "dale," "hill," etc., are also used.

Cardiff; villages in Jefferson County, Alabama; Garfield County, Colorado, and Onondaga County, New York, named from the city in Wales.

Cardwell; village in Dunklin County, Missouri, named for Frank Cardwell, of Paragould, Arkansas.

Carencro; town in Lafayette Parish, Louisiana, so named because large flocks of buzzards roosted in the cypress trees common in that neighborhood. A Creole word, meaning "buzzard."

Carlinville; city in Macoupin County, Illinois, named for Thomas Carlin, governor of the State in 1834-42.

Carlisle; county in Kentucky, named for John G. Carlisle, Secretary of the Treasury under President Cleveland.

Carlisle; town in Middlesex County, Massachusetts, named, according to Whitmore, for Charles Howard, Earl of Carlisle. Other authorities say for the town in Scotland.

Carlisle; borough in Cumberland County, Pennsylvania, named for the town in England.

Carlisle; town in Union County, South Carolina, named for a prominent family.

Carlstadt; borough in Bergen County, New Jersey, named by early German settlers for the town in Croatia.

Carlton; county and village in Minnesota, named for one of the first representatives in the legislature of the district, which was afterwards formed into Carlton County.

Carmel; town in Penobscot County, Maine, and several other small places, named from the mountain in Palestine.

Carnegie; borough in Allegheny County, Pennsylvania, named for Andrew Carnegie.

Carnesville; town in Franklin County, Georgia, named for Col. T. P. Carnes, sr.

Caro; village in Tuscola County, Michigan, a fanciful name given by its founder, W. E. Sherman.

Carolina; name given to two States, North and South Carolina. Near the middle of the sixteenth century, Jean Ribault visited the region and named it Carolina, in honor of his king, Charles IX of France, but the name never came into general use and soon disappeared. About 1628, this name was applied definitely to that part of the country lying between Virginia and Florida, having been given in honor of Charles I of England. In an old manuscript, now in London, the following may be found: "1629-30, Feb. 10. The Attorney-General is prayed to grant by Patent 2 Degrees in Carolina," etc. In 1663 the name was definitely applied to the province granted to proprietors by Charles H of England. This province was named in honor of the reigning king, and thus the old name given in honor of Charles I was retained.

Caroline; county in Maryland, named in honor of Caroline Calvert, daughter of Charles, Fifth Lord Baltimore.

Caroline; county in Virginia, named for the wife of George H. Carondelet; village in St. Louis County, Missouri, named for Baron Carondelet, Spanish commander in chief and governor of Louisiana in 1791.

Carp; river and railroad station in Marquette County, Michigan. A translation of the Indian name literally meaning "big carp river."

Carrington; island in Great Salt Lake, Utah, named for a member of an exploring party.

Carrington; island in Yellowstone Lake, Yellowstone Park, named for Campbell Carrington.

Carrituck; plantation in Somerset County, Maine. An Indian word, meaning "the place where the water forms a semicircle around the land."

Carroll; counties in Arkansas, Georgia, Illinois. Indiana, Iowa, Kentucky, Maryland, Mississippi, Missouri, New Hampshire, Ohio, and Virginia, and several small places, named for Charles Carroll, of Carrollton, Maryland.

Carroll; county in Tennessee, named for William Carroll, governor in 1821-27.

Carrollton; township in Carroll County, Arkansas; cities in Carroll County, Iowa, Carroll County, Kentucky, Carroll County, Missouri; towns in Carroll County, Mississippi, and Carroll County, Georgia, and villages in Carroll County, Maryland, and Carroll County, Ohio, named for the home of Charles Carroll.

Carrollton; town in Cattaraugus County, New York, named for G. Carroll, an original proprietor.

Carrying Place; plantation in Somerset County, Maine, so named because the Indians had to carry their canoes from one waterway to another on the route to Canada.

Carson; city, pass, lake, river, and valley in Nevada, and peak in Utah, named for the celebrated Rocky Mountain guide, Christopher, or Kit, Carson.

Carson; county in Texas, named for S. P. Carson, secretary of State under David G. Burnet.

Carter; county and village in Kentucky, named for William G. Carter, a member of the State senate.

Carter; county in Missouri, named for Zimri Carter, an early settler.

Carter; county and village in Tennessee, named for Gen. Landon Carter.

Carteret; county in North Carolina, named for Sir George Carteret, one of the proprietors.

Cartersville; city in Bartow County, Georgia, named for Col. F. Carter, of Milledgeville.

Carthage; city in Jasper county, Missouri, village in Jefferson County, New York, and many other places, named for the ancient city in Egypt.

Caruthersville; city in Pemiscot County, Missouri, named for Hon. Samuel Caruthers, of Madison County.

Carver; town in Plymouth County, Massachusetts, named for John Carver, first governor of Plymouth colony.

Carver; county and village in Minnesota, named for Capt. Jonathan Carver, early explorer.

Cary; village in Wake County, North Carolina, named for the temperance lecturer of Ohio.

Caryville; town in Genesee County, New York, named for Col. Alfred Cary, early settler.

Cascade; county in Montana, so named because it contains the great falls of the Missouri River.

Cascade; chain of mountains in Oregon and Washington, so called from the cascades in the Columbia River, breaking through the range.

Cascade Locks; town in Wasco County, Oregon, situated at the locks built at the cascades in the Columbia River.

Casco; bay and town in Cumberland County, Maine. From an Indian word, meaning, according to some authorities, "resting place," or "crane bay."

Casey; county in Kentucky; Caseyville; town in Union County, Kentucky. Named for Col. William Casey, a pioneer of the State.

Cash City; town in Clark County, Kansas, named for its founder, Cash Henderson.

Cashie; river in North Carolina, named for an Indian chief.

Cashion; town in Kingfisher County, Oklahoma, named for Roy Cashion, a Rough Rider in the Spanish-American war, and the only one of the Oklahoma contingent killed in the charge up San Juan hill.

Cass; counties in Illinois, Indiana, Iowa, Michigan, Minnesota, Missouri, Nebraska, and Texas; river in Michigan; lake in Minnesota, and village in Cass County, Texas, named for Gen. Lewis Cass, governor of Michigan in 1820.

Cass; county in North Dakota, named for Gen. George W. Cass, director of the Northern Pacific Railroad.

Cassadaga; lake, creek, and village in Chautauqua County, New York. Indian word, meaning "under the rocks."

Casselton; town in Cass County, North Dakota, named for Gen. George W. Cass, director of the Northern Pacific Railroad.

Cass Lake; village in Cass County, Minnesota.

Cassville; village in Grant County, Wisconsin, named for Gen. Lewis Cass.

Castalia; town in Erie County, Ohio, named for the ancient fountain at the foot of Mount Parnassus in Phocis.

Castile; town in Wyoming County, New York, named from the ancient kingdom of Spain.

Castine; town in Hancock County, Maine, named for Baron de St. Castine, a French nobleman, by whom it was settled.

Castle; peak in the Sierra Nevada, California, so named from its conical shape.

Castle; peak in Elk Mountains, Colorado, named from its castellated summit.

Castle; island in the Hudson River, New York, so called from a stockade built by the Dutch as a protection from the Indians.

Castle Rock; town in Summit County, Utah, so called from a vast rock which is thought to resemble a ruined castle. Towns in Douglas County, Colorado, and Grant County, Wisconsin, named from rocks near.

Castleton; village in Rensselaer County, New York, named from an ancient Indian castle on the adjacent hills.

Castleton; town in Rutland County, Vermont, named for one of the original proprietors.

Castor; bayou in Louisiana, and river in Missouri, so named because of the prevalence of beavers, a French word, meaning "castor."

Castro; county in Texas; Castroville; town in Medina County, Texas. Named for Henri Castro, who settled 600 immigrants in Texas under Government contract between 1842 and 1845.

Caswell; county in North Carolina, named for Richard Caswell, governor of the State in 1777-1779.

Catahoula; lake and parish in Louisiana, named for an extinct Indian tribe.

Cataract; village in Owen County, Indiana, so named on account of the falls in the river near.

Cataraque; river in New York. Indian word, meaning "fort in the water," the early name of Lake Ontario.

Catasauqua; creek and borough in Lehigh County, Pennsylvania. Indian word, corruption of Gottoshacki, "the earth thirsts for rain," or "parched land."

Catawba; river in North and South Carolina, county in North Carolina, town in said county, town in Marion County, West Virginia; creek in Botetourt County, and town in Roanoke County, Virginia; island in Lake Erie, and village in Clark County, Ohio, besides several other small places, named from the Indian tribe.

Catawissa; branch of the Susquehanna River, and borough in Columbia, Pennsylvania. Corruption of the Indian word Gattawisi, "growing fat," though some authorities say the name signifies "clear water;" a different derivation is from Ganawese, designating the region to which the tribe of Conoys retired.

Cathaneu; river of Maine. Indian word meaning "bent," or "crooked."

Catharine; town in Schuyler County, New York, named for Catharine Montour, wife of an Indian sachem.

Cathedral; peaks in California and Colorado, so named from their resemblance to cathedrals.

Catheys; creek in Humboldt County, California, named for an old settler.

Cathlamet; point and town in Wahkiakum County, Washington, named from the Indian tribe Cathlamah.

Cathlapootle; river in Washington, named for the Quathlapohtle Indian tribe.

Cato; town in Cayuga County, New York, named by the State land board in honor of the distinguished Roman.

Catoctin; stream in Virginia tributary to the Potomac. An Indian word, meaning "great village."

Catskill; creek, mountains, and town in Greene County, New York. The mountains were called Katsbergs by the Dutch, from the number of wild-cats found in them, and the creek, which flows from the mountains, Katerskill, "tomcats' creek."

Cattaraugus; county, village, and creek in New York. Indian word, meaning "bad smelling shore or beach."

Caucomgomoc; lake in Maine. Corruption of an Indian word, meaning "big gull lake."

Caugwaga; creek in Erie County, New York. A corruption of the Indian Gagwaga, "creek of the Cat nation."

Causton; bluff in Georgia, named for Thomas Causton.

Cavalier; county and town in Pembina County, North Dakota, named for Charles Cavalier, one of the old settlers in the Lower Red River Valley.

Cawanesque; branch of the Chemung River, New York. An Indian word, meaning "at the long island."

Cawanshanock; creek in Armstrong County, Pennsylvania. Indian, derived from Gawunechhanne, "green briar stream."

Cawker; city in Mitchell County, Kansas, named for K. H. Cawker.

Cayuga; county, village, and lake in New York. Indian word, the derivation of which is in dispute. The generally accepted theory is that it means" long lake," having been originally applied to the lake, which is 38 miles long and from 1 to 3 ½ miles wide. Morgan derives it from Gweugweh, "the mucky land," while others say that it signifies "canoes pulled out of the water." One of the six nations of Indians was so called. Six small places in the country bear this name.

Cayuse; village in Umatilla County, Oregon, named from the Indian ponies, which are numerous in the country.

Cazenovia; lake and town in Madison County, New York, named by its founder, Col. John Linklaen, for Theophilus Cazenove, general agent of the Holland Land Company.

Cazenovia; township in Woodford County, Illinois, .and villages in Pipestone County, Minnesota, and Richland County, Wisconsin, are named for the above.

Cecil; county in Maryland; Cecilton; town in Cecil County, Maryland. Named for Cecil Calvert, second Lord Baltimore.

Cedar; this word, with various suffixes, forms the name of numerous features throughout the country. Counties in Iowa, Missouri, and Nebraska, 153 post offices, with or without suffixes, and numberless rivers, creeks, etc., bear the name, referring to the presence of the tree in the vicinity.

Cedar Keys; town in Levy County, Florida, named from a group of islands in the harbor.

Celeron; island near Detroit, Michigan, named for Sieur Celeron, commandant at Detroit in early days.

Center; town in Sharp County, Arkansas, and county in Pennsylvania, so named because of their geographical situation in county or State. One hundred and fifty places in the country bear this name, alone or with various prefixes.

Center Harbor; town in Belknap County, New Hampshire, named for one of the first settlers, Col. Joseph Senter.

Central; town in Pickens County, South Carolina, so named because of its geographical situation in county or State. Twenty-eight other places, with and without suffixes, are so called.

Central City; town in Huntington County, West Virginia, so named because it is nearly halfway between Guyandotte and Catlettsburg.

Central Lake; village in Antrim County, Michigan, situated on a lake which is in the center of a chain of lakes and rivers in the county.

Ceredo; village in Wayne County, West Virginia, named by its founder because of the bountiful harvest of corn upon its site. The name is derived from Ceres, the goddess of corn and harvests.

Cerrillos; town in Santa Fe County, New Mexico. A Spanish word meaning "little eminences, or hills."

Cerro Colorado; a conical hill of reddish color in Colorado. The name was given by the Mexicans, and means "red hill."

Cerro Gordo; village in Piatt County, Illinois; county in Iowa; and village in Columbus County, North Carolina, named from the Mexican battlefield. The words mean "large (around) hill."

Ceylon; village in Erie County, Ohio, and five other places, named from the island off the coast of India.

Chadbourn; town in Columbus County, North Carolina, named for a prominent business man of Wilmington, North Carolina.

Chadds Ford; village in Chester County, Pennsylvania, named for the proprietor, Francis Chadsey.

Chadron; city in Dawes County, Nebraska, named for an old French squawman.

Chaffee; county in Colorado, named for Jerome B. Chaffee. United States Senator.

Chaffin; bluff in Virginia, named for the family who owned it.

Chagrin; river in Ohio. Two different theories obtain in regard to this name, one being that a party of surveyors under Harvey Rice, so named it because of their disappointment at finding that they were not following the course of the Cuyahoga River. Howe says that it is named from the Indian word shagrin, which is said to mean "clear." Chagrin Falls; village in Cuyahoga County, Ohio, named from the river.

Chamberlain; lake in Maine, named for an old settler.

Chambers; county in Alabama, named for Senator Henry C. Chambers of that State.

Chambers; county in Texas, named for Thomas J. Chambers, major-general in the Texas revolution.

Chambersburg; town in Franklin County, Pennsylvania, named for a Scotchman who founded it, Benjamin Chambers.

Champaign; counties in Illinois and Ohio, and city in the former State, so called from the general character of the country. A French word, meaning "a flat, open country."

Champion; town in Jefferson County, New York, named for Gen. Henry Champion, an early proprietor.

Champlain; lake and town in Clinton County, New York, named for the discoverer of the lake, Samuel de Champlain, a French naval officer, who explored that country in 1609.

Chancellorsville; village in Spottsylvania County, Virginia, named for a family in the neighborhood.

Chandeleur; bay and islands on the coast of Louisiana, so named because they were discovered on Candlemas or Chandeleur day.

Chandlerville; village in Cass County, Illinois, named for Dr. Charles Chandler, founder.

Chaney; creek in Mississippi, named for Robert Chaney, an early settler in Perry County.

Chanhassan; river in Minnesota and North Dakota. Indian name, "pale bark wood, sugar tree."

Chanhassen; village in Carver County, Minnesota. Indian word, meaning "firestone."

Chankie; creek in South Dakota. Coues says it is clipped from Tschehkanakasahtapah, "breech clout." Haines gives chanka, "firestone," so named from a very hard rock of vitrified sandstone found near its mouth.

Chanlers; purchase in Coos County, New Hampshire, named for Jeremiah Chanler, early owner.

Chanopa; lake in Minnesota. Indian word, meaning "two wood."

Chanshayapi; river in Minnesota. Indian word, meaning "red wood, or a post painted red."

Chanute; city in Neosho County, Kansas, named for O. Chanute, civil engineer with the Leavenworth, Lawrence and Galveston Railroad.

Chapa; river in Minnesota. Indian word, meaning "beaver."

Chapel Hill; town in Orange County, North Carolina, named from a colonial chapel of the Church of England, built on a hill.

Chapin; town in Lexington County, South Carolina, named for a family of that name.

Chapman; borough in Snyder County, Pennsylvania, named for William Chapman, who owned slate quarries there.

Chappaqua; town in Westchester County, New York. Indian word meaning "an edible root of some kind."

Chappaquiddick; island in Dukes County, Massachusetts. From an Indian word Cheppiaquidne, "separated island." So called because separated from Martha's Vineyard by a narrow strait.

Chardon; village in Geauga County, Ohio, named for a proprietor, Peter Chardon Brooks.

Chariton; county, river, and town in Putnam County, Missouri. The origin of the name is in doubt. The most generally accepted theory is that it was given by the early French, but that the original form of the word has been lost, hence the translation is impossible. Some persons say that there was a French trader who had his agency near the mouth of the river, whose name was similar.

Charlemont; town in Franklin County, Massachusetts, named for the Earl of Charlemont.

Charles; county in Maryland, named in honor of Charles Calvert, son of Cecilius Calvert, second Lord Baltimore.

Charles; river in Massachusetts, and point in Northampton County, Virginia; Charles City; county in Virginia. Named for Charles I of England.

Charles Mix: county in South Dakota, named for a pioneer citizen.

Charleston; town in Penobscot County, Maine, named for an early settler, Charles Vaughan.

Charleston; town in Tallahatchie County, Mississippi, named from Charleston, South Carolina.

Charleston; county and city in South Carolina. The city was named first and was originally called Charles Town, in honor of Charles II. of England.

Charleston; city in Kanawha County, West Virginia, named for Charles Clendman, father of George Clendman, the founder.

Charlestown; part of Boston, Massachusetts, named for Charles I of England.

Charlestown; town in Sullivan County, New Hampshire, named for Sir Charles Knowles.

Charlestown; town in Washington County, Rhode Island, named either for King Charles II. of England, or for Charles Edward, the pretender.

Charlestown; town in Jefferson County, West Virginia, named for the brother of George Washington, Charles Washington, who owned the land upon which the town was built.

Charlevoix; county and village in Michigan, named for Pere Francis X. Charlevoix, a missionary and historian.

Charley Apopka; creek in Florida. Corruption of an Indian word, tsalopopkohatchee, "catfish eating creek."

Charloe; village in Paulding County, Ohio, named for an Ottawa Indian chief.

Charlotte; county in Virginia and village in Monroe County, New York, named for Charlotte Augusta, Princess of Wales.

Charlotte; city in Mecklenburg County, North Carolina, named for the wife of George III. of England.

Charlottesville; city in Virginia, named for Charlotte Augusta, Princess of Wales.

Charlton; county and village in Georgia, named for Robert M. Charlton, poet, and United States Senator in 1852.

Charlton; town in Worcester County, Massachusetts, named for Sir Francis Charlton, gentleman of the privy chamber in 1755.

Chartiers; two creeks, township in Allegheny County, and two villages in western Pennsylvania, named for Peter Chartiers, a noted half-breed spy and Indian hunter.

Chase; counties in Kansas and Nebraska, named for Salmon P. Chase, Secretary of the Treasury under Lincoln.

Chaska; city in Carver County, Minnesota. An Indian name given to the firstborn, if a son.

Chateaugay; river, lake, and village in Franklin County, New York, the origin of the name of which is in dispute. Some authorities say it is from the French word, meaning "castle ford." Haines derives it from the Indian word Chatauqua, "place where one was lost"

Chatham; counties in Georgia and North Carolina, towns in Barnstable County, Massachusetts, and Carroll County, New Hampshire; borough in Morris County, New Jersey; village in Columbia County, New York, and many other places, named for William Pitt, earl of Chatham.

Chattahoochee; river, county, and village in Fulton County, Georgia, and town in Gadsden County, Florida; from an Indian word meaning "painted stone."

Chattanooga; city in Hamilton County, Tennessee, and creek in Georgia. Indian word, meaning "crow's nest" or " eagle's nest."

Chattooga; county and river in Georgia. It is said to be from the same Indian word as Chattahooche, "painted stone."

Chaumont; village in Jefferson County, New York, named for Le Ray de Cahumont, early proprietor.

Chautauqua; county in Kansas; county, lake, and town in New York. An Indian word which has been the subject of much controversy. Webster says it is a corruption of a word which means "foggy place." Another derivation gives the meaning as "bag tied in the middle," referring to the shape of the lake. It is also said to mean "place where a child was washed away." Dr. Peter Wilson, an educated Seneca, says it is literally "where the fish was taken out." Other meanings given are "place of easy death," "place where one was lost."

Chaves; county in New Mexico, named for Mariano Chaves, governor in 1836.

Cheanill; chain of hills in Oregon. Indian word meaning "bald hills."

Cheat; river in West Virginia, so called because of the variableness of the volume of water.

Cheatham; county in Tennessee, named for Benjamin Cheatham, Confederate general.

Chebanse; town in Iroquois County, Illinois, named for an Indian chief. The word means "little duck."

Chebeague Island; village in Cumberland County, Maine. The name is probably derived from Chebeeg, "great waters," or "wide expanse of water."

Cheboygan; river, county, and city in Michigan. An Indian word, variously interpreted. Haines says it is composed of two words, che, "great," and poygan, "pipe." Another derivation gives the meaning, "the river that comes out of the ground." The Michigan Historical Society gives Chabwegan, "a place of ore."

Checaque; river in Iowa. An Indian word, meaning "skunk."

Chectemunda; creek in Montgomery County, New York. An Indian word meaning "twin sister."

Cheektowaga; town in Erie County, New York. Derived from the Indian word, Juk do waali geh, "the place of the crabapple tree."

Cheesechankamuck; eastern branch of Farmington River, Connecticut. Indian word, meaning "the great fishing place at the weir."

Cheetiery Sopochnie; chain of volcanic mountains in the Aleutian Islands. An Indian word, meaning "four mountains."

Chefuncte; river in Louisiana. Indian word, meaning "chinkapin."

Chehalis; river, county, and city in Lewis County, Washington, named from an Indian tribe, Tsihalis. The word means "sand, or sandy land."

Chehtanbeh; river in Minnesota. Indian word, meaning "sparrow hawk's nest."

Chelmsford; town in Middlesex County, Massachusetts, named for the English town.

Chelsea; city of Massachusetts, named from the English town.

Chelsea; town in Washtenaw County, Michigan, and town in Orange County, Vermont; indirectly named for the town in England.

Chemawa; village in Marion County, Oregon. Indian word, meaning "our old home."

Chemehuevis; valley in Arizona named from a tribe of Indians.

Chemung; river, county, and town in New York. An Indian word, meaning "big horn in the water," or "big horn." The river was so called according to tradition from a fossil tooth found in it.

Chenango; river, county, and a town in Broome County, New York. An Indian word, meaning "bull thistles."

Chene; bayou in Louisiana. French word, meaning "oak."

Cheney; creek in Humboldt County, California, named for au old settler.

Cheney; city in Sedgwick County, Kansas, named for P. B. Cheney, stockholder of the Atchison, Topeka and Santa Fe Railroad.

Cheney; town in Spokane County, Washington, named for Benjamin P. Cheney, of Boston, one of the originators of the Northern Pacific Railroad.

Chepachet; river and village in Providence County, Rhode Island, and village in Herkimer County, New York. An Indian word meaning "where the stream divides," or "the place of separation."

Chepultepec; town in Blount County, Alabama. An Indian word meaning "grasshopper hill."

Cheputnaticook; lake in Maine. Indian word meaning "great hill lake."

Cheraw; town in Chesterfield County, South Carolina, named from an Indian tribe which is also known as the Sara. The meaning is "tall grass or weeds."

Cherokee; county and town in Alabama; township in Benton County, Arkansas; village in Butte County, California; county and village in Georgia; county and city in Iowa; nation in Indian Territory; county and city in Kansas; villages in Lawrence County, Kentucky, and Lowndes County, Mississippi; county and village in Swain County, North Carolina; post-office in Woods County, Oklahoma; county and post-office in Spartanburg County, South Carolina; village in Lauderdale County, Tennessee; county and village in San Saba County, Texas, and village in Marathon County,

Wisconsin, named for an Indian tribe. The word is derived from cheere, "fire," and is said to be the name of their "lower heaven."

Cherry; county in Nebraska, named for Lieutenant Cherry, United States Army.

Cherry Creek; town and creek in Chautauqua County, New York, named by Joshua Bentley, jr., a surveyor who found the center of the town to be on a small island in a stream where there was a small cherry tree.

Cherryvale; city in Montgomery County, Kansas, in the valley of Cherry Creek.

Cherry Valley; village in Otsego County, New York. The name "Cherry" occurs frequently with and without suffixes, generally referring to the presence of the tree.

Chesaning; village in Saginaw County, Michigan. An Indian word meaning "big rock," the name having been given because of a large rock near the place.

Chesapeake; bay in Maryland which gives name to several places in the country.

An Indian name variously explained. Heckewelder says it is corrupted from Tschischwapeki, which is compounded of kitshi, "highly salted," and peek, "a body of standing water, a pond, a bay." Others give che, "great," and sepi, "waters." Bosman interprets it as "mother of waters." W. W. Tooker says that the early form was Chesepiooc, from k'che-sepi-ack, "country on a great river."

Cheshire; county in New Hampshire, town in Berkshire County, Massachusetts, and four small places named for the county in England.

Chester; county in Pennsylvania, named by George Pearson, a friend of William Penn, in honor of the native place of Penn.

Chester; county and town in South Carolina, named from Chester County, Pennsylvania.

Chester; county in Tennessee, named for Robert I. Chester, an old settler.

Chesterfield; county in South Carolina and town in Hampden County, Massachusetts, named for Philip Dormer Stanhope, Fourth Earl of Chesterfield.

Chesterfield; counties in North Carolina and Virginia, named from the town in Derbyshire, England.

Chesterville; village in Albany County, New York, named for Rev. John Chester, of Albany.

Chestnut; twenty-seven post-offices and many natural features bear this name, indicating the presence of the tree.

Chesuncook; lake and town in Piscataquis County, Maine. An Indian word which, according to Judge Potter, means " the goose place." Thoreau gives, " the place where many streams empty in." Haines says that it signifies "great goose place."

Chetimaches; lake in Louisiana which is also known as Grand Lake, the name of an Indian tribe, the word meaning "red crabs."

Chetopa; city in Labette County, Kansas. An Indian word, meaning " four houses," the town having been built on the site of four houses occupied by the wives of an Osage chief.

Chewaukan; marsh in Oregon. Indian word, meaning "water potato."

Cheyenne; counties in Colorado, Kansas, and Nebraska, mountain in Colorado, rivers in Nebraska and South Dakota, city in Laramie County, Wyoming, and several small places, named for the Indian tribe. The word is probably a corruption of the French, chien, "dog," applied by some neighboring tribes to those at present known as Cheyennes. It was the custom for Indians to call themselves by the name which signified "men," and to call neighboring tribes by some opprobrious epithet. The word was doubtless introduced by the early French traders.

Chicacomico; creek on the eastern shore of Maryland. An Indian word, meaning "the place where turkeys are plenty."

Chicago; city and river. in Illinois. The origin of the word is from the Indian, being a derivation by elision and French annotation from the word Chi-kaug-ong. Col. Samuel A. Starrow used the name in a letter to Gen. Jacob Brown, in 1816, as follows: "The river Chicago (orin the English, " Wild Onion River)." Schoolcraft in 1820 said: "Its banks * * * stated to produce abundantly * * * the wild species of cepa or leek." Bishop Baraga gives: " From Chicag, or Sikag, "skunk," a kind of wild cat." John Turner defines skunk as she-gahg; onion, she-gau-ga-winzhe, "skunk weed." When the word first appeared the country was inhabited by a tribe of Miamis, in whose dialect the word for skunk was "se-kaw-kwaw." It is said that the wild cat, or skunk, was named from the plant.

Chicamauga; creek and town in Walker County, Georgia, named from an Indian tribe. The word by some is said to mean "sluggish or dead water," or "the river of death;" by others it is thought to signify "boiling pot," so called from a whirlpool in the river.

Chichester; town in Merrimack County, New Hampshire, and village in Ulster County, New York, named from the city in England.

Chickahominy; river in Virginia, which according to De Vere is named from the Indian word, Checahaminend, "land of much grain," so called because it flows through fertile lowlands. Heckewelder, however, says that it is corrupted from Tschikene-mahoni, "a lick frequented by turkeys."

Chickasaw; county and township in Iowa, county in Mississippi, and nation in Indian Territory, named from the Indian tribe. According to Edward Fontaine, the tribe divided on account of a feud, and one part took the name of one brother, Chickasaw, and the other took the name of the other brother, Choctaw. The word is said to mean "rebels," or "renegades."

Chickasha; town in Chickasaw Nation, Indian Territory. The name is derived from the word Chickasaw.

Chickies; creek and village in Lancaster County, Pennsylvania. Name derived from the Indian Chikiswalungo, "Place of crabs." Heckewelder says the meaning is " the place of crawfish."

Chickisalung-a: creek in Pennsylvania. Indian word, derived from Chickiswalunga, "the place of crawfish," or "the place of crabs or crab fish."

Chickomuxen; creek in Maryland. An Indian word, meaning "fishing place at a weir."

Chickwolnepy; creek in New Hampshire. Indian word, meaning "near great pond."

Chico; city in Butte County, California, situated on Chico Creek. A Spanish word, meaning " little."

Chicomico; creek in Connecticut. An Indian derivation from she, orche, "great," and komuk, or comaco, "house," or "inclosed place."

Chicopee; river, city, and falls in Massachusetts. An Indian word, meaning "cedar tree," or "birch-bark place."

Chicora; town in Berkeley County, South Carolina. From an Indian word, Yuchikere, meaning " Yuchi are there," or "Yuchi over there."

Chicot; county in Arkansas; creek in New York. French word, meaning "wood;" a term also applied to a stub or broken piece of wood.

Childress; county and town in Texas, named for George C. Childress, author of the Texas declaration of independence.

Chilhowee; mountain ridge in Tennessee and village in Johnson County, Missouri. Indian word, meaning "deer mountain," or by some thought to mean "fire deer," an allusion to the custom of the Indians hunting by fire, by which the deer were blinded and easily killed.

Chillicothe; cities in Ohio and Illinois, and towns in Wapello County, Iowa, and Livingston County, Missouri, named from an Indian tribe. The word is said to mean "town," or "city."

Chillisquaque: creek and village in Northumberland County, Pennsylvania. An Indian word, meaning "the place of snowbirds."

Chilmark; town in Dukes County, Massachusetts, named from the town in England.

Chilson; lake and village in Essex County, New York, named for a family of early settlers.

Chilton; county and village in Clarke County, Alabama, named for William P. Chilton, of that State.

Chilton; city in Calumet County, Wisconsin, named Chillington, the home of an early settler, for Chillington Hall, England, but the county clerk in recording the name, omitted the second syllable, hence Chilton.

Chimney Rock; town in Rutherford County, North Carolina, named from nearby cliffs, which bear a likeness to colossal chimneys.

Chinook; village in Pacific County, Washington, named from a tribe of Indians.

Chinquapin; town in Duplin County, North Carolina. The name is the Indian name for "nut," or "small chestnut."

Chippewa; river in Michigan and counties in Michigan, Minnesota, and Wisconsin, named from an Indian tribe. The word, according to some authorities, means "puckered moccasins." Other explanations are "he overcomes," or "he surmounts obstacles."

Chisago; county in Minnesota. An Indian word, possibly from the same source as Chicago.

Chissesessick; rivers in Virginia and Georgia. An Indian word, meaning "the place of blue birds."

Chittenango; creek and village in Madison County, New York. Morgan says it is an Indian word, meaning "where the sun shines out;" other authorities translate it "waters divide and run into."

Chittenden; county in Vermont, named for Thomas Chittenden, governor of the State in 1790-97.

Chittenden; peak in Yellowstone Park, named for George B. Chittenden.

Chivington; village in Kiowa County, Colorado, near the battle ground where General Chivington defeated the Cheyenne Indians.

Chocoma; peak in the White Mountains, New Hampshire, said to be named for a prophet-chief of the Sosokis Indians, who, being pursued to this lofty peak by a white hunter, leaped over the precipice and was dashed to pieces.

Choctaw; counties in Alabama and Mississippi, and nation in Indian Territory, also several small places, named for an Indian tribe. Gatschet says the word means " flat head." Dromenech gives " charming voice," because of the aptitude of the tribe for singing and music.

Choctawhatchee; bay and river in Florida. Indian word, meaning "river of the Choctaws."

Chohwajica; lake in Minnesota. Indian word, meaning "willow."

Chokin; lake in Minnesota. Indian word, meaning "place of roasting," the lake probably having been so named because the Dakota Indians roasted the teepwinna root, which they used for food, on the shore of the lake.

Chokio; village in Stevens County, Minnesota. Indian word, meaning "the middle."

Chokoloskee; town in Lee County, Florida. The named is derived from the Indian word, chokoliska, meaning "the red houses."

Choteau; county and township in Teton County, Montana, and county in South Dakota, named for the Chouteau family, two brothers of which, Auguste and Pierre, founded St. Louis.

Chouptyatanka; lake in Minnesota. Indian word, meaning "big dry wood."

Chowan; river and county in North Carolina, named from the Chowanoke Indian tribe. The word is thought to be equivalent to Shawnee, "southern people." One authority derives the word from sowan-ohke, "south country."

Christian; county in Kentucky, named for Col. William Christian, an officer of the Revolution.

Christian; counties in Illinois and Missouri, named from the county in Kentucky.

Christiana; creek and village in Delaware, and borough in Lancaster County, Pennsylvania, named for the King and Queen of Sweden, Christian and Christiana.

Chuctanunda; stream in Montgomery County, New York. An Indian word meaning "twin sisters."

Chula; village in Livingston County, Missouri; Chulafinmee; town in Cleburne County, Alabama; Chulahoma; town in Marshall County, Mississippi. From an Indian word meaning "red fox."

Chuluota; town in Orange County, Florida. Indian word, meaning "beautiful view."

Churchill; county in Nevada, which takes its name from Fort Churchill, named for an officer of the United States Army.

Churchville; village in Monroe County, New York, named for Samuel Church, pioneer settler.

Cibolo; river and village in Guadalupe County, Texas. A Spanish word, meaning "Mexican bull."

Cicero; town in Onondaga County, New York, named by the State land board for the celebrated Roman.

Cimarron; river in Oklahoma and Indian Territory and village in Colfax County, New Mexico. A Spanish word, meaning "wild, unruly."

Cincinnati; city in Ohio, laid out and named by Col. Israel Ludlow, in honor of an organization of officers formed after the Revolutionary war and named in honor of Cincinnatus, the Roman patriot.

Cincinnatus; town in Cortland County, New York, named by the State land board, for the celebrated Roman patriot.

Cinnabar; mountain just north of Yellowstone Park, named from its rocks, which ate colored red by iron, which was mistaken for cinnabar.

Cinnaminson; town in Burlington County, New Jersey. The name is derived from the Indian, china, or sinne, "a stone," and mona, or minna, "island," hence "stone island place."

Circleville; city in Jackson County, Kansas, so named because of a suggestion that it had been circling around the prairie in search of a location.

Circleville; village in Pickaway County, Ohio, so named from the circular Indian mounds in the neighborhood.

Cisco; many places in the United States bear tins name. An Indian word, meaning a kind of trout of an oily nature.

Citra; town in Marion County, Florida, noted for its orange groves.

Citrus; county in Florida, named from its orange groves.

Clackamas; county, village, and river in Oregon, named from an Indian tribe.

Claiborne; parish in Louisiana and counties in Tennessee and Mississippi, named for William C. C. Claiborne, governor of Mississippi Territory and of Louisiana as a Territory and State.

Clallam; county in Washington, named for an Indian tribe. The word means "strong people."

Clanton; town in Chilton County, Alabama, named for General Clanton, Confederate general.

Clapper; town in Monroe County, Missouri, named foo Henry Clapper, who was instrumental in bringing a railroad into the place.

Clare; county in Michigan. The origin of the name is in doubt, but the Michigan Historical Society says that it is probably named from county Clare in Ireland.

Claremont; town in Sullivan County, New Hampshire, named from the country seat of Lord Clive, an English general.

Clarence; city in Shelby County, Missouri, named for a son of John Duff, an early settler.

Clarendon; county and town in South Carolina, named for Edward, Earl of Clarendon.

Clarion; river, county, and borough in Pennsylvania. A French word, meaning "clear, bright," applied first to the river.

Clark; county in Arkansas, named for Governor William Clark.

Clark; peak in California, named for Fred Clark, a topographer.

Clark; counties in Indiana, Illinois, Kentucky, and Ohio, named for Gen. George Rogers Clark, who captured Vincennes.

Clark; county in Kansas, named for Capt. Charles F. Clarke, United States Volunteers, who died at Memphis, December 10, 1862.

Clark; county in Missouri, named for Capt. William Clarke of the Lewis and Clarke Expedition.

Clark; creek in Nebraska, named for Dr. M. H. Clark, first member of the Territorial council from Dodge County.

Clark; county in South Dakota, named for Newton Clark, legislator in 1873.

Clark; county in Wisconsin, named for A. W. Clark, early settler.

Clarke; county in Alabama. named for Governor John Clarke of Georgia.

Clarke; county in Georgia, named for Gen. Elijah Clarke, officer of the Revolution.

Clarke; county in Iowa, named for James Clarke, governor of the State in 1846.

Clarke; county in Mississippi, named for Joshua G. Clarke, first chancellor of the State.

Clarke; county in Virginia, named for Gen. George Rogers Clarke.

Clarke; county in Washington, and river in Montana, named for Capt. William Clarke, of the Lewis and Clarke expedition.

Clarkfork; town in Kootenai County, Idaho, named from the river, which was named for Capt. William Clarke, of the Lewis and Clarke expedition.

Clarkia; village in Kootenai County, Idaho, named for Capt. William Clarke, of the Lewis and Clarke expedition.

Clarks; village in Merrick County, Nebraska, named for S. H. H. Clark, superintendent of the Union Pacific Railroad.

Clarksburg; town in Berkshire County, Massachusetts, named for Judge Clarke, first chancellor of the State.

Clarksburg; town in Harrison County, West Virginia. Some authorities claim that it was named for Capt. William Clarke, of the Lewis and Clarke expedition, while others maintain that it was named for a pioneer.

Clarksdale; town in Coahoma County, Mississippi, named for Captain Clark, brother-in-law of Governor Alcorn.

Clarkson; town in Monroe County, New York, named for General Clarkson, large landowner.

Clarkston; village in Asotin County, Washington; Clarksville; city in Pike County, Missouri. Named for Capt. William Clarke, of the Lewis and Clarke expedition.

Clarksville; town in Habersham County, Georgia, named for Gen. John Clarke, governor of Georgia.

Clarksville; town in Hamilton County, Indiana, named for Gen. George Rogers Clark, who captured Vincennes.

Clarksville; town in Coos County, New Hampshire, named for Benjamin Clark.

Clarkton; town in Dunklin County, Missouri, named for Henry E. Clark, an early contractor.

Clatskanie; town in Columbia County, Oregon, named from the Indian tribe, Klatskanai.

Clatsop; county in Oregon, named for. an Indian tribe.

Claverack; town in Columbia County, New York, from the Dutch, klaver-akker, "clover field," said by some to have been so called from the immense fields of clover which abounded there at the time of its settlement. Another opinion is that it is of Dutch origin, the first part of the word meaning " an opening or side gorge;" the latter part being a division of the river which the Dutch skippers referred to; the Hudson was divided into 13 "racks" or "reaches."

Clay; county in Arkansas, named for John M. Clayton, State senator.

Clay; counties in Alabama, Florida, Georgia; county, and village in Illinois; county, and town in Indiana; county in Kansas; town in Webster County, Kentucky; counties in Mississippi, Missouri, North Carolina, South Dakota, Tennessee, Texas, and West Virginia; mount in New Hampshire, and many small places, named for Henry Clay.

The counties of Minnesota and Nebraska doubtless were named for him also, though no record can be found to that effect.

Clay; county in Iowa, named for Henry Clay, jr., who fell at the battle of Buena Vista. Clay; county in Kentucky, named for Gen. Green Clay.

Claymont; village in Newcastle County, Delaware, named from the character of the soil.

Clayton; town in Kent County, Delaware, named for Thomas Clayton, or his son, Col. Joshua Clayton.

Clayton; county, and town in Rabun County, Georgia, named for Augustin Smith Clayton.

Clayton; village in St. Louis County, Missouri, named for Ralph Clayton.

Clayton; county in Iowa, town in Jefferson County, New York, and town in Johnston County, North Carolina, named for John M. Clayton, Senator from Delaware.

Claytonville; town in Brown County, Kansas, named for Powell Clayton, United States Senator from Arkansas.

Clear Creek; county in Colorado, so called because it is drained by Clear Creek, an affluent of the South Platte.

Clearfield; creek, county, and borough in Pennsylvania. The creek received its name from the clearings along its banks.

Clear Lake; village in Polk County, Wisconsin, situated on a lake of that name.

Clearwater; descriptive name given to a river in Idaho and many smaller streams in the country, which have given names to twelve post-offices.

Cleburne; counties in Alabama and Arkansas, and town in Johnson County, Texas, named for Gen. Patrick Cleburne.

Clermont; county in Ohio, name probably derived from Clermont, France.

Clermont; village in Columbia County, New York, named by Chancellor Livingston, a friend of Fulton, for the first American steamboat.

Cleveland; counties in Arkansas and Oklahoma, named for President Grover Cleveland.

Cleveland; village in Oswego County, New York, named for James Cleveland, early settler.

Cleveland; county and village in Rowan County, North Carolina, named for Col. Benjamin Cleveland.

Cleveland; city in Cuyahoga County, Ohio, named for Gen. Moses Cleveland, of the Connecticut Land Company, who surveyed it.

Cleveland; town in Bradley County, Tennessee, named for John Cleveland, who came there from North Carolina.

Clifford; village in Lapeer County, Michigan, named for Clifford Lyman, the first child born in the village.

Clifton; village in Greene County, Ohio, named from the cliffs which bound the river at this point.

Climax; village in Kalamazoo County, Michigan, so called because when Daniel B. Eldred first visited the township he said, "This caps the climax."

Clinch; county in Georgia, and river in Virginia and Tennessee, named for Gen. Duncan L. Clinch.

Clingmans Dome; peak in Great Smoky Mountains, North Carolina, named for United States Senator Thomas L. Clingman, who determined its altitude.

Clinton; county, and city in Dewitt County, Illinois; counties in Indiana, Iowa, and Kentucky; town in Jones County, Georgia; county in Michigan, and town in Worcester County, Massachusetts, named for De Witt Clinton, governor of New York and projector of the Erie Canal.

Clinton; counties in Missouri, Ohio, and New York, town in Dutchess County, New York, and village in Oneida County, New York, named for George Clinton, governor of New York, and vice-president of the United States.

Clinton; county in Pennsylvania, supposed to have been named for Gen. Henry Clinton.

Clockville; village in Madison County, New York, named for John Klock, original grantee.

Cloquet; town in Carlton County, Minnesota, so named from the mills there. A French word, meaning "sound of the mill."

Cloud; county in Kansas, named for William F. Cloud, colonel Second Regiment of Kansas.

Clymer; village in Cass County, Indiana, named for George Clymer, its founder.

Clymer; town in Chautauqua County, New York, named for George Clymer, one of the signers of the Declaration of Independence.

Coahoma; county and town in Mississippi. An Indian word, meaning " red panther."

Coast; range of mountains in Oregon, so named because lying parallel with the Pacific coast.

Coatesville; borough in Chester County, Pennsylvania, named for Moses Coates, one of the early settlers.

Cobalt; village in Middlesex County, Connecticut, so named from mines of cobalt there.

Cobb; county in Georgia, named for Thomas W. Cobb, United States Senator from that State.

Cobbosseecontee; river and lake in Maine. An Indian word, meaning "place where sturgeon are taken."

Cobden; village in Union County, Illinois, named for Richard Cobden.

Cobleskill; creek and town in Schoharie County, New York, named for Cobel, an early mill owner.

Cobscook; arm of Passamaquoddy Bay, Maine. Hubbard derives it from the name of the Indian tribe, Passamaquoddy, which he says signifies "falls or rough water." Other derivations are Kabassak-hige, "sturgeon-catching place," and "a small, muddy stream."

Cocalico; creek in Lancaster County, Pennsylvania. Corrupted from Achgookwalico, "where snakes gather together in holes."

Cochecalechee; tributary of the Chattahoochee, in Georgia. An Indian word meaning "broken arrow."

Cocheco; river in New Hampshire. An Indian word meaning "rapid or violent."

Cochecton; town in Sullivan County, New York. An Indian word meaning, according to Haines, "low ground;" others say "finished small harbor."

Cochituate; village in Middlesex County, Massachusetts. An Indian word meaning "land on, or near, rapid streams or falls."

Cochran; county in Texas, named for a man who fell at the Alamo.

Cocke; county in Tennessee, named for Gen. William Cocke, United States Senator from that State in 1796-97 and 1799-1805.

Cock Robin; island in California, settled by a man named Robin, who, because of his bragging of his fighting qualities, was nicknamed "Cock Robin."

Coconino; county in Arizona, named from a band of Apache Indians.

Cocoosing; creeks in Connecticut and Pennsylvania. An Indian word, meaning "where owls are."

Cod; cape in Massachusetts, which received its name from Bartholomew Gosnold, who caught many codfish there.

Codington; county in South Dakota, named for Rev. R. B. Codington, legislator in 1875.

Codornices; creek in California. Derived from the Spanish, codorniz, "quail."

Codorus; creek in York County, Pennsylvania. An Indian word, said to mean " rapid water."

Coeur d'Alene; lake and town in Kootenai County, Idaho; named from a tribe of Indians. French name, meaning "needle hearts" or "awl hearts." Some authorities say that this name was given to these Indians because the expression was used by a chief of the tribe to denote his opinion of the Canadian trappers' meanness. Rev. M. Eells says. that the name was given to the tribe by members of the Hudson Bay Company, because of their sharpness in trade.

Coeyman; town in Albany County, New York, named for the patenteee, Barent Peterse Coeymans.

Coffee; counties in Alabama, Georgia, and Tennessee; Coffeeville; town in Yalobusha County, Mississippi. Named for Gen. John Coffee, noted Indian fighter.

Coffee; creek in Humboldt County, California, so named from the occasion of a sack of coffee having been spilled into it.

Coffey; county in Kansas; Coffeyville; city in Montgomery County, Kansas. Named for A. M. Coffey, member of the first Kansas territorial legislature.

Cohasset; town in Norfolk County, Massachusetts. An Indian word, said by some to mean "a fishing promontory," "a place of pines," or " young pine trees."

Cohocton; town in Steuben County, New York. From an Indian word, cohocta, "steam rising in a black alder swamp with overhanging trees," or "trees in water." Cohoes; city in Albany County, New York, named from Cohoes falls. An Indian word, meaning "shipwrecked canoe;" also said to signify "great bendings."

Cokato; village in Wright County, Minnesota. An Indian word, meaning "at the middle."

Coke; county and village in Wood County, Texas, named for Richard Coke, governor and United States Senator from Texas.

Cokesbury; town in Greenwood County, South Carolina. The name is formed by the combination of the names of two bishops of the Methodist Episcopal Church, Thomas Coke and Francis Asbury.

Colbert; county in Alabama, named for George and Levi Colbert.

Colby; city in Thomas County, Kansas, named for J. R. Colby, one of the old settlers.

Colby; city in Clark and Marathon counties, Wisconsin, named for Charles Colby, president of the Wisconsin Central Railroad.

Colchester; borough in New London County, Connecticut, and other places in the country; named from a town in England.

Colchester; town in Delaware County, New York, named for Colchester, Connecticut.

Colden; town in Erie County, New York, named for Cadwalader D. Colden, of the State senate.

Cold Spring; town in Cape May County, New Jersey, and many small places in the country; named from springs near.

Cold Spring; village in Putnam County, New York, named from spring formerly there.

Coldwater; city in Michigan, named from a stream of the same name. The name is applied descriptively to many places, the city in Kansas, however, having been named from the city in Michigan.

Coldwater; town in Tate County, Mississippi, named from a near-by creek, which was named descriptively.

Cole; county in Missouri, named for Capt. Stephen Cole, an Indian fighter.

Colebrook; town in Coos County, New Hampshire, named for Sir George Colebrook, original grantee.

Coleman; county and town in Texas, named for R. M. Coleman, captain of the first company of Texas rangers.

Colerain; town in Bertie County, North Carolina, named from the town in Ireland.

Coleraine; town in Franklin County, Massachusetts. Origin of the name is in doubt, but Gabriel Hanger was created Baron Coleraine in 1761, the date of the naming of the town.

Coles; county in Illinois, named for Edward Cole, governor of the State in 1823-1826.

Colesville; town in Broome County, New York, named for Nathaniel Cole, one of the first settlers.

Colfax; counties in Nebraska and New Mexico. and towns in Clinton County, Indiana, and Grant Parish, Louisiana, and Bay County, Michigan, named for Schuyler Colfax, Vice-President of the United States under President Grant.

Collegeville; borough in Montgomery County, Pennsylvania, seat of Ursinus College.

Colleton; county in South Carolina, named for Sir John Colleton, one of the eight original proprietors of Carolina.

Collettsville; town in Caldwell County, North Carolina, named for a family resident there.

Collin; county in Texas, named for Collin McKinney, early settler.

Collingsworth; county in Texas, named for Judge James Collingsworth, secretary of state of the republic in 1836.

Collinsville: city in Madison County, Illinois, settled by four brothers from Litchfield, Connecticut, named Collins.

Collinsville; town in Dundy County, Nebraska, named for Moses Collins, early settler.

Collinsville; village in Lewis County, New York, named for Homer Collins.

Coloma; town in Eldorado County, California, named from an Indian tribe.

Colony; city in Anderson County, Kansas, named for a colony from Ohio and Indiana, which settled in the neighborhood.

Colorado; the name of a State, two rivers, and several towns. A Spanish word, meaning "ruddy, blood red;" in a secondary sense, "colored."

Colquitt; county and town in Georgia, named for Walter T. Colquitt, United States Senator.

Colter; peak in Yellowstone Park, named for John Colter, a guide with the Lewis and Clarke expedition.

Colton; town in St. Lawrence County, New York, named for Jesse Colton Higley, early settler.

Coltsneck; town in Monmouth County, New Jersey. The name is probably derived from an innkeeper's sign upon which was printed the old seal of New Jersey—a horse's neck with a wreath around it.

Columbia; counties in Arkansas, Florida, Georgia, New York, Oregon, Pennsylvania, Washington, and Wisconsin, and river in Oregon and Washington. The river was named by Captain Gray for the vessel in which he entered its mouth.

Columbiana; county in Ohio;Columbus; county in North Carolina, and 26 places in the country. Named for Christopher Columbus.

Colusa; county and town in California, named from an Indian tribe.

Colville; town in Stevens County, Washington, named from the old Hudson Bay Company's fort near the Columbia River.

Colwich; city in Sedgwick County, Kansas. The name is a compound of Colorado and Wichita, with reference to the Colorado and Wichita Railroad.

Comal; county in Texas which takes its name from the river. A Spanish word, meaning "fiat earthen pan."

Comanche; counties in Kansas, Oklahoma, and Texas, named from the Indian tribe.

Commack village in Suffolk County, New York. From an Indian word winne-comac, " the beautiful place." Commencement; bay in Washington, named by Vancouver, because he thought it the beginning of the arm of an inlet.

Commerce; village in Scott County, Missouri, so named because it was a trading post as early as 1803.

Como; town in Park County, Colorado, so named by the early miners because there was a lake in the neighborhood, referring to Lake Como, Italy.

Como; town in Panola County, Mississippi, named from a highland pond upon the place of Dr. G. G. Tate, who settled it.

Communipaw; village in Bergen County, New Jersey, named for the original grantee, Michael Pauw, director of the Dutch West India Company. The word is a compound of "the commune of Pauw."

Comstock; famous silver and lead bearing lode in Nevada, named for Henry Page Comstock.

Conant; creek in Yellowstone Park, named for Al Conant, who nearly lost his life in it.

Concho; county and river in Texas. A Spanish word, meaning a "shell."

Concord; town in Middlesex County, Massachusetts, so called either from the Christian concord among the first company, or "from the peaceful manner of its acquisition," having been purchased from the Indians.

Concord; city in Cabarrus County, North Carolina, named from the battle of Concord.

Concord; town in Essex County, Vermont, named for the town in Massachusetts.

Concordia; city in Cloud County, Kansas, named so because there was a controversy for years over a permanent seat of county government, which was finally settled with unanimity.

Cone; peak in Siskiyou County, California, so named because of its regular conical shape.

Conedogwinit; stream in Pennsylvania. An Indian word, meaning "fora long way nothing but bends."

Conejos; county and town in Colorado, named from the Rio de los Conejos, which was so called because there were great numbers of jack rabbits found by the Mexican pioneers.

Conemaugh; river and town in Cambria County, Pennsylvania. An Indian word, meaning "otter creek."

Conequonessing; creek in Pennsylvania. An Indian word, meaning "for a long-time straight."

Conestoga; creek and village in Lancaster County, Pennsylvania, named for an Indian tribe. The word is said to mean, "the great maize land."

Conesus; lake and town in Livingston County, New York. Name derived from the Indian word, ganeasos, "place of many berries," or according to Morgan, "place of nanny berries."

Conewago; creek and village in Lancaster County, Pennsylvania. An Indian word, meaning "a long reach," or "a long strip."

Conewango; river in New York. The name is derived from the Indian word, ganowungo, "the rapids," or, according to some other authorities, "they have been gone a long time."

Coney; island at the extremity of Long Island, New York, which is said by some to have been so named because of the numbers of rabbits there. Another theory ascribes it to the winds having driven the sand into truncated cones. It appears, however, to have been originally called Congu, which may suggest another derivation.

Confluence; borough in Somerset County, Pennsylvania, so named because situated near the confluence of three streams.

Congaree; river, and town in Richland County, South Carolina, named from a tribe of Indians.

Conklin; town in Broome County, New York, named for Judge John Conklin.

Conly; creek in Humboldt County, California, named for an old settler.

Conneaut; lake and borough in Pennsylvania, and village and creek in Ashtabula County, Ohio. Heckewelder says it is a corruption of the Indian, gunniate, "it is a long time since he or they are gone." According to others it is a Seneca Indian word, signifying "many fish." A third theory gives "snow place."

Conneautville; borough in Crawford County, Pennsylvania, named from the same.

Connecticut; river and State. An Indian name, derived from Quonoktacut, meaning, according to some authorities, "a river whose water is driven in waves by tides or winds." Haines says, "land on the long tidal river." Other interpretations are, "on long river," "long river," and "the long, or without end river."

Connellsville; borough in Fayette County, Pennsylvania, named for Zachariah Connell, who laid it out.

Connersville; city in Fayette County, Indiana, named for John Conner, who laid out the place in 1817.

Connersville; village in Harrison County, Kentucky, named for Lewis Conner.

Conness; mount in California, named for John Conness, Senator from California in 1863-1869.

Cononodaw; creek in Pennsylvania. Name corrupted from the Indian word gunniada, "he tarries long."

Conoquenessing-; borough in Butler County, Pennsylvania. Name corrupted from the Indian word gunachquene'sink, "for a long way straight."

Conoy; creek and village in Lancaster County, Pennsylvania. Corruption of the Indian word guneu, "long."

Conquest; town in Cayuga County, New York, so named to commemorate the conquest achieved by those who favored a division of the old town of Cato.

Conshohocken; borough in Montgomery County, Pennsylvania, named from the Indian name which the place first bore.

Constable; village in Franklin County, New York, named for William Constable, agent and part proprietor.

Constableville; village in Lewis County, New York, named for William Constable, son of the original proprietor.

Constitution; island in the Hudson River, New York, named from the fort.

Contoocook; river in New Hampshire. An Indian word, meaning "crow river."

Contra Costa; county in California. A Spanish word, meaning "a coast opposite to another."

Converse; county in Wyoming, probably named for A. R. Converse, territorial treasurer.

Conway; county and town in Faulkner County, Arkansas, named for Henry W. Conway, Territorial Delegate in Congress.

Conway; town in Franklin County, Massachusetts, named for Henry Seymour Conway, secretary of state of England. Some authorities claim that the name was derived from the town in Wales.

Conway; town in Horry County, South Carolina, named for Gen. Robert Conway, early resident.

Cook; inlet of the Pacific Ocean on the coast of Alaska, named for Captain Cook, the navigator. .

Cook; county in Illinois, named for Daniel P. Cook, member of Congress.

Cooke; county in Texas, named for William G. Cooke, captain of New Orleans Grays at the storming of Bexar.

Cooksburg; village in Albany County, New York, named for Thomas B. Cook, early landholder.

Coolidge; city in Hamilton County, Kansas, named for Thomas Jefferson Coolidge, former president of the Atchison, Topeka and Santa Fe Railroad.

Cooper; township in Washington County, Maine, named for Gen. John Cooper, an early and esteemed settler.

Cooper; county in Missouri, named for Capt. Sanshell Cooper, early settler.

Cooper; river in South Carolina, named for the Earl of Shaftsbury, Lord Ashley Cooper, one of the proprietors.

Cooper; point in Washington, named for a man who took up a claim there, which he afterwards deserted.

Cooperstown; village in Otsego County, New York, named for the father of James Fenimore Cooper.

Cooperstown; borough in Venango County, Pennsylvania, named for its founder, William Cooper.

Cooperstown; town in Robertson County, Tennessee, so named because a great many barrels were made there for the Red River mills.

Coopersville; village in Clinton County, New York, named for Ebenezer Cooper, mill owner.

Coos; county in New Hampshire; Coos; bay, river, and county in Oregon. An Indian word, meaning either "lake," "lagoon," or "inland bay," or " place of pines."

Coosa; river and county in Alabama, named from a tribe of Indians.

Coosawhatchie; river and town in Beaufort County, South Carolina. An Indian word, meaning "the river of the Coosas."

Cope; town in Arapahoe County, Colorado, named for Jonathan Cope, who laid it out.

Cope; town in Orangeburg County, South Carolina, named for J. Martin Cope, founder.

Copemish; village in Manistee County, Michigan. An Indian word, meaning "beech tree."

Copenhagen; village in Lewis County, New York, named from the city in Denmark.

Copiah; county in Mississippi; Copiah Creek; village in Copiah County, Mississippi. An Indian word, meaning "calling panther."

Coplay; creek and borough in Lehigh County, Pennsylvania. An Indian word, meaning "that which runs evenly" or "a fine-running stream."

Copper; harbor in Michigan, so called from the copper mines near.

Copperopolis; town in Calaveras County, California, named from its extensive copper mines.

Coquille; river and town in Coos County, Oregon. A French word, meaning " shell." Coralville; town in Johnson County, Iowa, so named from the coral formation under the town.

Coram; village in Suffolk County, New York, named for an Indian chief.

Coraopolis; borough in Allegheny County, Pennsylvania, named for Cora Watson, wife of one of the proprietors.

Corapechen; creek in Maryland. An Indian word, meaning "fierce-running stream."

Corbett; post-office in Multnomah County, Oregon, named for H. W. Corbett, United States Senator from the State.

Corcoran; mount in California, named for W. W. Corcoran, of Washington, D. C.

Cordova; thirteen places in the country named from the city in Spain.

Corfu; village in Genesee County, New York, named for the ancient city of the Ionian Islands.

Corinna; town in Penobscot County, Maine, named for the Greek poetess of Boeotia.

Corinth; city in Alcorn County, Mississippi, named from the ancient city in Greece.

Cork; villages in Butts County, Georgia, Fulton County, New York, Ashtabula County, Ohio, and Tyler County, West Virginia, named from the city in Ireland.

Cornelius; town in Washington County, Oregon, named for Col. T. R. Cornelius, volunteer in Cayuse war.

Cornell; mount in New York, named for Stephen B. Cornell, founder of Cornell University.

Cornettsville; village in Davies County, Indiana, named for Myer and Samuel Cornett, who laid it out.

Corning; city in Steuben County, New York, and city in Nemaha County, Kansas, named for Erastus Corning.

Cornplanter; township in Venango County, and Indian reservation in Warren County, Pennsylvania, named for a Seneca Indian chief.

Cornville; town in Somerset County, Maine, so named from an unusually good yield of corn.

Coronaca; town in Greenwood County, South Carolina, which derived its name from the plantation of Joseph Salvador, a wealthy Jewish landowner of Charleston.

Coronado; cities in San Diego County, California, and Wichita County, Kansas, named for the Spanish explorer, Francisco Vasquez de Coronado.

Corpus Christi; bay and city in Texas, named with reference to a festival in the Roman Catholic Church.

Correctionville; town in Woodbury County, Iowa, situated on a correction line.

Corunna; city in Shiawassee County, Michigan, named from the city in Spain.

Corry; city in Erie County, Pennsylvania, named for a former owner, Hiram Corry.

Corsica; borough in Jefferson County, Pennsylvania, named from the island in the Mediterranean Sea.

Corsicana; city in Navarro County, Texas, named for the wife of Navarro, a Mexican, who owned a large tract of land in the county at one time.

Corson; inlet in New Jersey, named for a family who lived north of the inlet.

Cortland; city in Republic County, Kansas, named from the city in New York.

Cortland; county and city in New York, named for Lieutenant-Governor Pierre Van Cortlandt.

Cortlandt; town in Westchester County, New York, named for Pierre Van Cortlandt.

Corvallis; city in Benton County, Oregon. Name formed of two Spanish words, meaning " heart of valley," so named from its situation in Willamette Valley.

Corvette; ledge in Maryland, so named because a French corvette went ashore on the ledge.

Corwin; village in Warren County, Ohio, named for Thomas Corwin, governor of the State.

Cory; village in Clay County, Indiana, named for a resident of Terre Haute.

Coryell; county and village in Texas, named for James Coryell, large land owner.

Coshocton; county and village in Ohio, named from the Indian town of Goshocking.

The word means, according to some authorities, "habitation of owls." Heckewelder gives "forks of the Muskingum, or union of waters." Others say "finished small harbor."

Cossatot; river in Arkansas, supposed to be a corruption of the French word cassetete, "tomahawk."

Cossayuna; lake and village in Washington County, New York. An Indian word, said to signify "the lake at our points."

Costilla; county in Colorado, named from the Costilla estate, which extends into Taos County, New Mexico.

Cosumne; river and town in Sacramento County, California, named from a tribe of Indians. The word means "salmon."

Cote Blanche; bay in Louisiana. A French name, meaning "white coast."

Cottle; county in Texas, named for G. W. Cottle, who fell at the Alamo.

Cottleville; town in St. Charles County, Missouri, named for Lorenzo Cottle, early settler.

Cotton Plant; town in Dunklin County, Missouri, distinguished by fields of growing cotton.

Cottonwood; county in Minnesota and many natural features and post-offices, named from a species of poplar found in many parts of the country. A creek in Kansas was so named because it was there that the first trees of this species were seen by Zebulon M. Pike on his exploring expedition.

Cottrell; key in Florida, named for Jeremiah Cottrell, first keeper of the light-house there.

Coulter; village in Allegheny County, Pennsylvania, named for Eli Coulter, early settler.

Coulter; creek in Yellowstone Park. named for John M. Coulter, botanist with Hayden expedition.

Council Bluffs; city in Pottawattamie County, Iowa, so called from a council held near there by Lewis and Clarke with the Indians.

Council Grove; city in Morris County, Kansas, so named from a council held by the United States Commission with the Indians in a fine grove on the Neosho River.

Coupeville; village in Island County, Washington, named for a navigator, Captain Coupe.

Coventry; towns in several States, named from the town in England.

Covington; counties in Alabama and Mississippi, cities in Georgia and Kentucky, and town in Wyoming County, New York, named for Gen. Leonard Covington.

Cow; island in the Missouri River in Kansas, from the old name given by the French, Isle de Vache, "isle of the cow," from the buffalo found there.

Cowanesque; creek in Potter County, Pennsylvania. An Indian word, meaning "overgrown with briars."

Cowanshannock; creek in Pennsylvania. An Indian word, gawiensch-hanne, "green briar stream."

Cowautacuck; creek in Connecticut. An Indian word, meaning "pine woodland."

Cowen; mount in Montana, named for the Assistant Secretary of the Interior.

Cowen; town in Webster County, West Virginia, named for the president of the Baltimore and Ohio Railroad.

Coweta; county in Georgia, named for Gen. William Mcintosh, head chief of the Coweta towns, a half-breed Indian.

Cowhocton; river in New York. Indian word meaning "login the water."

Cowles; town in Webster County, Nebraska, named for W. D. Cowles, railroad man.

Cowley; county in Kansas, named for Matthew Cowley, first lieutenant Company I, Ninth Kansas.

Cowlitz; county and river in Washington, named from the Indian tribe Coweliske.

Cowpens; village in Spartanburg County, South Carolina, made famous by a battle fought there during the Revolution. It received its name from a herd of cattle kept there in early days.

Cox; bar in California, named for an old settler.

Cox; creek in Florida. named for a man who lived on its banks.

Coxsackie; town in Greene County, New York. The name is derived from the Indian kuk, "to cut," and auke, "earth," descriptive of the ridge cut and tumbled in by the waters of the Hudson pressing hard on the shore. Another theory derives the name from an Indian word meaning "hooting of owls."

Coyote; village in Santa Clara County, California, and town in Rio Arriba County, New Mexico. The word, in the dialect of the Cushina and other tribes inhabiting the upper portions of Sacramento Valley, means a species of dog. It is also derived from the Mexican coyote, "prairie wolf."

Cozad; town in Dawson County, Nebraska, named for the original owner of the site, John J. Cozad.

Crab Grass; creek in Florida, so called from a species of grass plentiful along its banks.

Crabtree; town in Linn County, Oregon, named for John J. Crabtree, early settler.

Craftsbury; town in Orleans County, Vermont, named for Ebenezer Crafts, one of the original grantees.

Craig; village in Routt County, Colorado, named for Rev. Bayard Craig, of Denver.

Craig; county and creek in Virginia, which took their name from a prominent family of Augusta County.

Craig; pass in Yellowstone Park, named for Mrs. Ida Craig Wilcox, the first tourist to cross the pass.

Craighead; county in Arkansas, named for Thomas B. Craighead, of the State senate.

Cranberry; islands in Hancock County, Maine, named so from a marsh of cranberries on the largest island.

Cranberry Isles; town in Hancock County, Maine, named from the islands.

Crane; county in Texas, named for William Carey Crane, Baptist minister.

Cranesville; village in Erie County, Pennsylvania, named for its founder, Fowler Crane.

Cranston; town in Providence County, Rhode Island, named for Samuel Cranston, governor of the State for nearly thirty years.

Crater; buttes in Idaho, so named from their volcanic origin.

Crater; lake in Oregon, so named because it occupies the crater of a former volcano.

Craven; county in North Carolina, named for William, Earl of Craven, a lord proprietor.

Crawford; county in Kansas, named for Samuel J. Crawford, colonel Second Kansas Regiment, and governor in 1865-69.

Crawford; counties in Indiana, Michigan, Ohio, and Pennsylvania, named for Col. William Crawford, who was captured by Indians and burned at the stake at Sandusky, Ohio, in 1782.

Crawford; counties in Arkansas, Georgia, Iowa, Illinois, Missouri, and Wisconsin, and town in Oglethorpe County, Georgia, named for William H. Crawford, Secretary of the Treasury under President Monroe.

Crawford; town in Lowndes County, Mississippi, named for Rev. Crawford, a Baptist preacher.

Crawford; purchase in Coos County, New Hampshire, named for the original owner, Ethan A. Crawford.

Crawford House; village in Coos County, New Hampshire, named from the purchase.

Crawford Notch; gap in White Mountains, New Hampshire, named from the purchase.

Crawfordsville; city in Indiana, named for William H. Crawford, Secretary of the Treasury under President Monroe.

Crawfordsville; town in Linn County, Oregon, named for George F. Crawford, early settler.

Crawfordville; town in Taliaferro County, Georgia, named from William H. Crawford, Secretary of the Treasury under President Monroe.

Creede; city in Mineral County, Colorado, named for the miner who made rich discoveries of gold there.

Creek; nation in Indian Territory, named from the tribe of Indians. The early English gave the name to the tribe because the country inhabited by them was full of creeks.

Crenshaw; county in Alabama, named for Anderson Crenshaw, of that State.

Cresskill; borough in Bergen County, New Jersey, named from a creek abounding in water cress. The word "kil" is Dutch for stream.

Cresson; village in Cambria County, Pennsylvania; Cressona; borough in Schuylkill County, Pennsylvania. Named for Elliott Cresson, a Philadelphia merchant.

Crested Butte; town in Gunnison County, Colorado, named for a conical, gray peak which dominates the valley. The mountain derives its name from its shape.

Crestline; village in Crawford County, Ohio, so called because it occupies the crest line of the middle elevation of the State.

Creston; city in Union County, Iowa, so named because it was the highest point on the Chicago, Burlington and Quincy Railroad.

Crestone; mountain in Colorado, named from its shape.

Creswell; town in Washington County, North Carolina, named for Postmaster-General Creswell.

Creve Coeur; village in St. Louis County, Missouri, named for an early French fort. The name means " heart break," or "heart breaker."

Crittenden; county in Arkansas, named for Robert Crittenden.

Crittenden; county and town in Grant County, Kentucky, named for John J. Crittenden, United States Senator from that State.

Crockett; counties in Tennessee and Texas and town in Houston County, Texas, named for Col. David Crockett, celebrated frontier Indian fighter, who fell at the Alamo.

Croghan; town in Lewis County, New York, named for Col. George Croghan.

Cronly; town in Columbus County, North Carolina, named for the former owner of the site.

Crook; counties in Oregon and Wyoming and town in Logan County, Colorado, named for Gen. George H. Crook.

Crooked; creek in Pennsylvania, named from the old Indian name, Woak-hanne, "crooked stream."

Crosby; county in Texas, named for Stephen Crosby, prominent citizen.

Crosman; valley in Nevada, named for Col. G. H. Crosman.

Cross; county in Arkansas, named for Judge Edward Cross, a pioneer.

Crosswicks; town in Burlington County, New Jersey. A corruption of the Indian " Crossweeksung, " house of separation." Croswell; village in Sanilac County, Michigan, named for Governor Croswell.

Crothersville; town in Jackson County, Indiana, named for Dr. Crothers.

Croton; village in Newaygo County, Michigan, named for the town in New York.

Croton; river in New York, named for an Indian chief whose name was Kenoten, Knoten, or Noton, meaning "the wind."

Croton Falls; town in Westchester County, New York, named from Croton River.

Crow; river in Minnesota. Translation of the Indian name Andaig.

Crowley; village in Polk County, Oregon, named for Solomon K. Crowley, early settler.

Crown Point; town in Essex County, New York. From the original French name, Point au Chevalure, "point of the hair or scalp," because it is said the French and Indians sent out "scalping parties" from this place.

Crow Wing; county and village in Minnesota, named from a stream which was called by the Indians Kayaugeweguan, "crow's feather or wing."

Croydon; town in Sullivan County, New Hampshire, named from the town in Surrey, England.

Crugers; village in Westchester County, New York, named for Col. John P. Cruger.

Crum Elbow; village in Dutchess County, New York, the name of which was given, it is said, from a sudden bend in the Hudson River at that place.

Cucharas; river and village in Huerfano County, Colorado. A Spanish word, meaning "spoon brook."

Cudahy; village in Milwaukee County, Wisconsin, named for the Cudahy brothers, who own a pork-packing establishment there.

Cuddeback; town in Humboldt, County, California, named for an old settler.

Cuerno Verde; mountain in Colorado, named for its shape and color. A Spanish name, meaning "green horn."

Cuero; town in Dewitt County, Texas. A Spanish word, meaning "hide, skin, leather."

Cuivre; river and village in Lincoln County, Missouri. A French word, meaning "copper."

Cullman; county and city in Alabama, named for General John G. Cullman of that State.

Culloden; village in Monroe County, Georgia, named for William Culloden, one of the first settlers in the county.

Cullom; village in Livingston County, Illinois, named for Shelby M. Cullom, United States Senator from that State.

Culpeper; county and town in Virginia, named for Lord Thomas Culpeper, governor in 1679-80.

Cumberland; county in Illinois, named from Cumberland road, which was projected to pass through it.

Cumberland; river and county in Kentucky. Dr. Thomas Walker, of Virginia, named the river in 1758, but whether for the Duke of Cumberland or for the English county it is not satisfactorily decided.

Cumberland; county in North Carolina, islands off the coast of Georgia, mountains and city in Maryland, and town in Providence County, Rhode Island, named for the Duke of Cumberland, victor of Culloden.

Cumberland; counties in Pennsylvania and Virginia, named for the county in England.

Cuming; county and town in Nebraska, named for T. B. Cuming, governor of the Territory in 1854-55.

Cumming; town in Forsyth County, Georgia, named for Col. William Cumming, of Augusta, Georgia.

Cummington; town in Hampshire County, Massachusetts, named for Col. John Cummings, former owner.

Cumminsville; village in Wheeler County, Nebraska, named for J. F. Cummings, county clerk.

Cumminsville; village in Hamilton County, Ohio, named for David Cummins, early settler.

Cundy; harbor and ledge in Maine, named for a family who settled there at an early date.

Cunningham; town in Chariton County, Missouri, named for Dr. John F. Cunningham, of Brunswick, Missouri.

Cupsuptic; lake in Maine. Indian word, meaning "the act of drawing a seine while fishing."

Currie; village in Murray County, Minnesota, named for a parish in Scotland.

Currituck; county in North Carolina, named from a tribe of Indians who once possessed the land.

Curry; county in Oregon, named for George L. Curry, governor of the Territory in 1855-1859.

Currytown; village in Montgomery County, New York, named for William Curry, patentee.

Curryville; town in Pike County, Missouri, named for Perry Curry, who laid out the town.

Curtin; village in Dauphin County, Pennsylvania, named for the Curtin family, of which Governor A. G. Curtin was a member.

Curwensville; borough in Clearfield County, Pennsylvania, named for John Curwen, of Montgomery County.

Cushing; town in Knox County, Maine, named for Thomas Cushing, lieutenant governor of Massachusetts.

Cusseta; town in Chambers County, Alabama, and village in Chattahoochee County, Georgia. An Indian word, meaning "coming from the sun," originally Hashita.

Custer; county and town in Colorado; county and town in Idaho; county, town, and creek in Montana; county and town in Nebraska; county and village in Beaver County, Oklahoma; county and city in South Dakota, and several other places, named for Gen. George A. Custer, who was killed by the Indians on the banks of Rosebud River in 1876.

Cuthbert; town in Randolph County, Georgia, named for Col. J. A. Cuthbert, member of Congress.

Cutler; town in Washington County, Maine, named for an early proprietor, Joseph Cutler, of Newburyport.

Cuttawa; town in Lyon County, Kentucky, named from the old Indian name of the Kentucky River, Kuttawa.

Cuttingsville; village in Rutland County, Vermont, named for one of the first settlers.

Cuttyhunk; island in Massachusetts. A contraction of the Indian word Poocutohhunkunnok, "thing that lies out in the water."

Cuyahoga; river and county in Ohio; Cuyahoga Falls; village in Summit County, Ohio, situated at falls on above river. The name is derived by some from Cayahaga, "crooked," but Atwater derives it from Cuyahogan-uk, "lake river."

Cynthiana; city in Harrison County, Kentucky, named for the two daughters of the original proprietors, Cynthia and Anna Harris.

Cypress; island in Washington; so named by Vancouver's party, from the abundance of that species of tree found there.

Cyr; plantation in Aroostook County, Maine, named for a family numerous in that section.

D

Dade; county and city in Pasco County, Florida, and counties in Georgia and Missouri; Dadeville; town in Tallapoosa County, Alabama. Named for Maj. Francis L. Dade, of the Seminole war.

Dagget; pond in Maine, named for an early settler.

Daggett; village in Owen County, Indiana, named for Charles Daggett, a prominent resident.

Dagsboro; town in Sussex County, Delaware, named for Sir John Dagworthy.

Dahlonega; towns in Lumpkin County, Georgia, and Wapello County, Iowa. An Indian name, meaning "yellow dollar," or "place of gold."

Dakota; two States—North and South Dakota—counties in Nebraska and Minnesota, and several small places, named for the Indian tribe. The name was originally spelled Lahkota or Dacorta, which means "friend," "ally," "leagued or united people," or "allied nation," the common name of the confederate Sioux tribes.

Dale; county in Alabama, named for Gen. Samuel Dale of that State.

Dallam; county in Texas, named for James W. Dallam, lawyer who made the first digest of Texas laws.

Dallas; county in Alabama, named for A. J. Dallas, Secretary of the Treasury under President Madison.

Dallas; counties in Arkansas, Iowa, Missouri, and Texas, and towns in Gaston County, North Carolina, and Dallas County, Texas; Dallas Center; town in Dallas County, Iowa. Named for George M. Dallas, Vice-President under James K. Polk.

Dalles; the name given by the Hudson Bay Company to deep chasms in rocks forming a narrow passage for rivers. A French word, meaning "flagstone, slab; also a spout for water or a trough." The most famous dalles are on the Columbia River, Oregon. A city in Wasco County, Oregon, takes its name from the above.

Dalmatia; town in Northumberland County, Pennsylvania, named from the titular kingdom of Austria.

Dalton; town in Berkshire County, Massachusetts, named for Gen. Tristram Dalton, speaker of the house of representatives of Massachusetts.

Dalton; village in Chariton County, Missouri, named for William Dalton.

Dalton; town in Coos County, New Hampshire, named for Hon. Tristram Dalton, a grantee.

Daly; mountain in Colorado, named for Judge Charles P. Daly, formerly president of the American Geographical Society.

Daly; county in Montana, named for Marcus Daly.

Damariscotta; river and town in Lincoln County, Maine. An Indian name, meaning "the alewife place," or "river of little fishes."

Damascus; fourteen places in the country bear the name of the famous city in Syria.

Dana; town in Worcester County, Massachusetts, named for the distinguished family of which Chief Justice Francis Dana was a member.

Danbury; city in Fairfield County, Connecticut, and several other places, named from the town in Essex, England.

Danby; town in Rutland County, Vermont, named from Danby, England.

Dandridge; town in Jefferson County, Tennessee, named for the maiden name of the wife of George Washington, Mrs. Martha Custis, née Dandridge.

Dane; county and village in Wisconsin, named for Nathan Dane, an American jurist, and member of Congress.

Danielsville; town in Madison County, Georgia, named for Gen. Allen Daniel.

Dannebrog; village in Howard County, Nebraska, which was settled by Danes from Milwaukee, Wisconsin.

Dannemora; town in Clinton County, New York, named from the celebrated iron region in Sweden.

Dansville; village in Ingham County, Michigan, named for Daniel L. Crossman, a resident.

Dansville; town in Steuben County, and village in Livingston County, New York, named for Daniel P. Faulkner, who laid the village out.

Danube; town in Herkimer County, New York, named from the river in Austria.

Danvers; town in Essex County, Massachusetts, said to have received its name from the Earl D'Anvers, but Nason says it is said to have received its name in honor of Sir Danvers Osborn, governor of New York in 1753.

Danville; town in Hendricks County, Indiana, named for Daniel Bales, proprietor.

Danville; city in Boyle County, Kentucky, named for its founder, Walker Daniel.

Danville; village in Montgomery County, Missouri, built on land which formerly belonged to Daniel M. Boone, son of Daniel Boone.

Danville; borough in Montour County, Pennsylvania, named for Gen. Daniel Montgomery.

Danville; town in Caledonia County, Vermont, named for the distinguished French admiral, D'Anville.

Danville; city in Pittsylvania County, Virginia, so named because situated on the river Dan.

Darby; borough in Delaware County, Pennsylvania, named from Derby, England, whence many of the early settlers came.

Darbyville; village in Pickaway County, Ohio, named for a Wyandotte Indian chief.

Dare; county in Virginia named for Virginia Dare, the first white child born in the New World, 1587.

Darke; county in Ohio; Darkesville; town in Berkeley County, West Virginia. Named for Gen. William Darke, an officer of the Revolution.

Darlington; borough in Beaver County, Pennsylvania, named for S. P. Darlington, a merchant of Pittsburg.

Darlington; county and village in South Carolina. The origin of the name is not known, but may have been given in honor of Colonel Darlington, Revolutionary leader.

Dartford; village in Green Lake County, Wisconsin, named for the first settler.

Dartmouth; town in Bristol County, Massachusetts, according to Whitmore, named from the seaport in Devonshire, England; other authorities give William, Earl of Dartmouth, founder of Dartmouth College at Hanover, New Hampshire.

Darwin; village in Clark County, Illinois, named for Charles Darwin, the English naturalist.

Darysaw; village and township in Grant County, Arkansas, so called from the French Des Ruisseaux, "streamlets."

Dauphin; county in Pennsylvania, named for the Dauphin of France, son of Louis XVI."

Davenport; city in Iowa, named for Colonel Davenport, early settler.

Davenport; village in Thayer County, Nebraska, named from Davenport, Iowa.

Davenport; town in Delaware County, New York, named for John Davenport, early settler.

Davidson; town in Boulder County, Colorado, named for Col. William A. Davidson, president of the Davidson Coal and Iron Mining Company, which platted the town.

Davidson; village in Josephine County, Oregon, named for Elijah B. Davidson, early settler.

Davidson; counties in North Carolina and Tennessee; Davidson College; town in Mecklenburg County, North Carolina. Named for Gen. William Davidson, an officer of the Revolution.

Davie; county in North Carolina, named for Gen. William R. Davie, governor in 1798-99.

Daviess; counties in Indiana, Kentucky, and Missouri, named for Col. Joseph Daviess, who fell at the battle of Tippecanoe.

Davis; creek in Humboldt County, California, named for an old settler.

Davis; county and town in Decatur County, Iowa, named for Garrett Davis, member of Congress.

Davis; town in Tucker County, West Virginia, named for Senator H. G. Davis.

Davison; county in South Dakota, named for Henry C. Davison, the first settler in the county.

Davitte; village in Polk County, Georgia, named for the original proprietor, J. S. Davitte.

Dawes; county in Nebraska, named for James W. Dawes, former governor of the State.

Dawson; county in Georgia, named for William C. Dawson, United States Senator from that State.

Dawson; county in Montana, named for Andrew Dawson, of the American Fur Company.

Dawson; village in Richardson County, Nebraska, named for Joshua Dawson, early settler.

Dawson; county in Texas, named for Nicholas Dawson, who led the forces at the battle of Salado, in 1836.

Dawsonville; town in Dawson County, Georgia, named for William C. Dawson.

Day; a county in Oklahoma. The counties in Oklahoma were originally named from the letters of the alphabet; later, names were given which began with the letter corresponding to the one by which the county had been known.

Day; county in South Dakota, named for Merritt H. Day, legislator.

Dayansville; village in Lewis County, New York, named for Charles Dayan, who founded it in 1826.

Dayton; town in York County, Maine, named for a prominent politician.

Dayton; city in Ohio, named for Jonathan Dayton, one of the original proprietors.

Daytona; town in Volusia County, Florida, named for W. T. Day, of Ohio.

Dead; mountain in Nevada, so called because it was supposed by the Mohave Indians to be the abode of departed spirits.

Deadwood; city in South Dakota, named from a forest of dead timber found near.

Deaf Smith; county in Texas, named for Erastus Smith, Indian and Mexican fighter, and scout, so called because his hearing was imperfect.

Deal; island in Maryland. Name corrupted from the old name, Devils Island.

Deal; borough in Monmouth County, New Jersey; Deal Beach; post office in Monmouth County, New Jersey. Named from Deal, England.

Deal Island; village in Somerset County, Maryland, named from the island.

Deansville; village in Oneida County, New York, named for Thomas Dean, agent of the Brothertown Indians.

Dearborn; county in Indiana; town in Wayne County; Michigan, river in Montana; and mount in South Carolina, named for Gen. Henry Dearborn, Secretary of War under President Thomas Jefferson.

Death; valley in California, so called because a party of immigrants perished there from thirst and starvation.

Deblois; town in Washington County, Maine, named for Thomas Amory Deblois, bank president.

Decatur; counties in Florida, Georgia, Indiana, Iowa, Kansas, and Tennessee, towns in Newton County, Mississippi, and Otsego County, New York, also many other places, named for Commodore Stephen Decatur.

Deckertown; borough in Sussex County, New Jersey, named for a family numerous in the neighborhood.

Decorah; city in Winneshiek County, Iowa, named for an Indian chief, Decorie.

Dedham; town in Hancock County, Maine, named for the Massachusetts town.

Dedham; town in Norfolk County, Massachusetts, named from the parish in England.

Deep; river in North Carolina. A translation of the Indian name Sapponah, "deep river."

Deep River; town in Poweshiek County, Iowa, named from a creek near.

Deerfield; descriptive name given to many places. The town in Rockingham County, New Hampshire, was so named because when the petition for a town was pending Mr. Batchelder killed a deer, and upon presenting it to Governor Wentworth obtained the act and name.

Deering; town in Hillsboro County, New Hampshire, named by Governor Benning Wentworth for the maiden name of his wife.

Deer Isle; town in Hancock County, Maine, named from three islands upon which deer were very abundant.

Deerlodge; county and town in Powell County, Montana, named from a salt lick where deer came in droves.

Defiance; county and city in Ohio, named from a fort erected by Gen. Anthony Wayne in defiance of the British and Indians.

De Funiak Springs; celebrated resort in Walton County, Florida, named for a resident of Nashville.

Dekalb; counties in Alabama, Georgia, Illinois, Indiana, Missouri, and Tennessee, and numerous places in the country, named for Baron De Kalb, who fell at the battle of Camden.

De Lacy; creek in Yellowstone Park, named for William W. De Lacy, the first white man known to have passed along the valley.

Delancey; village in Delaware County, New York, named for James De Lancey, an early patentee.

De Land; town in Volusia County, Florida, named for H. A. De Land, a manufacturer of Fairport, New York, who founded it.

Delano; mountains in Montana and Utah, named for Columbus Delano, Secretary of the Interior under President Grant.

Delavan; city in Walworth County, Wisconsin, named for E. C. Delavan, a temperance advocate of Albany, New York.

Delaware; river, State, counties in Indiana, Iowa, New York, Ohio, and Pennsylvania, named for Lord de la Warr, governor and first captain-general of Virginia. Many small places also bear this name. A tribe of Indians were known by this name, and in the case of the county in Indiana, the name was given because this tribe had villages within the boundaries of the county.

Deleon; town in Comanche County, Texas; Deleon Springs; town in Volusia County, Florida. Named for Ponce de Leon.

Delgada; point in California, named for an old Spanish explorer.

Delhi; village in Delaware County, New York, named for the city in India. Several other places bear this name.

Dellenbaugh; mount in Arizona, named for F. S. Dellenbaugh, the artist, by the Powell survey.

Delmar; town on the border between Delaware and Maryland, named from the first syllables of the names of each State.

Del Norte; county in California, situated in the northwest corner of the State. Spanish name, meaning "of the north."

Del Norte; town in Rio Grande County, Colorado, named from the river Rio Grande del Norte, "grand river of the north."

Delphi; town in Carroll County, Indiana, and village in Onondaga County, New York, named for the ancient town in Phocis.

Delphos; city in Allen County, Ohio, and several other places named from the classical Delphos of Greece.

Del Rio; town in Valverde County, Texas, named from its situation on Rio Grande, Spanish name, meaning "of the river."

Delta; county in Colorado, named from a delta of arable land at the mouth of the Uncompahgre River where it flows into Gunnison River.

Delta; counties in Michigan and Texas, so named because triangular in shape.

Demopolis; city in Marengo County, Alabama. Greek word, meaning "city of the people."

Denbigh; town in Warwick County, Virginia, named from a county in Wales.

Denison; city in Crawford County, Iowa, named for J. W. Denison; who laid it out.

Denison; city in Grayson County, Texas, settled by persons from the north, and probably named for Rev. C. W. Denison, of early antislavery fame.

Denmark; town in Lewis County, New York, named for the kingdom in Europe.

Denmark; town in Bamberg County, South Carolina, named for B. A. Denmark, a railroad director.

Denning; town in Ulster County, New York, named for William H. Denning, former proprietor.

Dennis; village in Barnstable County, Massachusetts, named for its first minister, Rev. Josiah Dennis.

Dennison; village in Tuscarawas County, Ohio, named, probably, for Gov. William Dennison.

Dennys; river in Maine, named for an Indian who used to hunt in the vicinity.

Dennysville; town in Washington County, Maine, named from Dennys River.

Dent; county in Missouri, named for Lewis Dent, early resident.

Denton; town in Caroline County, Maryland, named for Sir Robert Eden, governor of the province in 1769-1776. It was first called Eden Town, from which it was shortened to the present form.

Denton; river, county, and city in Texas, named for Capt. John B. Denton, who was killed in battle with the Indians.

Denver; city in Colorado, named for James W. Denver, former governor of Kansas. Many small places take their name from this city.

Depauville; village in Jefferson County, New York, named for Francis Depau, a large proprietor.

Depere; city in Brown County, Wisconsin, so named because situated on Rapides des Peres.

Depew; village in Erie County, New York, named for Chauncey M. Depew, United States Senator.

Depeyster; town in St. Lawrence County, New York, named for Frederick Depeyster, member of a celebrated New York family.

Deposit; village in Delaware and Broome counties, New York, named so because it was formerly a place of deposit for lumber.

Deptford; township in Gloucester County, New Jersey, named from a port in England.

Derby; city in New Haven County, Connecticut, and town in Orleans County, Vermont, named for the town and county in England. Many other places also bear this name, given either directly or indirectly from the same.

Derrick City; village in McKean County, Pennsylvania, so named from the great numbers of derricks which mark the oil wells in the vicinity.

Derry; town in Rockingham County, New Hampshire, and borough in Montour County, Pennsylvania; also one or two small places named for the town in Ireland, now called Londonderry.

Deruyter; village in Madison County, New York, named for Admiral De Ruyter, of the Dutch navy.

Deschutes; river and village in Sherman County, Oregon. From early French name, riviere des chutes, meaning " river of falls."

Desha; county in Arkansas, named for Capt. Ben Desha, prominent citizen of the State.

Desmet; town in Kootenai County, Idaho, and village in Kingsbury County, South Dakota, named for Peter John De Smet, a Jesuit missionary.

Des Moines; river, county, and city in Iowa. This name is thought to have been derived from the Indian word, mikonang, meaning "the road." This name was applied by the Indians to a place in the form of Moingona, which the French shortened into Moin, calling the river "riviere des moins." Finally the name became associated with the Trappist monks, and the river by a spurious etymology was called "la riviere des moines," "the river of the monks."

De Soto; counties in Florida, and Mississippi, and parish in Louisiana, village in Sumter County, Georgia, and twelve other places, named for the discoverer of the Mississippi River, Hernando de Soto.

Des Plaines; river and village in Cook County, Illinois. Derived from the presence of a species of maple called by the French, "plaine."

Destruction; island on the northwest coast of North America, so named because of the massacre of a boat crew upon this coast.

Detour; village in Chippewa County, Michigan, so named from its position, it being necessary to make a detour in order to reach it.

Detroit; river and city in Michigan. A French word, meaning "a strait, or narrow passage," given to the river by the early French explorers because it is a short, narrow river connecting Lake St. Clair with Lake Erie.

Deuel; county in Nebraska, named for Harry P. Deuel, superintendent of the Union Pacific Railroad.

Deuel; county in South Dakota, named for Jacob Deuel, a legislator in 1862.

Devils; lake in Sauk County, Wisconsin, so named because it is situated in a deep chasm with no visible inlet or outlet.

Devils Lake; village, Sauk County, Wisconsin, named from the lake.

Devine; town in Medina County, Texas, named for Hon. Thomas J. Devine, an old resident of San Antonio.

Devoe, creek in Arkansas, so called from the name given by the early French, De Veau, "the calf."

Dewey; county in Oklahoma, named for Admiral George Dewey. A number of towns also bear his name.

Dewey; county in South Dakota, named for William P. Dewey, surveyor-general in 1873.

Dewitt; county and village in Illinois, and town in Carroll County, Missouri, named for Dewitt Clinton, one time governor of New York.

Dewitt; town in Onondaga County, New York, named for Moses De Witt. early settler.

Dewitt; county in Texas, named for Green De Witt, colonizer, who settled families at Gonzales in 1827.

Dexter; city in Cowley County, Kansas, named for a trotting horse of Robert Bonner, of New York.

Dexter; town in Penobscot County, Maine, named for Judge Samuel Dexter, candidate for governor of Massachusetts in 1816.

Dexter; village in Washtenaw County, Michigan, named for Samuel W. Dexter, who settled there in 1829.

Dexter; village in Jefferson County, New York, named for S. Newton Dexter, a prominent business man of Whitesboro.

D'Hanis; town in Medina County, Texas, named for Count von D'Hanis, who founded the town about 1845.

Diana; town in Lewis County, New York, named for the Greek goddess.

Dickens; county in Texas, named for J. Dickens, who fell at the Alamo.

Dickey; county and village in Lamoure County, North Dakota, named for Hon. George Dickey, member of the legislature.

Dickey; river in Washington. The name is derived from the Indian name, Dickohdockteader.

Dickinson; counties in Iowa and Kansas, named for Daniel S. Dickinson, United States Senator from New York in 1844.

Dickinson; county in Michigan, named for Don M. Dickinson, Postmaster-General under President Cleveland.

Dickinson; town in Stark County, North Dakota, named for W. S. Dickinson of Malone, New York, who founded it.

Dickinson; county in Virginia, named for a prominent member of the legislature.

Dicksburg; village in Knox County, Indiana, named for Thomas Dick, former owner of the ground.

Dickson; county and town in Tennessee, named for William Dickson.

Die All; island in California, so named because all the Indians on the island died.

Dighton; city in Lane County, Kansas, named for Dick Deighton, a surveyor.

Dighton; village in Bristol County, Massachusetts, named for Frances Dighton, wife of Richard Williams, one of the first settlers.

Diller; village in Jefferson County, Nebraska, named for H. H. Diller, early settler.

Dillon; city in Beaverhead County, Montana, named for Sydney Dillon, railroad president.

Dillon; town in Marion County, South Carolina, named for a prominent family.

Dillsboro; town in Dearborn County, Indiana, named for Gen. James Dill, early settler.

Dillsboro; town in Jackson County, North Carolina, named for George W. Dill, early settler.

Dimmit; county in Texas, named for Philip Dimmit, one of the earliest settlers in the State.

Dinwiddie; county and town in Virginia, named for Robert Dinwiddie, lieutenant governor of the State in 1752-1758.

Dirty Devil; creek in Arizona, so named by Powell during his first trip down the canyon of the Colorado, because of the muddiness of its waters.

Disappointment; cape at the mouth of the Columbia River, Washington, so named by John Meares, the English navigator, who thought no river existed in the region.

Dismal; swamp in Virginia and North Carolina, so named because of its dismal appearance, due to the dense forest of juniper, cypress, etc., which cover it.

Dismaugh; lake in Laporte County, Indiana. From an Indian word, meaning "lake of the monks."

District of Columbia. See Columbia.

Dix; mount and town in Schuyler County, New York, named for Gen. John A. Dix, United States Senator.

Dixfield; town in Oxford County, Maine.

Dixmont; town in Penobscot County, Maine, named for Dr. Elijah Dix, of Boston.

Dixmont; village in Allegheny County, Pennsylvania, named for Miss Dorothea Dix, American philanthropist.

Dixon; city in Lee County, Illinois, named for John Dixon, the founder.

Dixon; town in Webster County, Kentucky, named for Hon. Archibald Dixon.

Dixville; town in Coos County, New Hampshire, named for Col. Timothy Dix, first settler.

Doane; mount in Yellowstone Park, named for Lieut. Gustavus C. Doane, U. S. Army, who commanded the military escort of an expedition in 1870.

Dobbins; town in Yuba County, California, named for a settler.

Dobbs Ferry; village in Westchester County, New York, named for a Swede who owned a ferry there.

Dobson; town in Surry County, North Carolina, named for W. P. Dobson, State senator.

Doctortown; town in Wayne County, Georgia, built upon the site of an old Indian settlement, which was the abode of a great "medicine man."

Doddridge; county in West Virginia, named for Philip Doddridge, a distinguished statesman of western Virginia.

Dodge; county in Georgia, named for W. E. Dodge, of New York, who, with W. P. Eastman, presented a court-house to the county. See Eastman.

Dodge; counties in Minnesota and Wisconsin, and city in Ford County, Kansas, on the site of old Fort Dodge, named for Gen. Henry Dodge, governor of Wisconsin Territory.

Dodge; county in Nebraska, named for Augustus Caesar Dodge, United States Senator from Iowa.

Dodge Center; village in Dodge County. Minnesota; Dodgeville; city in Iowa County, Wisconsin. Named for Gen. Henry Dodge, governor of Wisconsin territory.

Dolores; county in Colorado, named from the Rio Dolores. A Spanish word, meaning "grief," which has a special significance among the Spaniards, being one of the titles of the Virgin Mary.

Dolph; village in Tillamook County, Oregon, named for J. N. Dolph, United States Senator.

Dominguez; creek in Colorado, named for a Spanish priest, who was one of the early explorers in this region.

Donaldsonville; town in Ascension parish, Louisiana, named for William Donaldson.

Donderberg; mountain in New York, on the Hudson. A Dutch word, meaning "thunder mountain," so called by the early Dutch settlers because of the frequent thunder storms which gather around its summit.

Donegal; borough and township in Westmoreland County, Pennsylvania, named from the Irish city.

Doniphan; county and city in Kansas, city in Ripley County, Missouri, and village in Hall County, Nebraska, named for Col. Alexander William Doniphan, a distinguished Western soldier.

Donley; county in Texas named for Stockton P. Donley, justice of the supreme court of the State.

Donner; lake in California, named for a leader of a party of immigrants, nearly all of whom perished from starvation.

Dooly; county in Georgia named for Col. John Dooly, an officer in the Revolution.

Doon; town in Lyon County, Iowa, named from a river in Scotland.

Door; county in Wisconsin, so named because of its proximity to "Death's Door," entrance to Green Bay.

Dorchester; county in Maryland, named for the Earl of Dorchester, whom Scharf says was a family friend of the Calverts.

Dorchester; town in Norfolk County, Massachusetts, named for Dorchester, England; county in South Carolina, named for the town in Massachusetts.

Dormansville; village in Albany County, New York, named for Daniel Dorman, former inn and store keeper.

Dorrance; borough in Luzerne County, Pennsylvania, named for a family of early settlers.

Dosoris; village in Queens County, New York. The name is a contraction of "dos uxoris," "dowry of a wife," the property having come to the first settler through his wife.

Dossett; village in Anderson County, Tennessee, named for the owner of the property, Jacob Dossett.

Dougherty; county in Georgia, named for Charles Dougherty.

Dougherty; township in Cerro Gordo County, Iowa, named for Daniel Dougherty, one of the prominent residents.

Douglas; counties in Colorado, Georgia, Illinois, Kansas, Minnesota, Missouri, Nevada, South Dakota, and Wisconsin, and probably the counties in Nebraska, Oregon, and Washington, named for Stephen A. Douglas, of Illinois.

Douglas; creek in Colorado, named for Chief Douglas, of the White River Utes.

Douglas; town in Worcester County, Massachusetts, named for Dr. William Douglas, author of a history of New England.

Douglas; mount in Montana, named for E. M. Douglas, of the United States Geological Survey.

Douglass; city in Butler County, Kansas, named for Joseph Douglass, by whom it was laid out.

Dover; city in Delaware; town in Morris County, New Jersey; and city in Strafford County, New Hampshire, named from the town in England.

Dowagiac; river and city in Cass County, Michigan. An Indian word, meaning "fishing river."

Downieville; town in Sierra County, California, named for a pioneer.

Downingtown; borough in Chester County, Pennsylvania, named for Thomas Downing.

Downs; city in Osborne County, Kansas, named for William F. Downs, of Atchison.

Downsville; village in Delaware County, New York, situated on Downs Creek. Both are named for Abel Downs, who had a tannery there.

Dows; town in Wright County, Iowa, named for a railroad contractor.

Doylestown; borough in Bucks County, Pennsylvania, named for William Doyle, an early settler.

Dracut; town in Middlesex County, Massachusetts, named from the home of the Varnum family, in Wales.

Drakes; bay in California, named for Sir Francis Drake, the navigator.

Drakesville; town in Davis County, Iowa, named for John A. Drake, who laid it out.

Drayton; town in Dooly County, Georgia, named for Colonel Drayton, of South Carolina.

Dresden; fifteen places in the country bear the name of the city in Germany.

Drew; county in Arkansas, named for Thomas S. Drew, governor in 1844-1848.

Drew; village in Sunflower County, Mississippi, named for a railroad man.

Drewry; bluff on James River, Virginia; Drewry Bluff; post-office in Chesterfield County, Virginia. Named for Maj. Augustus Drewry.

Drummond; lake in the center of Dismal Swamp in Virginia, named for William Drummond, former governor of North Carolina. Another authority says that it was named for a hunter who discovered it.

Dryden; town in Tompkins County, New York, named for the poet, John Dryden.

Dry Tortugas; ten small islands off the coast of Florida. The name was given from the lack of springs and abundance of sea turtles. Tortugas is a Spanish word, meaning "tortoises."

Duane; town in Franklin County, New York, named for James Duane, proprietor and first settler.

Duanesburg; town in Schenectady County, New York. French says that it was named for James Duane, principal proprietor. Gordon says it was named for Judge Duane.

Dublin; city in Laurens County, Georgia, named from the city in Ireland. Several other places are named from the same.

Dubois; county in Indiana, named for Toussaint Dubois, who had charge of the guides and spies in the Tippecanoe campaign.

Dubois; borough in Pennsylvania, named for its founder, John Dubois.

Dubuque; county and city in Iowa, named for a French trader, Julien Dubuque.

Duck Hill; town in Montgomery County, Mississippi, named from a hill near the town where ducks were plentiful in early days.

Dudley; town in Worcester County, Massachusetts, named for two brothers, Paul and William Dudley, who were among the first proprietors.

Dufur; village in Wasco County, Oregon, named for an old settler.

Dukes; county in Massachusetts, so named because it was under the government of the Duke of York, afterwards James H. Duluth; city in Minnesota, named for Sieur Daniel Graysolon Duluth, a French traveler.

Dumfries; town in Prince William County, Virginia, named for the town in Scotland.

Dummer; town in Coos County, New Hampshire; Dummerston; town in Windham County, Vermont. Named for William Dummer, lieutenant-governor of Vermont and acting governor of Massachusetts in 1723-1728, 1728-1730 Dumont; village in Clear Creek County, Colorado, named for John M. Dumont, a mine operator.

Dunbar; village in Otoe County, Nebraska, named for John Dunbar, large landowner.

Dunbar; borough in Fayette County, Pennsylvania, named for the town in Scotland.

Dunbar; village in Marlboro County, South Carolina, named for a family in the neighborhood.

Dunbarton; town in Merrimack County, New Hampshire, named by Archibald Stark, one of the first proprietors, who emigrated from Dunbarton, Scotland.

Duncan; town in Bolivar County, Mississippi, named for a leading citizen.

Duncan Falls; town in Muskingum County, Ohio, named for a trader, Major Duncan.

Duncannon; borough in Perry County, Pennsylvania, named from the town in Wexford, Ireland.

Duncombe; town in Webster County, Iowa, named for Hon. J. F. Duncombe.

Dundaff; borough in Susquehanna County, Pennsylvania, named from the town in Wales.

Dundee; village in Yates County, New York, named from the town in Scotland. A number of other places also bear this name.

Dundy; county in Nebraska, named for Judge Elmer S. Dundy.

Dungeness; town in Clallam County, Washington. This name was given to a low point of land in the county, by Vancouver, because of its resemblance to Dungeness in the British channel, and subsequently applied to the town.

Dunkirk; city in Chautauqua County, New York, named indirectly from the town in France.

Dunklin; county in Missouri, named for Daniel Dunklin, governor of Missouri in 1832-1836.

Dunlap; town in Harrison County, Iowa, named for the superintendent of the Chicago and Northwestern Railway.

Dunlap; city in Morris County, Kansas, named for Joseph Dunlap, a trader among the Indians and founder of the town.

Dunlapsville; town in Union County, Indiana, laid out by John Dunlap, one of the first settlers.

Dunmore; lake in Vermont, named by the Earl of Dunmore, who waded into it and formally christened it for himself.

Dunmore; town in Pocahontas County, West Virginia, named for John (Lord) Dunmore, governor of Virginia, 1772—1770.

Dunn; town in Harnett County, North Carolina, named for a resident.

Dunn; county in Wisconsin, named for Charles Dunn, first chief justice of the Territory.

Dunnsville; town in Albany County, New York, named for Christopher Dunn, original owner.

Dunraven; peak in Yellowstone Park, named for the Earl of Dun raven.

Dunstable; town in Middlesex County, Massachusetts. The history of the town states that it was named for the mother of one of the petitioners, Mary Tyng, but there is no record of her maiden name or birthplace. There is, however, record of a large family by the name of Long, who came from Dunstable, England, in 1635. This fact gives a direct connection, and it is probable that the town took its name from the English town.

Dupage; county in Illinois, named for a river which flows through the county. The origin of the name of the river is unknown.

Duplin; county in North Carolina, named for Lord Duplin, or Dupplin, of the board of trade.

Duquesne; borough in Allegheny County, Pennsylvania, named from old Fort Duquesne, which was named for a distinguished French officer.

Duquoin; city in Perry County, Illinois, said to have been named for an Indian chief of the Kaskaskia tribe.

Durand; village in Shiawassee County, Michigan, named for George H. Durand, of Flint, Michigan, member of Congress.

Durand; city in Pepin County, Wisconsin, named for Miles Durand Prindle, an early settler.

Durant; town in Cedar County, Iowa, named for Thomas Durant.

Durants; neck of land in Perquimans County, North Carolina, granted to George Durant in 1662.

Durham; town in Middlesex County, Connecticut, named from the town in England.

Durham; town in Androscoggin County, Maine. named from the former residence of the royal family, early settlers.

Durham; county and town in North Carolina, named for Dr. Durham, owner of the town site of Durham.

Dushore; borough in Sullivan County, Pennsylvania, named for its founder, the name being a corruption of Dupetit-Thouars.

Duston; island in New Hampshire, named for an early settler.

Dutchess; county in New York, named for Mary of Modena, Duchess of York. Previous to the appearance of Johnson's Dictionary the title of the wife of a duke was spelled with a "t;" hence the name of the county is so spelled.

Dutton; mount in Utah, named by Powell for Maj. C. E. J Hitton.

Duval; county in Florida, named for William P. Duval, Territorial governor in 1822-1834.

Duval; county in Texas, named for the Duval family, prominent in the State. One member, Burr H. Duval, fell in Fannin's massacre.

Duwamish; river in Washington, named from an Indian tribe.

Duxbury; town in Plymouth County, Massachusetts, settled by Miles Standish. It is said to have received its name from the seat of the Standish family in England, Duxbury Hall.

Dwight; village in Hampshire County, Massachusetts, named for the Dwight family, prominent early settlers.

Dycusburg; village in Crittenden County, Kentucky, named for William E. Dycus, its founder.

Dyer; county in Tennessee; Dyersburg; city in Tennessee. Named for Col. Henry Dyer, who fell at the battle of New Orleans.

Dyersville; town in Dubuque County, Iowa, named for a former owner, James Dyer.

Dyerville; town in Humboldt County, California, named for a settler.

Dysart; town in Tama County, Iowa, named for a town in Scotland.

E

Eagle; this word, either alone or with suffixes, forms the name of 81 post-offices in the United States—in many cases so called because of the former presence of the bird.

Eagle; county in Colorado. Hall's History gives the origin as from the river of that name flowing through this county.

Eagle River; village in Keweenaw County, Michigan, named from the Indian, Migisiwisibi, meaning "eagle."

Earl Park; town in Benton County, Indiana, laid out by Adams Earl and A. D. Raub.

Earlville; town in Delaware County, Iowa, named for its first settler, G. M. Earl.

Earlville; village in Madison County, New York, named for Jonas Earl, canal commissioner.

Early; county in Georgia, named in honor of Peter Early, governor of the State in 1813.

Easley; town in Pickens County, South Carolina, named for General Easley, a prominent South Carolinian.

East Baton Rouge; parish in Louisiana. See Baton Rouge.

East Bend; town in Yadkin County, North Carolina, named from the bend in the Yadkin River at that point.

East Brady; borough in Clarion County, Pennsylvania, on the Allegheny River, east of Bradys Bend.

East Bridgewater; town in Plymouth County, Massachusetts, named from the original name of Brockton, Massachusetts, which first received the name of Bridgewater in honor of a celebrated English duke.

East Carroll; parish in Louisiana, named in honor of Charles Carroll of Carrollton.

East Fallowfield; townships in Crawford and Washington counties, Pennsylvania, said to be named for Lancelot Fallowfield, one of the first purchasers of land from William Penn.

East Feliciana; parish in Louisiana. A Spanish word, meaning "dome."

East Greenbush; town in Rensselaer County, New York, named by the Dutch Het Groen Bosch, meaning "green bush," because of the pine woods near, which were continually green.

East Greenwich; town in Kent County, Rhode Island, named for the district of London in Kent County, England.

Eastham; town in Barnstable County, Massachusetts, named from its extreme eastern situation in the county.

Eastland; county and town in Texas, named for M. W. Eastland.

Eastman; town in Dodge County, Georgia, named for W. P. Eastman, who, with W. E. Dodge, presented the county with a court-house.

Easton; city in Northampton County, Pennsylvania, named from the estate of an English nobleman.

Easton Center; village in Bristol County, Massachusetts, perhaps named in honor of Hon. John Easton, governor of Rhode Island.

Eastport; city in Washington County, Maine, which was originally called Moose Island, hut was later incorporated under its present name in honor of being the most eastern city in the United States.

East River; a body of water at New York, properly a strait connecting Long Island Sound with New York Bay; called a river no doubt from the river-like action of its tides; the name is used to distinguish it from North River, that is, the Hudson.

Eastwood; village in Onondaga County, New York, a suburb of Syracuse, and named from its eastward position from that place.

Eaton; town in Weld County, Colorado, named for Benjamin H. Eaton and Aaron J. Eaton of the Eaton Milling and Elevator Company.

Eaton; county in Michigan, named for John H. Eaton, Secretary of War under President Jackson.

Eaton; town in Madison County, New York, and village in Preble County, Ohio, named for Gen. Wm. Eaton, of Massachusetts, Revolutionary officer and commander of the United States military forces in Tripoli.

Eaton Rapids; town in Eaton County, Michigan, so named on account of the rapids in Grand River.

Eatonton; city in Putnam County, Georgia, named for Gen. Wm. Eaton.

Eatontown; township in Monmouth County, New Jersey, named for an old settler.

Eau Claire; river in Michigan. The name is French and signifies "clear water."

Eau Claire; county and city in Wisconsin, named from the river in Michigan.

Eau Galle; river in Wisconsin, from which township and village in Wisconsin are named. French word, signifying "bitter water."

Eau Pleine; river and town in Portage County, Wisconsin. French name, meaning "full water," or "stocked river."

Ebeeme; mountain and gorge in Piscataquis County, Maine. An Indian word, meaning "where they get high-bush cranberries."

Ebenecook; village in Lincoln County, Maine. A corruption of the Indian Abanauk, meaning "bread place," or according to another authority, "highbush cranberry place."

Ebenezer; town in Holmes County, Mississippi, named by the early settlers for the old Jewish city.

Ebensburg; borough of Cambria County, Pennsylvania, laid out by the Rev. Rees Lloyd, and named by him for his eldest son, Eben.

Echaconnee; town in Bibb County, Georgia, named from the creek on which it is situated, and which in turn is derived from the Indian, meaning " beaver creek."

Echo; canyon in the Wasatch Mountains of Utah.

Echo; peak in Yellowstone Park, so named because of its remarkable echo.

Echo Canyon; town in Summit County, Utah, named from the canyon.

Echols; county in Georgia, named for Robert M. Echols.

Eckley; town in Yuma County, Colorado, said to be so named for Amos Eckles, cattle foreman for J. W. Bowles.

Ecola; creek and summer resort in Clatsop County, Oregon, so named by Captain Clark because a whale was washed up there—ecola, an Indian word meaning "whale."

Economy; township in Beaver County, Pennsylvania, established in 1825 by a Harmonist society, and named to indicate the principles of their government and their habits of living.

Ecore Fabre; stream in Arkansas. The name is derived from the French word "ecore," meaning a shore, bank, or bluff, and Fabre, a proper name.

Ecorse; town in Wayne County, Michigan, named from the river, which was so called by the Indians on account of the birch and other kinds of bark found on its banks. The word is French, meaning "bark of a tree."

Ector; county in Texas, named for Matthew Ector, Confederate commander and judge.

Eddington; town in Penobscot County, Maine, named for Colonel Eddy, a prominent settler.

Eddy; county in New Mexico, named in honor of C. B. Eddy, a prominent citizen.

Eddy; county in North Dakota, named for one of the early bankers of Fargo.

Eddyville; town in Wapello County, Iowa, named for J. P. Eddy, who established a post there at an early day.

Eddyville; city in Lyon County, Kentucky, so named for the large eddies in the Cumberland River at this point.

Eden; town in Hancock County, Maine, named probably for Richard Eden, an early English author.

Eden; town in Concho County, Texas, named for Fred Ede, who owned the land.

Edenton; town in Chowan County, North Carolina, named for Charles Eden, governor of the State in 1714-1722.

Edgar; county in Illinois, named for Gen. John Edgar, an early and distinguished pioneer of the State.

Edgecomb; town in Lincoln County, Maine, named for Lord Edgecombe, a friend of the American colonies.

Edgecombe; county in North Carolina, named for Richard, Baron of Mount Edgecombe, of the board of trade.

Edgefield; town and county in South Carolina, named, as Simms supposes, because of the geographical situation at the edge of the State. There is also a supposition that the county derives its name from the fact that it borders on an older county.

Edgerton; city in Johnson County, Kansas, named for Edgerton, the chief engineer of the Atchison, Topeka and Santa Fe Railroad.

Edgerton; village in Williams County, Ohio, named for Alfred P. Edgerton.

Edgerton; city in Rock County, Wisconsin, probably named for E. W. Edgerton, an early settler.

Edina; city in Knox County, Missouri. A poetical name given to Edinburgh.

Edinburg; nine post-offices in the United States are named for the Scottish town.

Edison; village in Morrow County, Ohio, named for Thomas A. Edison.

Edisto; river and island in South Carolina, named from an Indian tribe; the tribe was also known as "Orista."

Edmeston; town in Otsego County, New York, named for Robert Edmeston, an early pioneer.

Edmonson; county of Kentucky, named for Capt. Jack Edmonson, who fell at the battle of Raisin River.

Edmunds; county in South Dakota, named in honor of Newton Edmunds, governor in 1863.

Edna; city in Labette County, Kansas, named for a child, Edna Gragery, in 1876.

Edwards; county in Illinois, named for Ninian Edwards, governor of Illinois Territory in 1809.

Edwards; county in Kansas, named for W. C. Edwards, of Hutchinson, first settler, who took active part in its organization.

Edwards; town in Hinds County, Mississippi, named for Dick Edwards, owner and proprietor of the Edwards House, Jackson, Mississippi.

Edwards; town in St. Lawrence County, New York, named for Edward McCormack, brother of the founder.

Edwards; town in Beaufort County, North Carolina, named for a prominent family of the neighborhood.

Edwards; county in Texas, named for Harden Edwards, who established, under grant from the Mexican Government, a colony at Nacogdoches in 1825.

Edwardsport; village in Knox County, Indiana, named for Edwards Wilkins.

Edwardsville; city in Madison County, Illinois, named for Ninian Edwards, Territorial governor in 1809.

Edwardsville; village in St. Lawrence County, New York, named for Jonathan S. Edwards, the first postmaster.

Eel; river in California, named from the Indian word Wishosk, "eel river," so called because of its crookedness.

Eel; river in Indiana, called by the Indians Shoamaque, "slippery fish." The Indiana State Historical Geology, 1882, gives the Indian name as Ke-wa-begwinn-maig, and the meaning "snake-fish-river."

Effingham; county in Georgia, named for Lord Effingham.

Effingham; county and city in Illinois. The city was named for the county which, in turn, was named for Gen. Edward Effingham.

Effingham; city in Atchison County, Kansas, named for Effingham Nichols, of Boston, a promoter of the Central Branch, Union Pacific Railroad.

Egbertsville; village in Richmond County, New York, named for James Egbertsville, a former resident.

Egg Harbor; township and city in Atlantic County, New Jersey, bordering on the ocean and Great Egg Harbor Bay. It was so called because of the number of gull's eggs found near the bay.

Egremont; town in Berkshire County, Massachusetts, supposed to have received its name from Charles Wyndham, Earl of Egremont, who was secretary of state in 1671.

Egypt; fourteen places of the United States are named for the ancient country in Africa.

Ehrenberg; town in Yuma County, Arizona, founded in 1850 by Herman Ehrenberg.

Ehrhardt; town in Bamberg County, South Carolina, named for a prominent family.

Elba; there are 16 places of this name in the United States, most of which were named for the island in the Mediterranean.

Elbert; county and peak in Colorado, named for Samuel W. Elbert, governor of the Territory in 1873-74.

Elbert; county in Georgia; Elberton; city in the above county. Named for Samuel Elbert, formerly a governor of the State.

Elbow; lake in Maine, so called because of its shape.

Elbridge; town in Onondaga County, New York, probably named after Elbridge Gerry, one of the signers of the Declaration of Independence.

El Capitan; cliff in the Yosemite Valley, California. The name is Spanish, meaning "the captain."

Eldora; city in Hardin County, Iowa. A corruption of the Spanish word El Dorado, meaning "the golden or gilded land."

Eldorado; city in Butler County, Kansas, and the first county in California in which gold was discovered. See Eldora.

Electric; peak in Yellowstone Park, named by Mr. Henry Gannett, United States geographer, on account of a severe electrical storm encountered there.

Eleven Mile; creek in Genesee County, New York, so called because it crosses the Buffalo road 11 miles from Buffalo.

Elgin; city in Kane County, Illinois, named for the Earl of Elgin.

Elizabeth; cape in Maine, and group of islands in Massachusetts, named in honor of Queen Elizabeth of England. This word, either alone or with suffixes, forms the names of 25 places in the United States, most of which were so named.

Elizabeth; city in Union County, New Jersey, named for the wife of Lord Carteret.

Elizabeth; borough in Allegheny County, Pennsylvania, named by the founder, Stephen Bayard, for his wife.

Elizabeth; town in Wirt County, West Virginia, named for Elizabeth, the wife of David Beauchamp.

Elizabeth City; county in Virginia, and town in Pasquotank County, North Carolina, named for Queen Elizabeth of England.

Elizabethtown; town in Bartholomew County, Indiana, named for Elizabeth Branham, the wife of the founder.

Elizabethtown; town in Bladen County, North Carolina, named for the wife of Lord Carteret, Elizabeth.

Elk; this word, either alone or as a prefix, forms the name of 63 places in the United States, most of them doubtless given on account of the numerous elk which made their home there.

Elk Falls; town in Elk County, Kansas, receives its name from a waterfall in Elk River, near the site of the town.

Elk Garden; town in Mineral County, West Virginia, so named by Senator Davis, because of the former abundance of elk.

Elkhart; county and city in Indiana, which take their name from the river.

Elkhart; village in Sheboygan County, Wisconsin, named from the lake, which at this point resembles an elk's heart.

Elkhorn; village in Douglas County, Nebraska, named for the river.

Elkhorn; city in Walworth County, Wisconsin. This city is named from the prairie, Elkhorn, which was named thus by Samuel F. Phoenix in July, 1836, when he found an elk's horn upon a tree there.

Elkins; town in Randolph County, West Virginia, named for Senator S. B. Elkins.

Elko; county in Nevada. The origin of this name is not certain, for according to some it is an Indian word, and according to others was so named on account of the abundance of elk found there.

Elk Park; village in Mitchell County, North Carolina, so named because of the number of elk killed there.

Elkton; village in Huron County, Michigan, named by an early settler, Martin Baker, who saw two large elk there when the first building was erected.

Ellen; mountain in Utah, named by J. W. Powell, United States Geological Survey, for the wife of Mr. A. H. Thompson, also of the Geological Survey.

Ellenburg; town in Clinton County, New York, named for the daughter of John R. Murray, of New York, the principal owner of township 5 of the military tract.

Ellendale; village in Sussex County, Delaware, named for the wife of Dr. J. S. Prettyman, who laid it out.

Ellery; town in Chautauqua County, New York, named for William Ellery, one of the signers of the Declaration of Independence.

Ellicott; city in Howard and Baltimore counties, Maryland, first settled and named by the brothers Andrew and John Ellicott.

Ellicott; town in Chautauqua County, New York; Ellicottville; village in Cattaraugus County, New York. Named for Joseph Ellicott, of the Holland Land Company.

Ellijay; town in Gilmer County, Georgia. The word is Indian, meaning "narrow valley."

Ellinwood; city in Barton County, Kansas, named for Col. John R. Ellinwood, engineer, Atchison, Topeka and Santa Fe Railroad.

Elliott; county in Kentucky, named for Judge John M. Elliott.

Elliottsville; village in-Richmond County, New York, named for Dr. Samuel M. Elliott.

Ellis; county and city in Kansas, named in honor of George Ellis, first lieutenant, Twelfth Kansas Infantry.

Ellis; county in Texas, named for Richard Ellis, president pro tempore of the first senate of the republic.

Ellisburg; town in Jefferson County, New York, which derives its name from Lyman Ellis, of Troy, New York, who settled there as a proprietor in 1797.

Ellisville; town in Jones County, Mississippi, named for Powhatan Ellis, member of the Supreme Court and United States Senator.

Ellsworth.; town in Hamilton County, Iowa, named for a banker at Iowa Falls.

Ellsworth; county and city in Kansas, named from the fort, Ellsworth, which in turn was named for Lieut. Allen Ellsworth.

Ellsworth; city in Hancock County, Maine, named for Oliver Ellsworth, one of the delegates to the National Constitutional Convention.

Elm; this word, with the suffixes "hurst," "wood," "dale," "hall," "grove," "creek," "city," "bury," "branch," forms the name of 29 places in the United States, in most cases given on account of the presence of this species of tree in the vicinity.

Elma; village in Erie County, New York, named for a large elm tree which stands near the village.

Elmira; city in Chemung County, New York, said to have been named for Elmira Teall, daughter of Nathan Teall, a tavern keeper.

Elmore; county in Alabama, named for John A. Elmore, of that State.

Elmore; county in Idaho, named for a celebrated mine in the county.

Elmore; village and town in Lamoille County, Vermont, named for the original grantee, Col. Samuel Elmore.

Elon College; town in Alamance County, North Carolina, named, probably, for Judge Elon.

El Paso; county in Colorado. The name is a Spanish one, meaning "the pass," "passage," or "gap," and was given this county with reference to Ute Pass, which is within its limits.

El Paso; city in Woodford County, Illinois; El Paso; county and city in Texas. County and city take their name from the presence of a pass or gap—that of the Rio Grande.

Elreno; city in Canadian County, Oklahoma. A Spanish word, meaning "reindeer."

Elsie; village in Clinton County, Michigan, named for Miss Elsie Tillotson, the daughter of an early pioneer.

Elsie; town in Perkins County, Nebraska, named for the daughter of C. E. Perkins.

Elyria; city in Lorain County, Ohio, named for Hernan Ely in 1817.

Emanuel; county in Georgia, named for David Emanuel, at one-time president of the Georgia senate.

Emaus; borough in Lehigh County, Pennsylvania, named by the Moravians in memory of the little village in Palestine.

Embarrass; river and village in Waupaca County, Wisconsin. A French word, meaning "obstruction."

Emerick; village in Madison County, Nebraska, named for John Emerick, an early settler.

Emery; county in Utah, named for George W. Emery, governor in 1875-1880.

Emlenton; borough in Venango County, Pennsylvania, named for Emlen, the wife of Joseph M. Fox, one of the original proprietors.

Emma; mountain in Arizona, named by J. W. Powell, of the U. S. Geological Survey, for his wife, Emma.

Emmet; counties in Iowa and Michigan and village in Saint Clair County, Michigan; Emmetsburg; city in Palo Alto County, Iowa. Named for the Irish patriot, Robert W. Emmett.

Emmitsburg; town in Frederick County, Maryland, named for William Emmitt, its founder.

Emmons; mountains in Colorado, New York, and Utah, named for S. F. Emmons, the geologist.

Emmons; county in North Dakota, named for James A. Emmons, a pioneer steamboatman and merchant at Bismarck.

Emory; town in Washington County, Virginia, named from Emory and Henry College, which is situated there and which received part of its name from Bishop Emory.

Empire; city in Cherokee County, Kansas, so named by the founder, S. L. Cheney, on account of the town topping a ridge.

Emporia; city in Lyon County, Kansas; Emporium; borough in Cameron County, Pennsylvania. A Lath. word, meaning "center of trade."

Emuckfaw; village in Tallapoosa County, Alabama. An Indian word, meaning "horseshoe bend."

Enfield; town in Hampshire County, Massachusetts, named, according to Dr. J. G. Holland, for Robert Field.

Enfield; towns in Grafton County, New Hampshire, and in Halifax County, North Carolina, named from the birthplace of John Wesley in England.

Engelmann; canyon and peak in Colorado, named for the botanist.

Englewood; city in Bergen County, New Jersey, named from the English "wood ingle," a woody nook or corner.

Englund; village in Marshall County, Minnesota, named for its first postmaster.

Enno; town in Wake County, North Carolina, named for an Indian tribe.

Enon; village in Clark County, Ohio, named for the place in Palestine where John was baptized.

Enoree; river in South Carolina, named for an Indian tribe.

Enosburg; town in Franklin County, Vermont, named for Roger Enos, to whom the land was originally granted.

Enterprise; this name is given to about 25 places in the United States to denote their policy.

Enterprise; city in Dickinson County, Kansas, named by the son of one of the proprietors.

Ephrata; town in Lancaster County, Pennsylvania; Ephratah; town in Fulton County, New York. Named for the ancient city of Palestine.

Eppes; creek and island in the James River, Charles City County, Virginia, named for Dr. Eppes, the owner.

Epping; town in Rockingham County, New Hampshire, named from the town in Essex, England.

Epsom; village in Daviess County, Indiana, so named because of a well nearby which contains water much resembling epsom salts in taste.

Epsom; town in Merrimack County, New Hampshire, named for the town in Surrey, England.

Epworth; town in Dubuque County, Iowa, named from the town in Lincolnshire, England.

Equinunk; villages in Delaware County, New York, and Wayne County, Pennsylvania. An Indian word, meaning "place where clothing is distributed."

Erath; county in Texas, named for an early settler and Indian fighter, George B. Erath.

Erie; one of the Great Lakes, drained by the St. Lawrence, is an Indian word, which, in the form of "Erige" or "Erilke," was the name of a now extinct Indian tribe of the Hurons, exterminated by the Iroquois, the word signifying "cat" or " wild-cat;" another authority gives the meaning as "mad."

Erie; city in Neosho County, Kansas, named from a small lake nearby, of that name.

Erie; counties in Ohio, Pennsylvania, and New York, and city in Pennsylvania; Erieville; village in Madison County, New York. Named from the lake Erin; the name of numerous towns and villages in the United States, named from the ancient name of Ireland.

Errol; town in Coos County, New Hampshire, named for a parish in Scotland.

Erskine; village in Passaic County, New Jersey, named for a parish in Scotland.

Erving; town in Franklin County, Massachusetts, named for the man who owned "Ervings Grant," in early days.

Erwin; town in Steuben County, New York, named for Col. Arthur Erwin of Pennsylvania.

Escambia; county and river in Alabama, and county and river in Florida, the counties having been named from the rivers, which are supposed to be named from the Spanish word, cambiar, meaning "barter or exchange."

Escanaba; river and city in Delta County, Michigan, the city taking its name from the river. According to Haines, an Indian word meaning "flat rock," but according to other authorities, means a "young male quadruped."

Eschscholtz; inlet of Kotzebue Sound, Alaska, named for J. F. Eschscholtz, the naturalist.

Escoheag; town in Kent County, Rhode Island. An Indian word, supposed to mean "origin of three rivers."

Escondido; city in San Diego County, California. A Spanish word meaning "hidden treasure."

Esculapia; watering place in Lewis County, Kentucky, named for the god of the medical art—Esculapius.

Eskridge; city in Wabaunsee County, Kansas, named for C. V. Eskridge, the first purchaser of a town lot.

Eskutassis; stream in Piscataquis County, Maine. An Indian word, meaning "small trout."

Eskweskwewadjo; mountain in Maine. An Indian word, meaning "she-bear mountain."

Esmeralda; county in Nevada, and mining camps in California and Idaho. Spanish word for emerald, the places being so named on account of the presence of these precious stones.

Esopus; stream in New York. A difference of opinion exists as to whether the Indian tribe of this name took the name from the river or whether the river was named for the tribe. Schoolcraft gives "Seepus" or "seepu" as the word nearest like it in the Indian languages.

Esperance; town in Schoharie County, New York. A French word, meaning "hope."

Essex; counties in Massachusetts, New Jersey, New York, Vermont, and Virginia, named for the English county of Essex.

Essexville; village in Bay County, Michigan, named for an early settler, Ransom Essex.

Estaboga; town in Talladega County, Alabama. An Indian word, meaning "where people reside."

Estherville; city in Emmet County, Iowa, named for Esther A. Ridley, wife of one of the original proprietors.

Estill; county in Kentucky and ii town in Madison County, Kentucky, named for Capt. James Estill, an Indian fighter.

Estill; town in Howard County, Missouri, named for Col. John R. Estill.

Ethel; town in Attala County, Mississippi, named for the daughter of Capt. S. B. McConnico.

Etna; many places in the United States are named for the celebrated volcano in Sicily.

Etowah; county in Alabama, and river in Georgia. From an Indian word, Etawa, meaning "poling a boat."

Etruria; township in Halifax County, North Carolina, named for the division of ancient Italy.

Euclid; town in Cuyahoga County, Ohio, and village in Onondaga County, New York, named for the celebrated geometer of Alexandria.

Eudora; city in Douglas County, Kansas, named for the daughter of Pascal Fish.

Eugene; city in Lane County, Oregon, named for Eugene Skinner, its first settler.

Eulalia; township in Potter County, Pennsylvania, named for the first child born within its limits.

Eureka; county in Nevada, and cities in California and Kansas. A Greek word, meaning "I have found it."

Eustis; town in Franklin County, Maine, named for Charles L. Eustis, an early proprietor.

Eutaw; town in Greene County, Alabama. According to Gatchet it is named from the Indian tribe, also known as Etiwaw, or from "itawa," "pine tree."

Eutawville; town in Berkeley County, South Carolina, named from the famous Eutaw Spring.

Evangeline; township in Charlevoix County, Michigan, named for the heroine of Longfellow's poem.

Evans; town in Weld County, Colorado, named for John Evans, former governor of Colorado.

Evans; town in Erie County, New York, named for David E. Evans, agent of the Holland Land Company.

Evansburg; village in Coshocton County, Ohio, named for Isaac Evans, who laid it out.

Evans Mills; village in Jefferson County, New York, named for Ethni Evans, a resident mill owner.

Evanston; city in Uinta County, Wyoming, and town in Cook County, Illinois, named for John Evans, former governor of Colorado.

Evansville; city in Vanderburg County, Indiana, named for Gen. Robert Evans, who laid it out.

Evart; village in Osceola County, Michigan, named for Frank Evart, a pioneer.

Evarts; mountain in Yellowstone Park, named for Truman C. Evarts.

Evening Shade; town in Sharp County, Arkansas, so named from the density of shade cast by the tall pine timber on an adjacent hill.

Everett; city in Middlesex County, Massachusetts, and a town in Bedford County, Pennsylvania, named for Edward Everett.

Everetts; town in Martin County, North Carolina, named for a resident family.

Ewings; creek in Missouri. Ewing is probably a contraction of " E. Wing," which designated this creek upon an early map.

Excelsior Springs; city in Clay County, Missouri, named from the medicinal springs there.

Exeter; many places in the United States received this name from the Exeter of England, the towns in Washington County, Rhode Island, and in Rockingham County, New Hampshire, being among them.

Eyota; village in Olmstead County, Minnesota. From an Indian word Iyotak, meaning "greatest," "most."

Ezel; town in Morgan County, Kentucky, named from the Bible.

Fabius; river in Missouri and town in Onondaga County, New York, named for the celebrated Roman consul. The town was named by the State land board of New York.

F

Factory; hill in Yellowstone Park, covered with geysers and hot springs, so named because of the noise and steam proceeding from them, resembling in these respects an active factory town.

Fair; a name used with various suffixes, such as "brook," "land," "port," etc., to indicate an attractive appearance.

Fairbank; township in Sullivan County, Indiana, named for General Fairbanks.

Fairbury; city in Jefferson County, Nebraska, named by an early settler, Mr. McDonell, for his home, Fairbury, Illinois.

Fairchild; creek in Park County, Colorado, named for A. Fairchild, a prospector.

Fairfax; county and town in Virginia, named for Lord Fairfax, grandson of Lord Culpeper.

Fairfield; county and town in Connecticut, counties in Ohio and South Carolina, and town in Somerset County, Maine, so named from the beauty of their fields.

Fairplay; town in Park County, Colorado, established by gold miners who named it as a living reproof to their "grab-all" neighbors.

Faison; town in Duplin County, North Carolina, named for a prominent family.

Fall; river in Massachusetts, so named because it is only about 2 miles in length and falls about 140 feet in a half mile.

Fall River; city in Bristol County, Massachusetts, situated on the Fall River.

Fallowfield; township in Washington County, Pennsylvania, named for Lancelot Fallowfield, one of the first purchasers of the land from William Penn.

Falls; county in Texas, named from the falls in Brazos River.

Fallston; borough in Beaver County, Pennsylvania, named from the falls in Beaver River.

Falmouth; towns in Cumberland County, Maine, and Barnstable County, Massachusetts, named from the seaport town in Cornwall.

Fannin; counties in Georgia and Texas, and village in Goliad County, Texas, named for Col. James W. Fannin, of North Carolina, who fought in the Texan war.

Farallone; group of small islands on the coast of California, named by the early Spanish explorers. The word farallon means "needle," or "small, pointed island."

Fargo; city in Cass County, North Dakota, named for one of the members of the Wells, Fargo Express Company. Several other places bear his name.

Faribault; county and city in Rice County, Minnesota, named for a settler from Canada, Jean Baptist Faribault.

Farley; town in Dubuque County, Iowa, named for the superintendent of the Sioux City Railroad.

Farmer; name applied to many small places, either with or without suffixes, indicative of rural conditions and appearance.

Farmington; town and river in Hartford County, Connecticut, named from a place in England.

Farmington; village in Oakland County, Michigan, named from Farmington, New York.

Farmington; town in Ontario County, New York, named from Farmington, Connecticut.

Farnham; village in Erie County, New York, named for Le Roy Farnham, the first merchant.

Farnham; town in Richmond County, Virginia, named from the town in Surrey, England.

Farragut; town in Fremont County, Iowa, named for Admiral Farragut.

Farrandsville; village in Clinton County, Pennsylvania, laid out by and named for William P. Farrand, of Philadelphia.

Farrar; town in North Carolina, named for a wealthy citizen.

Farwell; village in Clare County, Michigan, named for Samuel B. Farwell, an officer of the old Flint and Pere Marquette Railroad.

Faulk; county in South Dakota, named for Andrew J. Faulk, governor from 1866 to 1869.

Faulkner; county and village in Arkansas, named for Sandy Faulkner, the real "Arkansas Traveller."

Fauquier; county in Virginia; auquier Springs; village in above county. Named for Francis Fauquier, governor of the State.

Fausse Riviere; village in Louisiana, so called because it is situated on what was formerly the bed of the Mississippi River. Many years ago the river wore through an isthmus and left its former bed dry for a distance of about 30 miles. A French name, meaning "false river."

Faustburg; village in South Carolina, named for the first settler.

Fayette; counties in Alabama, Georgia, Illinois, Indiana, Iowa, Kentucky, Ohio, Pennsylvania, Tennessee, Texas, find West Virginia, and many places throughout the country, named for the Marquis de la Fayette. The name is also seen with suffixes, such as " ville" and "corner."

Fear; cape and river in North Carolina. Sir Richard Grenville narrowly escaped being wrecked near the cape, in consequence of which he so named it.

Feather; river in California. A translation of the early Spanish name, Plumas.

February; village in Washington County, Tennessee, named for a resident of the place.

Federal; name given to several places in the country, in reference to the national form of government.

Federalsburg; village in Caroline County, Maryland, so named because settled by persons from the Northern States.

Felix; townships in Grundy counties, Illinois and Iowa, named for Felix Grundy, Senator from Tennessee.

Fells; point in Maryland named for the purchaser, a ship carpenter, William Fell.

Felts Mills; village in Jefferson County, New York, named for John Felt, early proprietor.

Fence; rivers in Wisconsin and Michigan. A translation of the Indian word, mitchigan, a wooden fence constructed near its banks by the Indians for catching deer.

Fenner; town in Madison County, New York, named for Governor Fenner, of Rhode Island.

Fennimore; village in Grant County, Wisconsin, named for a settler who disappeared during the Black Hawk war.

Fennville; village in Allegan County, Michigan, named for a lumberman, Elam Fenner, who founded the village.

Fenton; village in Genesee County, Michigan, named for Colonel Fenton, who owned a large tract of land on the present site.

Fentonville; village in Chaulguqua County, New York, named for Reuben Eaton Fenton, governor of the State in 1865-1869.

Fentress; county in Tennessee, named for James Fentress, member of a commission appointed to fix upon a place for the seat of justice for Shelby County.

Fergus; county in Montana, named for James Fergus, a pioneer of the State.

Fergusonville; village in Delaware County, New York, named for the Ferguson brothers, who were largely engaged in business there.

Fermanagh; township in Juniata County, Pennsylvania, named for a county in Ireland.

Fern; name used with various suffixes, generally given because of the presence of the plant. Eighteen places bear this name, some with suffixes, such as "dale," "bank," and "ridge."

Fernandina; city in Nassau County, Florida, named for a Spaniard, Fernandez.

Ferrisburg; town in Addison County, Vermont, named for Benjamin Ferris, who applied for a charter in 1762.

Ferry; county in Washington, named for Elisha P. Ferry, governor of the Territory.

Fetterman; town in Taylor County, West Virginia, named for a resident of Pittsburg, Pennsylvania, who owned the land.

Fever; river in Illinois, named by the early French, La Riviere de Feve, "the river of the bean," because of the immense quantity of wild beans upon its banks. The name was corrupted to Fievre, "fever," which gave rise to the impression that the place was unhealthy.

Fidalgo; island and village in Skagit County, Washington, and harbor in Alaska, named for the Spanish explorer.

Fields Landing; village in Humboldt County, California, named for a settler.

Fifty Eight; village in Orangeburg County, South Carolina, named so because it is 58 miles from Charleston.

Fillmore; mount in California, named for a naval officer.

Fillmore; counties in Minnesota and Nebraska, and many places in the country named for Millard Fillmore, President of the United States.

Fillmore; station in Wyoming, named for a superintendent of the Southern Pacific Railroad.

Fincastle; town in Botetourt County, Virginia, and several other places directly or indirectly named for Governor Lord Dunmore and his son George, Lord Fincastle.

Findlay; city in Hancock County, Ohio, named from Fort Findlay, built by Col. James Findlay, of Cincinnati.

Findley; township in Allegheny County, Pennsylvania, named for William Findley, governor of the State in 1817-1820.

Fine; town in St. Lawrence County, New York, named for John Fine, the principal proprietor.

Finney; county in Kansas, named for David W. Finney, lieutenant-governor in 1881-1885.

Fire; hill in Humboldt County, California, so named because in early days it was used as a station from which to signal with fire.

Fire; creek in Missouri, originally called Fire-prairie Creek, because of the fires that swept over the prairies.

Firehole; river in Yellowstone Park. The word "bole" was used by the early explorers to designate depressions among the mountains, while the first part of the name refers to the remarkable geyser region from which the river flows.

Fisher; county and village in Texas, named for S. Rhodes Fisher, secretary of the navy in Houston's cabinet.

Fishkill; town, village, creek, plains, and mountains in Dutchess County, New York, named by the early Dutch settlers, Vischkill, "fish creek."

Fitchburg; city in Worcester County, Massachusetts, named for John Fitch, one of the committee that procured the act of incorporation.

Fithian; village in Vermilion County, Illinois, named for Dr. William Fithian.

Fitzwilliam; town in Cheshire County, New Hampshire, named for the Earl of Fitzwilliam.

Five Corners; village in Miami County, Indiana, so named because it is at the junction of several roads.

Flackville; village in St. Lawrence County, New York, named for John P. Flack, first postmaster.

Flagstaff; town in Coconino County, Arizona, named from a pole set by a party of emigrants who camped near and celebrated the Fourth of July.

Flambeau; lakes, town, and river in Wisconsin. The lakes were so called on account of the torches used to catch fish at night.

Flatbush; part of Brooklyn, New York, so named from woods that grew on fiat country.

Flathead; lake, county, and river in Montana, named from an Indian tribe. The name originated with the early settlers who called several different tribes of Indians by this name on account of their custom of flattening the heads of infants by fastening a piece of board or a pad of grass upon the forehead. After this had been worn several months it caused a flat appearance of the head.

Flattery; promontory in Washington so named by Captain Cook, "in token of an improvement in our prospects."

Flavel; summer resort in Clatsop County, Oregon, named for a prominent resident of Astoria.

Fleming; town in Cayuga County, New York, named for Gen. George Fleming, an old resident.

Fleming; county in Kentucky; Flemingsburg; town in Fleming County. Named for Col. John Fleming, an early settler in the State.

Flint; river in Georgia, named from the Indian name, Thronatuska, also Lonoto, "flint."

Flint; city in Michigan, named from a river, which was called by the Indians Pawon-nuk-ening, "river of the flint."

Flirt; lake in Florida, named for a Government schooner.

Flora; town in Madison County, Mississippi, named by W. B. Jones for his wife.

Florence; city in Marion County, Kansas, named for Miss Florence Crawford, of Topeka.

Florence; village in Douglas County, Nebraska. named for Miss Florence Kilbourn.

Florence; town in Oneida County, New York, and village in Hampshire County, Massachusetts, named from the city in Italy.

Florence; county and town in South Carolina, named for the daughter of Gen. W. W. Hardlee.

Florence; county in Wisconsin, named for the Florence Mining Company.

Flores; creek in Idaho, named from the flowers on its banks.

Florida; one of the States of the Union, named by Ponce de Leon "the florid or flowery land." He chose this name for two reasons: First, because the country presented a pleasant aspect; and, second, because he landed on the festival which the Spaniards call Pascuade Flores, or Pascua Florida, "feast of flowers," which corresponds co Palm Sunday. The second reason is generally considered to have more weight.

Florissant; town in El Paso County, Colorado, named by Judge James Castello for his old home in Missouri.

Florissant; city in St. Louis County, Missouri, named from the flowery valley in which it is situated.

Floyd; county in Georgia, named for Gen. John Floyd, at one-time member of Congress from that State.

Floyd; county in Indiana, said by some authorities to have been named for Col. John Floyd, while others claim that it was named for Davis Floyd.

Floyd; county, town, and river in Iowa, named for Sergt. Charles Floyd, of the Lewis and Clarke exploring party.

Floyd; county in Kentucky, named for Col. John Floyd, an officer of the Revolution.

Floyd; town in Oneida County, New York, named for William Floyd, one of the signers of the Declaration of Independence.

Floyd; county in Texas, named for Dolfin Floyd, who fell at the Alamo.

Floyd; county and town in Virginia, named for John Buchanan Floyd, governor in 1847-1852.

Floyds; creek in Adair County, Missouri, named for an early settler who came from Kentucky.

Flushing; town in Queens County, New York, now a part of New York City, called by the early Dutch settlers, "Vlissengen" of which the present name is a corruption. Some authorities claim that the early settlers came from Flushing, Holland.

Fluvanna; county in Virginia, named from a river which was named for Queen Anne, of England.

Foard; county in Texas, named for Robert L. Foard.

Folsom; town in Sacramento County, California, named for the owner of the ranch on which it was laid out.

Folsom; peak in Yellowstone Park, named for David E. Folsom, leader of an expedition in 1869.

Fonda; village in Montgomery County, New York, named for Douw Fonda.

Fond du Lac; town in Minnesota and county and city in Wisconsin, so named because of their situation. A French word, meaning "end of lake."

Fontaine-qui-Bouille; creek in Colorado, so named because its head is a spring of water highly aerated.

Fontana; city in Miami County, Kansas, named from a spring 1 mile west of the town site.

Fontanelle; town in Adair County, Iowa, and creek in Wyoming, named for a trapper in the employ of the American Fur Company.

Ford; county in Illinois, named for Thomas Ford, governor of the State in 1842-1846.

Ford; county and city in Kansas, named for James H. Ford, colonel of Second Colorado Cavalry.

Ford; village in Holt County, Nebraska, named for an early settler.

Forellen; peak in Yellowstone Park. A German name, meaning "trout."

Forest; counties in Pennsylvania and Wisconsin, so named from the forests within their limits. The name occurs, either alone or with suffixes, as the name of ninety places in the country.

Forrest; town in St. Francis County, Arkansas, named for Gen. N. B. Forrest, who built the first house there.

Forsyth; county and city in Monroe County, Georgia, named for Governor John Forsyth.

Forsyth; county in North Carolina, named for Major Forsyth, a distinguished officer of the State, killed in the war of 1812.

Fort Ann; village in Washington County, New York, named from an old fortification built in 1756, during the wars with the French.

Fort Atkinson; city in Jefferson County, Wisconsin, named for Gen. Henry Atkinson, who commanded a stockade there during the Black Hawk war.

Fort Bend; county in Texas," named for a fort on Brazos River.

Fort Benton; town in Choteau County, Montana, on the side of an old fort which was named for Thomas H. Benton, of Missouri.

Fort Covington; village in Franklin County, New York, named for Gen. Leonard Covington.

Fort Crook; village in Sarpy County, Nebraska, named from a fort which was named for Gen. George Crook.

Fort Dade; village in Hernando County, Florida, so named because situated near the spot where Major Dade and companions perished while defending themselves against a party of Seminoles.

Fort Dodge; city in Webster County, Iowa, named for Senator Dodge, of Wisconsin.

Fort Edward; town in Washington County, New York, named from an old fort built in 1709, named in honor of Edward, Duke of York.

Fort Fairfield; town in Aroostook County, Maine, named for an old fort which took its name from John Fairfield, who was governor of Maine for many years.

Fort Fetterman; village in Albany County, Wyoming, named for Lieut. Col. W.J. Fetterman, killed by the Indians in 1866.

Fort Gaines; town in Clay County, Georgia, named for Gen. E. P. Gaines.

Fort Hall; part of an Indian reservation in Bingham County, Idaho, named from a fort which was built by Capt. N. J. Wyeth and named for one of his partners.

Fort Hamilton; village in Kings County, now a part of New York City, named for Alexander Hamilton.

Fort Kent: town in Aroostook County, Maine, named from a fort which was named for Governor Edward Kent, of Maine.

Fort Keogh; village in Custer County, Montana, named from a fort which took its name from Captain Keogh, who fell with General Custer.

Fort Klamath; town in Klamath County, Oregon, named from an Indian tribe.

Fort Leavenworth; town in Leavenworth County, Kansas, named for Gen. Henry Leavenworth, who erected the fort.

Fort Lupton; town in Weld County, Colorado, named for an early settler on Adobe Creek in 1840.

Fort Madison; city in Lee County, Iowa, named for James Madison, President of the United States.

Fort Morgan; town in Morgan County, Colorado, named for Col. C. A. Morgan.

Fort Motte; town in Orangeburg County, South Carolina, named so because situated upon the site of Motte's house, which was fortified by the British during the Revolution.

Fort Myers; town in Lee County, Florida, first a military post, named for Capt. Abraham C. Myers.

Fort Pierre; village in Stanley County, South Dakota, named for Pierre Choteau.

Fort Plain; village in Montgomery County, New York, named from an old fortress erected on a plain at the junction of the Mohawk and Osquaga rivers.

Fort Recovery; village in Mercer County, Ohio, named from an old fort built by General Wayne.

Fort Scott; city in Kansas, named for Gen. Winfield Scott.

Fort Sheridan; village in Lake County, Illinois, named from the military post near, which was named for Gen. P. H. Sheridan.

Fort Smith; town in Sebastian County, Arkansas, named for a fort built under the direction of General Smith, for whom it was named.

Fort Wayne; city in Indiana, named from a fort built by Lieutenant-Colonel Hamtramck in 1794, named for Gen. Anthony Wayne.

Fort Worth; city in Tarrant County, Texas, named for General Worth, prominent in the Mexican war.

Fortyfort; borough in Luzerne County, Pennsylvania, named from the old fort of Revolutionary days.

Foster; county in North Dakota, named for Hon. George I. Foster, a pioneer, prominent in the territorial legislature.

Foster; town in Providence County, Rhode Island, named for Theodore Foster, United States Senator from that State.

Fostoria; city in Seneca County, Ohio, named for Governor Charles Foster.

Fountain; name given to many places, mostly because of springs.

Fountain; county in Indiana, named for Major Fountain, of Kentucky, killed at the battle of Maumee in 1790.

Four Oaks; town in Johnston County, North Carolina, named from four great oaks near.

Fowler; village in Clinton County, Michigan, named for John N. Fowler.

Fowler; town in St. Lawrence County, New York, named for Theodocius Fowler, former proprietor.

Fowlerville; village in Livingston County, Michigan, named fur Ralph Fowler, the first settler.

Fowlerville; village in Livingston County, New York, named for Wells Fowler, first settler.

Foxburg; village in Clarion County, Pennsylvania, named for the original proprietor, H. M. Fox.

Foxcroft; town in Piscataquis County, Maine, named for Col. Joseph E. Foxcroft, of New Gloucester, an early proprietor.

Fox Lake; village in Dodge County, Wisconsin, named from the Indian name of the Lake, Hosh a rac ah tah, "fox."

Frackville; borough in Schuylkill County, Pennsylvania, named for Daniel Frack, one of the original settlers.

Framboise; island in the Missouri River. A French word, meaning "raspberry."

Framingham; town in Middlesex County, Massachusetts. The name is evidently a corruption of Framlingham, Suffolk County, England.

Francestown; town in Hillsboro County, New Hampshire, named for the wife of Governor Benning Wentworth, whose maiden name was Frances Deering.

Franceville; town in El Paso County, Colorado, named for Hon. Matt France, of Colorado Springs.

Franceway; creek in Grant County, Arkansas. The name is a corruption of the name Francois, given by the early French.

Francis; creek in Humboldt County, California, named for a settler.

Franconia; town in Grafton County, New Hampshire, named from the duchy in Germany.

Frank; island in Yellowstone Park, named for the brother of Henry W. Elliott, of the Hayden expedition.

Frankfort; city in Marshall County, Kansas, named for Frank Schmidt, of Marysville, owner of the town site.

Frankfort; village in Herkimer County, New York, named for Lawrence Frank, an early settler.

Franklin; counties in Alabama, Arkansas, Florida, county and town in Heard County, Georgia, counties in Illinois and Indiana, county and town in Lee County, Iowa, county in Kansas, county and city in Kentucky, parish in Louisiana, county and town in Hancock County, Maine, county and town in Norfolk County, Massachusetts, counties in Mississippi and Missouri, county and town in Nebraska, county and village in Delaware County, New York, county and town in Macon County, North Carolina, county in Ohio, county and boroughs in Cambria and Venango counties, Pennsylvania, counties in Tennessee, Vermont, Virginia, and Washington, and mountain in New Hampshire, named for Benjamin Franklin. Many other places throughout the country bear his name.

Franklin; town in Delaware County, New York, named for Temple Franklin.

Franklin; county in Texas, named for B. C. Franklin, first judge of the district court of the republic.

Frankstown; village in Blair County, Pennsylvania, named for Stephen Franks, a German trader.

Franktown; town in Douglas County, Colorado, named for Hon. J. Frank Gardner, early resident.

Fraser; village in Macomb County, Michigan, named for a lawyer from Detroit, Michigan.

Frazer; creek in Humboldt County, California, named for an early settler.

Frazer; village in Delaware County, New York, named for Hugh Frazer, an early patentee.

Frederic; town in Crawford County, Michigan, named for Frederick Barker, a pioneer of that place.

Frederica; town in Glynn County, Georgia, named for Frederick, Prince of Wales.

Frederick; county in Maryland, named for Frederick, son of Charles, Fifth Lord Baltimore. It may have been given also in reference to Frederick, Prince of Wales.

Frederick; county in Virginia, named for Frederick, Prince of Wales.

Fredericksburg; city in Spottsylvania County, Virginia, named for Frederick, Prince of Wales.

Fredericktown; city in Madison County, Missouri, named for George Frederick Bollinger, a former member of the State legislature.

Fredonia; city in Wilson County, Kansas, named for Fredonia, New York.

Fredonia; village in Chautauqua County, New York. The name was devised to signify "land of freedom," and proposed as a name for the United States.

Freeborn; county and township in Minnesota, named for William Freeborn, member of the council in 1855.

Freehold; town in Monmouth County, New Jersey, originally a freehold.

Freelandsville; village in Knox County, Indiana, named for Dr. John F. Freeland.

Freeman; town in Franklin County, Maine, named for Samuel Freeman, of Portland, Maine.

Freemansburg; borough in Northampton County, Pennsylvania, named for Jacob Freeman.

Freeo; creek in Arkansas, a corruption of the Spanish word frio, "cold."

Freeport; town in Cumberland County, Maine, so named because it was intended that it should be a free port. The name is found frequently in the country, generally having been given in the spirit of liberty.

Freetown; town in Bristol County, Massachusetts, called by the original settlers Freeman's Land.

Fremont; county and pass in Colorado, counties in Idaho and Iowa, town in Rockingham County, New Hampshire, town in Steuben County, New York, island in Utah, and county and peak in Wyoming, besides numerous small places in the country, named for Gen. John C. Fremont.

French; river in Massachusetts, so named from a settlement of French Protestants in the town of Oxford.

French Broad; river in North Carolina, so named because the country west of the Blue Ridge was held by the French, according to some authorities. Others hold that the river was named by a party of hunters for their captain, whose name was French. The latter part of the name is used descriptively.

Frenchburg; town in Menifee County, Kentucky, named for Judge Richard French, prominent politician.

French Camp; town in Choctaw County, Mississippi, so named from an old settlement made by French.

Frenchman; bay on the coast of Maine, so named because a settlement was made here by Frenchmen.

Frenchs Mills; village in Albany County, New York, named for Abel French, who owned a factory there.

Fresno; county, river, and city in California, so named from a species of ash.

Friar Point; town in Coahoma County, Mississippi, named for an old woodchopper, early settler there.

Frio; county and town in Texas, named from the Rio Frio. A Spanish word meaning "cold."

Frontier; county in Nebraska, so named because it was on the frontier at the time of its naming.

Frostburg; town in Allegany County, Maryland, named for a family who owned the land.

Fruita; town in Mesa County, Colorado, situated in a large fruit-growing district.

Frustum; mount in Colorado, named from its shape.

Fryburg; town in North Dakota, named for General Fry, United States Army.

Fryeburg; town in Oxford County, Maine, named for its founder, Gen. Joseph Frye, a veteran officer of the French wars, who received a grant of land in Maine as a reward for his services.

Fulford; village in Eagle County, Colorado, named for A. H. Fulford, a pioneer.

Fullerton; city in Nance County, Nebraska, named for Randall Fuller, early stockman.

Fulton; county in Arkansas, named for William Savin Fulton, governor of the Territory.

Fulton; counties in Georgia, Illinois, Indiana, Kentucky; county and villages in Montgomery and Oswego counties, New York, and county in Pennsylvania, named for Robert Fulton. His name has been given to numerous places throughout the country.

Fulton; city in Bourbon County, Kansas, named from Fulton, Illinois.

Funk; town in Phelps County, Nebraska, named for P. C. Funk.

Funkstown; town in Washington County, Maryland, named for Jacob Funk, original proprietor.

Furnas; county in Nebraska, named for Robert W. Furnas, governor in 1873-75.

G

Gabilan; mountain ridge, spur of the coast range in California. A Spanish word, meaning "sparrow hawk."

Gadsden; county in Florida and town in Etowah County, Alabama, named for James Gadsden, American statesman.

Gaffney; city in Cherokee County, South Carolina, named for a family in the State.

Gagetown; village in Tuscola County, Michigan, named for James Gage, the first settler.

Gaines; town in Orleans County, New York, named for Gen. E. P. Gaines.

Gaines; county in Texas, named for James Gaines, who fought in the war for Texan independence.

Gainesville; town in Hall County, Georgia; city in Alachua County, Florida, and town in Wyoming County, New York, named for Gen. E P. Gaines.

Galen; town in Wayne County, New York, named by the State land board for Claudius Galenus, an illustrious physician of antiquity.

Galena; city in Illinois and mount in Colorado, named from the lead ore found in the vicinity.

Galesburg; city in Knox County, Illinois, named for Rev. George W. Gale, the founder.

Galesburg; village in Kalamazoo County, Michigan, named for Gen. L. Gale, early settler.

Galesville; village in Trempealeau County, Wisconsin, named for Hon. George Gale, who laid it out.

Gallatin; counties in Illinois and Kentucky; county and river in Montana; town in Columbia County, New York, and town in Copiah County, Mississippi, named for Albert Gallatin, Secretary of the Treasury under Thomas Jefferson.

Gallaway; town in Fayette County, Tennessee, named for Governor Gallaway.

Gallia; county in Ohio, settled in 1790 by a colony of Frenchmen, and named by them from the Latin appellation of France.

Gallinas; river in New Mexico. A Spanish word, gallina, "hen," used figuratively to denote a coward.

Gallipolis; city in Gallia County, Ohio, so named because settled by French.

Gallitzin; borough in Cambria County, Pennsylvania, named for its founder, Prince Demetrius Augustine Gallitzin.

Gallman; town in Copiah County, Mississippi, named for a leading citizen.

Galloo; islands in Lake Ontario, Jefferson County, New York, named for an old resident.

Galva; city in McPherson County, Kansas, named by Mrs. J. E. Doyle for her old home in Illinois.

Galveston; county and city in Texas, named for Don Jose Galvez, Spanish viceroy of Texas; in 1797 proclaimed king by the people of Mexico.

Galway; village in Saratoga County, New York, named from the county in Ireland.

Gambier; village in Knox County, Ohio, named for Lord James Gambier, a British admiral, who was a benefactor of Kenyon College, located at this place.

Gannett; station on the Union Pacific Railroad in Nebraska, named for J. W. Gannett, auditor of the road.

Gans; town in Humboldt County, California, named for a settler.

Gansevoort; village in Saratoga County, New York, named for Col. Peter Gansvoort, who located there soon after the war.

Garberville; town in Humboldt County, California, named for J. C. Garber.

Garden; thirty places in the country bear this name, used descriptively, either with or without suffixes.

Garden of the Gods; locality near Pikes Peak, Colorado. Lewis N. Tappan and three others went from Denver to select a site for a town. They stood upon a rocky prominence and exclaimed, "A fit garden for the gods," hence the name.

Gardiner; city in Kennebec County, Maine, named for Sylvester Gardiner, one of the proprietors of the old Plymouth patent.

Gardiner; town in Ulster County, New York, named for Addison Gardiner, formerly lieutenant-governor.

Gardiner; river in Yellowstone Park, probably named for an old trapper who was a companion of Joseph Meek.

Gardiners; island lying east of Long Island, named for the first settler, Lyon Gardiner, a Scotchman.

Gardner; city in Johnson County, Kansas, named for Henry J. Gardner, governor of Massachusetts in 1855.

Gardner; town in Worcester County, Massachusetts, named for Col. Thos. Gardner, who fell at the battle of Bunker Hill.

Garfield; county and mountain in Colorado; mountain in Idaho; town in Lasalle County, Illinois; town in Pawnee County, Kansas; plantation in Aroostook County, Maine; county in Nebraska; borough in New Jersey; town in Mahoning County, Ohio; county in Oklahoma; town in Clackamas County, Oregon, and counties in Utah and Washington, named for President James A. Garfield. His name is also borne by many other places in the country.

Garfield; town in Humboldt County, California, named for the son of Gilbert Garfield, a settler.

Garland; county in Arkansas, named for A. H. Garland, governor of the State in 1874.

Garland; town in Penobscot County. Maine, named for Joseph Garland, who was the first man to settle there.

Garnett; city in Anderson County, Kansas, named for W. A. Garnett, of Louisville Kentucky.

Garrard; county in Kentucky, named for Col. James Garrard, governor of the State in 1796.

Garrett; city in Dekalb County, Indiana, county in Maryland, and borough in Pennsylvania, named for John W. Garrett, president of the Baltimore and Ohio Bail road.

Garrison; village in Nacogdoches County, Texas, named for Z. B. Garrison, early settler, although the name was probably also given in reference to others of that name in the first settlement.

Garysburg; town in Northampton County, North Carolina, named for Roderick B. Gary.

Garza; county in Texas, named for the family of that name of which Governor Garza, who founded San Antonio, was a member.

Gasconade; river and county in Missouri. The word is from Gascon, an inhabitant of Gascony. The people of that province were noted for their boastfulness. The early French gave the name to a tribe of Indians who were very boastful, and from them it was transferred to the river and county.

Gasport; village in Niagara County, New York, so named from springs which emit an inflammable gas.

Gaston; camp in California, named for a military commander.

Gaston; county in North Carolina, named for William Gaston, a judge of the supreme court of the State.

Gaston; town in Lexington County, South Carolina, named for the Gaston family.

Gastonia; town in Gaston County, North Carolina, named for William Gaston, a judge of the supreme court of the State.

Gates; town in Monroe County, New York, and county in North Carolina; Gatesville; town in Gates County, North Carolina. Named for Gen. Horatio Gates, Revolutionary commander.

Gay Head; headland and town in Dukes County, Massachusetts, so named from the brilliant colors of the cliffs.

Gaylesville; town in Cherokee County, Alabama, named for George W. Gayle, a prominent politician of the State.

Gaylord; city in Smith County, Kansas, named for C. E. Gaylord, of Marshall County.

Gaylord; village in Otsego County, Michigan, named for an attorney of the Michigan Central Railroad.

Gayoso; village in Pemiscot County, Missouri, named for Governor Don Manuel Gayoso de Lemos.

Geary; county and town in Doniphan County, Kansas, named for John W. Geary, governor of the Territory in 1856-57.

Geauga; county in Ohio. The name is thought by some to have been derived from the same source as Cuyahoga; others say it is derived from the Indian word, Sheauga-sipe, meaning "raccoon river," a name originally applied to Grand River. Haines says that it was the name of a chief of one of the Six Nations. Still another theory derives it from Cageauga, "dogs round the fire."

Geddes; town in Onondaga County, New York, named for James Geddes, first settler.

Genesee; county, river, and town in Wyoming County, New York, and county in Michigan, besides several other small places, named from the Indian, meaning "shining or beautiful valley."

Geneseo; town in Livingston County, New York, on the Genesee River. The name is a modification of the name of the river, and is given to cities in Rice County, Kansas, and Henry County, Illinois.

Geneva; county and town in Alabama. The name has been given to 21 places in the country, transferred from the city in Switzerland.

Genoa; 16 places in the country bear the name of the city in Italy.

Gentry; county and town in Missouri, named for Col. Richard Gentry, killed at the battle of Okeechobee, Florida.

Georgetown; town in Clear Creek County, Colorado, named for George Griffith, clerk of the court.

Georgetown; town in Sussex County, Delaware, named for Commissioner George Mitchell, prominent resident.

Georgetown; formerly a city, now a part of the District of Columbia, named for George Boone, an Englishman who purchased several tracts of land in the neighborhood.

Georgetown; village in Brown County, Indiana, named for George Grove, its founder.

Georgetown; town in Scott County, Kentucky, named for President George Washington.

Georgetown; town in Sagadahoc County, Maine, and county and city in South Carolina, named for George I, King of England.

Georgetown; lake in New York, named for George H, King of England.

Georgetown; town in Williamson County, Texas, said to have been named for George Glasscock, early settler.

Georgia; State of the Union, named by King George II. for himself.

Georgia; strait between Washington and Vancouver Island, named for George III., King of England.

German; town in Chenango County, New York, named for Gen. Obadiah German, original proprietor.

German Flats; town in Herkimer County, New York, named so from the German settlers on the Mohawk Flats.

Germanton; village in Stokes County, North Carolina, settled by Germans.

Gerry; town in Chautauqua County, New York, named for Elbridge Gerry, a signer of the Declaration of Independence.

Gervais; town in Marion County, Oregon, named for Joseph Gervais, a pioneer.

Gethsemane; town in Nelson County, Kentucky, named for the garden at the foot of the Mount of Olives.

Gettysburg; borough in Adams County, Pennsylvania, named for James Gettys, who laid it out.

Geuda; city in Sumner County, Kansas, named from the mineral springs near.

Gibbon; river and hill in Yellowstone Park and village in Umatilla County, Oregon; Gibbonsville; town in Lemhi County, Idaho, named for Gen. John Gibbon, United States Army.

Gibraltar; several towns in the country are named from the city in Spain.

Gibson; county in Indiana, named for John Gibson, secretary and acting governor of Indiana Territory in 1811-1813.

Gibson; county and town in Tennessee, named for Col. Thomas Gibson.

Gibsonville; town in Guilford County, North Carolina, named for a prominent resident.

Gila; county in Arizona and river of Arizona and New Mexico. The name is said to be of Spanish origin, but the meaning is lost.

Gilberton; borough in Schuylkill County, Pennsylvania, named for John Gilbert, who owned coal mines there.

Gilboa; town in Schoharie County, New York, and Putnam County, Ohio, named from the mountain in Palestine.

Gildehouse; village in Franklin County, Missouri, named for a family who first settled there.

Gilead; town in Oxford County, Maine, named from the large Balm of Gilead tree standing in the middle of the town.

Giles; village in Brown County, Nebraska, named for the first postmaster, Giles Mead.

Giles; county in Virginia, named for William Branch Giles, governor of the State in 1827-1830. The county in Tennessee was probably named for the same.

Gilford; town in Belknap County, New Hampshire, named for S. S. Oilman, who made the first settlements there.

Gill; town in Franklin County, Massachusetts, named for Moses (Jill, one time lieutenant-governor of the State.

Gillespie; county in Texas, named for Robert A. Gillespie, who fell at the battle of Monterey.

Gilliam; village in Saline County, Missouri, named for a farmer residing in the neighborhood.

Gilliam; county in Oregon, named for Col. Cornelius Gilliam, member of the volunteers of Willamette Valley.

Gilman; town in Eagle County, Colorado, named for H. M. Oilman, a prominent resident.

Gilman; town in Marshall County, Iowa, named for a railroad contractor.

Gilman; town in Hamilton County, New York, named for John M. Gilman, early settler, from New Hampshire.

Gilmanton; town in Belknap County, New Hampshire, named for the former owners of the site.

Gilmer; county in Georgia, named for George P. Gilmer, governor of the State in 1830.

Gilmer; comity in West Virginia, named for Thomas W. Gilmer, member of Congress from Virginia.

Gilpin; county and mountain in Colorado, named for William Gilpin, first Territorial governor.

Gilsum; town in Cheshire County, New Hampshire, named for the first proprietors, Gilbert and Sumner.

Girard; city in Crawford County, Kansas, named for the borough in Pennsylvania.

Girard; borough in Erie County, Pennsylvania; Girardville; borough in Schuylkill County, Pennsylvania, and several other towns and villages. Named for Stephen Girard, at one time the wealthiest man in the United States.

Gladstone; city in Delta County, Michigan, and town in Stark County, North Dakota, named for the English statesman.

Gladwin; county and city in Michigan, named for Maj. Henry Gladwin, in command at Detroit at the time of Pontiac's conspiracy.

Glasco; city in Cloud County, Kansas, named from the city in Scotland, and spelled by the first postmaster "Glasco."

Glascock; county in Georgia, named for Thomas Glascock, an officer of the War of 1812.

Glasgow; city in Barren County, Kentucky, and several other places, named from the city in Scotland.

Glassboro; town in Gloucester County, New Jersey, named from its glass factories.

Glasscock; county in Texas, named for George W. Glasscock, who took part in the storming of San Antonio.

Glastonbury; town in Hartford County, Connecticut, named from the town in England.

Glazypool; mountain and creek in Arkansas. A corruption of the French name, Glaise a Paul, "Paul's clay pit."

Glen; two hundred and fifty-six places in the country bear this name alone or with suffixes. In the majority of cases the word is used descriptively, though in a few cases it is a proper name.

Glen; town in Montgomery County, New York, named for Jacob Glen, a prominent citizen.

Glenn; county in California, named for Hugh J. Glenn, a prominent resident of the county.

Glenn Springs; town in Spartanburg County, South Carolina, named from a famous spring owned by the Glenn family.

Glens Falls; village in Warren County, New York, named by John Glenn for himself.

Glenville; town in Schenectady County, New York, named from the manor of Sandir Leenderste Glen, which formerly occupied the site.

Glidden; town in Carroll County, Iowa, named for a manufacturer of barbed wire.

Gloucester; city in Essex County, Massachusetts, county and city in New Jersey, and county in Virginia, as well as several other places; named for Gloucestershire, England.

Glover; town in Orleans County, Vermont, named for Gen. John Glover, of Marblehead, a principal proprietor.

Gloversville; city in Fulton County, New York, named from its glove factories.

Glynn; county in Georgia, named for John Glynn, an English lawyer and warm friend of the American colonies.

Gnadenhutten; town in Tuscarawas County, Ohio, settled by Moravian missionaries. A German word, meaning "tents of grace."

Goddard; city in Sedgwick County, Kansas, named for J. F. Goddard, general manager of the Atchison, Topeka and Santa Fe Railroad.

Godfrey; village in Madison County, Illinois, named for Capt. Benjamin Godfrey.

Goff; city in Nemaha County, Kansas, named for Edward II. Goff of the Union Pacific Railroad.

Goffstown; town in Hillsboro County, New Hampshire, named for Col. John Goffe.

Gogebic; county and lake in Michigan. An Indian word. According to some authorities, a contraction of Agojebic, "rocky," or "rocky shore;" others say it is from Gogebing, "dividing lake."

Golconda; city in Pope County, Illinois, and town in Humboldt County, Nevada, named from the city in India.

Gold; a name of frequent occurrence throughout the country. It appears with numerous suffixes and in most cases was given to denote the presence of the metal.

Golden Gate; bay in California, named by Colonel Fremont, before the discovery of gold in the country, because of the brilliant effect of the setting sun on the cliffs and hills.

Gold Point; town in Martin County, North Carolina, named from the gold leaf tobacco.

Goldsboro; city in Wayne County, North Carolina, named for M. T. Goldsboro, of Maryland.

Goldthwaite; town in Mills County, Texas, named for a man prominent in the organization of a railroad running into the town.

Goliad; county in Texas, named by making an anagram of the name, "Hidago," the Mexican revolutionary hero.

Gonzales; county in Texas, named for Raphael Gonzales, at one-time provisional governor of the State.

Goochland; county in Virginia, named for William Gooch, lieutenant-governor of Virginia in 1727-1749.

Goodhue; county and village in Minnesota, named for James M. Goodhue, the first journalist of the Territory, who founded the Pioneer, of St. Paul.

Goodman; town in Holmes County, Mississippi, named for the first president of the Mississippi Central Railroad.

Goose; river in Maine, named from a pond at the source, so called by an early settler from a wild-goose nest which he found on a rock on the bank of the pond.

Gooski; lake in Florida, named for an old settler, a Pole.

Gordon; county in Georgia, named for William W. Gordon, first president of the Central Railroad.

Gore; pass in Colorado, named for a gunsmith of Denver.

Gorham; town in Cumberland County, Maine. Some authorities say it was named for Col. Shubael Gorham, one of the original proprietors, but Whitmore says that it was named for Capt. John Gorham, one of the early proprietors.

Gorham; town in Coos County, New Hampshire, named for Captain Gorham, who was in the Narragansett fight.

Gorham; town in Ontario County, New York, named for Nathaniel Gorham.

Gorman; township in Ottertail County, Minnesota, named for Willis A. Gorman, former governor of the State.

Goshen; city in Elkhart County, Indiana, and village in Orange County, New York, named from the "Land of Goshen." The name is found in many parts of the country, applied as a synonym of fruitfulness and fertility.

Gosiute; peak and lake in Nevada, named for an Indian tribe.

Gosnold; town in Dukes County, Massachusetts, settled by Bartholomew Gosnold.

Gosper; county in Nebraska, named for John J. Gosper, secretary of state.

Gothic; mountains in the Adirondacks, New York, and Elk Mountains, Colorado, so named because of pinnacles resembling Gothic architecture.

Gouldsboro; town in Hancock County, Maine, named for Robert Gould, one of the original proprietors.

Gouverneur; town in St. Lawrence County, New York, named for Gouverneur Morris, an American statesman.

Govan; town in Bamberg County, South Carolina, named for a family prominent in South Carolina history.

Gove; county and city in Kansas, named for Grenville L. Gove, captain in the Eleventh Kansas Regiment.

Governors; island in Boston Harbor, Massachusetts, named for Governor Winthrop, to whose descendants it still belongs.

Governors; island in New York Harbor, named for Governor Van Twiller, who owned it at an early date.

Gowanda; village in Cattaraugus County, New York. An Indian word, meaning "a town among the hills by the water side."

Grafton; town in Worcester County, Massachusetts, named for Charles Fitz-Roy, Duke of Grafton.

Grafton; county and town in New Hampshire, named for Augustus Henry Fitz-Roy, Duke of Grafton.

Grafton; city in Taylor County, West Virginia, named by the Baltimore and Ohio Railroad, because they grafted a branch from this point to Wheeling.

Graham; county in Kansas, named for John L. Graham, captain of the Eighth Kansas Regiment.

Graham; county, and town in Alamance County, North Carolina, named for Senator William A. Graham, Secretary of the Navy under President Fillmore.

Graham; city in Young County, Texas, named for one of two brothers, who owned salt works near where the town was built.

Grahamsville; village in Sullivan County, New York, named for Lieutenant Graham, who was killed by Indians near the present site of the village.

Grahamton; town in Meade County, Kentucky, named for an early pioneer.

Grahamville; town in Beaufort County, South Carolina, named for the founder.

Grainger; county in Tennessee, named for Mary Grainger.

Granby; town in Hampshire County, Massachusetts, said to have been named for John, Marquis of Granby.

Granby; town in Essex County, Vermont, named for Earl Granby in 1761.

Grand; county in Colorado, named from Grand Lake, the source of Grand River.

Grand Coteau; town in St. Landry Parish, Louisiana, so named because of its position. A French name, meaning "great hill."

Grand Forks; county and city in North Dakota, which take their name from the junction of the Red River of the North with Red Lake River.

Grand Haven; city in Ottawa County, Michigan, ho named because it is situated on the best harbor on the eastern shore of Lake Michigan.

Grand Island; city in Nebraska on Platte River, which is divided into two channels at that point by an island nearly 50 miles long.

Grand Isle; town in Aroostook County, Maine, named from an island in the river at that point.

Grand Isle; county and village in Vermont, named from an island in Lake Champlain, since called South Hero. The early French called it Grand Isle.

Grand Junction; town in Greene County, Iowa, so named from its position at the junction of the Keokuk and Des Moines and Chicago and Northwestern railroads.

Grand Lake Stream; plantation in Washington County, Maine, named from a lake in the northern part of the State.

Grand Rapids; cities in Michigan and Wisconsin, named from rapids and falls in the Grand and Wisconsin rivers.

Grand Ronde; river and valley in Oregon. Is a French name, meaning "great round," and was applied by the early French trappers to the valley because of its circular shape.

Grand Tower; city in Jackson County, Illinois, named from a high rocky island which resembles a tower, in the Mississippi River.

Grand Traverse; county in Michigan, named from Grand Traverse Bay.

Granite; county in Montana, named from a mountain which contains the celebrated Granite Mountain silver mine.

Graniteville; village in Iron County, Missouri, named for a quarry near, considered one of the most remarkable in the world.

Grant; military post in Arizona, county in Arkansas, town in Humboldt County, California; town in Montgomery County, Iowa; county in Kansas, parish in Louisiana, county in Minnesota, county and village in Nebraska, counties in New Mexico, Oklahoma, Oregon, South Dakota, and West Virginia, and many small places throughout the country, named for Gen. U. S. Grant.

Grant; county in Indiana, named for Samuel and Moses Grant, of Kentucky, killed in battle with the Indiana.

Grant; county in Kentucky. According to John McGee it was named for Col. John Grant, an early settler, but according to J. Worthing McCann, the county was named for Samuel Grant.

Grant; river and county in Wisconsin, named for a trapper who had a cabin on its banks.

Grantsville; town in Calhoun County, West Virginia, named for U. S. Grant.

Granville; county in North Carolina and town in Hampden County, Massachusetts, named for John Carteret, Earl of Granville.

Grass; river in St. Lawrence County, New York, from the name given it by the early French, LaGrasse Riviere, meaning "the fertile river."

Grass Valley; city in Nevada County, California, named from a valley covered with grass.

Gratiot; county in Michigan, named for Capt. Charles Gratiot, United States Army, who constructed Fort Gratiot in 1814.

Gratiot; village in Lafayette County, Wisconsin, named for Col. Henry Gratiot, an Indian agent.

Grattan; township in Kent County, Michigan, named for the Irish orator.

Gratz; borough in Dauphin County, Pennsylvania, named from the Prussian town.

Graves; county in Kentucky, named for Capt. Benjamin Graves, who fell at the battle of Raisin River.

Gravesend; village in Kings County, New York, now a part of New York City, named by persons from Gravesend, England.

Gravette; town in Benton County, Arkansas, named for E. T. Gravette.

Gray; county in Kansas, named for Alfred Gray, secretary of the Kansas State board of agriculture in 1873-1880.

Gray; town in Cumberland County, Maine, said to have been named for Thomas Gray, one of the proprietors.

Gray; county in Texas, named for Peter W. Gray, prominent lawyer of Houston.

Grayling; town in Crawford County, Michigan, named from the fish for which the Au Sable River was famous.

Graymount; town in Colorado near the foot of Grays Peak; hence the name.

Grays; peak in Colorado, named by Dr. Parry for Dr. Asa Gray, botanist.

Grays; harbor in Washington, named for the discoverer, Capt. Robert Gray, of Boston.

Grayson; county in Kentucky and county in Virginia, named for Col. William Grayson, United States Senator from Virginia.

Grayson; town in Carter County, Kentucky, named for Col. Robert Grayson.

Grayson; county in Texas, named for Peter W. Grayson, attorney-general of the Texan Republic in 1836.

Graysville; village in Sullivan County, Indiana, named for Joe Gray, its founder.

Graysville; village in Herkimer County, New York, named for Latham Gray, a resident.

Great Barrington; town in Berkshire County, Massachusetts, named for William, Viscount Barrington.

Great Basin; an area of territory in Utah whose waters do not reach the sea; hence it is called a "basin."

Great Bend; city in Barton County, Kansas, which takes its name from a bend in the Arkansas River south of there.

Great Bend; borough in Susquehanna County, Pennsylvania, named from a bend in the Susquehanna River at that point.

Great Black; river in Maine, which takes its name from the Indian designation, Chimkazaootook, meaning "big black stream."

Great Butte des Morts; lake in Wisconsin, so called from mounds near, which are said to contain the bodies of Indians slain in battle.

Great Falls; city in Cascade County, Montana, named from the falls in the Missouri, near the city.

Great Quabbin; mountain in Massachusetts, named for a celebrated Indian sachem. The word is supposed to mean "many waters."

Great Salt; lake in Utah, named from the salinity of its waters.

Great Sinabar; creek in Missouri, a corruption of the old French name Chenal au Barre, meaning "channel of the bar," or "through the bar."

Greeley; city in Colorado, county and city in Kansas, and county in Nebraska, named for Horace Greeley.

Greeley; village in Holt County, Nebraska, named for Peter Greeley.

Green; descriptive word found frequently with and without various suffixes. The river in Wyoming and Utah was so called from the green shale through which it flows.

Green; river rising in the Wind River range of the Rockies, formerly known as Popo Agie, a word of the Crow dialect, meaning "head of river."

Green; mountains in New England, so named from their forests of evergreen trees.

Green; counties in Kentucky and Wisconsin, named for Gen. Nathaniel Greene.

Green Bay; city in Brown County, Wisconsin, named from the bay which was called by the early French "la grande baie," "the large bay," which was corrupted into the present name.

Greenbrier; county in West Virginia, named from the river, which was so called by Col. John Lewis.

Greenbush; town in Rensselaer County, New York, translation original Dutch name Groen Bosch, from the pine woods which originally covered the flats.

Greencastle; city in Indiana, named from the town in Ireland.

Green Cove Springs; town in Clay County, Florida, named from a large sulphur spring, supposed by some to be the "fountain of youth" of Spanish and Indian legends.

Greene; counties in Georgia, Illinois, Indiana, Iowa; town in Androscoggin County, Maine; counties in Mississippi, Missouri, and New York, and village in Chenango County, New York; counties in North Carolina, Ohio, Pennsylvania, and Tennessee; named for Gen. Nathaniel Greene, Revolutionary soldier.

Greene; town in Butler County, Iowa. named for Judge George Green, of Linn County.

Greenesville; county in Virginia; Greeneville; town in Greene County, Tennessee. Named for Gen. Nathaniel Greene.

Greenfield; town in Franklin County, Massachusetts, which derives its name from the river which intersects it.

Green Island; town in Albany County, New York, so named because situated on an island of that name in Hudson River.

Green Lake; county in Wisconsin, so named from a lake which was called so from the color of its waters.

Greenleaf; city in Washington County, Kansas, named for the treasurer of the Union Pacific Railroad, A. W. Greenleaf.

Greensburg; city in Kiowa County, Kansas, named for Col. D. R. Green.

Greenup; county and town in Kentucky, named for Christopher Greenup, governor of the State in 1804-1808.

Greenville; city in Muhlenberg County, Kentucky, and town in Pitt County, North Carolina, named for Gen. Nathaniel Greene.

Greenville; city in Montcalm County, Michigan, named for John Green, one of the first settlers.

Greenville; town in Washington County, Mississippi, named for the first settler.

Greenville; county and city in South Carolina, named from the physical appearance. The name was first given to the city and from that applied to the county.

Greenwich; town in Hampshire County, Massachusetts, and village in Washington County, New York, named from the town in England.

Greenwood; town in Sebastian County, Arkansas, named for Moses Greenwood, a prominent merchant of early days.

Greenwood; county in Kansas, named for Alfred B. Greenwood, Commissioner of Indian affairs in 1859-60.

Greenwood; city in Leflore County, Mississippi, named for Greenwood Leflore, a noted Choctaw Indian chief.

Greenwood; village in Cass County, Nebraska, named for an early settler, J. S. Green.

Greenwood; county in South Carolina, descriptively named.

Greer; county in Oklahoma, named for John A. Greer, governor of Texas in 1849 - 1853.

Greer; town in Greenville County, South Carolina, named for a resident family.

Gregg; county in Texas, named for a prominent citizen, John Gregg, killed in the civil war.

Gregory; county in South Dakota, named for J. Shaw Gregory, legislator.

Greig; town in Lewis County, New York, named for the late John Greig, of Canandaigua.

Grenada; county and town in Mississippi, named from the Spanish province.

Grenola; city in Elk. County, Kansas, named by compounding the first part of the name of two rival towns in the neighborhood—Greenfield and Kanola.

Gridley; town in McLean County, Illinois, named for Asahel Gridley.

Griffin; city in Spalding County, Georgia, named for Gen. L. L. Griffin.

Grifton; town in Pitt County, North Carolina, named for the Grifton family.

Grifton Corners; village in Delaware County, New York, named for the Griffin family.

Griggs; county in North Dakota, named for Hon. Alex. Griggs, a pioneer of Grand Forks, member of the constitutional convention of North Dakota.

Grimes; town in Colusa County, California, named for the man who founded it.

Grimes; town in Polk County, Iowa, named for Senator Grimes.

Grimes; county in Texas, named for Jesse Grimes, member of the council of provisional government.

Grimesland; town in Pitt County, North Carolina, named for Gen. Bryan Grimes.

Grinnell; city in Poweshiek County, Iowa, named for Hon. W. H. Grinnell, a citizen.

Griswold; town in New London County, Connecticut, named for Roger Griswold, governor of the State in 1811.

Grizzly; peak in Colorado, named by a party of scientists from an adventure with a grizzly bear.

Gross; point in Maine on the Penobscot River, named for the first settler, Zachariah Gross.

Grosse Isle; village in "Wayne County, Michigan, which takes its name from an island in Detroit River, which was -called by the early French Grosse Isle, " great isle." Grossepoint; town in Wayne County, Michigan, so named from a large point which projects into Lake St. Clair, named by the French, Grosse Pointe, "great or large point."

Grosvenor; mount in Arizona, named for H. C. Grosvenor, who was killed there in 1861.

Groton; town in Middlesex County, Massachusetts, named from the place in England owned by the family of Deane Winthrop, whose name headed the petition for the grant.

Groton; village in Tompkins County, New York, named from the above.

Grover; village in Cleveland County, North Carolina, and town in Dorchester County, South Carolina, named for Grover Cleveland.

Grubbs; village in Newcastle County, Delaware, named for the early owner, John Grubbs.

Grundy; counties in Illinois, Iowa, Missouri, and Tennessee; Grundy Center; town in Grundy County, Iowa. Named for Felix Grundy, United States Senator from Tennessee.

Guadalupe; county in New Mexico and river and town in Victoria County, Texas, named for Don Felix Victoria, first president of Mexico, known as "Guadalupe Victoria." Guernsey; county in Ohio, named by emigrants from the island of Guernsey in the English Channel.

Guero; mount in Colorado, named for a Ute Indian.

Guilford; borough in New Haven County, Connecticut, named from a town in England.

Guilford; county in North Carolina, named for the Earl of Guilford, father of Lord North.

Gulfport; town in Harrison County, Mississippi, named by W. H. Hardy, because of its situation.

Gulpha; creek in Hot Springs, Arkansas. The name is a corruption of Calfat, a proper name, probably belonging to an early settler.

Gunnison; county, town, mountain, and river in Colorado, and island in Great Salt Lake, Utah, named for Capt. J. W. Gunnison, an early explorer.

Gurnet; point at the entrance to Plymouth Harbor, Massachusetts, named from the gurnet, a sea fish.

Guthrie; creek in Humboldt County, California, named for an early settler.

Guthrie; county in Iowa, named for Capt. Edwin B. Guthrie.

Guthrie; town in Callaway County, Missouri, named for Guthrie brothers, early settlers.

Guthrie Center; town in Guthrie County, Iowa, named for Capt. Edwin B. Guthrie.

Guttenburg; city in Clayton County, Iowa, and town in Hudson County, New Jersey, named for the inventor of printing.

Guyandot; town in Cabell County, West Virginia, and river in same State. The French form of Wyandotte, the tribe of Indians.

Guyot; mounts in Colorado, New Hampshire, and Tennessee, named for Arnold Guyot, the geographer.

Gwinnett; county in Georgia, named for Button Gwinnett, one of the signers of the Declaration of Independence.

H

Habana; city in Mason County, Illinois, named for the city in Cuba. The word is Spanish, meaning "harbor."

Habersham; county in Georgia, named for Col. Joseph Habersham, speaker of the general assembly of Georgia in 1785.

Hackensack; town in Bergen County, New Jersey. An Indian word. Authorities differ as to the meaning of this word, the many different versions being "hook mouth," "a stream that unites with another on low ground," "on low ground," "the land of the big snake."

Hackettstown; town in Warren County, New Jersey, named for Samuel Hackett, a large landowner.

Hackneyville; town in Tallapoosa County, Alabama, named from the suburb in London.

Haddam; city in Washington County, Kansas, named for the town in Connecticut.

Haddonfield; borough in Camden County, New Jersey, named for Elizabeth Haddon.

Hadley; peak in Humboldt County, California, named for an early settler.

Hadley; town in Hampshire County, Massachusetts, named from the parish in Essex, England.

Hadlyme; town in New London County, Connecticut. The name is formed of a combination of the names of the two townships in which it is located—Haddam and Lyme.

Hagerstown; city in Washington County, Maryland, named for a German named Hager, one of the original proprietors.

Hague; several towns and villages in the United States are named for the city in Holland.

Hague; peak in Colorado, named for Arnold Hague of the United States Geological Survey.

Hahn; peak in Colorado; Hahn Peak; village in Routt County, Colorado. Named for Joe Hahn, an early settler.

Hainesville; village in Holt County, Nebraska, named for S. S. Haines, early settler.

Halcott; town in Greene County, New York, named for George W. Halcott, sheriff.

Hale; county in Alabama, named for Stephen F. Hale, prominent in the State.

Hale; village in Carroll County, Missouri, named for John P. Hale, of Carrollton.

Hale, county in Texas. named for Lieut. J. C. Hale, of the Confederate army.

Hale Eddy; village in Delaware County, New York, named for a family of early settlers.

Half Dome; mountain of granite in California, on the walls of the Yosemite Valley, so named because it has the appearance of a half dome.

Halfmoon; bay in California, so named from its crescent shape.

Halfmoon; town in Saratoga County, New York, so named from a crescent-shaped piece of land between the Hudson and the Mohawk.

Halibut; island off the coast of Alaska, so named on account of the large number of halibut found there.

Halifax; counties in North Carolina and Virginia, and towns in Plymouth County, Massachusetts, and Windham County, Vermont, named for George Montagu, Earl of Halifax.

Hall; county in Georgia, named for Dr. Lyman Hall, one of the signers of the Declaration of Independence.

Hall; county in Nebraska, named for Augustus Hall, former Congressman from Iowa.

Hall; county in Texas, named for an early settler and captain in the war of independence, Warren O. C. Hall.

Halletts Cove; part of New York City, formerly a village in Queens County, New York, which received its name from the original patentee.

Hallowell; city in Kennebec County, Maine, named for Benjamin Hallowed, a large proprietor in the Kennebec patent.

Hallstead; borough in Susquehanna County, Pennsylvania, named for William F. Hallstead, general manager of the Delaware, Lackawanna and Western Railroad.

Hallsville; village in Montgomery County, New York, named for Capt. Robert Hall.

Halseyville; village in Tompkins County, New York, named for the first settler, Nicholl Halsey.

Halstead; city in Harvey County, Kansas, named for the journalist, Murat Halstead.

Hamblen; county in Tennessee, named for Hezekiah Hamblen.

Hamburg; name given to several. places in the United States after the city in Germany, among them being towns in Erie County, New York, and Aiken County, South Carolina.

Hamersville; village in Brown County, Ohio, named for Gen. Thomas Lyon Hamer.

Hamilton; many places in the United States are named for the statesman, Alexander Hamilton, among them being counties in the States of Florida, Illinois, Indiana, Kansas, New York, Ohio, Tennessee, a town in Essex County, Massachusetts, and probably the county of that name in Nebraska.

Hamilton; town in Harris County, Georgia, named for General Hamilton, governor of South Carolina.

Hamilton; county in Iowa, named for William W. Hamilton, president of the senate in 1857.

Hamilton; county in Texas, named for James Hamilton, of South Carolina, a sympathizer-and helper of Texas in its war.

Hamlet; village in Richmond County, North Carolina, named for its founder.

Hamlin; several places in the United States are named for Hannibal Hamlin, among which are a plantation in Aroostook County, Maine, a county in South Dakota, and city in Brown County, Kansas.

Hammond; village in Piatt County, Illinois, named for Charles Goodrich Hammond, railway manager.

Hammond; city in Lake County, Indiana, named for Abram Hammond, twelfth governor, 1860-61.

Hammond; town in Presque County, Michigan, named for Stephen Hammond.

Hammond; town in St. Lawrence County, New York, named for Abijah Hammond, an early proprietor.

Hammonton; town in Atlantic County, New Jersey, named for a family of former residents.

Hammonville; town in Hart County, Kentucky, named for a resident.

Hampden; county and town in Massachusetts and a town in Penobscot County, Maine, named for the English patriot, John Hampden.

Hampshire; counties in Massachusetts and West Virginia, named for the county in England.

Hampstead; many villages in New Hampshire, Maryland, and Virginia, named for the parish in England.

Hampton; name of several places in the United States, named for the parish in Middlesex, England, a town in Rockingham County, New Hampshire, being one of these.

Hampton; county and town in South Carolina, named for Gen. Wade Hampton.

Hamptonburg; town in Orange County, New York, named from the birthplace— Wolverhampton—of William Bull, first settler.

Hancock; counties in Georgia, Illinois, Indiana, Iowa, and Kentucky, county and town in Maine, town in Berkshire County, Massachusetts, county in Mississippi, mountain in New Hampshire, town in Delaware County, New York, and counties in Ohio, Tennessee, and West Virginia, named for John Hancock, one of the signers of the Declaration of Independence. Many other places in the United States are named for the same man.

Hancock; mount in Yellowstone Park, named for Gen. Winfield Scott Hancock.

Hand; county in South Dakota, named for George A. Hand, Territorial secretary in 1880.

Handsboro; town in Harrison County, Mississippi, named for a Northern man who established a foundry there before the civil war.

Hanging Rock; village in Lawrence County, Ohio, named from the presence of a cliff at the back of the town.

Hangmans; creek in Washington, tributary of the Spokane River, so named because some Indians were hanged on its bank.

Hanna; reef and island in Texas, probably named for Captain Hanna, captain of the Leonidas, in 1837.

Hannacrois; creek in New York, said to have been named by the Dutch, "hannekraai," meaning "cock-crowing creek," from the legend that a rooster came floating down this creek on a cake of ice.

Hannibal; town in Oswego County, New York, named by the State land board, being situated in the military tract given to the surviving soldiers of the Revolution; Hannibal; city in Marion County, Missouri. Named for the Carthaginian general.

Hanover; many places in the United States are named for the Duke of Hanover, who became George I of England, or from the Prussian city and province belonging to him. Among these are a town in Plymouth County, Massachusetts, city in Washington County, Kansas, and a county in Virginia.

Hansford; county in Texas, named for John M. Hansford, who was a judge and lawyer there during the days of the republic.

Hanson; county in South Dakota, named for Joseph R. Hanson, clerk of the first legislature.

Haralson; county and village in Georgia, named for Gen. Hugh A. Haralson, former Congressman from that State.

Harbeson; village in Sussex County, Delaware, named for Harbeson Hickman, a large landowner.

Harbine; village in Thayer County, Nebraska, named for Col. John Harbine.

Hardeman; county in Texas, named for two brothers, Bailey and T. J. Hardeman, prominent citizens in the days of the Republic; and a county in Tennessee, named for one of the brothers, Col. T. J. Hardeman.

Hardenburg; town in Ulster County, New York, named for Johannes Hardenburg, an early patentee in Delaware and Sullivan counties.

Hardin; several places in the United States have received this name, among them a number of counties, most of which were named for Col. John Hardin. Among these are the counties in Illinois, Iowa, Ohio, Tennessee, and Kentucky.

Hardin; city in Ray County, Missouri, named for Governor Charles II. Hardin, 1875-1877.

Hardin; county in Texas, named for the family of William Hardin, of Liberty.

Hardin Factory; town in Gaston County, North Carolina, named for the builder of the factory.

Hardinsburg; town in Breckinridge County, Kentucky, named for Capt. William Hardin, a pioneer.

Hardwick; town in Worcester County, Massachusetts, named for Philip Yorke, Lord Hardwicke, a member of the privy council.

Hardy; town in Sharp County, Arkansas, named for a railroad official.

Hardy; county in West Virginia, named for Samuel Hardy, a member of Congress from Virginia in 1784.

Hardy Station; town in Grenada County, Mississippi, named by the railroad company for Richard Hardy, the owner of the land upon which the depot was built.

Harford; county and village in Maryland, named for Henry Harford, the natural son of Lord Baltimore, the sixth, and proprietor at the time of the Revolution.

Harlan; city in Shelby County, Iowa, named for Senator Harlan.

Harlan; village in Smith County, Kansas, named for John C. Harlan, one of the first settlers.

Harlan; county and town in Kentucky, named for Maj. Silas Harlan.

Harlan; county in Nebraska, named for James Harlan, Secretary of the Interior 1865-6(5.

Harlem; part of New York City and the channel which extends northward from Hell Gate, connecting with the Hudson, named for the town in Holland.

Harleyville; town in Dorchester County, South Carolina, named for a resident family.

Harman; village in Arapahoe County, Colorado, named for L. B. Harman, its founder.

Harmer; township and village .in Allegheny County, Pennsylvania, named for the Hon. Harmer Denny.

Harmony; borough in Butler County, Pennsylvania, named by a colony of Germans to indicate the principle of its organization.

Harnett; county of North Carolina, named for Cornelius Harnett, an American statesman.

Harney; county, city, and lake in Oregon, named for General Harney.

Harper; county in Kansas, named for Marion Harper, first sergeant Company E, Second Kansas Regiment.

Harpers Ferry; town in Jefferson County, West Virginia, named for Robert Harper, who settled there in 1734 and established a ferry.

Harpersfield; town in Delaware County, New York, named for Joseph Harper, an "original patentee.

Harperville; village in Scott County, Mississippi, named for G. W. Harper, an old resident.

Harpswell; town in Cumberland County, Maine, probably named for the town in England.

Harrellsville; town in Hertford County, North Carolina, named for a former resident.

Harriet; lake in Minnesota, named for the wife of Colonel Leavenworth.

Harrietstown; town in Franklin County, New York, named for the wife of James Duane.

Harrietta; village in Wexford County, Michigan, a combination of the names of the manager of the Ann Arbor Railroad, Harry, and that of his wife, Henrietta.

Harrington; town in Kent County, Delaware, named for the Hon. Samuel M. Harrington, at one-time chancellor of the State.

Harris; town in Humboldt County, California, named for an early settler.

Harris; county in Georgia, named for Charles Harris, a prominent lawyer and judge.

Harris; county in Texas, named for John R. Harris, who erected the first steam sawmill in Texas (1829).

Harrisburg; town in Lewis County, New York, named for Richard Harrison, of New York.

Harrisburg; the capital of Pennsylvania, named for John Harris, the original proprietor.

Harrison; twenty places in the United States bear this name, among them being the counties of Indiana, Iowa, Mississippi, and Ohio, and a town in Gloucester County, New Jersey, named for William Henry Harrison, former President of the United States.

Harrison; counties in Kentucky and West Virginia, named for Col. Benjamin Harrison, father of William Henry Harrison.

Harrison; town in Cumberland County, Maine, named for Harrison Gray Otis, of Boston.

Harrison; town in Tallahatchie County, Mississippi, named for James T. Harrison, prominent lawyer.

Harrison; county in Missouri, named for Albert G. Harrison, of Callaway County.

Harrison; town in Westchester County, New York, named for John Harrison.

Harrison; county in Texas, named for an early pioneer.

Harrisonburg; village in Catahoula Parish, Louisiana, and town in Rockingham County, Virginia, named for the Harrisons of Virginia.

Harrisville; town in Cheshire County, New Hampshire, named for Milan Harris, who established a mill there.

Harrisville; town in Lewis County, New York, named after Fosket Harris, first settler.

Harrisville; village in Meigs County, Ohio, named for Joseph Harris, a pioneer.

Harrisville; town in Ritchie County, West Virginia, named for Thomas Harris.

Harrodsburg; city in Mercer County, Kentucky, named for Col. James Harrod, who built the first cabin there.

Hart; county in Georgia, named for Nancy Hart, the celebrated Georgia heroine of the Revolution.

Hart; county in Kentucky, named for Nathaniel Hart, an officer of the war of 1812.

Hart; river and lake in Yellowstone Park, named for Hart Hunney, an old hunter. Others say it was named "Heart," from its shape.

Hartford; name transferred from England to many places in the United States, the capital of Connecticut being one of these.

Hartford; city in Lyon County, Kansas, town in Windsor County, Vermont, and village in Mason County, West Virginia, named for the city in Connecticut.

Hartley; county in Texas, named for O. C. and R. K. Hartley, distinguished members of the bar in the days of Texas's revolution.

Hartsville; town in Bartholomew County, Indiana, named for Gideon B. Hart, a pioneer.

Hartsville; town in Darlington County, South Carolina, named for a resident family.

Hartwick; town in Otsego County, New York, named for Christopher Hartwick, patentee.

Harvard; mountain in Colorado, and city in McHenry County, Illinois, named from the university.

Harvard; university in Cambridge, Massachusetts, and a town in Worcester County, of the same State, named for the Rev. John Harvard, who founded the university.

Harvey, county in Kansas, named for James M. Harvey, captain Company G, Tenth Kansas, governor, and United States Senator.

Harwich; town in Barnstable County, Massachusetts, named for the seaport in Essex County, England.

Hasbrouck Heights; borough in Bergen County, New Jersey, named for Mr. Hasbrouck, the principal owner of the land upon which the borough is located.

Hasenclever; village in Herkimer County, New York, named for a German who received a grant of land there.

Haskell; county in Kansas, named for Dudley C. Haskell, a former member of Congress.

Haskell; county in Texas, named for Charles Haskell, of Tennessee.

Hastings; city in Barry County, Michigan, named for Eurotas P. Hastings, formerly auditor-general of the State.

Hatboro; borough in Montgomery County, Pennsylvania, so named because of its extensive hat factories.

Hatchechubee; town in Russell County, Alabama. A combination of the Indian words hatchie, "a creek," and chubba, "half way," "the middle."

Hatchie; river in Tennessee. An Indian word, hatch ie, meaning "a small river."

Hatfield; town in Hampshire County, Massachusetts, named for a town in England.

Hatteras; township and cape in Dare County, North Carolina, named for a tribe of Lennape Indians.

Hattiesburg; town in Perry County, Mississippi, named for the wife of Capt. W. H. Hardy, its founder.

Havensville; city in Pottawatomie County, Kansas, named for Paul E. Havens, of Leavenworth.

Haverford; township in Delaware County, Pennsylvania, named for the town in Wales.

Haverhill; city in Essex County, Massachusetts, named for the town in England.

Haverhill; town in Grafton County, New Hampshire, named for the town in Massachusetts.

Haverstraw; town in Rockland County, New York, named by the early Dutch Haverstroo, meaning "oats straw."

Havilah; town in Kern County, California, named from the Bible, the word meaning "land of gold."

Havilandsville; village in Harrison County, Kentucky, named for Robert Haviland.

Havre de Grace; town in Harford County, Maryland. A French word meaning "harbor of grace, or safety."

Haw; river and town in Alabama County, North Carolina, named from the Indian tribe Sissipahaw.

Hawesville; city in Hancock County, Kentucky, named for Richard Hawes.

Hawkeye; town in Fayette County, Iowa, named for a noted Indian chief.

Hawkins; county in Tennessee, named for Benjamin Hawkins, United States Senator from North Carolina.

Hawks Nest; town in Fayette County, West Virginia, named for a cliff on New River.

Hawley; town in Franklin County, Massachusetts, named for Joseph Hawley, of Northampton.

Hawthorne; borough in Passaic County, New Jersey, named for Nathaniel Hawthorne.

Hayden; town in Grand County, Colorado; mountain in the Grand Teton range in Wyoming, and valley in Yellowstone Park; Hayden Hill; village in Lassen County, California. Named for Dr. Ferdinand V. Hayden, the geologist.

Haydensville; village in Hampshire County, Massachusetts, named for Joel Hayden, its founder.

Hayes; county in Nebraska and mount in New Hampshire,. named for Rutherford B. Hayes.

Hayesville; town in Clay County, North Carolina, named for George W. Hayes, State senator.

Hays; city in Ellis County, Kansas, named for Gen. William Hays, United States Army.

Hays; county in Texas, named for John C. Hays, colonel in the Texan service in the war between Mexico and the United States.

Haywood; county in North Carolina, named for John Haywood, State treasurer.

Haywood; county in Tennessee, named for Judge John Haywood, author of a history of Tennessee.

Hazardville; village in Hartford County, Connecticut, named for Colonel Hazard, owner of powder works.

Hazelton; city in Barber County, Kansas, named for its founder, Rev. J. H. Hazelton.

Hazlerigg; village in Boone County, Indiana, named for H. G. Hazlerigg, its founder.

Hazleton; city in Luzerne County, Pennsylvania, so named from the great abundance of hazel bushes.

Healdsburg; city in Sonoma County, California, named for Col. Harmon Heald, an early settler.

Healing Springs; village in Bath County, Virginia, named for the thermal mineral springs situated there.

Heard; county in Georgia, named for Stephen Heard, an officer of the American Revolution.

Heath.; town in Franklin County, Massachusetts, named for Gen. William M. Heath.

Heath Springs; town in Lancaster County, South Carolina, named after a firm of capitalists, Heath & Springs.

Heber; city in Wasatch County, Utah, named for Heber O. Kimball, a leader of the Mormons.

Hebron; twenty-five cities in the United States bear the name of this ancient city in Palestine.

Heceta; village in Lane County, Oregon, probably named for the early explorer, Capt. Bruno de Heceta.

Hector; town in Schuyler County, New York, named for the character in the Iliad.

Hedges; peak in Yellowstone Park, named for Cornelius Hedges.

Hedrick; town in Keokuk County, Iowa, named for General Hedrick.

Heidelberg; name of several places in the United States settled by colonists from that city in Germany.

Helderberg; plateau in New York, so named because of the fine prospect from it. A Dutch word meaning "clear mountain."

Helena; city in Lewis and Clarke County, Montana. Opinions differ as to the origin of the name, for by some it is supposed to lie named for Helen of Troy, but according to the Helena Historical .Directory of 1879 was named by John Somerville, of Minnesota, St. Helena, from the resemblance in its location to that of the original St. Helena. It was then voted to drop the prefix Saint, and that was done.

Helena; village in St. Lawrence County, New York, named for the daughter of Joseph Pitcairn, of New York.

Helicon; village in Winston County, Alabama, named from the ancient mountain in Boeotia.

Hellertown; borough in Northampton County, Pennsylvania, named for a family of early settlers.

Hell Gate; narrow pass in the East River, New York. Dutch word Hellegate, meaning "gate of hell." So named on account of the whirlpools, which made navigation dangerous.

Hellgate; river in Montana, named by Father de Smet Porte de L'Enfer, "gate of hell," because by this way the Blackfeet reached his people.

Hell Roaring; creek in Yellowstone Park, so named by a prospecting party, because one of them described it as a "hell roarer."

Helvetia; name of a few places in the United States settled by the Swiss and by them given the ancient name of Switzerland.

Hemlock; lake in New York. Translation of the Indian word Onehda.

Hemphill; county in Texas, named for John Hemphill, former Congressman from Texas.

Hempstead; county in Arkansas, named for Edward Hempstead, first delegate to Congress from Missouri Territory.

Hempstead; town in Nassau County, New York. Derived from the Dutch word Heemstede, meaning "homestead."

Henderson; county and river in Illinois; city and county in Kentucky; county and village in Chester County, Tennessee, named for Col. Richard Henderson, of Kentucky.

Henderson; town in Wexford County, Michigan, named for its first settler.

Henderson; village in York County, Nebraska, named for David Henderson, one of its first settlers.

Henderson; town in Jefferson County, New York, named for William Henderson, proprietor.

Henderson; county in North Carolina, named for Chief Justice Leonard Henderson.

Henderson; county in Texas, named for James Pinckney Henderson, foreign minister in the days of the republic; its first governor.

Henderson; village in Mason County, West Virginia, named for a family of early settlers.

Hendersonville; town in Henderson County, North Carolina, named for Chief Justice Leonard Henderson.

Hendricks; county in Indiana, named for William Hendricks, one of the early governors of the State.

Henlopen; cape on the coast of Delaware. Derived from the Dutch words Hin loop or Inlopen, meaning "to run in."

Hennepin; county in Minnesota, and village in Putnam County, Illinois, named for Louis Hennepin, a Franciscan missionary.

Hennessey; city in Kingfisher County, Oklahoma, named for Pat Hennessey, an Indian fighter, who was killed upon the ground which later became the town site.

Henniker; town in Merrimack County, New Hampshire, named for John Henniker, esq., a merchant of London.

Henrico; county in Virginia, named for the Prince of Wales, son of James I.

Henrietta; town in Monroe County, New York, named for Henrietta Laura, Countess of Bath.

Henrietta; town in Rutherford County, North Carolina, named for the wife of S. B. Tanner.

Henry; many counties in the United States, among them those in the States of Alabama, Georgia, Illinois, Indiana, Kentucky, Missouri, Tennessee, and Virginia, and mountain in Tennessee, named for Patrick Henry.

Henry; lake in Idaho, and fork of Snake River, named for one of the partners of the Northwest Fur Company.

Henry; county in Iowa, named for Gen. Henry Dodge, governor of the Territory of Wisconsin.

Henry; cape on coast of Virginia, named for the Prince of Wales, son of James I.

Henry; lake in Yellowstone Park, named for a celebrated fur trader, Andrew Henry, who established a trading post there.

Henson; town in Hinsdale County, Colorado, named from the creek, which was named for an early settler.

Hepburn; town in Page County, Iowa, named for Congressman Hepburn.

Hepler; city in Crawford County, Kansas, named for B. F. Hepler, of Fort Scott.

Herculaneum; village in Jefferson County, Missouri, named for the ancient city in Italy.

Herington; city in Dickinson County, Kansas, named for M. D. Herington, its founder.

Herkimer; county in New York. named for Gen. Nicholas Herkimer. a German, one of the patentees.

Herman; village in Washington County, Nebraska, named for Samuel Herman, conductor on the Omaha and Northwestern Railroad.

Hermann; town in Gasconade County, Missouri, settled by Germans, and named by them for their countryman, who fought so bravely at the time of the Roman invasion.

Hermitage; town in Hickory County, Missouri, named for the residence of Andrew Jackson.

Hermon; village in St. Lawrence County, New York, named for the mountain in Syria.

Hernando; county in Florida and city in De Soto County, Mississippi, named for Hernando De Soto, discoverer of the Mississippi River.

Hersey; village in Nohles County, Minnesota, named for General Hersey, of Maine, largely interested in the Territory.

Hertford; county, and a town in Perquimans County, North Carolina, named for Conway, Marquis of Hertford.

Heuvelton; village in St. Lawrence County, New York, named for Jacob Van Heuvel.

Hewes; point in Penobscot Bay, Maine, named for its first settler, Paola Hewes.

Hiawatha; city in Brown County, Kansas, named for the hero of Longfellow's poem.

Hibernia; several places in the United States bear this name of ancient Ireland.

Hickman; county and city in Fulton County, Kentucky, named for Capt. Paschal Hickman.

Hickman; county in Tennessee, named for Edmund Hickman.

Hickory; this name, either alone or with suffixes, is borne by 46 places in the United States. When alone, as in the cases of the county in Missouri, and the towns in Newton County, Mississippi, and Catawba County, North Carolina, the places were named for Andrew Jackson—"Old Hickory."

Hickory Flats; town in Benton County, Mississippi, named for a near-by hickory grove.

Hicks; island at entrance to Napeague Bay, Long Island, New York, named for the owner.

Hicksville; village in Queens County, New York. named for Charles Hicks, the Quaker reformer.

Hicksville; village in Defiance County, Ohio, named for Henry W. Hicks, who was one of the founders.

Hidalgo; county in Texas, said to be named for Hidalgo y Costilla, a priest, and leader in Mexican war of independence.

Higganum; village in Middlesex County, Connecticut. A corruption of the Indian word, Tomhegan-ompakut, meaning "at the tomahawk rock."

Higginsport; village in Brown County, Ohio, named for Col. Robert Higgins, who laid it out.

Highbridge; borough in Hunterdon County, New Jersey, named for its remarkable railroad bridge.

Highgate; town in Franklin County, Vermont, named from the chapelry in Middlesex, England.

Highland; counties in Ohio and Virginia, and city in Doniphan County, Kansas, so named on account of the high location.

Highlands; borough in Monmouth County, New Jersey, adjacent to the Atlantic Highlands, and taking its name therefrom.

Highlands; broken hills on the Hudson River, New York. Derived from the name of Hogeland, or Hoogland, meaning "highland," originally given them by the Dutch.

Highlands; town in Mason County, North Carolina, so named because it is the highest village east of the Mississippi.

High Point; village in Guilford County, North Carolina, so named because it is the highest point on the North Carolina Railroad.

Hightower; village in Forsyth County, Georgia, on the Etowah River. The name is a corruption of the name of the river.

Hightstown; borough in Mercer County, New Jersey, named for the Hight family.

Hildebran; village in Burke County, North Carolina, named for Pope Gregory VII.

Hilgard; mountain in Utah, named for J. E. Hilgard, formerly superintendent United States Coast and Geodetic Survey.

Hill; city in Graham County, Kansas, named for W. R. Hill. who located the town.

Hill; town in Merrimack County, New Hampshire, named for Isaac Hill, governor 1836-1839.

Hill; county in Texas, named for George W. Hill.

Hillburn; town in Rockland County, New York, originally named Woodburn, changed in 1882 to Hillburn in order not to conflict with a post-office of same name in that State. Both names are descriptive.

Hillers; mountain in Utah, named for John H. Hillers, photographer.

Hillsboro; counties in Florida and New Hampshire, and town in Orange County, North Carolina, named for the Karl of Hillsborough.

Hillsboro; city in Marion County, Kansas, named for a former mayor, John G. Hill.

Hillsboro; village in Vernon County, Wisconsin, named for the Hillsboro brothers, who made the first claim within the town.

Hillsdale; county in Michigan, so named because of its rolling surface—hills and valleys.

Hiltonhead; village in Beaufort County, North Carolina, said to have been named for the captain of the ship in which Colonel Sayle came over to make discoveries.

Hinckley; lake and village in Oneida County, New York, named for a resident family.

Hinds; county in Mississippi. named for Gen. Thomas Hinds, former Congressman from that State.

Hinesburg; town in Chittenden County, Vermont, named for an original proprietor, Abel Hines.

Hinesville; town in Liberty County, Georgia, named for Charlton Hines, esq.

Hingham; town in Plymouth County, Massachusetts, named for the town in England.

Hinsdale; county in Colorado, named for Lieutenant-Governor George A. Hinsdale.

Hinsdale; town in Berkshire County, Massachusetts, named for Rev. Theodore Hinsdale.

Hinsdale; town in Cheshire County, New Hampshire, named for Col. Ebenezer Hinsdale, one of its principal inhabitants.

Hinton; city in Summers County, West Virginia, named for the former owner of the town site.

Hippocrass; island in Maine, probably so named by seamen, the word meaning "spiced wine"

Hiram; town in Oxford County, Maine, named for Hiram, King of Tyre."

Hitchcock; county in Nebraska, named for Phineas W. Hitchcock, Senator from Nebraska.

Hoback; peak and river in Wyoming, named for an early trapper with the Missouri Fur Company.

Hobart; town in Wexford County, Michigan, named for the first settler.

Hobart; town in Delaware County, New York, named for Bishop Hobart, of New Jersey.

Hobgood; town in Halifax County, North Carolina, named for the principal of the Oxford Female Seminary.

Hoboken; city in Hudson County, New Jersey. Derived from the Indian word Hopocan, meaning a "tobacco pipe."

Hockanum; river and village in Hartford County, Connecticut. An Indian word, meaning "hook-shaped," "a hook;" so named because of the change in the course of the river at this point.

Hockendaqua; stream in Northampton County, Pennsylvania. Indian word, meaning "searching for land."

Hockessin; village in Newcastle County, Delaware. An Indian word, meaning "good bark;" applied to this locality on account of the good quality of white oak found there.

Hocking; river and county in Ohio. Derived from the Indian word Hockhock, "a gourd" or "a bottle," and ing, meaning "a place;" so called localize at this point the river suddenly assumes the shape of a bottle.

Hodgdon; town in Aroostook County, Maine, named for the proprietor, John Hodgdon.

Hodgeman; county in Kansas, named for Amos Hodgeman, captain Company H, Seventh Kansas.

Hodgensville; town in Larue County, Kentucky, named for Robert Hodgen.

Hodges; ledge of rock in Massachusetts, named for Isaac Hodges.

Hodges; town in Greenwood County, South Carolina, named for a resident family.

Hoffman; mount in California, named for Charles F. Hoffman, State geological survey.

Hoffman; village in Richmond County, North Carolina, named for a resident family.

Hoffmans Ferry; village in Schenectady County, New York, named for John Hoffman, owner of a ferry there.

Hog Creek; village in Allen County, Ohio, named for a stream with the Indian name Koskosepe, meaning "hog river."

Hohenlinden; village in Chickasaw County, Missouri, named for the village in Bavaria.

Hohokus; town in Bergen County, New Jersey, said to be derived from the Indian word Ho-hokes, meaning "a shout," or "some kind of a bark of a tree."

Hoisington; city in Barton County, Kansas, named for A. J. Hoisington, of Great Bend.

Hokab; village in Houston County, Minnesota, named from the river. An Indian word, meaning "a horn."

Hokaman; name of several lakes in Minnesota. An Indian word, meaning "where herons set."

Holbrook; town in Norfolk County, Massachusetts, named for Elisha Holbrook, a prominent citizen.

Holden; town in Worcester County, Massachusetts, named for the Hon. Samuel Holden, one of the directors of the Bank of England.

Holderness; town in Grafton County, New Hampshire, named after the district in Yorkshire, England.

Holdridge; town in Phelps County, Nebraska, named for G. W. Holdridge, superintendent Burlington and Missouri River Railway.

Holland; village in Dubois County, Indiana, and city in Ottawa County, Michigan, named by early settlers for the country of Europe.

Hollandale; town in Washington County, Mississippi, named for Dr. Holland, whose plantation the town site now occupies.

Holland Patent; village in Oneida County, New York, named for Henry, Lord Holland, patentee.

Holley; village in Orleans County, New York, named for Myron Holley, one of the first canal commissioners.

Holliday; town in Johnson County, Kansas, named for Cyrus K. Holliday, of Topeka.

Holliday; village in Monroe County, Missouri, named for Samuel Holliday, of St. Louis.

Hollidaysburg; borough in Blair County, Pennsylvania, named for William and Adam Holliday, the first settlers.

Hollis; town in Hillsboro County, New Hampshire, named for Thomas Hollis, a benefactor of Harvard College; or, according to Togg, for the Duke of Newcastle.

Hollister; town in San Benito County, California, named for Col. W. W. Hollister, an early settler.

Hollister; town in Middlesex County, Massachusetts, named for Thomas Hollis, of London, a patron of Harvard College.

Holly Beach; borough in Cape May County, New Jersey, named for a beach within its precincts where holly is supposed to have been found abundantly.

Holly Springs; city in Marshall County, Mississippi, and village in Wake County, North Carolina, so named on account of the prevalence of these two features.

Holmes; county in Mississippi, named for David Holmes, governor of the Territory and State, 1809-1817.

Holmes; county in Ohio, named for Major Holmes, an officer of the war of 1812.

Holmes; mounts in Utah and Yellowstone Park, named for the geologist, W. H. Holmes.

Holmesville; village in Cage County, Nebraska, named for L. M. Holmes, its founder.

Holmesville; village in Holmes County, Ohio, named for Major Holmes.

Holston; branch of the Tennessee River, named, according to Haywood, for its discoverer.

Holt; county in Missouri, named for David Rice Holt, member of the State legislature.

Holt; town in Clay County, Missouri, named for Jerry Holt, upon whose land the town was established.

Holton; city in Jackson County, Kansas, named for Hon. Edward Holton.

Holts Summit; village in Callaway County, Missouri, named for Timothy Holt.

Holy Cross; mountain peak in Colorado, so named for a cross of snow upon its eastern face.

Holyoke; city in Hampden County, Massachusetts, and mountain in same county, named for Rev. Edward Holyoke, an early president of Harvard College.

Homer; name given to several places in the United States for the Greek poet, among them being a village in Cortland County, New York.

Homosassa; town in Citrus County. Florida. An Indian word, the meaning differing according to different authorities, two versions being "river of fishes" and "pepper ridge."

Honesdale; borough in Wayne County, Pennsylvania, named for Philip Dale, a patron of the Delaware and Hudson Canal Company.

Honeoye; lake in Ontario County, New York; Honeoye Falls; village in Monroe County, New York. From the Indian word, Hayeayeh, meaning "a finger lying."

Honolulu; name transferred from the city in Hawaii to a village in Craven County, North Carolina, meaning "fair haven," from hono, "a harbor," and lulu, "smooth, quiet."

Hood; river and mountain in Oregon and a canal in Washington, named for Alexander Arthur Hood, afterwards Lord Brinport.

Hood; county in Texas, named for Gen. John B. Hood, a frontiersman.

Hookerton; town in Greene County, North Carolina, named for a prominent citizen.

Hookstown; borough in Beaver County, Pennsylvania, named for Matthias Hook, an early resident.

Hookton; village in Humboldt County, California, named for Major Hook.

Hoopa; town and valley in Humboldt County, California, named for the Hoopa Indians, a tribe on the lower Trinity River.

Hoosic; river in Massachusetts, New York, and Vermont. Derived from the Mohican Indian, wudjoo, meaning "a mountain," and abic, "a rock."

Hoosic; town in Renssalaer County, New York, named from the river.

Hoover; village in Cass County, Indiana, named for Riley Hoover, its founder.

Hopatcong; lake in New Jersey. An Indian name, meaning "stone over water," because of an artificial causeway of stone which connected an island of the lake with the shore.

Hope; town in Bartholomew County, Indiana, so named by its Moravian settlers as a monument to the sentiment which caused them to emigrate there.

Hope; city in Dickinson County, Kansas, formerly called Wagram; renamed Hope for a post-office in the vicinity, when it became a station on the Atchison, Topeka and Santa Fe Railroad.

Hopewell; borough in Mercer County, New Jersey, named according to the Puritan system of nomenclature, the place having been settled early in the eighteenth century by families from Long Island, formerly from Connecticut.

Hopkins; county in Kentucky, named for Samuel Hopkins, a Revolutionary officer.

Hopkins; county in Texas, named for a pioneer family.

Hopkinsville; city in Christian County, Kentucky, named for Gen. Samuel Hopkins, a Revolutionary officer.

Hopkinton; town in Middlesex County, Massachusetts, named for Edward Hopkins, early governor and patron of Harvard College.

Hopkinton; town in Merrimack County, New Hampshire, named for the town in Massachusetts.

Hopkinton; town in St. Lawrence County, New York, named for Roswell Hopkins, first settler.

Hopkinton; town in Washington County, Rhode Island, said to have been named for Stephen Hopkins, governor.

Hoppeny; creek in Pennsylvania. Indian word, meaning " where the wild potato grows."

Hoppogue; village in Suffolk County, Long Island, New York. A corruption of its original Indian name of Winganhappague, meaning "sweet water."

Hoquiam; river and city in Chehalis County, Washington. The name from the Indian Ho-qui-umptse, meaning "hungry for wood;" the river being so called on account of the great amount of driftwood at its mouth.

Horace; city in Greeley County, Kansas, named for Horace Greeley.

Horicon; lake and city in Dodge County, Wisconsin, and town in Warren County, New York. An Indian word meaning "clear."

Hornby; town in Steuben County, New York, named for John Hornby, an early English landholder.

Hornellsville; city in Steuben County, New York, named for its first settler, George Hornell.

Hornersville; village in Dunklin County, Missouri, named for William II. Horner, founder.

Horry; county in South Carolina, named for Gen. Peter Horry.

Horse; creek, a branch of Green River in Wyoming which, at the time of receiving its name, was the grazing ground of a herd of wild horses.

Horseheads; town in Chemung County, New York, so named because at this point, during an expedition against the Indians, General Sullivan caused his pack horses to be killed and the heads piled up.

Horton; city in Brown County, Kansas, named for Chief Justice A. H. Horton.

Hortonville; village in Outagamie County, Wisconsin, named for its founder.

Hosensack; creek in Pennsylvania. A German word, meaning "breeches pocket," and so called by a hunter who became bewildered in its valley.

Hosensack; village in Lehigh County, Pennsylvania, named for the creek.

Hospital Creek; stream in Vermont, so named because of the hospital built upon its banks, by General Gates.

Hot Springs; county in Arkansas, so named for the famous springs formerly within its limits.

Houghton; county in Michigan, named for Douglas Houghton, formerly State geologist.

Houlton; town in Aroostook County, Maine, named for an early settler, Joseph Houlton.

Hounsfield; town in Jefferson County, New York, named for Ezra Hounsfield, early proprietor.

Housatonic; river of Massachusetts and Connecticut. From the Indian words wussi, "beyond," and adene, "mountain," meaning "beyond the mountains." According to other authorities from the Indian words wassa, "proud," aton, "stream," and ick, from azhubic, meaning "rocks," the wdiole meaning "proud river flowing through the rocks."

Housatonic; village in Berkshire County, Massachusetts, named from the river.

Houseville; village in Lewis County, New York, named for its founder, Eleazer House.

Houston; this name is borne by many places in the United States, generally given in honor of Gen. Samuel Houston, among them being counties in Minnesota, Tennessee, and Texas; city in Chickasaw County, Mississippi, and the city in Texas County, Missouri; named for Gen. Samuel Houston.

Houston; village in Kent County, Delaware, named for John W. Houston.

Houstonia; village in Pettis County, Missouri, named for Gen. Samuel Houston.

Houstoun; county in Georgia, named for John Houstoun, an early governor.

Houtzdale; borough in Clearfield County, Pennsylvania, named for Dr. Houtz, who owned the land upon which the town is built.

Hovenweep; creek in Mineral County, Colorado. An Indian word meaning "deserted valley."

Howard; county in Arkansas, named for James Howard, State senator.

Howard; counties in Indiana and Iowa, named for Gen. T. A. Howard, of Indiana.

Howard; city in Elk County, Kansas, named for Gen. O. O. Howard.

Howard; county in Maryland, named for Gen. John Eager Howard, of Revolutionary fame.

Howard; county in Missouri, named for Gen. Benjamin Howard, an early governor.

Howard; county in Texas, named for Volney Howard, United States Congressman.

Howe; creek in Humboldt County, California, named for an early settler.

Howell; town in Vanderburg County, Indiana, named for Capt. Lee Howell, local railroad man.

Howell; county in Missouri, named for an early settler.

Howell; town in Monmouth County, New Jersey, probably named for Richard Howell, an early governor.

Howell; town in Marion County, Oregon, named for an early settler.

Hoxie; city in Sheridan County, Kansas, named for H. M. Hoxie, general manager of the Missouri Pacific Railroad.

Hoyt; mount in Wyoming, named for Hon. John W. Hoyt, formerly governor of Wyoming.

Hubbard; county in Minnesota, named for Lucius P. Hubbard, former governor.

Hubbard; village in Dakota County, Nebraska, named for Judge A. W. Hubbard.

Hubbardston; town in Worcester County, Massachusetts; Hubbardton; town in Rutland County, Vermont. Named for Thomas Hubbard of Boston, one of its charter citizens.

Hudson; town in Middlesex County, Massachusetts, named for the Hon. Charles Hudson.

Hudson; county in New Jersey, river, and city in Columbia County, New York, named for Henry Hudson, the discoverer.

Hudson; village in Summit County, Ohio, named for David Hudson, an early settler.

Huerfano; county, town, river, and canyon in Colorado, named from an isolated mountain in the river valley. A Spanish word, meaning "orphan."

Hughes; county in South Dakota, named in honor of Alexander Hughes, legislator, 1873.

Hughesville; town in Gilpin County, Colorado, named for Patrick Hughes, upon whose ranch the town is located.

Hugoton; city in Stevens County, Kansas, named for Victor Hugo, "ton" being added to prevent conflict with Hugo, Colorado.

Hulberton; village in Orleans County, New York, named for Hulbert, a former resident.

Hull; town in Sioux County, Iowa, named for John Hull.

Hull; town in Plymouth County, Massachusetts, named for the town in England.

Humboldt; name of a number of places in the United States, named for the geographer, Baron Alexander von Humboldt, among them being the counties in California and Iowa, city in Allen County, Kansas, and county and river in Nevada.

Hummelstown; borough in Dauphin County, Pennsylvania, named for Frederick Hummel, by whom it was laid out.

Humphrey; peak of the San Francisco Mountains in Arizona, and mount in Yellowstone Park, named for Gen. A. A. Humphreys, Chief of Engineers, United States Army.

Humphrey; town in Cattaraugus County, New York, named for Charles Humphrey, speaker of the assembly when the town was founded.

Humphreys; county in Tennessee, named for Parry W. Humphreys.

Humphreysville; village in New Haven County, Connecticut, named for the Hon. David Humphreys.

Humptulips; river in Chehalis County, Washington. An Indian word, meaning "chilly region."

Hunnewell; city in Sumner County, Kansas, and city in Shelby County, Missouri, named for H. H. Hunnewell, of Boston.

Hunniwell; point at the mouth of the Kennebec River, Maine, named for a former resident of the vicinity.

Hunt; county in Texas, named for Memucan Hunt, one-time minister from the Republic of Texas Hunter; town in Greene County, New York, named for John Hunter, a proprietor.

Hunterdon; county in New Jersey, named for Governor Robert Hunter, of New York.

Huntersville; town in Mecklenburg County, North Carolina, named for a prominent citizen.

Huntersville; village in Pocahontas County, West Virginia, so called because the site was originally occupied by hunters' cabins.

Huntingdon; county in Pennsylvania, named for a town in the same State, which, in turn, was named for Selena, Countess of Huntingdon.

Huntingdon; town in Carroll County, Tennessee, named for Memucan Hunt, whose heirs donated the land for its site.

Huntington; county in Indiana, named for Samuel Huntington, of Connecticut, one of the signers of the Declaration of Independence.

Huntington; town in Hampshire County, Massachusetts, named for Charles P. Huntington, of Northampton.

Huntington; town in Baker County, Oregon, named for J. B. Huntington, upon whose ranch the town was built.

Huntington; city in Cabell County, West Virginia, named for C. P. Huntington, of the Chesapeake and Ohio Railway.

Huntsville; town in Madison County, Alabama, named for John Hunt, its first settler.

Huntsville; city in Randolph County, Missouri, named for David Hunt, of Kentucky, first settler.

Hurley; town in Ulster County, New York, named for the Lovelace family, who were Barons Hurley, of Ireland.

Huron; one of the Great Lakes of North America. Opinions differ as to the classification of the name. whether French or Indian, and to its meaning. According to some authorities it is a corruption of the name " Hure," given a tribe of Indians by the French, the word meaning " head of a wild boar," applicable on account of their unkempt appearance; another authority says it is derived from the Indian word, Onkwe honwe, "true man;" by others to have been corrupted by the French from the Indian Irri ronon, "cat tribe."

Huron; city in Atchison County, Kansas, and county in Michigan, named for the Huron Indians.

Huron; county and village in Erie County, Ohio, named for the lake.

Hustisford; village in Dodge County, Wisconsin, named for John Hustis, an early settler.

Hutchinson; city in Reno County, Kansas, named for C. C. Hutchinson, its founder.

Hutchinson; village in McLeod County, Minnesota, named for the Hutchinson brothers, its founders.

Hutchinson; county in South Dakota, named for John Hutchinson, first Territorial secretary.

Hutchinson; county in Texas, named for Anderson Hutchinson, prominent citizen in days of the Republic.

Hyde; county in North Carolina, named for Edward Hyde, governor during colonial days.

Hyde; county in South Dakota, named for James Hyde. member of the legislature in 1873.

Hyde Park; town in Dutchess County, New York, named for Hyde Park, London.

Hyde Park; town in Lamoille County, Vermont, named for Jedediah Hyde, an early settler.

Hydesville; town in Humboldt County, California, named for an early settler.

Hyndman; peak in Idaho, named for an old resident of the vicinity.

Iberia; parish in Louisiana. derives its name from the ancient name of Spain.

Iberville; parish in Louisiana. named for Pierre le Moyne lbervilie, a Canadian naval commander who built the first fort on the Mississippi.

Icy; cape in Alaska. so named because of the ice along the coast at this point.

Idaho; State of the United States and county in same State. An Indian word, meaning "gem of the mountains."

Ichoconnaugh; creek in Georgia. An Indian word, meaning "deer trap."

Iliff; town in Logan County, Colorado, named for John W. Iliff, one of Colorado's cattle kings, near whose ranch the town was located.

Ilion; village in Herkimer County, New York, named from the place mentioned in Homer's poem.

Illinois; State of the United States. One authority gives it as a combination of the Indian word Illini, meaning " men," and the French suffix ois, meaning " tribe," "band of men."

Illyria; village in Fayette County, Iowa, named for the ancient Kingdom of Austria.

Imlay City; village in Lapeer County, Michigan, named for Judge Imlay, of New York, who owned a mill in the township.

Independence; name borne by 27 places in the United States, given them in commemoration of the Declaration of Independence, among them being a county, and the city in Montgomery County, Kansas.

Indiana; State of the United States, so named because a company of traders bought this tract of land lying along the Ohio from the Indians.

Indiana; county in Pennsylvania, named from the general appellation of the Indian tribes.

Indian Cattle; village in Herkimer County, New York, named from the Indian fort, part of a chain of defenses which guarded the approach to Canada.

Industry; town in Franklin County, Maine, so named on account of the industrious character of the people.

Ingalls; town in Payne County, Oklahoma, named for the Senator from Kansas.

Ingham; county in Michigan, named for Samuel D. Ingham, Secretary of the Treasury under Jackson.

Ingold; village in Sampson County, North Carolina, named for a resident family.

Inkpa; tributary of the Minnesota River. An Indian word, Eenk-pa, or Piah, meaning "end" or "point."

Inman; city in McPherson County, Kansas, named for Maj. Henry Inman.

Inman; station in Holt County, Nebraska, named for W. H. Inman, an early settler.

Inman; town in Spartanburg County, South Carolina, named for a resident family.

Interlaken; city in Putnam County, Honda, so named on account of the surrounding lakes. From Interlachen, meaning "among the lakes."

Inverness; township in Cheboygan County, Michigan, named for the city in Scotland.

Inverury; village in Sevier County, Utah, named for the town in Scotland.

Inyankara; town in Crook County, Wyoming. From an Indian word, Isanyati, meaning "rocky hills."

Iola; city in Allen County, Kansas, named for the wife of J. F. Col born.

Ionia; name transferred from Greece to many places in the United States, among them being the county in Michigan.

Iosco; county in Michigan. An Indian word, meaning "water of light," or "shining water."

Iowa; State of the United States, county in that State, and a county in Wisconsin. The name is derived from an Indian word, meaning "sleepy ones," or "the drowsy ones."

Iowa Falls; city in Hardin County, Iowa, named for the falls in the river.

Ipswich; town in Essex County, Massachusetts, named for the capital of Suffolk, England.

Ira; town in Rutland County, Vermont; Irasburg; town in Orleans County, Vermont. Probably named for Ira Allen, a grantee.

Iredell; county in North Carolina, named for James Iredell, judge of the Supreme Court.

Irion; county in Texas, named for an early settler.

Iron; counties in Michigan, Missouri, Utah, and Wisconsin, so named on account of the great amount of this ore found within their limits.

Irondequoit; town in Monroe County, New York. An Indian word, which, according to some authorities, means "the place where the waves gasp and die," and according to others, "a bay."

Iroquois, county in Illinois, river in Indiana, town in Kingsbury County, South Dakota. An Indian word, meaning "heart people," or "people of God," or from the Indian Hiro, "I have said," and koue, a vocable, which expressed joy or sorrow, according to the rapidity with which it is pronounced; the name of a tribe.

Irvine; town in Estill County, Kentucky, named for Col. William Irvine.

Irving; city in Marshall County, Kansas; Irvington; town in Essex County, New Jersey, and village in Westchester County New York. Named for Washington Irving.

Irwin; village in Gunnison County, Colorado, named for Richard Irwin, a noted mining man.

Irwin; county in Georgia; Irwinton; town in Wilkinson County, Georgia. Named for Gen. Jared Irwin, former governor of the State.

Isa; lake in Yellowstone Park, named for Miss Isabel Jelke, of Cincinnati.

Isaac; branch of St. Jones Creek, Delaware, named for Isaac Webb, an early settler.

Isabella; county in Michigan, named for the daughter of John Hurst, who was the first white child born within its limits.

Isanti; county in Minnesota, named from the Indian tribe who were dwellers at Isantamde, "knife lake." Said by Haines to have been the original name of the Santees.

Ishawooa; town in Bighorn County, Wyoming. An Indian word, meaning "much cascara."

Island; county in Washington, so named because it is composed entirely of islands.

Island Tails; town in Aroostook County, Maine, so named on account of an island which is midway of the stream at the verge of the falls.

Island Mine; village on Isle Royale, Michigan, so named because of a copper mine there.

Island Pond; village in Essex County, Vermont, so named because of an island in the center of a little lake between the spurs of the mountains.

Isle au Chene; island in Lake Superior, Wisconsin; one of the Apostle Islands. French phrase, meaning "island of the oak."

Isle au Haut; island at the entrance to Penobscot Bay, Maine. composed of high, steep cliffs. A French phrase, meaning "island of the height."

Isle au Haut; town in Hancock County, Maine, named from the island.

Isle Lamotte; town in Grand Isle County, Vermont, named for a French officer, La Motte.

Isle of Wight; county in Virginia named for the island in the English Channel.

Islesboro; township in Waldo County, Maine, so named because it consists of a long, narrow island in Penobscot Bay; Islington; village in Norfolk County, Massachusetts, named for the parish in England.

Islip; town in Suffolk County, New York, named for a parish in England.

Israels; stream in Coos County, New Hampshire, named for a noted trapper, Israel Glines.

Issaquena; county in Mississippi. An Indian word meaning "deer river."

Istachatta; town in Hernando County, Florida. An Indian word meaning "man snake."

Italian; mountain peak in Colorado, so named because at a distance it displays the national colors of Italy—red, white, and green.

Itasca; village in Dupage County, Illinois, named for the Minnesota lake.

Itasca; county and lake in Minnesota, into which flows the headwaters of the Mississippi, and named on this account Itasca, from the two Latin words Veritas caput, "the true head."

Itawamba; county in Mississippi, said to have been named for the daughter of a Chickasaw Indian chief.

Ithaca; city of Tompkins County, New York, and village in Gratiot County, Michigan, named for one of the Ionian Islands, supposed to be the one celebrated in the Homeric poems as the Kingdom of Ulysses.

Ivanhoe; many places in the United States have been named for Scott's novel, among them being a town in Lake County, Illinois.

Izard; county in Arkansas, named for George Izard, former governor.

Izuza; tributary of the Minnesota River. An Indian word, meaning "white stone."

Jacinto; village in Alcorn County, Mississippi. A Spanish word, meaning "hyacinth."

Jack; county and town in Texas, named for William Houston and Patrick Jack, brothers, who were early settlers and prominent citizens in the days of the Republic.

Jackson; many places in the United States bear the name of Andrew Jackson, among them being counties in Arkansas, Florida, Illinois, Indiana, Iowa, Kansas, Kentucky; parish in Louisiana; counties in Michigan, Mississippi, and Missouri; town in Carroll County, New Hampshire; city in Jackson County, Ohio; counties in Tennessee, Texas, West Virginia, and Wisconsin; named for Gen. Andrew Jackson.

Jackson; mountain in the Sawatch Range in Colorado, named for the photographer, W. H. Jackson.

Jackson; county in Georgia, named for Gen. James Jackson, United States Senator from that State.

Jackson; town in Waldo County, Maine, named for Henry Jackson, a contemporary of Colonel Knox in the Revolution.

Jackson; village in Jackson County, Minnesota, said to have been named for Henry Jackson, a proprietor.

Jackson; lake in Wyoming, named for David Jackson, a noted mountaineer.

Jacksonville; city in Morgan County, Illinois; town in Randolph County, Missouri, and village in Onslow County, North Carolina, named for Gen. Andrew Jackson.

Jacoby; creek in Humboldt County, California, named for an early settler.

Jaffray; town in Cheshire County, New Hampshire, and southern point of entrance to Portsmouth Harbor, named for George Jaffray, one of the original proprietors, and later a chief justice of the State.

Jamaica; town in Queens County, New York. An Indian word, meaning, according to some authorities, "a country abounding in springs;" according to others, " land of water and wood." James; peak in Colorado, named for the botanist.

James; river in Virginia, named for James I of England.

Jamesburg; borough in Middlesex County, New Jersey, named for a resident family.

James City; county in Virginia, named for the first English settlement, Jamestown.

Jamestown; town in Boone County, Indiana, named for James Mattock, its founder.

Jamestown; city in Cloud County, Kansas, named for James P. Pomeroy, of the Central Branch Union Pacific Railroad.

Jamestown; city in Chautauqua County, New York, named for James Pendergast, an early settler.

Jamestown; town in Newport County, Rhode Island, named for the Duke of York and Albany, later James II. of England.

Jamestown; town in James City County, Virginia, named for King James I, and the first English settlement in America.

Jamesville; village in Onondaga County, New York, named for James De Witt.

Jamesville; town in Martin County, North Carolina, named for a prominent citizen.

Janesville; town in Lassen County, California, and city in Rock County, Wisconsin, named for Henry F. Janes.

Janesville; town in Bremer County, Iowa, named for the wife of John T. Barrick, its founder.

Jara; creek in Colorado. A Spanish word, literally "rock rose," but in connection with the creek meaning "willow brush."

Jarrolds; village in West Virginia, named for a resident family.

Jasonville; village in Greene County, Indiana, named for Jason Rogers, one of its founders.

Jasper; many counties, towns, and villages in the United States bear the name of Sergeant Jasper, of Fort Moultrie (S. C.) fame, who was killed in the siege of Savannah, among these being counties in Georgia, Illinois, Indiana, Iowa, Mississippi, Missouri, Texas, and towns in Pickens County, Georgia, and Steuben County, New York.

Java; town in Wyoming County, New York, named for the island in the Malay Archipelago.

Jay; county in Indiana; towns in Franklin County, Maine; Essex County, New York, and Orleans County, Vermont, named for Hon. John Jay, an eminent statesman, proprietor, and early governor of New York.

Jeddo; village in Orleans County, New York, and borough in Luzerne County, Pennsylvania, named for the capital of Japan, the old name of Tokyo.

Jeff Davis; county in Texas, named for Jefferson Davis.

Jefferson; many places in the United States have been named for Thomas Jefferson, third President, among them being counties in Arkansas, Colorado, Georgia, Illinois, Indiana, Iowa, Kansas, Kentucky, Mississippi, Missouri, Montana, New York, Pennsylvania, Tennessee, Washington, West Virginia, and Wisconsin, a parish in Louisiana, town in Coos County, New Hampshire, mount in Oregon, and a peak in the White Mountains of New Hampshire.

Jefferson; town in Ashe County, North Carolina, named for a prominent citizen.

Jefferson; county in Texas, named for Jefferson Beaumont, an early settler and prominent citizen.

Jekyl; island in Georgia, named for Sir Joseph Jekyl.

Jenkintown; borough in Montgomery County, Pennsylvania, named for William Jenkins, early settler.

Jennings; county in Indiana, named for Jonathan Jennings, first governor of the State.

Jenny; lake in Yellowstone Park, named for the Shoshone wife of Richard Leigh.

Jenny Lind; town in Calaveras County, California, named for the Swedish songstress.

Jerauld; county in South Dakota, named for H. J. Jerauld, legislator.

Jericho; town in Chittenden County, Vermont, named for the ancient city in Palestine.

Jerome; town in Bladen County, North Carolina, named for a prominent citizen.

Jeromeville; village in Ashland County, Ohio, named for John Baptiste Jerome, a French trader.

Jersey; county in Illinois, named from the State of New Jersey.

Jersey City; city in Hudson County, New Jersey, originally called the "city of Jersey," named from one of the channel islands of England.

Jerseyville; city in Jersey County, Illinois, named from the State of New Jersey.

Jerusalem; town in Yates County, New York, named from the city of Palestine.

Jessamine; county and creek in Kentucky, named for Jessamine Douglass, the daughter of an early settler.

Jessup; village in Antelope County, Nebraska, named for ex-Governor Jessup, of Iowa.

Jesup; town in Buchanan County, Iowa, named for Morris K. Jesup, of New York.

Jetmore; city in Hodgeman County, Kansas, named for Col. A. B. Jetmore, of Topeka.

Jewell; county and city in Kansas, named for Lieut. Col. Lewis R. Jewell, Sixth Kansas Cavalry.

Jewett; town in Greene County, New York, named for Freeborn G. Jewett, justice of the supreme court.

Jewett; village in Harrison County, Ohio, named for T. M. Jewett, former president of the Pittsburg, Cincinnati and St. Louis Railroad.

Jo Daviess; county in Illinois, named for Col. Joseph Hamilton Daviess, of Kentucky.

Joe Gee; hill in Orange County, New York, named for the last Indian who had his cabin on the hill.

Joes; brook near Walden, Vermont, named for Captain Joe, a friendly Indian of the St. Francis tribe.

John Day; river in Oregon, and town in Grant County of the same State, named for a member of Hunt's Astoria overland expedition.

Johns; creek in Humboldt County, California, named for an early settler.

Johnsburg; town in Warren County, New York, named for John Thurman, an early settler.

Johnson; county in Arkansas, named for Judge Benjamin Johnson.

Johnson; county in Georgia, named for Governor H. V. Johnson.

Johnson; county in Indiana, named for John Johnson, judge of the supreme court of the State.

Johnson; counties in Illinois, Kentucky, Missouri, and Nebraska, named for Richard Johnson, Vice-President of the United States.

Johnson; county in Iowa, named for Andrew Johnson.

Johnson; county in Kansas, named for Rev. Thomas Johnson, missionary to the Shawnees.

Johnson; city in Stanton County, Kansas. named for Col. Alexander S. Johnson, of Topeka.

Johnson; village in Nemaha County, Nebraska, named for Julius A. Johnson. large landowner.

Johnson; county in Tennessee, named for Samuel Johnson.

Johnson; county in Texas, named for M. G. Johnson, member of Texas congress.

Johnson; town in Lamoille County, Vermont, named for the proprietor, William S. Johnson.

Johnsons; creek in New York, named for Sir William Johnson, who encamped on its banks when on his way to Fort Niagara.

Johnsonville; town in Humphreys County, Tennessee, named for Andrew Johnson.

Johnston; town in Rhode Island, named for Augustus J. Johnston, attorney-general of the colony.

Johnston; pass in Utah, named for Gen. A. S. Johnston.

Johnstons; county in North Carolina, named for Gabriel Johnston, governor.

Johnstown; city in Fulton County, New York, named for its founder, Sir William Johnson.

Johnstown; city and borough in Cambria County, Pennsylvania, named for an early settler, Joseph Jahns or Yahns.

Joliet; city in Will County, Illinois, named for Louis Joliet, a French trader.

Jones; county in Georgia, named for James Jones, member of Congress from that State.

Jones; county in Iowa, named for George W. Jones, United States Senator from that State.

Jones; county in Mississippi, named for Commodore John Paul Jones.

Jones; county in North Carolina, named for William Jones, a North Carolina statesman.

Jones; county in Texas, named for Anson Jones, one of the first Senators in the United States Congress from Texas.

Jones; creek in Yellowstone Park, named for Col. W. A. Jones, United States Army, its first explorer.

Jonesboro; town in Washington County, Maine, named for John C. Jones, one of the original proprietors.

Jonesboro; town in Washington County, Tennessee, named for William Jones, a North Carolinian statesman.

Jonesport; town in Washington County, Maine, named for John C. Jones, one of the original proprietors.

Jonesville; town in Bartholomew County, Indiana, named for Benjamin Jones, its founder.

Jonesville; town in Union County, South Carolina, named for a resident family.

Joplin; city in Jasper County, Missouri, named from Joplin Creek, which was named for Rev. H. G. Joplin, who lived on its banks.

Joppa; name which is borne by 11 places in the United States, and which was transferred from the ancient city in Palestine.

Jordan; this name, either alone or with suffixes, is borne by 27 places in the United States, and was transferred from the river of Palestine. Among these places are villages in New London County, Connecticut, Onondaga County, New York. and a stream in Utah.

Joseph; peak in Yellowstone Park, named for the famous Nez Perce, Chief Joseph.

Josephine; county in Oregon, named for Josephine Rollins, the daughter of the discoverer of the first gold found in that county.

Juab; county in Utah, named for a friendly Indian of the region.

Juan de Fuca; strait separating Washington from Vancouver Island, named for a Greek navigator in the Spanish service, who explored it.

Judith; river in Montana, named for Miss Hancock, of Fincastle, Virginia.

Judsonia; town in White County, Arkansas, named for Rev. Adoniram Judson, a Baptist missionary.

Juhelville; village in Jefferson County, New York, named for Madame Juhel, relative of the Le Ray family.

Julesburg; town in Sedgwick County, Colorado, said to be named for Jules Benard, a frontiersman.

Julien; township in Dubuque County, Iowa, named for Julien Dubuque, the French trader for whom the county was named.

Jump-off-Joe; stream in southern Oregon, so named because a trapper, Joe McLoughlin, fell from the bluff of the stream and was badly injured.

Junction; city in Geary County, Kansas, so named because it is near the junction of the Republican and Smoky Hill rivers.

Junction; borough in Hunterdon County, New Jersey, so named because it is situated at the junction of two railroads.

Junction; butte in Yellowstone Park, so named because it is at the junction of the Yellowstone and Lamar rivers.

Juneau; county and city in Dodge County, Wisconsin, named for the founder of Milwaukee.

Juniata; county, river, borough, and a township in Perry County, Pennsylvania; Juniataville; village in Fayette County, Pennsylvania. From Indian word which means "they stay long," or, according to another derivation, "beyond the great bend."

Junius; town in Seneca County, New York, named by the State land board for Junius, of the classics.

K

Kahoka; city in Clark County, Missouri. See Cahokia.

Kaibab; plateau in Arizona. An Indian word meaning "mountain lying down."

Kalama; town in Cowlitz County, Washington, probably named from the Indian, Okala kalama, meaning "a goose."

Kalamazoo; city. river, and county in Michigan. According to one authority derived from the Indian word Negikanamazo, meaning "otter tail;" "beautiful water" and "boiling water" are other versions.

Kalispel; city in Flathead County, Montana, named for an Indian tribe.

Kamas; town in Summit County, Utah. The Indian name for root, which is used as food by the Indians of the Pacific coast.

Kamrar; town in Hamilton County, Iowa, named for Senator Kamrar.

Kanab; town, creek, and plateau in Kane County, Utah. Indian word, meaning "willow."

Kanabec; county in Minnesota. An Indian word, meaning "snake."

Kanawha; river in North Carolina, river and county in West Virginia. Derived from an Indian word, meaning "river of the woods."

Kandiyohi; town and county in Minnesota. From the Indian kandi, "buffalo flesh," and lyohl, "to reach me."

Kane; county in Illinois, named for Elias Kent Kane.

Kane; county in Utah; Kaneville; town in Kane County, Illinois. Named for Gen. Thomas L. Kane, of Philadelphia.

Kankakee; county, city, and river in Illinois. An Indian word, meaning, according to different authorities, "wolf land river," "raven," or "among the meadows."

Kanopolis; city in Elsworth County, Kansas. The name is a combination of Kansas and Centropolis, Ellsworth being the central county of the State.

Kansas; State, city, and river in the same State, and city in Missouri, named for an Indian tribe of the Sioux family, or from kanosas, "willow."

Kaolin; village in Chester County, Pennsylvania, so named because of the large deposits of kaolin.

Karnes; county in Texas, named for Henry Karnes, an early settler and Indian fighter.

Karsaootuk; stream in northern Maine. An Indian word, meaning "black river," or "pine stream."

Kaska; village in Schuylkill County, Pennsylvania. An Indian word, meaning "wonderful land river."

Kaskaskia; town in Randolph County, Illinois, and river in the same State. An Indian word, meaning "bad hearts," the name of a tribe of Illinois Indians.

Kasota; village in Lesueur County, Minnesota. An Indian word, meaning "cleared," "cleared off," or "the sky clear from clouds."

Kasson; village in Dodge County, Minnesota. An Indian word, meaning "to use all up."

Katahdin; mountain in Maine. An Indian word, meaning, according to different authorities, "highest land," "big mountain," "greatest or chief mountain."

Katchenaha; lake in Florida. An Indian word, meaning "turkey lake."

Katonah; village in Westchester County, New York, named for an Indian chief.

Kaufman; city and county in Texas, named for David S. Kaufman, former Congressman.

Kaukauna; city in Outagamie County, Wisconsin. An Indian word, which, according to different authorities, means "a portage," "a long portage," "the place where pickerel are caught," "place of pike."

Kay; county in Oklahoma, formerly written "K," a letter of the alphabet.

Kearney; county in Nebraska, city in Buffalo County, same State, and town in Hudson County, New Jersey, named for (Jen. Philip Kearny.

Kearney; city in Clay County, Missouri, named for Gen. Stephen W. Kearny.

Kearny; county in Kansas, named for Gen. Philip Kearny.

Kearsarge; mountain in New Hampshire. Indian word, meaning "pine or peaked mountain," or koowas, "pointed mountain," "the highest place;" another authority gives, "proud or selfish."

Keene; city in Cheshire County, New Hampshire, named for Sir Benjamin Keene.

Keeseville; village in Essex County, New York, named for its founder, Richard Keese.

Keith; county in Nebraska, named for John Keith, of North Platte, Nebraska.

Kelleys Island; township and village in Erie County, Ohio, named from an island in Lake Erie, which was owned by Datus and Irad Kelly.

Kellogg; town in Jasper County, Iowa, named for an early settler.

Kemper; county in Mississippi, named for Col. Reuben Kemper, an American soldier in the Florida and Mexican wars.

Kemper City; town in Victoria County, Texas, named for Captain Kemper.

Kenansville; town in Duplin County, North Carolina, named for Hon. James Kenan, member of Congress.

Kendall; county in Illinois and town in Orleans County, New York, named for Hon. Amos Kendall, Postmaster-General United States.

Kendall; county in Texas, named for George W. Kendall, prominent citizen.

Kenduskeag; town and river in Penobscot County, Maine. An Indian word meaning "little eel river," or "place for taking salmon."

Kenesaw; town in Cobb County, Georgia, named for an Indian chief.

Kenesaw; village in Adams County, Nehraska, named for Kenesaw Mountain.

Kenly; town in Johnston County, North Carolina, named for a prominent railroad official.

Kennard; town in Washington County, Nebraska, named for Hon. Thomas P. Kennard, secretary of state, 1867.

Kennebec; county and river in Maine, named for powerful Indian chief of the tribe of Canabas.

Kennebunk; town in York County, Maine; Kennebunk Port; town in York County, Maine. Named for the Indian, meaning "long water place," or, "where he thanked him."

Kenner; city in Jefferson County, Louisiana, named for Duncan F. Kenner, an eminent lawyer of that State.

Kennett Square; borough in Chester County, Pennsylvania, named from the village of Kennett, Wiltshire, England.

Kenosha; city and county in Wisconsin. An Indian word, meaning "fish," "pickerel," "pike."

Kenoza; lake in Haverhill, Massachusetts. An Indian word, meaning "pickerel."

Kensington; town in Rockingham County, New Hampshire, named from the parish in England.

Kent; counties in Delaware, Maryland, and Rhode Island, named from the county of Kent in England.

Kent; county in Michigan, named for Chancellor Kent of New York.

Kent; town in Putnam County, New York, named for a family of early settlers.

Kent; county in Texas, named for R. Kent, an early settler.

Kenton; county in Kentucky and city in Hardin County, Ohio, named for Gen. Simon Kenton, a distinguished pioneer "of Kentucky.

Kentucky; state of the Union. An Indian word, meaning "dark and bloody ground," or "the prairies."

Kentwood; town in Tangipahoa Parish, Louisiana, named for a local merchant, Amacker Kent.

Keokuk; city and county in Iowa, named for an Indian chief, the word meaning "running, or watchful fox."

Keosauqua; town in Van Buren county, Iowa. An Indian word, meaning "the great bend," so named for a bend in the Des Moines River.

Keota; town in Keokuk County, Iowa. An Indian word, meaning either "gone to visit" or "the fire is gone out."

Kern; county, city, and river in California, named for three brothers.

Kernersville; town in Forsyth County, North Carolina, named for a prominent citizen.

Kerr; county and town in Texas, named for James Kerr, prominent early settler.

Kershaw; county and town in Lancaster County, South Carolina, named for the Kershaw family, early settlers.

Keshena; town in Shawano County, Wisconsin, named for an Indian chief, the word meaning "swift flying."

Ketten Chow; valley in California. An Indian word meaning "cammas valley."

Kewaskum; village in Washington, named for an old Indian chief, the word meaning "returning track."

Kewaunee; county, city, and river in Wisconsin. An Indian word, meaning "prairie hen or wild duck," or according to another authority, "to go round."

Keweenaw; county in Michigan; the vicinity so named by the Indians because of the point of land which projects into Lake Superior; the word meaning "canoe carried back," "carrying place," hence a portage.

Keyapaha; county and river in Nebraska. An Indian word, meaning "turtle hills."

Keyser; town in Moore, County, North Carolina, named for a prominent citizen.

Keyser; town in Mineral County, West Virginia, named for a prominent man who was an officer of the Baltimore and Ohio Railroad at one time.

Keystone; towns in Wells County, Indiana, and Dickey County, North Dakota, named by its Pennsylvania settlers for their State, the Keystone State.

Keytesville; city in Chariton County, Missouri. named for Rev. Keyte, an early settler.

Key West; city in Monroe County, Florida. A corruption of Cayo Hueso, a Spanish word, meaning "a bone reef or island;" the place so named because of the number of bones found upon the reef.

Kezar; village in Gunnison County, Colorado, named for Gardner H. Kezar.

Kezar; ponds in Oxford County, Maine, named for an old hunter.

Kickapoo; town, in Peoria County, Illinois, Anderson County, Texas, and Leavenworth County, Kansas. An Indian word, meaning "easily navigable," or according to another authority, "ghost of an otter."

Kidder; village in Caldwell County, Missouri, named from the Kidder Land Company, of Boston, who laid out the town.

Kidder; county in North Dakota, named for Hon. Jefferson P. Kidder, prominent in the State's political affairs.

Kidron; town in Coweta County, Georgia, named for the brook near Jerusalem.

Kilbourn City; village in Columbia County, Wisconsin, named for Byron Kilbourn, a pioneer.

Kilbuck; town in Allegheny County, Pennsylvania, named for a chief of the Delaware Indians.

Kildare; township in Juneau County, Wisconsin, named for the Irish town.

Kilkenny; village in Lesueur County, Minnesota, named for the town in Ireland.

Killbuck; town in Wayne County. Ohio, named for a chief of the Delaware Indians.

Killing-worth; town in Middlesex County, Connecticut, intended by its Scotch settlers to be named Kenilworth, but, by the mistake of the clerk of the court, named as above.

Kilmarnock; town in Lancaster County, Virginia, named for the town in Scotland.

Kimball; county in Nebraska, named for John P. Kimball.

Kimble; county in Texas, named for George C. Kimble, an early settler.

Kimbolton; village in Guernsey County, Ohio, named from the town in England.

Kincaid; city in Anderson County, Kansas, named for Robert Kincaid, of Mound City.

Kinderhook; town in Columbia County, Sew York; anglicized form of Kinder Hoeck, the name given the place by Henry Hudson, meaning "children's point," on account of the many Indian children he saw there.

Kineo; mountain in Maine. An Indian word, meaning "high bluff."

King", county in Texas, named for William King, a prominent citizen.

King; county in Washington, named for William Rufus King, former vice-president of the United States.

King and Queen; county in Virginia, named for William and Mary, king and queen of England.

Kingfisher; county in Oklahoma; so named on account of the great number of birds of this species which live on the banks of Kingfisher Creek within the county.

King George; county in Virginia, named for King George, of England.

Kingman; city in Kingman County, Kansas, named for Chief Justice S. A. Kingman.

Kingman; town in Penobscot County, Maine, named for R. S. Kingman.

Kingman; pass in Yellowstone Park, named for Lieut. D. C. Kingman, United States Army.

Kings; peak in Humboldt County, California, named for Captain King.

Kings; county in New York, named for the Stuart dynasty.

Kingsbury; plantation in Piscataquis County, Maine, named for Hon. Sanford Kingsbury, of Gardiner.

Kingsbury; county in South Dakota, named for C. W. Kingsbury, early legislator.

Kingsley; village in Grand Traverse County, Michigan, named for Judson Kingsley, who gave the site for the railway depot.

Kingston; town in Barton County, Georgia, named for J. P. King, of Augusta.

Kingston; town in Plymouth County, Massachusetts, named for Evelyn Pierrepont, first Duke of Kingston.

Kingston; village in Tuscola County, Michigan, named for two families, King and Kingsbury.

Kingston; city in Caldwell County, Missouri, named for an early governor, Austin A. King.

Kingstree; town in Williamsburg County, South Carolina; so named because of the presence of a large pine tree on the bank of Black River.

Kingsville; village in Johnson County, Missouri, named for Gen. William M. King, who located it.

King "William; county in Virginia, named for William HI of England.

Kinmans; pond in Humboldt County, California, named for Seth Kinman, an early settler.

Kinney county in Texas. named for an early settler, H. I. Kinney.

Kinsale; village in Westmoreland County, Virginia, named from a town in Ireland.

Kinsey; creek in Humboldt County, California, named for an early settler.

Kinsley; city in Edwards County, Kansas, named for W. E. W. Kinsley, of Boston, Massachusetts.

Kinston; town in Lenoir County, North Carolina, named for King George III.

Kinzua; village in Warren County, Pennsylvania, named from the river, which doubtless received this Indian name, signifying "they gobble," on account of the wild turkeys which frequent its banks.

Kiowa; counties in Colorado and Kansas, and city in Barber County, Kansas. An Indian word, meaning "great medicine."

Kirkland; town in Oneida County, New York, named for Rev. Samuel Kirkland.

Kirklin; town in Clinton County, Indiana, named for Nathan Kirk, its founder.

Kirklin; town in Clinton County, New York, named for Martin Kirk, proprietor.

Kirksville; city in Adair County, Missouri, named for Jesse Kirk.

Kirkwood; village in Newcastle County, Delaware, and township in Belmont County, Ohio, named for Maj. Kobert Kirkwood, a Revolutionary officer.

Kirkwood; town in St. Louis County, Missouri, named for the first chief engineer of the Missouri Pacific Railway, which runs through the place.

Kirwin; city in Phillips County, Kansas, named for Col. John Kirwin, of the Regular Army.

Kishacolquillas; creek and village in Mifflin County, Pennsylvania, named for an Indian chief, the meaning said to be "the snakes are already in their dens."

Kishwaukee; river and town in Winnebago County, Illinois. An Indian word, which means "sycamore tree."

Kiskiminitas; township in Armstrong County, Pennsylvania. An Indian word, meaning "make daylight."

Kit Carson; town in Cheyenne County, Colorado, named for the celebrated Rocky Mountain guide.

Kittanning; borough in Armstrong County, Pennsylvania, situated on the site of the Indian village of that name, meaning "greatest river."

Kittrell; town in Vance County, North Carolina, named for a prominent resident.

Kittson; county in Minnesota, named for W. W. Kittson, a prominent resident.

Klamath; river in California, lake and county in Oregon; Klamath Falls; town in Klamath County, Oregon. Named for the Indian tribe.

Klej Grange; town in Worcester County, Maryland, the name formed of a combination of the first letters of the names of the daughters of J. W. Drexel, of New York—Kate, Louise, Emma, and Josephine.

Klickitat; county in Washington, named from a tribe of Indians distinguished for their predatory habits, the name signifying "robber."

Kline; town in Barnwell County, South Carolina, named for a resident.

Kneeland; prairie in Humboldt County, California, named for an early settler.

Knife; river in North Dakota, the original name being couteau, French, meaning "knife."

Knightsville; town in Clay County, Indiana. named for A. W. Knight, its founder.

Knott; county in Kentucky, named for Proctor Knott.

Knowersville; town in Albany County, New York, named for the Knower family.

Knox; many counties in the United States bear this name, among them counties in Illinois, Indiana, Kentucky, Maine, Missouri, Nebraska, Ohio, Tennessee, Texas, and a town in Waldo County, Maine; Knoxville; village in Crawford County, Georgia, and town in Albany County, New York. Named for Gen. Henry Knox, Secretary of War during the Administration of Washington.

Knoxville; town in Franklin County, Mississippi, named by Tennessee emigrants for the town in their own State.

Knoxville; village in Madison County, New York, named for Herman Knox, an early resident.

Knoxville; village in Steuben County, New York, and borough in Allegheny County, Pennsylvania, named for Chief Justice John Knox, of the Supreme Court.

Kokomo; city in Howard County, Indiana. An Indian word, meaning "young grandmother."

Konkapot; two streams in Connecticut, named for Capt. John Konkapot, chief of the Stockbridge Indians.

Kooskia; town in Idaho County, Idaho, named for the Clearwater River, whose Indian name, Kooskootske, means "small water or stream."

Korbel; town in Humboldt County, California, named for an early settler.

Kortright; town in Delaware County, New York, named for Lawrence Kortright, a patentee.

Kosciusko; county in Indiana. and town in Attala County, Mississippi, named for Tadeusz Kosciusko, the Polish patriot.

Koshkonong; lake, creek, and town in Wisconsin, and village in Oregon County, Missouri. An Indian word, meaning "the lake we live on," or, according to Haines, "frightful place," "ugly place."

Kossuth; county in Iowa, plantation in Washington County, Maine, town in Alcorn County, Mississippi, and village in Auglaize County, Ohio, named for Louis Kossuth, the Polish patriot.

Kotzebue; sound of Alaska, named for its discoverer, the Russian navigator, Otto von Kotzebue.

Kreischerville; village in Richmond County, New York, named for B. Kreischer.

Krenitzin; five islands in the Aleutian Archipelago, named for the navigator who first discovered them.

Kubbakwana; lake at the sources of the Mississippi. An Indian word, meaning "rest in the path."

Kutztown; borough in Berks County, Pennsylvania, named for George Kutz, who laid out the town.

Kwichluak; an arm of the Yukon River in Alaska. An Indian word, meaning "crooked river."

L

La Bajada; town in New Mexico, on the road from Santa Fe, which at this point makes a rapid descent. It was named by the Spanish on this account La Bajada, meaning "the descent or landing."

Labonte; creek and town in Converse County, Wyoming, named for La Bonte, an early French trapper.

Laceyville; village in Harrison County, Ohio, named for Maj. John S. Lacey.

Lackawanna; county and river in Pennsylvania. An Indian word, meaning "stream that forks."

Lackawannock; mountain and township in Mercer County, Pennsylvania. named from the Lackawanna River, and with the suffix signifying "at the river fork."

Lackawaxen; township in Pike County. Pennsylvania, at the confluence of the Lackawanna and Delaware, and on this account given the Indian name, which means "where the roads fork."

Laclede; county in Missouri, and town in Linn County, Missouri, named for Pierre Laclede Ligueste, founder of St. Louis.

Laconia; city in Belknap County, New Hampshire, named for a portion of Greece.

La Conner; town in Skagit County, Washington, named for J. J. Connor, an early settler.

Lac qui Parle; county, lake, and river in Minnesota. A French name, meaning "the lake that talks," or "speaking lake."

La Crosse; city and county in Wisconsin. A French name given the town because before its settlement the ground was a favorite place for ball playing with the Indians, the game being called by the French "la crosse."

Lac Traverse; lake in Minnesota. A French word, meaning "cross lake."

Lacygne; city in Linn County, Kansas, named from the river Marais des Cygnes, a French name, meaning "swans' marsh."

Laddonia; city in Audrain County, Missouri, named for Amos Ladd, an early settler.

Ladys Creek; stream in Missouri, named for "William Lady.

La Fave; stream in Perry County, Arkansas, named for a French family, La Feve, who lived at its mouth.

Lafayette; the name of six counties and many townships, towns, and villages in the United States, given them in honor of Marquis de Lafayette, who served in the American Army during the Revolution. Among these are the counties in Arkansas, Florida, Mississippi, Missouri, Wisconsin, parish in Louisiana, town in Yamhill County, Oregon, and mountain in New Hampshire.

Laflin; borough in Luzerne County, Pennsylvania, probably named for Laflin, of the firm of Laflin & Rand, powder manufacturers.

Lafourche; parish in Louisiana, named for the Bayou La Fourche, which intersects it; the name, a French one, meaning "the fork."

L'Agles; stream in Bradley County, Arkansas, named from the French word l'aigle, " eagle." Lagrange; county in Indiana, and towns in Dutchess County, New York, and Lenoir County, North Carolina, named for the home of Lafayette, near Paris.

Lagrue; stream in Arkansas; a French word, meaning "the crane."

Laingsburg; village in Shiawassee County, Michigan, named for Dr. Laing, early settler and founder of the village.

Lairdsville; village in Oneida County, New York, named for Samuel Laird, early settler.

La Junta; town in Otero County, Colorado, at the junction of two railroads; a Spanish name, meaning "junction" or "meeting."

Lake; a name given to 11 counties in the United States because of the presence of such bodies of water either within or near them. These are in the States of California, Colorado, Florida, Illinois, Indiana, Michigan, Minnesota, Ohio, Oregon, South Dakota, and Tennessee.

Lake; city in Columbia County, Florida, so named on account of the presence in the vicinity of 10 lakes.

Lake; city in Calhoun County, Iowa, named for a lake near the town.

Lake Ann; village and lake in Benzie County, Michigan, named for the wife of the first settler, A. P. Wheelock.

Lake Geneva; city in Walworth County, Wisconsin, so named because of the resemblance in its geographical situation to the city in New York.

Lake Helen; village in Volusia County, Florida, named for the daughter of its founder, H. A. De Land.

Lake Linden; village in Houghton County, Michigan, named for an early settler.

Lake Mills; town and village in Jefferson County, Wisconsin, so named because situated on Rock Lake, which is the source of power for saw and grist mills.

Lake Odessa; township and village in Ionia County, Michigan, named from the city in Russia.

Lake of the Woods; lake in Minnesota. Originally named Lac des Bois by the French, "lake of the woods," because of the heavily wooded islands in the lake.

Lakeville; town in Plymouth County, Massachusetts, so named because a great portion of the township is occupied by a chain of lakes.

Lakin; city in Kearny County, Kansas, named for David L. Lakin, of Topeka.

Lamar; county in Alabama, city in Barton County, Missouri, towns in Prowers County, Colorado, and Benton County, Mississippi, and river in Yellowstone Park, named for L. Q. C. Lamar, a former Secretary of the Interior.

Lamar; town in Darlington County, South Carolina, named for a resident family.

Lamar; county in Texas, named for Mirabeau B. Lamar, a prominent Texas statesman.

Lamartino; town in Fond du Lac County, Wisconsin, named for the French historian.

Lamb; county in Texas, named for Lieutenant Lamb.

Lambertville; city in Hunterdon County, New Jersey, named for John Lambert, an early settler.

Lamoille; county and river in Vermont; the name probably a mistaken rendition of La Mouette, the name originally given the river by Champlain.

Lamoine; town in Hancock County, Maine, named for an early French resident.

La Motte; island iii Lake Champlain, New York, named for Capt. Pierre Sieur de la Motto, who built a fort there.

Lamoure; county in North Dakota, named for Hon. Judson Lamoure, an early settler and a prominent man in Territorial politics.

Lampasas; county, town, in same county, and creek in Texas. A Spanish word meaning, "a water lily."

Lampeter; village in Lancaster County, Pennsylvania, named for the town in Wales.

Lamy; village in Santa Fe County, New Mexico, named for Archbishop Lamy.

Lana; stream in Vermont, named for General Wool, United States Army; lana being latin for wool.

Lanark; city in Carroll County, Illinois, named for the town in Scotland.

Lancaster; name of many counties, towns, and villages in the United States, transferred from the county in England; among these, counties in Nebraska, Pennsylvania, South Carolina and Virginia; town in Lancaster County, South Carolina; cities in Atchison County, Kansas, and Lancaster County, Pennsylvania, and a village in Erie County, New York.

Landaff; town in Grafton County, New Hampshire, named for the town in Wales.

Lander; county in Nevada, named for Gen. F. W. Lander.

Landisburg; borough in Perry County, Pennsylvania, named for James Landis, its founder.

Landrum; town in Spartanburg County, South Carolina, named for a resident family.

Lane; county in Kansas, named for James II. Lane, Senator from that State.

Lane; comity in Oregon, named for Joseph Lane, twice governor of the Territory.

Lanesboro; town in Berkshire County, Massachusetts, named for James Lane, Viscount Lanesborough.

Lanesboro; borough in Susquehanna County, Pennsylvania, named for Martin Lane, an early settler.

Langdon: town in Sullivan County, New Hampshire, named for Governor John Langdon.

Langford; mountain in Yellowstone Park, named for the first superintendent of the park, Nathaniel Pitt Langford.

Langhorne; borough in Bucks County, Pennsylvania; Langhorne Manor; borough in Bucks County, Pennsylvania. Named for Jeremiah Langhorne, an early settler and prominent in State politics.

Langlade; county in Wisconsin, named for the first white settler in the State.

L'Anguille; stream and township in Arkansas. A French word, meaning "aneel."

Lanier; town in Bryan County, Georgia, named for Clement Lanier.

Lansingburg; town in Rensselaer County, New York, named for Abraham Lansing, its founder.

Lapeer; county and city in Michigan. A corruption of the French word, lapier, meaning "flint."

Lapile; stream and town in Union County, Arkansas. French word, meaning "a pier."

La Plata; county in Colorado, which contains the Sierra La Plata. A Spanish word, meaning "mountain of silver."

La Playa; village in Santa Barbara County, California. A Spanish word, meaning "the shore or strand," and given to this village on account of its location on the Pacific coast.

Lapompique; branch of the Aroostook River, Maine. An Indian word, meaning "rope stream."

Laporte; county in Indiana. A French word, meaning "door" or "opening" between two stretches of forest connecting two prairies.

Laporte; borough in Sullivan County, Pennsylvania, named for a French family who were large land owners.

Lapwai; town in Nez Perces County, Idaho. An Indian word, meaning "place of division," or "a boundary."

Laramie; village in Shelby County, Ohio, and river in the same State, named for Peter Laramie, a French Canadian trader.

Laramie; county, and city in Laramie County, Wyoming, named for Jacques Laramie, a French trapper.

Laredo; city in Webb County, Texas, named for the seaport town in Spain.

Laribee; town in Humboldt County, California, named for an early settler.

Larimer; county in Colorado, named for Gen. William Larimer, early pioneer in Colorado and Nebraska.

Larned; city in Pawnee County, Kansas, named for Gen. B. F. Larned.

Larrabee; town in Cherokee County, Iowa, named for Governor William Larrabee.

Larue; county in Kentucky, named for John La Rue, an early settler.

Lasalle; counties in Illinois and Texas; city in Lasalle County, Illinois, and village in Niagara County, New York, named for Rene Robert Cavalier, Sieur de La Salle.

Las Animas; county in Colorado, and town in Bent County in the same State. A contraction of the name originally given the river by the Spaniards, El Rio de las Animas Perditas, "the river of lost souls," because traditionally a Spanish regiment on its way to Florida was lost here.

Lassecks; peak in Humboldt County, California. named for an Indian chief.

Lassen; county and peak in California, named for Peter Lassen, an early explorer.

Las Vegas; city in San Miguel County, New Mexico. A Spanish name, meaning "the plains," or the "meadows," and given this city on account of its situation in the midst of a fertile meadow.

Latrobe; borough in Westmoreland County, Pennsylvania, named for Benjamin H. Latrobe, jr.

Latta; town in Marion County, South Carolina, named for a prominent family.

Lattimore; town in Cleveland County, North Carolina, named for a prominent resident.

Latty; village in Paulding County, Ohio, named for the first settler, Judge A. S. Latty.

Lauderdale; counties in Alabama, Mississippi, and Tennessee, and town in Lauderdale County, Mississippi, named for Col. James Lauderdale.

Laughery; river and town in Ohio County, Indiana, so named from the massacre of Captain Laughery's company by the Indians.

Laughing Fish Pond; point in Schoolcraft County, Michigan, so named from the Indian name, Stikameg bapid, meaning " laughing white fish."

Laura; village in Knott County, Nebraska, named for the wife of the first settler, whose name was Estep or Estop.

Laurel; county in Kentucky and town in Jones County, Mississippi, so named on account of the dense laurel thickets growing within their limits.

Laurens; county in Georgia, named for Col. John Laurens, of South Carolina, the Bayard of the American Revolution; Laurens; county in South Carolina and town in same county, named for Col. Henry Laurens and his son, John.

Lausanne; township in Carbon County, Pennsylvania, named from the town in Switzerland.

Lavaca; river, county, and bay in Texas. A corruption of the name, Les Vaches, given the river by the Spanish explorer, La Salle, on account of the number of buffalo found there; Les Vaches meaning "the cows."

Lavallette; city in Ocean County, New Jersey, named for a resident family.

Lawrence; many places in the United States bear the name of James Lawrence, captain in the memorable battle with the British on Lake Erie. Among these are counties in Alabama, Arkansas, Illinois, Indiana, Kentucky, Mississippi, Missouri, Pennsylvania, and Tennessee.

Lawrence; creek in Humboldt County, California, named for an early settler.

Lawrence; city in Douglas County, Kansas, named for Amos Lawrence, of Boston.

Lawrence; city in Essex County, Massachusetts, named for Hon. Abbott Lawrence, of Boston.

Lawrence; county in South Dakota, named for John Lawrence, former member of State legislature.

Lawrenceburg; city in Dearborn County, Indiana, named for the wife of Captain Vance, whose maiden name was Lawrence.

Lawrenceburg; town in Lawrence County, Tennessee; Lawrenceville; town in Gwinnett County, Georgia, and city in Lawrence County, Illinois. Named for Capt. James Lawrence.

Lawson; village in Clear Creek County, Colorado, named fur Alexander Lawson, keeper of a wayside inn.

Lawton; village in Van Buren County, Michigan, named for Nathaniel Lawton, who donated the right of way to the Michigan Central Railroad.

Leadbetter; point in Shoalwater Bay, Washington, named for Lieutenant Lead better, United States Army.

Lead; city in Lawrence County, South Dakota; Lead Hill; town in Davidson County, North Carolina; Leadville; city in Lake County, Colorado. So named on account of the species of ore found within their limits.

Leake; county in Mississippi; Leakesville; town in Greene County, Mississippi. Named for the Hon. Walter Leake, an early governor of the State.

Leaksville; village in Rockingham County, North Carolina, named for a prominent resident.

Leakton; village in Newton County, Georgia, named for the man who kept the village store in early times.

Leavenworth; town in Crawford County, Indiana, named for the proprietors, S. M. and Z. Leavenworth.

Leavenworth; city and county in Kansas, named for Gen. Henry Leavenworth, for whom Fort Leavenworth is named.

Lebanon. This name, either alone or with the suffixes "Church," "Junction,"

"Lake," or "Spring," forms the name of 33 places in the United States, named either directly or indirectly from the mountain of Palestine; Lebanon County in Pennsylvania and city in the same county being of these.

Lebo; city in Coffey County, Kansas, named for an early settler.

Leboeuf; township in Erie County. Pennsylvania, named from the creek which was so named by the French on account of the number of buffalo found upon its banks.

Le Claire; town in Scott County, Iowa, named for Antoine Le Clair, French founder of Davenport.

Lecompton; city in Douglas County, Kansas, named for Judge D. S. Leeompte, chief justice of the Territory.

Leconte; mountain in Tennessee, named for Joseph Leconte, a geologist.

Ledyard; town in New London County, Connecticut, named for Col. William Ledyard, of the State militia.

Ledyard; town in Cayuga County, New York, named for Benjamin Ledyard, agent for the disposal of the lands of the military tract.

Lee; counties in Alabama, Arkansas, Florida, Kentucky, Mississippi, and Texas, named for Robert E. Lee, commander of the armies of the Confederacy.

Lee; counties in Georgia and Illinois, named for Gen. Richard Henry Lee, of the Revolution.

Lee; towns in Berkshire County, Massachusetts, and Oneida County, New York, named for Gen. Charles Lee, of Massachusetts.

Lee; county in Iowa, named for member of the New York land company, Albany, New York.

Lee; county in Virginia, named for Henry Lee, former governor of the State.

Leechburg; borough in Armstrong County, Pennsylvania, named for David Leech.

Leech Lake; lake in Minnesota. Translation of the Indian name, which meant "the place of leeches."

Leeds; many towns in the United States, among them that in Hampshire County, Massachusetts, have been named for the manufacturing town in Yorkshire, England.

Leesburg; town in Loudoun County, Virginia; Leesville; town in Lexington County, South Carolina. Named for the Lee family, of Virginia.

Leflore; county in Mississippi, named for Greenwood Leflore.

Left Hand; creek in Boulder County, Colorado, named for a chief of the Arapahoe Indians.

Lehi; city in Utah County, Utah, named for a character in the Book of Mormon.

Lehigh; river and county in Pennsylvania; Lehighton; a borough in Carbon County, Pennsylvania. Named by the Delaware Indians, Lechauwekink, "where there are forks," of which the present name is a corruption.

Leicester; town in Worcester County, Massachusetts, named for Robert Dudley, Earl of Leicester.

Leicester; town in Livingston County, New York, named for Leicester Phelps, son of Judge Oliver Phelps.

Leidy; mountains in Utah and Wyoming, named for the paleontologist, Joseph Leidy.

Leigh; township in Prince Edward and Amelia counties, Virginia, named for the Leigh family of Virginia.

Leigh; lake in Yellowstone Park, named for Richard Leigh. "Beaver Dick," hunter and guide in the Teton Mountains.

Leipsic; villages in Kent County, Delaware, and Putnam County, Ohio, named for the city in Saxony.

Leitchfield; town in Grayson County, Kentucky, named for Maj. David Leitch.

Leland; village in La Salle County, Illinois, named for Edwin S. Leland.

Le Mars; city in Plymouth County, Iowa. The name is composed of the initials of the ladies who accompanied its founder on his first visit to the spot.

Lenape; villages in Leavenworth County, Kansas, and Chester County, Pennsylvania. The name is the original name of the Delaware Indians, and means "original or first people."

Lenoir; county, and town in Caldwell County, North Carolina, named for Gen. William Lenoir, Revolutionary officer.

Lenora; city in Norton County, Kansas, named for Mrs. Lenora Hauser.

Lenox; town in Berkshire County, Massachusetts, the family name of the Duke of Richmond, who was secretary of state at the time.

Leominster; town in Worcester County, Massachusetts, named for the town in Hertfordshire, England.

Leon: county in Florida, and city in Butler County, Kansas, named for Ponce de Leon.

Leon; county in Texas, named for Alonzo de Leon, a Spanish captain and builder of missions in Texas.

Leonard; village in Oakland County, Michigan, named for Leonard Rowland.

Leonardville; city in Riley County, Kansas, named for Leonard T. Smith, an officer of the Kansas Central Railroad.

Leopold; town in Perry County, Indiana, named for Leopold, King of the Belgians.

Leoti; city in Wichita County, Kansas, named for a white girl captured by the Indians, the name meaning "prairie flower."

Le Ray; town in Jefferson County, New York, named for Mr. Le Ray Chaumont.

Le Raysville; borough in Bradford County, Pennsylvania, named for Vincent Le Ray, the son of a large landowner.

Le Roy; town in Osceola County, Michigan, named for an Indian chief who lived near the town.

Leroy; town in Genesee County, New York, named for Herman Le Roy, a large proprietor.

Les Cheneaux; strait in Mackinaw County, Michigan. A French name, meaning "gutter, valley, the channel."

Leslie; county in Kentucky, named for Governor Preston H. Leslie.

Lesueur; county and borough in Minnesota, named for Le Sueur, an early explorer.

Letcher; county in Kentucky, named for Robert P. Letcher, former governor of the State.

Leverett; town in Franklin County, Massachusetts, named for Sir John Leverett, colonial governor.

Levy; county in Florida, named for a prominent politician.

Lewiedale; town in Lexington County, South Carolina. named for a member of a prominent resident family.

Lewis; creek in Colorado, named for a pioneer ranch owner.

Lewis; counties in Kentucky, Missouri, Tennessee, and Washington; named for Meriwether Lewis.

Lewis; county in New York, named for Morgan Lewis, former governor of the State.

Lewis; county in West Virginia, named for Col. Charles Lewis.

Lewis and Clarke; river in Clatsop County, Oregon, and county in Montana, named for Capt. Meriwether Lewis and Capt. William Clarke, of the Lewis and Clarke expedition.

Lewisberry; borough in York County, Pennsylvania, named for the Lewis family, of which Dr. Ellis Lewis was a member.

Lewisboro; town in Westchester County, New York, named for John Lewis, a prominent resident.

Lewisburg; town in Greenbrier County, West Virginia, named for Samuel Lewis.

Lewis Fork; southern branch of Columbia River in Idaho; Lewiston; city in Nez Perce County, Idaho. Named for Meriwether Lewis.

Lewiston; city in Androscoggin County, Maine, named for the founders, the Lewis families.

Lewiston; village in Niagara County, New York, named for Morgan Lewis, former governor of the State.

Lewiston; town in Bertie County, North Carolina, named for a prominent resident.

Lewistown; town in Logan County, Ohio, named for Capt. John Lewis, a noted Shawnee chief.

Lexington; twenty-seven places in the United States bear this name, a majority of them having been given in commemoration of the famous Revolutionary battle. Among these is the county in South Carolina.

Lexington; town in Middlesex County, Massachusetts, named for the parish of Lexington, England.

Leyden; towns in Franklin County, Massachusetts, and Lewis County, New York, named for the town in the Netherlands, the refuge of the Pilgrim Fathers prior to their arrival in America.

Liberal; cities in Seward County, Kansas, and Barton County, Missouri, so named to characterize the ideas of the people.

Liberty; counties in Florida, Georgia, and Texas, and city in Montgomery County, Kansas, named for the sentiment which is so dear to the American people.

Liberty Center; village in Wells County, Indiana, so named because it is located in the center of Liberty Township.

Licking; county in Ohio, so named because the deer and elk found the saline deposits of the Licking River a favorite feeding ground.

Ligonier; borough in Westmoreland County, Pennsylvania, named for Sir John Ligonier, Lord Viscount of Enniskillen.

Lilesville; town in Anson County, North Carolina, named for a merchant of the place.

Lillington; town in Harnett County, and village in Pender County, North Carolina, named for Col. John A. Lillington, of the Revolution.

Lily; bay and township in Piscataquis County, Maine, so named on account of the many lilies found there.

Lime; lake in Cattaraugus county, New York, an anglicization of the Indian name Tecarnowundo, meaning " lime lake."

Limerick; town in York County, Maine, and township in Montgomery County, Pennsylvania, named for the town in Ireland.

Limesprings; town in Howard County, Iowa, so named from the springs in the rocks.

Limestone; counties in Alabama and Texas, and village in Cattaraugus County, New York, so named on account of the nature of the rock found within its limits.

Lincklaen; town in Chenango County, New York, named for John Lincklaen, an early proprietor of the township.

Lincoln; counties in Arkansas, Colorado, Idaho, Kansas, Minnesota, Mississippi, Nebraska, Nevada, New Mexico, Oklahoma, Oregon, South Dakota, Washington, West Virginia, and Wisconsin; parish in Louisiana; city in Lancaster County, Nebraska; town in Providence County, Rhode Island, and mountains in Colorado and New Hampshire, named for President Abraham Lincoln.

Lincoln; counties in Georgia, Kentucky, Missouri, North Carolina, and Tennessee, named for Gen. Benjamin Lincoln, an officer of the Revolution.

Lincoln; town in Whitmore County, Massachusetts, named for the ninth Earl of Lincoln.

Lincoln; county in Maine, and town in Middlesex County, Massachusetts, named for Lincolnshire, England.

Lincoln; town in Penobscot County, Maine, named for Governor Enoch Lincoln.

Lincolnton; towns in Lincoln County, Georgia, and Lincoln County, North Carolina; Lincolnville; town in Waldo County, Maine. Named for Gen. Benjamin Lincoln, an officer of the Revolution.

Lincolnville; town in Berkeley County, South Carolina, named for President Abraham Lincoln.

Lindley; town in Steuben County, New York, named for Col. Eleazar Lindley.

Lindsay; creek in Humboldt County, California, named for an early settler.

Lindsborg; city in McPherson County, Kansas, so named because the first syllable of the names of many of the early settlers was "linds," the "borg" being added, which in Swedish means "castle."

Line Port; town in Stewart County, Tennessee, so named because it is situated both upon the Cumberland River and on the lines between the States of Kentucky and Tennessee.

Linn; counties in Iowa, Kansas, Missouri, and Oregon; village in Osage County, Missouri, and mountain in California; Linneus; city in Linn County, Missouri. Named for Hon. Lewis F. Linn, United States Senator from Missouri.

Linton; city in Greene County, Indiana, named for a resident of Terre Haute.

Linwood; city in Leavenworth County, Kansas, and village in Butler County, Nebraska, so named on account of the presence of this kind of wood.

Lipscomb; county in Texas, named for Abner Lipscomb, a prominent early resident, and associate justice of the Supreme Court.

Lisbon; twenty-one places in the United States bear this name, transferred from the town in Spain.

Lisle; towns in Broome County, New York, and Dupage County, Illinois, named for the city in France.

Litchfield; county in Connecticut and town in Herkimer County, New York, named for the city in England.

Lititz; borough in Lancaster County, Pennsylvania, named from the barony of Lititz in Bohemia.

Little; village in Holt County, Nebraska, named for L. B. Little.

Little Beaver; stream on the boundary between Pennsylvania and Ohio. Translation of the Indian name Tangamochke.

Little Ferry; borough in Bergen County, New Jersey, so named on account of the ferry over Overpeck Creek.

Little Mountain; town in Newberry County, South Carolina, so named because it is situated near Little Mountain.

Little River; county in Arkansas, named from the river which forms its northern boundary.

Little Rock; capital of Arkansas, so named because it is built upon a bed of rock.

Little Sioux; river in Iowa. A translation of the name originally given it by the French, Petite Riviere des Sioux.

Little Tabeau; river in Missouri; the name a corruption of the original French name, Terre Beau, "beautiful land."

Littleton; town in Arapahoe County, Colorado, named for Richard S. Little.

Littleton; town in Middlesex County, Massachusetts, named for George Littleton, a member of the British Parliament.

Littleton; town in Grafton County, New Hampshire, named for Col. Moses Little.

Live Oak; county in Texas, named from the abundance of this species of oak.

Livermore; town in Androscoggin County, Maine, named for Deacon Elijah Livermore, an early settler.

Livermore; town in Grafton County, New Hampshire, named for a prominent resident family.

Liverpool; many places in the United States bear this name, transferred to them from the town in England, among them being a village in Onondaga County, New York.

Livingston; counties in Illinois, Michigan, and Missouri, named for Edward Livingston, former Secretary of State.

Livingston; counties in Kentucky and New York and parish in Louisiana, named for Robert R. Livingston, a prominent politician.

Livingston; town in Orangeburg County, South Carolina, named for a prominent resident family.

Livonia; townships in Livingston County, New York, and Wayne County, Michigan, named for the division of Russia.

Lizard; river in Iowa; the name a translation of the Indian name Wassakaponipah, "the river with the lizards."

Llano; county and river in Texas. A Spanish word meaning "plain," and so called because of the character of its surface.

Llano Estacado; an elevated plateau in northwest Texas and New Mexico; Spanish words meaning "staked plain," applied to this plateau on account of the stake-like boles of the yucca plant, which grows there.

Loachapoka; town in Macon County, Alabama. An Indian word meaning "here terrapins are killed."

Locke; town in Cayuga County, New York, named for the philosopher, John Locke.

Lock Haven; city in Clinton County, Pennsylvania, so named localise of the two locks and a safe harbor near it.

Lockport; village in Lafourche Parish, Louisiana, so named because it was once a favorite tying-up place for the river boats.

Lockport; city in Niagara County, New York, so named for the double tier of locks at this point.

Lodi; several places in the United States have been named for the city in Italy.

Logan; county in Arkansas, named for James Logan, a pioneer.

Logan; counties in Colorado, Kansas, Nebraska. North Dakota, Oklahoma, and mountain in Arizona, named for Gen. John A. Logan.

Logan; county in Illinois, named for Dr. John Logan, father of Gen. John A. Logan.

Logan; county in Kentucky, named for Gen. Benjamin Logan, a pioneer of the State.

Logan; creek in Nebraska, named for Logan Fontanelle, a friendly Omaha chief.

Logan; county in West Virginia, named for Logan, an Indian chief of the Mingo tribe.

Logansport; city in Cass County, Indiana, named for Captain Logan, Indian chief, nephew of Tecumseh.

Loleta; town in Humboldt County, California. An Indian word meaning "a pleasant place."

London; several towns and villages in the United States have been named for the city in England.

Londonderry; towns in Rockingham County, New Hampshire, and Windham County, Vermont, so named in compliment to Rev. Matthew Clark, who distinguished himself in the defense of Londonderry, Ireland.

Lone Rock; village in Richland County, Wisconsin, so named on account of the remarkable mound of sandstone situated near the town.

Lone Tree; town in Johnson County, Iowa, named for a single tree which stands in the prairie. .

Long Branch; celebrated watering place in New Jersey, taking its name from a branch of South Shrewsbury River.

Long Island; island on the Atlantic coast, part of the State of New York. An anglicization of the Dutch name Lange Eylandt.

Longmeadow; town in Hampden County, Massachusetts, so named on account of the presence of a long meadow within the township.

Longmont; town in Boulder County, Colorado. A combination of the name of the discoverer of Longs Peak and the French mont, "mountain."

Longton; city in Elk County, Kansas, named for the town in England.

Longs; peak in Colorado, named for Capt. Stephen D. Long.

Long Tom; stream in the Willamette Valley; the name a corruption of the Indian name, Lung-tum-ler.

Lonoke; county in Arkansas. Said by one authority to have been named for the Indian tribe, the word meaning "the people," but according to another authority it was so named on account of the presence of a lone oak tree which stood near its present site.

Lonsdale; village in Providence County, Rhode Island, named for the division in England.

Lookout; capes in North Carolina and Oregon, so named because of the dangers of navigation at these points.

Lookout; mountain in Tennessee; so named on account of the extensive prospect from its summit.

Loretto; borough in Cambria County, Pennsylvania, named from the city in Italy.

Los Angeles; county and city in California. A Spanish name meaning "the angels." Los Gatos; city in Santa Clara County, California. A Spanish name meaning "the cats," and doubtless applied to the city because of the presence of wild-cats in the country.

Los Pinos; river in Colorado. A Spanish name meaning "the pines."

Lost; river in Washington County, Indiana, which for several miles is lost in a subterranean channel.

Lost River; stream in Virginia, so called because of its abrupt disappearance at the foot of a mountain.

Lott; town in Falls County, Texas, named for a prominent citizen.

Loudon; town in Merrimack County, New Hampshire, named for the Earl of Loudon.

Loudon; county in Tennessee, named for Fort Loudon.

Loudoun; county in Virginia, named for the Earl of Loudon.

Louisa; county in Iowa, named for Louisa Massey.

Louisa; county and town in same county, in Virginia, named for the daughter of George H.

Louisburg; town in Franklin County, North Carolina, named for the fortress.

Louisiana; State in the Union, named for Louis XIV of France.

Louisiana; city in Pike County, Missouri, named for Louisiana Territory, of which it was a part when founded.

Louisville; city in Pottawatomie County, Kansas, named for Louis Wilson, the son of the original preemptor of the town site.

Louisville; city in Jefferson County, Kentucky, named for Louis XVI of France.

Louisville; town in Winston County, Mississippi, named for Col. Louis Winston, a prominent early settler.

Loup; county in Nebraska, named for the tribe of Pawnee Loups.

Love; town in De Soto County, Mississippi, named for Colonel Love.

Loveland; village in Larimer County, Colorado, named for Hon. W. A. H. Loveland.

Lovell; town in Oxford County, Maine.

Lovewell; mountain and pond in New Hampshire, named for Capt. John Lovewell, the hero of a fight with the Indians.

Loving; county in Texas, named for Oliver Loving, an early pioneer.

Lowell; military post in Arizona, named for Gen. C. R. Lowell.

Lowell; town in Penobscot County, Maine, named for Lowell Hayden, the first person born within its limits.

Lowell, city in Middlesex County, Massachusetts; plantation in' Franklin County, Maine; town in Gaston County, North Carolina, and village in Kent County, Michigan, named for Francis Cabot Lowell, of Boston.

Low Freight; stream in Clark County, Arkansas; the name a corruption of the original French name, l'eau froid, meaning " cold water."

Lowndes; counties in Alabama, Georgia, and Mississippi, named for William Jones Lowndes, member of Congress from South Carolina.

Lowndesville; town in Abbeville County, South Carolina, named for the Lowndes family, prominent in that State.

Lowville; town in Lewis County, New York, named for Nicholas Low.

Loyalhanna; stream and township in Pennsylvania. The name a corruption of the Indian word Laweel-hanna, meaning "the middle stream."

Loyalsock; branch of the Susquehanna River and a township in Lycoming County, Pennsylvania. A corruption of the Indian Lawi-saquik, meaning "the middle creek."

Loydsville; town in Belmont County, Ohio, named for a Welsh family.

Lubbock; county in Texas, named for Tom Lubbock, a colonel in the civil war.

Lucas; county and town in same county in Iowa, and county in Ohio, named for Robert Lucas, governor of Ohio and first governor of Iowa Territory.

Luce; county in Michigan, named for Governor Cyrus G. Luce.

Lucerne; town in Columbiana County, Ohio; Lucerneville; village in Knox County, Ohio. Named for the lake in Switzerland.

Ludington; city in Mason County, Michigan, named for James Ludington, of Milwaukee.

Ludlow; town in Kenton County, Kentucky, named for Israel Ludlow, a prominent pioneer.

Ludlow; town in Hampden County, Massachusetts, named for the town in Shropshire, England.

Lumberton; town in Pearl River County, Mississippi, so named on account of its principal industry.

Lumpkin; county and town in Stewart County, Georgia, named for Wilson Lumpkin, an early governor.

Luna; county in New Mexico, named for a prominent resident family.

Lunenburg; town in Worcester County, Massachusetts, and town in Essex County, Vermont, named for the Duke of Lunenburg, George H of England.

Lunenburg; county in Virginia, named for the town in Prussia, from which its settlers came.

Lutesville; village in Bollinger County, Missouri, named for its founder, Eli Lutes.

Luther; village in Lake County, Michigan, named for William A. Luther, an early settler.

Luthersburg; village in Clearfield County, Pennsylvania, named for W. H. Luther, an old resident.

Luzerne; county and borough in same county in Pennsylvania, named for Chevalier della Luzerne, former minister from France to the United States.

Lycoming; branch of the Susquehanna, a county and a town in Pennsylvania. An Indian word meaning "sandy stream."

Lyell; mountain in California, named for the English geologist, Sir Charles Lyell.

Lykens; borough in Dauphin County, Pennsylvania; a corruption of the name of the man for whom it was named—Andrew Lycan.

Lyman; town in York County, Maine, named for Theodore Lyman, of Boston.

Lyman; town in Grafton County, New Hampshire, named for Daniel Lyman, one of the early proprietors.

Lyman; county in South Dakota, named for W. P. Lyman, legislator and soldier.

Lyme; towns in New London County, Connecticut; Jefferson County, New York, and Grafton County, New Hampshire, named either directly or indirectly from the borough of Lyme-Regis, England.

Lynchburg; city in Campbell County, Virginia, named for a rich settler and officer in the Revolution.

Lynchtown; township in Oxford County, Maine, named for the owner of Lynch's mills.

Lyndeboro; town in Hillsboro County, New Hampshire, named for Benjamin Lynde, a large landowner.

Lyndon; town in Caledonia County; Lyndon Center; village in Caledonia County; Lyndonville; village in Caledonia County, Vermont. Named for Josiah Lyndon, son of an early proprietor.

Lynn; town in Essex County, Massachusetts, named for Lynn-Regis, England.

Lynn; county in Texas, named for G. W. Lynn, an early settler.

Lynnville; town in Jasper County, Iowa, so named on account of the proximity of a basswood grove.

Lynxville; village in Crawford County, Wisconsin, named for the steamer Lynx, which brought the Government surveyors to the place.

Lyon; counties in Iowa, Kansas, and Nevada, named for Gen. Nathaniel Lyon, United States Army.

Lyon; county in Kentucky, named for Col. Crittenden Lyon.

Lyons; city in Rice County, Kansas, named for Truman J. Lyon, the owner of the town site.

Lyons; village in Burt County, Nebraska, named for Waldo Lyon, an early resident.

Lyonsdale; village in Lewis County, New York, named for its first settler, Calen Lyon.

Lysander; town in Onondaga County, New York, named for the Spartan general.

M

Mabbettsville; village in Dutchess County, New York, named for James Mabbett, the former proprietor.

McAdenville; town in Gaston County, North Carolina, named for Hon. R. Y. McAden, speaker of the house of representatives.

McArthur; village in Vinton County, Ohio, named for Gen. Duncan McArthur, an officer in the Indian wars.

McBride; village in Montcalm County, Michigan, named for an early settler.

McClellandville; village in Newcastle County, Delaware, named for William McClelland, an early settler.

McColl; town in Marlboro County, South Carolina, named for D. D. McColl, a capitalist.

McComb; town in Pike County, Mississippi, named for a former owner of the Mississippi Central Railroad.

McConnellsburg; borough in Fulton County, Pennsylvania, named for its founder.

McConnellstown; village in Huntingdon County, Pennsylvania, named for its founder.

McConnelsville; village in Morgan County, Ohio, named for Robert McConnel.

McCook; county in South Dakota, named for Edwin S. McCook, of Ohio, distinguished in the civil war.

McCool; town in Attala County, Mississippi, named for Hon. James F. McCool.

McCracken; city in Rush County, Kansas, named for William McCracken, of New York City, an official of the Missouri Pacific Railway.

McCracken; county in Kentucky, named for Capt. Virgil McCracken.

McCulloch; county in Texas, named for Benjamin McCulloch, a brigadier-general in the Confederate army.

McCune; city in Crawford County, Kansas, named for Isaac McCune, its founder.

McDonald; county in Missouri, named for Sergeant McDonald, of South Carolina.

McDonough; town in Henry County, Georgia; MacDonough; county in Illinois, town in Chenango County, New York, and village in Newcastle County, Delaware. Named for the eminent naval commander, Commodore Thomas McDonough.

McDowell; county in North Carolina, named for the two generals, Joseph and Charles McDowell, of Revolutionary fame.

McDowell; county in West Virginia, and town in Highland County, Virginia, said to have been named for James McDowell, former governor of Virginia.

McDuffie; county in Georgia, named for George McDuffie, an early governor of South Carolina.

Macedon; town in Wayne County, New York, named for the ancient Macedonia of the Greeks.

Macedonia; name transferred from Greece to many places in the United States.

McFarlan; town in Anson County, North Carolina, named for a prominent citizen.

McGrawville; village in Alleghany County, New York, named in honor of a Mr. McGraw, who owned considerable property there.

McGregor; city in Clayton County, Iowa, named for an early proprietor, Alexander McGregor.

McHenry; county in Illinois, named for (Ten. William McHenry, member State legislature.

McHenry; fort near Baltimore, Maryland, named for James McHenry, Secretary of War under Washington and Adams.

McHenry; county in North Dakota, named for Hon. James McHenry, an early pioneer.

Machhanna; the largest of the three streams which, united, form the Lehigh River. An Indian word meaning "the largest stream."

Machias; river and town in Washington County, Maine; Machiasport; town in Washington County, Maine; probably a corruption of the French word, Magi, and given to the river on account of tieing discovered upon the festival of the Magi, or, according to another authority, derived from the Indian word Machisses, "bad small falls."

Machigamic; river in northern Wisconsin, so called because it flows from the lake bearing the Indian name, Mitchigamic, meaning "large lake."

Macinaw; town in Tazewell County, Illinois. An Indian word, meaning "turtle."

Macintire; mountain in the Adirondacks, named for an iron speculator of the region.

Mcintosh; county in Georgia, named for the Mcintosh family, members of which accompanied Oglethorpe in his first expedition into the State.

Mcintosh; county in North Dakota, named for Hon. E. H. Mcintosh, a member of the Territorial legislature.

McKean; county in Pennsylvania, named for Thomas McKean, an early governor, and one of the signers of the Declaration of Independence.

McKee; town in Jackson County, Kentucky, named for Judge George R. McKee.

McKeesport; city in Allegheny County, Pennsylvania, named for David McKee, who once kept a ferry there.

Mackinac; county in Michigan and town in same county. Derived from the Indian word "michilimackinac," meaning "island of the great turtle," or in other dialects, "island of the giant fairies."

McKinley; county in New Mexico, named for late President William McKinley.

Macksville; city in Stafford County, Kansas, named for George Mack, the first postmaster in the county.

McLaurin; village in Perry County, Mississippi, named for General McLaurin, first president of the Gulf and Ship Island Railroad.

McLean; county in Kentucky, named for Judge Alney McLean.

McLean: county in Illinois, named for John McLean, member of Congress from that State.

McLean; county in North Dakota, named for lion. John R. McLean, a prominent State politician.

McLennan; county in Texas, named for Neil McLennan.

Maclenny; town in Baker County, Florida, named for H. C. MacClenny, its founder.

McLeod; county in Minnesota, named for Hon. Martin McLeod, president of the State council.

McLouth: city in Jefferson County, Kansas, named for the owner of the town site.

McMechen; town in Marshall County, West Virginia, named for a former resident.

McMinn; county in Tennessee; McMinnville; town in Warren County, Tennessee. Named for Gen. Joseph McMinn, an early governor.

McMullen; county in Texas, named for John McMullen, a colonizer of western Texas.

McNairy; county in Tennessee, named for Judge John McNairy.

McNeils; island in Washington, named for the captain of a steamer of the Hudson Bay Company.

Macomb; county in Michigan and town in St. Lawrence County, New York, named for Gen. Alexander Macomb.

Macon; counties in Alabama, Georgia, Illinois, Missouri, North Carolina, and Tennessee, and cities in Georgia and Missouri, towns in Mississippi and North Carolina, and a village in Macon County, Illinois, named for Gen. Nathaniel Macon, United States Senator from North Carolina.

Macoupin; county and creek in Illinois, so named by the Indians because the white potato, signified by the name, was found abundantly along the banks of the creek.

McPherson; counties in Kansas and Nebraska, and town in McPherson County, Kansas, named for Maj. Gen. J. B. McPherson.

Macungie; borough in Lehigh County, Pennsylvania. An Indian name, meaning "the feeding place of bears."

Madawaska; branches of the St. John and Aroostook rivers in Maine and a town in Aroostook County. An Indian word, meaning " porcupine place," or, "where one river enters another."

Madden; creek in Humboldt County, California, named for Captain Madden.

Madera; county and town in California; the county, having been formed from a part of Fresno County after the building of the town of Madera, was named for that town, which was quite a lumber center. A Spanish word, meaning "lumber."

Madison; counties in Alabama, Arkansas, Florida, Georgia, Illinois, Indiana, Iowa, Kentucky, Mississippi, Missouri, Montana, Nebraska, New York, North Carolina, Ohio, Tennessee, Texas, and Virginia, parish in Louisiana, cities in Georgia and Kansas, towns in Somerset County, Maine, and Carroll County.

New Hampshire, and a peak in the White Mountains, named for James Madison, fourth President of the United States.

Magalloway; river in New Hampshire. An Indian word, meaning "large tail."Magataukamde; lake in Minnesota. An Indian word meaning "swan lake."

Magnolia; many towns in the United States, named directly or indirectly for Dr. Pierre Magnol, for whom the tree of this species was named.

Magoffin; county in Kentucky, named for Beriah Magoffin, a former governor.

Magothy; river in Maryland. An Indian word, meaning "a small plain devoid of timber."

Mahanoy City; borough in Schuylkill County, Pennsylvania. A corruption of the Indian word, Mahoni, meaning "a lick."

Mahantango; branch of the Susquehanna River, Pennsylvania. An Indian word, meaning "where we had plenty of meat to eat."

Mahaska; county in Iowa, named for the greatest chief of the Iowas.

Mahomet; village in Champaign County, Illinois, named for the founder of the Mohammedan religion.

Mahon; village in Marshall County, Mississippi, named for John Mahon.

Mahoning: river and county in Ohio; Mahony; township and city in Schuylkill County, Pennsylvania, and branch of the Susquehanna River, in the same State. Name derived from an Indian word, meaning "a lick."

Mahtowa; town in Carlton County, Minnesota, named from the Indian word, meaning "grass lands."

Maiden Rock; village in Pierce County, Wisconsin, named for the rock, famous in Indian legends, from which an Indian maiden leaped to escape marriage with a warrior of another tribe.

Maidstone; town in Essex County, Vermont, named for the town in Kent, England.

Maine; a State in the Union said to be named for the private estate of Henrietta Maria, in Maine, a province of France; or, according to another authority, so called because the fishermen of the islands along the coast referred to the mainland as the "main," and in some early documents it was spelled "Mayn."

Makage; western tributary of the Minnesota River. From an Indian word, Makagi, meaning "brown earth."

Makiapier; pond in New Jersey. An Indian word, meaning "water of a reddish color."

Malade; river and village in Oneida County, Idaho. A French word, meaning "sick or infirm."

Malaga; towns in Gloucester County, New Jersey, and Monroe County, Ohio, named for the city of Spain.

Malcom; town in Poweshiek County, Iowa, named for an early Scotch settler.

Maiden; city in Middlesex County, Massachusetts, named for the town in England.

Malheur; river and county in Oregon. A French word, meaning "misfortune."

Malmaison; village in Pittsylvania County, Virginia, named for a chateau in France.

Malta; towns in Morgan County, Ohio, and Saratoga County, New York, named for the island in the Mediterranean Sea.

Malvern; several towns in the United States have been named for the watering place in England.

Mamajuda; island in the Detroit River, Michigan, named for an Indian squaw.

Mamakating; town in Sullivan County, New York, named for an Indian chief.

Mamaroneck; town in Westchester County, New York, named for an Indian chief.

Mammoth; cave in Kentucky, so named on account of its great size.

Manada; stream in Dauphin County, Pennsylvania. An Indian word, meaning "an island."

Manahan; stream in York County, Pennsylvania. An Indian word, meaning "where liquor has been drunk."

Manahawkin; town in Ocean County, New Jersey, and a creek in the same state. An Indian name, meaning "good corn land," and applied to this section on account of the productiveness of the land.

Manalapan; river in New Jersey. An Indian word, meaning "good bread or good country."

Manan; islands on the coast of Maine. The Indian word for island.

Manasquan; village in Monmouth County, New Jersey. An Indian word, said to mean "an island with an enclosure for squaws."

Manatawny; branch of the Schuylkill River in Pennsylvania. Derived from the Indian word, menhaltanink, "here we drank" (liquor).

Manatee; county, town, and river in Florida, ho named because the sea cow is found on the coast.

Manaticut; river in Massachusetts, named from the Indian and probably meaning "a place of observation." Manato-Kikewe; stream in Wisconsin. An Indian word, meaning "stooping spirit river." Mancebona; village in Antrim County, Michigan, named for the youngest daughter of the first settler, Mancebona Andrews.

Manchester; cities in Chesterfield County, Virginia, Essex County, Massachusetts, and Hillsboro County, New Hampshire, and village in Ontario County, New York, named for the city in England.

Mandan; city in Morton County, North Dakota, named for the Indian tribe.

Mandarin; town in Duval County, Florida, so named because its chief orange crop is of this species.

Mandeville; town in St. Tammany Parish, Louisiana, named for Mandeville de Marigny, a descendant of the French officer of the first colonization.

Manhasset; formerly a village in Queens County, New York, and now a part of New York City. An Indian name, meaning "little island."

Manhattan; an island in New York. An Indian word, said by some authorities to mean "little island;" others think it means "the people of the whirlpool," referring to Hell Gate, and another authority gives its origin as from the word Manna-ha-ta, "place of drunkenness," since Verrazano landed upon the lower extremity of Manhattan Island and gave the Indians liquor, on which they became drunk.

Manheim; towns in Herkimer County, New York, and Lancaster County, Pennsylvania, named for the town in Germany.

Manidowish; river in Wisconsin. An Indian word, meaning "evil spirit."

Manistee; county, city, and river in Michigan. An Indian word, meaning "vermilion river," or, according to another authority, "lost river."

Manistique; town in Schoolcraft County, Michigan, from the same source as the above.

Manitou; county in Michigan, river in Wisconsin, and town in El Paso County, Colorado. An Indian name given to any object of religious reverence.

Manitowoc; city in Wisconsin and county in Michigan. An Indian word, meaning "spirit land."

Mankato; cities in Jewell County, Kansas, and Blue Earth County, Minnesota. An Indian word, meaning "bule," or, more properly, "green earth."

Mankisitah-Watpa: river in South Dakota, strongly impregnated with white slime, hence given this name by the Indians, it meaning "river of white water."

Manlius; town in Onondaga County, New York, named for a Roman general.

Manly; village in Moore County, North Carolina, named for Governor Charles Manly.

Manning; town in Carroll County, Iowa. named for a merchant of the place.

Manning; town in Clarendon County, South Carolina, named for the Manning family so prominent in South Carolina history.

Mannsville; village in Jefferson County, New York, named for Col. H. B. Mann.

Mannussing; island in Long Island Sound. From an Indian word, munnohan, meaning "an island."

Mansfield; town in Holland County, Connecticut, named for Moses Mansfield, mayor of New Haven.

Mansfield; town in Bristol County, Massachusetts, named for William Murray, Earl of Mansfield.

Mansfield; city in Richland County, Ohio, named for Col. Jared Mansfield, at one-time surveyor-general, United States.

Mansfield; town in Tioga County, Pennsylvania, named for Asa Mann, original owner of the land.

Manson; town in Calhoun County, Iowa, named for a resident.

Manteno; village in Kankakee County, Illinois. Probably a corruption of the Indian word Manitou, meaning "spirit."

Manteo; town in Dare County, North Carolina, named for an Indian chief, who was the first Indian baptized.

Manton; village in Michigan, named for the first white settler, George Manton.

Mantua; towns in Portage County, Ohio, and Gloucester County, New Jersey, named for the town in Italy.

Manuelito; station in McKinley County, New Mexico, named for a former chief of the Navajos. A Spanish word, meaning "little Manuel."

Maple Forest; town in Crawford County, Michigan, so named because of its beautiful forests.

Maquoketa; city in Jackson County, Iowa, and river in same State. The name is derived from an Indian word, variously translated as "high bank," "feather," " a bear."

Maquon; town in Knox County, Illinois. This name was given William Penn by the Indians because in his treaty with them on the banks of the Delaware he used a quill pen, this word with them signifying "a quill or feather."

Marais; town in Orange County, Missouri. French word, meaning "swamp or morass."

Marais des Cygnes; river in Wabaunsee County, Kansas. A French phrase, meaning "swans' marsh."

Marathon; town in Cortland County, New York, and county in Wisconsin, named for the battlefield in Greece.

Marblehead; town in Essex County, Massachusetts, which was so named on account of the variegated porphyry-colored stones found there.

Marcellus; towns in Onondaga County, New York, and Cass County, Michigan, named for the illustrious Roman, M. Claudius Marcellus.

Marcus Hook; borough in Delaware County, Pennsylvania, named for, but a corruption of the name of, an Indian chief, Maarte, who lived in that section.

Marcy; town in Oneida County, New York, and mountain in the same State, named for a former governor, William L. Marcy.

Mare; island in San Pablo Bay, California, said to be so named on account of a wild mare which formerly inhabited the island.

Marengo; county in Alabama and cities in McHenry County, Illinois, and Iowa County, Iowa, named from the battlefield of Italy.

Margaretsville; town in Northampton County, North Carolina, named for Mrs. Margaret Ridley.

Margaretville; village in Delaware County, New York, named for the owner of the land, Margaret Lewis, the daughter of Governor Morgan Lewis.

Marias; river in Montana, named for Miss Maria Wood.

Mariaville; town in Hancock County, Maine, named for the daughter of Mr. Bingham, a large landowner.

Mariaville; town in Schenectady County, New York, named for the daughter of James Duane.

Maricopa; county in Arizona, named for an Indian tribe.

Marie Saline; township in Ashley County, Arkansas. From the French marias saline, meaning "salt marsh."

Maries; county in Missouri, named for the Big and Little Maries rivers, which name is of French origin.

Marietta; city in Ohio, named for Queen Marie Antoinette of France.

Marietta; town in Lancaster County, Pennsylvania, named for the wives of the two proprietors.

Marilla; town in Erie County, New York, named for Mrs. Marilla Rogers, of Alden.

Marin; county in California, named for the celebrated chief of the Lecatuit, or Likatuit, tribe.

Marine; village in Madison County, Illinois, ho named because settled by several sea captains from the east.

Marine; village in Washington County, Minnesota, named for the Marine Lumber Company of Delaware and Vermont, which settled the village.

Marinette; county in Wisconsin, named for the daughter of an Indian chief, Marinette Jacobs, the name being a composite of the names Marie and Antoinette.

Marion; counties in Alabama, Arkansas, Florida, Georgia, Illinois, Indiana, Iowa, Kansas, Kentucky, Mississippi, Missouri, Ohio, Oregon, South Carolina, Tennessee, Texas, and West Virginia, town in Marion County, South Carolina, and fort in Florida; Marionville; city in Lawrence County, Missouri. Named for Gen. Francis Marion.

Mariposa; river, county, and town in same county in California, named for a flower which grows abundantly there. A Spanish word, meaning "butterfly."

Markleville; town in Madison County, Indiana, named for John Markle, who laid it out.

Marlboro; many places in the United States were given this name; some of them for the Duke of Marlborough and others from the town in England.

Marlinton; village in Pocahontas County, West Virginia, named for the first settler.

Marlow; town in Cheshire County, New Hampshire, named for the borough in England.

Marmiton; stream in Missouri. From the French word, marmiton, "scullion," from marmite, "pot or kettle."

Maroon; peak in the Elk Mountains, Colorado, so named on account of the peculiar color of the sandstone.

Marquam; village in Clackamas County, Oregon, named for P. A. Marquam, an old resident of Portland.

Marquette; counties in Michigan and Wisconsin, city in the same county in Michigan, town in Green Lake County, Wisconsin, city in McPherson County, Kansas, and river in Michigan, named for the Jesuit missionary, Jacques Marquette.

Marseilles; village in Wyandot County, Ohio, named for the city in France.

Marshall; counties in Alabama, Illinois, Indiana, Iowa, Mississippi, Kentucky, Tennessee, and West Virginia, named for Chief Justice John Marshall.

Marshall; town in Boulder County, Colorado, named for Joseph M. Marshall, who discovered coal in this section.

Marshall; county in Kansas, named for Francis J. Marshall, member of the first Territorial legislature.

Marshall; county and village in same county in Minnesota, named for Governor William R. Marshall.

Marshall; county in South Dakota, named for Thomas F. Marshall, Congressman from North Dakota.

Marshallton; village in Newcastle County, Delaware, named for John Marshall, who first started a rolling null there.

Marshfield; town in Plymouth County, Massachusetts, so named on account of its situation.

Marshfield; city in Webster County, Missouri, named for the home of Daniel Webster.

Marshfield; town in Washington County, Vermont, named for Capt. Isaac Marsh, who purchased the town site from the Indians.

Marshfield; city in Wood County, Wisconsin, so named because unusually large marshes cover the township.

Martha's Vineyard; island comprising Dukes County, Massachusetts. Martha, said to be a corruption of Martin, the name of a friend of the discoverer of the island, the Vineyard being added on account of the abundance of wild grapes found there.

Martin; county in Kentucky. Named for Col. John P. Martin.

Martin; county in Minnesota, named for Henry Martin, an early settler.

Martin; town in Claiborne County, Mississippi, named for Gen. W. T. Martin, of Natchez, Mississippi.

Martin; county in North Carolina, named for colonial governor, Josiah Martin.

Martin; county in Texas, named for Wyly Martin, an early settler.

Martinez; town in Contra Costa County, California, named for a prominent Spanish settler.

Martins; creek in Humboldt County, California, named for an early settler.

Martins; location in Coos County, New Hampshire, granted to Thomas Martin, 1773.

Martinsburg; village in Dixon County, Nebraska, named for Jonathan Martin, its first settler.

Martinsburg; borough in Blair County, Pennsylvania, named for its founder.

Martinsburg; town in Berkeley County, West Virginia, named for Col. Tom Martin, a nephew of Lord Fairfax, a wealthy landowner.

Martins Ferry; city in Belmont County, Ohio, named for the family who established the ferry there.

Martinsville; city in Morgan County, Indiana, named for the oldest of the locating commissioners, John Martin.

Martinsville; village in Harrison County, Missouri, named for Zadoc Martin, a miller.

Martinsville; town in Spartanburg County, South Carolina, named for the founder.

Marvine; mountains in Colorado and Utah, named for the geologist, A. R. Marvine.

Mary; bay in Yellowstone Lake, Yellowstone Park, named for Miss Mary Force.

Mary; lake in Yellowstone Park, named for Miss Mary Clark.

Maryland; one of the thirteen original States, named for Henrietta Maria, wife of Charles I, of England.

Marysville; city in Yuba County, California, named for Mrs. Mary Covilland, one of the founders of the place.

Marysville; city in Marshall County, Kansas, named for the wife of Francis J. Marshall, for whom the county was named.

Marysville; village in Union County, Ohio, named for the daughter of the original proprietor.

Mascoutah; city in St. Clair County, Illinois. An Indian word, meaning "prairie," or "grassy plain."

Masgeek-Hanna; stream of Pennsylvania, an Indian word, meaning "stream flowing through swampy ground."

Mashamoquet; stream in Connecticut. An Indian word, meaning "near the great mountain," oraccording to another authority, "at the great fishing place."

Mashapaug; village in Tolland County, Connecticut; Mashpee; town in Barnstable County, Massachusetts. From an Indian word, Mashapaug, meaning either "standing water," or "great pond."

Maskegon; river in Michigan. An Indian word, meaning " swamp" or "bog."

Mason; village in Effingham County, Illinois, named for Roswell B. Mason, chief engineer Illinois Central Railroad.

Mason; counties in Illinois, Kentucky, and Michigan, named for Stevens T. Mason, the last Territorial governor and first State governor of Michigan.

Mason; bayou in Chicot County, Kansas, named for the early proprietor, the Marquis of Maison Rouge.

Mason; town in Hillsboro County, New Hampshire, named for John Mason, the founder of the colony.

Mason; county in Texas, named for Captain Mason, United States Army.

Mason; county in Washington, named for Charles H. Mason, the first State secretary.

Mason; county in West Virginia, named for George Mason, governor of the State.

Mason; creek in Yellowstone Park, named for Maj. Julius W. Mason, United States Army.

Masonville; town in Delaware County, New York, named for Rev. John M. Mason, of New York.

Massabesic; village in Hillsboro County, New Hampshire. An Indian word, meaning "a place at a great river or brook."

Massac; county in Illinois, named for Fort Massac, which was the scene of an Indian massacre, from which circumstance it derived its name.

Massachaug; pond in Rhode Island. An Indian word, meaning "place where rushes grow."

Massachusetts; one of the thirteen original States. An Indian word, meaning "at or near the great hills." According to other authorities, "the hill in the shape of an arrow head," "great hill mouth," "the blue hills."

Massapeag; village in New London County, Connecticut. An Indian word, meaning "great water land."

Massena; village in St. Lawrence County, New York, named for Andre Massena, a marshal of France.

Massillon: city in Ohio. named for Jean Baptiste Massillion, a celebrated French divine.

Masten; village in Kent County, Delaware, named for William Masten, an early settler.

Masthope; town in Pike County, Pennsylvania. A corruption of the Indian mashapi, meaning "beads of glass."

Matagoodus; tributary of the Penobscot River in Maine. An Indian word meaning "meadow ground."

Matagorda; county, and village in same county, in Texas. A Spanish word meaning " thick brush."

Matamoras; village in Pike County, Pennsylvania. A Spanish word meaning "Moor slayer."

Matanaucook; branch of the Penobscot in Maine. An Indian word meaning "place of bad lands."

Matawan; town in Monmouth County, New Jersey. An Indian word to which various meanings are ascribed, among them "magician," "charmed skin," "it arrives in a lake."

Mathews; county in Virginia, named for Gen. George Mathews, an officer of the Revolution and governor of Georgia.

Matoaca; village in Chesterfield County, Virginia. The original name of the Indian princess, Pocahontas, for whom it is named.

Mattahumkeag; lake in Maine. An Indian word meaning "sand creek pond."

Mattapan; station in Boston, Massachusetts. An Indian word meaning "sitting-down place."

Mattapoisett; town in Plymouth County, Massachusetts. An Indian word given various meanings, "at the great rivulet," "a place of rest," "a place unfavorable for the passage or shelter of canoes."

Mattaponi; river in Virginia. The name said by one authority to be formed by the names of four streams which join, the Mat, Te, Po, and the Ny; another states that it is a corruption of the Indian word mattachpona, "no bread at all," and still another of the word mattapan, meaning "he sits down."

Mattawamkeag; river and a town in Penobscot County, Maine. An Indian word meaning "down a stream which empties into the main river."

Matteawan; stream and village in Dutchess County, New York, which in early days was noted for its peltrie, hence the Indian name meaning "good fur," or "charmed, enchanted skin."

Matthews; town in Mecklenburg County, North Carolina, named for a prominent resident.

Mattison; village in Cook County, Illinois, named for George Joel Aldrich Mattison.

Mattituck; village in Suffolk County, New York. An Indian word, meaning "place without wood, or land not wooded."

Mattoon; city in Coles County, Illinois, named for William Mattoon.

Mauch Chunk; borough and river in Carbon County, Pennsylvania. An Indian word, meaning, according to different authorities, "on the mountain," or "bear's cave."

Maumee; village in Lucas County, Ohio. From an Indian word, "omaumeeg," meaning "people who live on the peninsula."

Maurepas; lake in Louisiana, named for Frederic Phillipeaux, Count of Maurepas.

Maurice; stream in New Jersey, named for the stadtholder of the United Dutch provinces, Maurice, Count of Nassau and Prince of Orange.

Maury; county in Tennessee, named for Abram Maury.

Maury; island in Washington, named for a naval officer.

Mauston; city in Juneau County, Wisconsin, named for Gen. M. M. Maughs, former proprietor of the original village.

Mauvaiseo Terres; tract on the White River, in North Dakota. A French name, meaning "bad lands."

Maverick; county in Texas, named for Samuel A. Maverick, a prominent early settler.

Maxatawny; stream in Berks County, Pennsylvania. From an Indian word, Machsithanna, meaning "bear's path stream."

Maxwell; town in Colusa County, California, named for its founder.

May; cape on the southern extremity of New Jersey, named for Cornelius Jacobson May, a Dutch navigator of the West Indian Company.

Mayaimi; lake in Florida. An Indian word, meaning "very large water."

Mayersville; town in Issaquena County, Mississippi, named for David Meyers, a large landowner.

Mayesville; town in Sumter County, South Carolina, named for the Mayes family, prominent in the county.

Mayodan; village in Rockingham County, North Carolina. A combination of the name of a prominent resident of Richmond, Virginia, and of the river, Dan.

Mays; creek in Michigan, named for Judge May.

Mays Landing-; town in Atlantic County, New Jersey, named for Cornelius Jacobson May, a Dutch navigator of the West Indian Company.

Maysville; city in Mason County, Kentucky, named for the original proprietor, John May.

Maysville; village in Jones County, North Carolina, named for a prominent citizen.

Mayville; village in Tuscola County, Michigan, named for the month of May.

Mayville; city in Dodge County, Wisconsin, named for "Uncle" May, an early settler.

Mazon; town in Grundy County, Illinois. An Indian name, meaning "a kind of weed," which grew along a stream near the town.

Meade; county in Kentucky, named for Capt. James Meade.

Meade; counties in Kansas and South Dakota, peak in Idaho, and city in same county in Kansas, named for Gen. George G. Meade.

Meadville; town in Franklin County, Mississippi, named for Cowles Meade, second secretary of the Territory.

Meadville; city in Crawford County, Pennsylvania, named for Gen. David Mead, its founder.

Meagher; county in Montana, named for Gen. Thomas Francis Meagher, a State official.

Meares; cape in Washington, named for the explorer, John Meares.

Mebane, town in Alamance County, North Carolina, named for Gen. Alexander Mebane.

Mecca; town in Trumbull County, Ohio, named for the capital of Arabia.

Mecklenburg; county in North Carolina, named for the Queen of George III, Charlotte of Mecklenburg.

Mecklenburg; county in Virginia, named for the province in Germany.

Medary; town in Brookings County, South Dakota, named for Samuel Medary, governor of Kansas Territory.

Medfield; town in Norfolk County, Massachusetts. A contraction of its original name of Meadfield, given it on account of the beautiful meadows there.

Mediapolis; town in Des Moines County, Iowa, so named because it is half way between Burlington and Washington.

Medina; county and river in Texas, named for a Mexican-Spaniard, P. Medina, an early settler.

Medo; village in Blue Earth County, Minnesota. The Indian name for a root which in appearance and taste resembles the sweet potato.

Medora; town in Billings County, North Dakota, named for the wife of the Marquis de Mores.

Meeker; town in Clear Creek County, Colorado, named for N. C. Meeker, of the New York Tribune.

Meeker; county in Minnesota, named for Bradley Meeker, associate justice of the supreme court.

Meherrin; river in Virginia. An Indian word, meaning "an island."

Meigs; peak in Colorado, named for Gen. M. C. Meigs.

Meigs; counties in Ohio and Tennessee, named for Col. Return J. Meigs.

Melrose; city in Middlesex County, Massachusetts, named for the borough in Scotland.

Melvern; city in Osage County, Kansas, named for Malvern Hills, Scotland.

Memaloose; island in the Columbia River, near The Dalles, Oregon, so named because it was an Indian burial place, the word meaning "isle of the dead."

Memphis; city in Shelby County, Tennessee, so named because situated upon the river in a manner very similar to that of the city in Egypt.

Memphremagog; lake in Vermont. An Indian word, said to mean "beautiful water," "lake of abundance."

Menan; island off Steuben Harbor, Maine. An Indian word, meaning "island."

Menard; county in Illinois, named for Pierre Menard, a French pioneer.

Menard; county in Texas, named for M. B. Menard, a prominent early settler.

Menasha; city in Winnebago County, Wisconsin. An Indian word, meaning "a thorn."

Mendham; town in Mason County, New Jersey, named for the town in England.

Mendocino; county, and a cape in Humboldt County, California, named for Don Antonia de Mendoza, the viceroy of Mexico.

Mendon; town in Worcester County, Massachusetts, named from the town of Mendham, England.

Mendota; city in Lasalle County, Illinois, and village in Dakota County, Minnesota. An Indian word, meaning "the mouth of a river."

Mendoza; village in Caldwell County, Texas, named for Don Antonio de Mendoza, the viceroy of Mexico.

Menifee; county in Kentucky, named for Richard H. Menifee.

Menoken; town in Shawnee County, Kansas. An Indian word, meaning "it grows well," "good growing place," "fortunate."

Menominee; town in Jo Daviess County, Illinois, river, city, and county in Michigan, and city in Dunn County, Wisconsin. The Indian name for the wild rice which grew abundantly in these regions.

Mentor; township and village in Lake County, Ohio, named for Mento, the counselor of Telemachus.

Mentz; town in Cayuga County, New York, named for the city in Germany.

Mequon; river and township in Ozaukee County, Wisconsin. An Indian name, meaning "ladle," and given the river because a bend in the river resembles a paddle.

Meramec; river in Missouri. A corruption of the Indian name which signifies "catfish river."

Merced; county, and city in same county in California. A Spanish word, meaning "mercy."

Mercer; counties in Illinois, Kentucky, Missouri, New Jersey, Ohio, Pennsylvania, and West Virginia, named for General Hugh Mercer.

Mercer; county in North Dakota, named for William Henry Harrison Mercer, an early pioneer and ranchman.

Mercersburg; borough in Franklin County, Pennsylvania, named for Gen. Hugh Mercer.

Merchantville; borough in Camden County, New Jersey, named for the Merchant family.

Meredith; town in Belknap County, New Hampshire, named for a British nobleman.

Meredith; town in Delaware County, New York, named for Samuel Meredith, of Pennsylvania.

Meredosia; town in Morgan County, Illinois. A corruption of the French name Marais d'Ogee, meaning "marsh of the pointed arch."

Meriwether; county in Georgia, named for David Meriwether, former member of Congress from Georgia.

Merom; town in Sullivan County, Indiana, named for the waters of Merom in Palestine.

Merrill; city in Lincoln County, Wisconsin, named for S. S. Merrill of the Wisconsin Central Railroad Company.

Merrimac; town in Essex County, Massachusetts, and village in Sauk County, Wisconsin; Merrimack; river, county, and town in Hillsboro County, New Hampshire. From the Indian, meaning "sturgeon," or "swift water."

Mesa; county in Colorado, so named because of its topographical situation; the name a Spanish one, meaning "elevated table-laud."

Mesa Inclinado; plateau in western Colorado. The name Spanish and significant of its slope.

Meshoppen; stream in Pennsylvania. An Indian name, meaning "glass beads," and given this stream because of the barter of trinkets made upon its banks.

Mesick; town in Wexford County, Michigan, named for its first settler.

Mesilla; town in Dona Ana County, New Mexico. An Indian word, meaning "little table-land."

Meskaskeeseehunk; branch of the Mattwamkeag River, Maine. An Indian word, meaning "little spruce brook."

Mesongo; stream in Maryland. An Indian word, meaning "where we killed deer."

Mesquite; village in Dallas County, Texas. The Spanish name for a tree of the locust family.

Metamora; village in Woodford County, Illinois, named for the Indian chief who was the hero of Edwin Forrest's play.

Metcalfe; county in Kentucky, named for Thomas Metcalfe, an early governor of the State.

Metea; village in Cass County, Indiana, named for Pottawattomie, an Indian chief; or possibly from meda or meta, which means "a prophet or priest."

Metuchen; borough in Middlesex County, New Jersey, named for the chief of the Raritans.

Metz; five villages in the United States bear the name of the town in Germany.

Mexia; town in Limestone County, Texas, named from Mexico.

Mexico; city in Audrain County, Missouri. Named from the country, which is said to be derived from the Aztec word Mexitili, the name of a tutelary divinity, but according to another authority meaning the "habitation of the god of war."

Meyer; county in South Dakota, named for Fred Meyer, civil engineer and land surveyor.

Meyersdale; borough in Somerset County, Pennsylvania, named for an early settler.

Miami; counties in Indiana, Kansas, and Ohio, cities in Dade County, Florida. and Saline County, Missouri, town in Ottawa Reservation, Indian Territory, and rivers in Florida and Ohio. The French orthography of the Indian word "Maumee," meaning "mother;" or, according to another authority, " pigeon."

Mianus; village and river in Fairfield County, Connecticut. A corruption of the name of the Indian chief Mayanno, meaning "he who gathers together."

Micanopy; town in Alachua County, Florida, named for a chief of the Seminole Indians, whose name signifies "chief of chiefs."

Michaux; town in Powhatan County, Virginia. An Indian word. meaning "great."

Michigamme; village in Marquette County, Michigan. An Indian word, meaning "large lake."

Michigan; lake and State in the United States. An Indian word, said by some to mean "big lake;" by others, "place for catching fish."

Middleboro; town in Plymouth County, Massachusetts, so named because it was situated between the Pilgrim settlement at Plymouth and the village of the Indian sachem, Massasoit, near Bristol, Rhode Island.

Middleburg; town in Vance County, North Carolina, so named because it is the middle point between two rivers.

Middlebury; town in Addison County, Vermont, so named because it was the central of three towns surveyed simultaneously.

Middlegrove; town in Monroe County, Missouri, so named because it is midway between the Big Muddy and Mississippi rivers.

Middleport; village in Niagara County, New York, so named on account of its situation on the canal half way between Albion and Lockport.

Middlesex; many places in the United States have been named for the county in England, among them being counties in Connecticut, Massachusetts, New Jersey, and Virginia.

Midland; county in Michigan, so named because of its situation in the east-central portion of the southern peninsula.

Midlothian; town in Chesterfield County, Virginia, named for the county in Scotland.

Mifflin; county in Pennsylvania, named for a former governor.

Milam; county in Texas, named for Benjamin R. Milam, an early settler and distinguished Indian fighter.

Milan; name of many places in the United States, transferred from Italy.

Milburn; town in Ballard County, Kentucky, named for William Milburn.

Miles; city in Jackson County, Iowa, named for the man who laid it out.

Miles; city in Custer County, Montana, named for Gen. Nelson A. Miles.

Milesburg; borough in Center County, Pennsylvania, named for its founder, Col. Samuel Miles.

Milford; town in Worcester County, Massachusetts, so named on account of the many mills erected upon Mill River.

Milford; town in Hillsboro County, New Hampshire, named for the town in England.

Milk; river in Montana, so named because of its whitish appearance.

Millard; county in Utah, named for Millard Fillmore.

Millard; village in Douglas County, Nebraska, named for Ezra Millard, its founder.

Millbury; town in Worcester County, Massachusetts, so named because the Blackstone River at this point is the site of many mills.

Milledgeville; city in Georgia, named for John Milledge, an early governor of the State.

Millelacs; lake and county in Minnesota. From the French, mille lacs, meaning "thousand lakes."

Miller; county in Arkansas, named for James Miller, former governor of the State.

Miller; county in Georgia, named for a distinguished citizen of the State, Andrew J. Miller.

Miller; county in Missouri, named for John Miller, a former governor.

Miller; village in Knox County, Nebraska, named for the first settler, Capt. J. M. Miller.

Miller; creek in Yellowstone Park, named for an early pioneer.

Millerplace; village in Suffolk County, New York, named for Andrew Miller, the son of an early pioneer of Easthampton.

Millersburg; town in Callaway County, Missouri, named for Thomas Miller, an early settler.

Millersburg; village in Holmes County, Ohio, named for Charles Miller, its founder.

Millersburg; borough in Dauphin County, Pennsylvania. named for Daniel Miller, its founder.

Millerstown; borough in Perry County, Pennsylvania. named for its founder, David Miller.

Millerton; town in Dutchess County, New York, named from Samuel G. Miller, one of the contractors and builders of the extension of the New York and Harlem Railroad from Dover Plains to Chatham.

Millinocket; lake on the Penobscot River, Maine. An Indian word, meaning "place full of islands."

Mills; county in Iowa, named for Major Mills, of the State.

Mills; county in Texas, named for John S. Mills, prominent in law and politics of the State.

Millsfield; town in Coos County, New Hampshire, named for Sir Thomas Mills.

Millstone; borough in Somerset County, New Jersey, probably so named for the stone found there which is suitable for milling purposes.

Milltown; borough in Middlesex County, New Jersey, so named because of the number of mills located there.

Milo; towns in Piscataquis County, Maine, and Yates County, New York, named for the Greek island.

Milton; county in Georgia, named for Homer V. Milton.

Milton; town in Norfolk County, Massachusetts, so named because of the number of mills operating on the Neponset at this point.

Milton; towns in Ulster County, New York; Chittenden County, Vermont, and Cabell County, West Virginia; village in Caswell County, North Carolina; named for John Milton, the poet.

Miltonvale; city in Cloud County, Kansas named for Milton Tootle, of St. Joseph, the former owner of the town site.

Milwaukee; county and city in Wisconsin, the name said to have been derived from the Indian word Milioke, which means "good earth" or '-good country."

Mimbres; river and mountains in New Mexico. A Spanish word, meaning "the willows."

Mine; river in Missouri. A contraction of the original French name, Riviere a la Mine.

Miner; county in South Dakota, named for Capt. Nelson Miner and Mr. Ephriam Miner, who were members of the legislature which created the county.

Mineral; counties in Colorado and West Virginia; Mineral Point; city in Iowa County, Wisconsin. So named on account of the abundance of ore in the vicinity.

Minersville; borough in Schuylkill County, Pennsylvania, so named because it is the center of the coal fields.

Minerva; towns in Stark County, Ohio, and Essex County, New York, named for the goddess of wisdom.

Mingo; county in West Virginia and village in Jefferson County, Ohio, named for an Indian tribe, the name said to signify "spring people."

Minisink; town in Orange County, New York. An Indian name said by some to mean "islanders;" by others, "home of the Minsies."

Minneapolis; cities in Ottawa County, Kansas, and Hennepin County, Minnesota. A combination of the Indian word, minni, "water," and the Creek word, polis, "city."

Minnehaha; county in South Dakota, and celebrated falls in Hennepin County, Minnesota. An Indian word, meaning " laughing water."

Minneiska; stream, and a village in Wabasha County, Minnesota. An Indian word, meaning "clear water."

Minnequa; village and summer resort in Bradford County, Pennsylvania. An Indian word, meaning "to drink."

Minnesota; State in the Union. An Indian word, meaning "much water" or "cloudy water."

Minnetonka; lake in Minnesota. An Indian word with various meanings ascribed to it, such as "big water," "great water," "pond of water," or "lake."

Minnicotta; lake in Minnesota. An Indian word, meaning "warm water."

Minniwakan; lake in North Dakota. An Indian word, meaning "spirit water."

Minonk; city in Woodford County, Illinois. An Indian word, given various meanings, such as "an island," "star," "place or locality."

Minooka; village in Grundy County, Illinois. An Indian word, meaning "maple forest," or "good earth."

Minor; creek in Humboldt County, California, named for Isaac Minor."

Minot; town in Androscoggin County, Maine, named for Judge Minot, a member of the general court.

Minto; village in Marion County, Oregon, named for John Minto, an early pioneer.

Minturn; village in Madera County, California, named for Jonas Minturn, an old settler.

Mirabile; town in Caldwell County, Missouri. A Latin word, meaning "wonderful."

Mishawaka; town in St. Joseph County, Indiana, probably named for the Indian chief, Mishiniwaka.

Mispan; branch of the Delaware River. An Indian word, meaning "raccoon."

Missaukee; county in Michigan, probably named from the Indian tribe, Mississauga, which means "people of the wide mouth river."

Missionary; ridge extending along the northeast border of Georgia, so called because Roman Catholic missions were established there at an early date.

Missisquoi; river in Vermont. An Indian word, meaning "the big woman."

Mississinewa; river in Indiana. An Indian word, meaning "river of great stones."

Mississippi; state of the Union, counties in Arkansas and Missouri, and river, one of the largest in the United States. An Indian word, meaning "great water" or "gathering in of all the waters," and "an almost endless river spread out."

Missoula; county, river, and city in Montana. The name said to mean the same as Missouri, "muddy water."

Missouri; state and river in the United States. The meaning as above.

Mitchell; town in Eagle County, Colorado, named for George R. Mitchell, a noted resident of Gilpin County.

Mitchell; county in Georgia, named for David Bradie Mitchell, governor of the State in early days.

Mitchell; county and town in Iowa, named for John Mitchell, the Irish patriot.

Mitchell; county in Kansas, named for Gen. William D. Mitchell.

Mitchell; county in North Carolina, named for Elisha Mitchell.

Mitchell; town in Wheeler County, Oregon, named for Senator John H. Mitchell.

Mitchell; county in Texas, named for the brothers A. and E. Mitchell, prominent Texans of early days.

Mitchells; peak in North Carolina, named for Elisha Mitchell, who lost his life while making a survey of it.

Mitchellville; town in Polk County, Iowa, named for Thomas Mitchell.

Mitchigami; lake in northern Wisconsin. An Indian word, meaning "large lake."

Moberly; city in Randolph County, Missouri, named for Col. William E. Moberly of Brunswick.

Mobile; city, county, river, and bay in Alabama, said to have been named from Maubila, an Indian city in the vicinity.

Mobjack; bay in Maryland, said to be so called because a pirate named Jack was mobbed and thrown overboard into this body of water.

Moccasin; village in Effingham County, Illinois. The Indian name for a shoe or covering for the foot.

Mocksville; town in Davie County, North Carolina, named for the former owner of the land.

Modena; village in Ulster County, New York, named for a city in Italy.

Modoc; county in California, and towns in Edgefield County, South Carolina, and Randolph County, Indiana. An Indian word, meaning "the head of the river."

Moffat; town in Saguache County, Colorado, named for D. H. Moffat, late president of the Denver and Rio Grande Railroad.

Mogollon; plateau in Arizona and range of mountains in New Mexico. A Spanish word, meaning "hanger-on, parasite."

Mohave; county in Arizona, said to have been named for a tribe of Indians whose name was Hamunkh-habi, "three hills."

Mohawk; river, township and village in Herkimer County, New York, said by one authority to have been named for a tribe of Indians, the word meaning "eats what lives," indicating that they were cannibals; but another authority states that it is a corruption of Maquaas, "muskrat."

Mohican; town and river in Ashland County, Ohio, named for the Indian tribe, the word meaning " wolf."

Moira; town in Franklin County, New York, named for the Earl of Moira.

Mokane; village in Callaway County, Missouri, on the Missouri, Kansas and Eastern Railroad; the name being formed of a combination of the first letters of these names.

Mokelumne; river in California. A corruption of the Indian name, Wakalumni, meaning "river."

Mokena; village in Will County, Illinois. An Indian word, meaning "turtle."

Molino; several towns and villages in the United States. A Spanish word, sometimes written "moline," meaning "mill."

Molunkus; river and plantation in Aroostook County, Maine. An Indian word, meaning "a short stretch of high land oil a small stream."

Monadnock; mountain in New Hampshire. An Indian word, meaning "spirit place," or, possibly, "bad," as signifying the difficulty of the ascent. Another authority gives the interpretation "at the silver mountain."

Monaghan; township in York County, Pennsylvania, named for the county in Ireland.

Mondamin; town in Harrison County, Iowa. An Indian word, meaning "corn" or "cornfield."

Monee; village in Will County, Illinois, named for the wife of an Indian trader, Joseph Bailes, the name being the Indian corruption of the English baptismal name of Mary.

Monhegan; island in Lincoln County, Maine. An Indian word, meaning "grand island."

Moniteau; county and creek in Missouri, so named by the Indians because of the painted figure of a man upon a rock in the vicinity, the word in their language meaning "spirit."

Monks Corner; town in Berkeley County, South Carolina, named for Thomas Monk, a prominent colonial settler.

Monmouth; town in Kennebec County, Maine, named from the battle of Monmouth, New Jersey.

Monmouth; county in New Jersey, named for Monmouthshire, England.

Mono; county and lake in California. A Spanish word, meaning "pretty," "nice."

Monocacy; river in Maryland, and creek in Pennsylvania. An Indian word meaning "stream containing many large bends."

Monongah; town in Marion County, West Virginia. An abbreviation of the names of Monongahela River and Monongalia County.

Monongalia; county in West Virginia. A Latinized form of the Indian word Monongahela.

Monroe; many places in the United States named for its fifth President, James Monroe; among them counties in Alabama, Arkansas, Florida, Georgia, Illinois, Indiana, Iowa, Kentucky, Michigan, Mississippi, Missouri, New York, Ohio, Pennsylvania, Tennessee, West Virginia, and Wisconsin; city in Walton County, Georgia; town in Waldo County, Maine; village in Orange County, New York; fort at Old Point Comfort, Virginia, and mountain in New Hampshire.

Monroe City; town in Knox County, Indiana, named for Monroe Alton, its founder.

Monroeville; village in Salem County, New Jersey, named for S. T. Monroe, minister of an early church.

Monrovia; village in Morgan County, Indiana, the name being a variation of the name of the township in which it is located.

Monsey; village in Rockland County, New York. A corruption of the Indian, Minsi, meaning "wolf."

Monson; town in Hampden County, Massachusetts, named for John, the second Lord Monson.

Montague; town in Franklin County, Massachusetts, named for Capt. William Montague.

Montague; town in Lewis County, New York, named for the daughter of H. P. Pierrepont.

Montague; county in Texas, named for Daniel Montague.

Montana; State in the Union. A Latin word, meaning "mountainous region," and applicable to this State on account of the nature of its topography.

Montauk; headland at the extreme eastern point of Long Island, New York. A corruption of the Indian, Minnawtawkit. meaning "island place," or "in the island country."

Montcalm; county in Michigan, named for General Montcalm.

Montclair; town in Essex County, New Jersey, named from "Clear Mountain."

Monte Diablo; mountain in California. A Spanish name, meaning "mountain of the devil."

Monterey; county, and city in same county, in California, named for Count de Monterey, viceroy of Mexico.

Monterey; town in Berkshire County, Massachusetts, named for a battle in the Mexican war.

Montezuma; county, and town in Summit County, Colorado, named for the Emperor of Mexico.

Montgomery; many counties and towns in the United States, named for Gen. Richard Montgomery, who was killed in the assault on Quebec. Among these are counties in Arkansas, Georgia, Illinois, Indiana, Iowa, Kansas, Kentucky, Maryland, Mississippi, Missouri, New York, North Carolina, Ohio, Pennsylvania, and Virginia, and village in Orange County, New York.

Montgomery; county in Alabama, named for Lieut. Lemuel P. Montgomery, of Montgomery, Alabama.

Montgomery; town in Daviess County, Indiana, named for Valentine B. Montgomery, its founder.

Montgomery; county in Tennessee, named for Col. John Montgomery.

Montgomery; county in Texas, named for Gen. James Montgomery.

Monticello; many places in the United States, among them the towns in Jasper County, Georgia, and Lawrence County. Mississippi, and village in Sullivan County, New York, named for the home of Thomas Jefferson in Albemarle County, Virginia.

Montour; county. ridge, and a borough in Lycoming County, in Pennsylvania, named for Madame Montour, an early French settler from Quebec.

Montpelier; city, the capital of Vermont, named from the city in France.

Montrose; county, and town in same county in Colorado, named for Sir Walter Scott's legend of " Montrose."

Montrose; village in Genesee County, New York, named from the town in Scotland.

Montrose; borough in Susquehanna County, Pennsylvania, named for Dr. Robert H. Rose.

Moodus; village in Middlesex County, Connecticut. A contraction of the Indian, Machemoodus, meaning " place of noises."

Moody; county in South Dakota, named tor Gideon G. Moody, United States Senator.

Mooers; town and village in Clinton County, New York, named for Gen. Benjamin Mooers.

Moore; county in North Carolina, named for Alfred Moore, an associate justice of the United States.

Moore; county in Tennessee, named for Gen. William Moore, prominent member of the general assembly of the State.

Moore; county in Texas, named for E. W. Moore, commodore of the Texas navy.

Moorefield; town in Hardy County, West Virginia, named for Conrad Moore.

Mooresville; town in Morgan County, Indiana, named for Samuel Moore, its founder.

Mooresville; town in Livingston County, Missouri, named for its founder, W. B. Moore.

Moorhead; city in Clay County, Minnesota, named for Gen. J. K. Moorhead of Pittsburg, Pennsylvania.

Moorhead; town in Custer County, Montana, named for W. G. Moorehead of the Northern Pacific Railroad.

Moosabec; light-house on the coast of Maine. An Indian word, meaning "the bald pond place."

Moose; river and plantation in Somerset County, Maine. Derivation of the Indian word Moosoa, " wood eaters." Moose; stream in Pennsylvania. Derived from the Indian word Chinklacamoose, meaning "it almost joins," and applicable to this river because there is a horseshoe bend in it where the extremities almost meet.

Mooselookmeguntic; lake in Maine. An Indian word, meaning "where the hunters watch the moose at night."

Moosup; river and village in Windham County, Connecticut, named for the Indian sachem, Maussup.

Mora; county in New Mexico. The Spanish name for raspberries.

Moran; city in Allen County, Kansas, named for Daniel Comyan Moran, a capitalist.

Moran; mountain in the Teton Range, Wyoming, named for Thomas Moran, the artist.

Moravia; town in Cayuga County, New York, named for the province in Austria.

Moreau; river in Missouri. A French word, signifying "extremely well."

Moreau; town in Saratoga County, New York, named for Marshall Moreau, of France.

Morehead; town in Rowan County, Kentucky, named for Gov. James T. Morehead.

Morehead; town in Carteret County, North Carolina, named for John M. Morehead, former governor of the State.

Morehouse; parish in Louisiana, named for the man who obtained the grant from Baron Bastrop, 1704.

Morehouse; town in Hamilton County, New York, named for the first settler.

Moresville; village in Delaware County, New York, named for the first settler.

Morgan; counties in Alabama, Georgia, Illinois, Indiana, Kentucky, Missouri, Tennessee, and West Virginia, named for Gen. Daniel Morgan, an officer in the Revolution.

Morgan; county in Colorado, named for Col. Christopher A. Morgan. of the Colorado Volunteers.

Morgan; town in Orleans County, Vermont, named for John Morgan, an original proprietor.

Morganfield; city in Union County, Kentucky; Morganton; town in Burke County, North Carolina. Named for Gen. Daniel Morgan, an officer of the Revolution.

Morgantown; town in Monongalia County, West Virginia, named for Gen. Zacquell Morgan, the original owner of the land.

Morganville; city in Clay County, Kansas, named for its founder, Ebenezer Morgan.

Moriah; township in Essex County, New York, and peak in the White Mountains, New Hampshire, named for the district in Palestine.

Morrill; city in Brown County, Kansas, named for Governor E. N. Morrill.

Morrill; town in Waldo County, Maine, named for Anson P. Morrill, former governor of the State.

Morrillton; city in Conway County, Arkansas, named for the early pioneers, E. J. and George H. Morrill.

Morris; county in Kansas, named for Thomas Morris, United States Senator from Ohio.

Morris; county in New Jersey, named for Lewis Morris.

Morris; county in Texas, named for W. W. Morris.

Morrison; town in Jefferson County, Colorado, named from the Morrison Stone and Lime Company.

Morrison; county in Minnesota, probably named for William Morrison, the first white man to discover the sources of the Mississippi.

Morissania; village and township in Westchester County, New York; Morristown; town in Morris County, New Jersey. Named for Lewis Morris, an American statesman.

Morristown; village in St. Lawrence County, New York, named for the principal proprietor.

Morrisville; village in Madison County, New York, named for a family of early settlers.

Morrisville; village in Wake County, North Carolina, named for the owner of the land.

Morrisville; borough in Bucks County, Pennsylvania, named for Robert Morris, the financier, who formerly resided there.

Morrow; county in Oregon, and town in Nez Perces County, Idaho, named for Gen. Henry A. Morrow.

Morrow; county in Ohio, and village in Warren County, same State, named for Governor Jeremiah Morrow.

Morton; counties in Kansas and North Dakota, named for Oliver P. Morton, United States Senator from Indiana.

Morton; village in Scott County, Mississippi, given the maiden name of the wife of Col. E. W. Taylor.

Morven; town in Anson County, North Carolina, named for the mountain in Scotland.

Moscow; many towns and villages in the United States, named for the city in Russia, among them being the town in Somerset County, Maine.

Moshannon; creek in Pennsylvania. A corruption of an Indian word meaning "elk creek."

Mosinee; village in Marathon County, Wisconsin. Derived from the Indian word meaning "moose."

Motley; county in Texas, named for Dr. William Motley, one of the signers of the Declaration of Independence.

Moulton; town in Appanoose County, Iowa, named for an engineer on the Chicago, Burlington and Quincy Railroad.

Moultonboro; town in Carroll County, New Hampshire, named for Col. Jonathan Moulton, one of the first settlers.

Moultrie; county in Illinois, and fortification on Sullivan Island, in Charleston Harbor, South Carolina; Moultrieville; town in Charleston County, South Carolina. Named for Gen. William Moultrie.

Mound; city in Linn County, ridge in McPherson County, and valley in Labette County, Kansas, so named on account of the topography of the country.

Mound Bayou; town in Bolivar County, Mississippi, named for the Indian mounds on the bayou.

Moundsville; city in Marshall County, West Virginia, so named because the largest mound of the mound builders is situated here.

Mount Carmel; many towns and villages in the United States are named for the mountain in Palestine.

Mount Clemens; city in Macomb County, Michigan, named for Judge Clemens, its founder.

Mount Gilead; town in Montgomery County, North Carolina, named from a country church.

Mount Morris; town in Livingston County, New York, named for Mr. Thomas Morris, of Philadelphia.

Mount Vernon; residence of Gen. George Washington, and city in Lawrence County, Missouri, named for the foregoing, which was originally built by Lawrence Washington for Admiral Vernon, for whom it was named.

Movestar; stream in Illinois. A corruption of the French, Mauvaise Terre, "bad land."

Moweaqua; village in Shelby County, Illinois, named from the Indian, which is given the various meanings of "weeping woman," "wolf woman," "woman of the wolf token."

Mower; county in Minnesota, named for J. E. Mower, a member of the Council.

Muhlenberg; county in Kentucky, named for Gen. J. P. G. Muhlenberg, an officer of the revolutionary war.

Muir; village in Ionia County, Michigan, named for W. K. Muir, superintendent of the Detroit and Mackinac Railway.

Mullan; town in Shoshone County, Idaho, named for Lieut. John Mullan.

Mullins; town in Marion County, South Carolina, named for the Mullin family, prominent in that country.

Multnomah; county in Oregon. An Indian word, meaning "down river."

Mulvane; city in Sumner County, Kansas, named for John R. Mulvane, of Topeka, Kansas.

Muncie; city in Delaware County, Indiana, and village in Vermilion County, Illinois, named from the Indian tribe, the word meaning "death," given to them on account of an epidemic of smallpox which nearly exterminated the tribe.

Mundy; township in Genesee County, Michigan, named for Edward Mundy, former lieutenant-governor of the State.

Munfordville; town in Hart County, Kentucky, named for Richard I. Munford, former proprietor.

Munising; village in Alger County, Michigan. A corruption of the Indian word miniss, "island."

Munnsville; village in Madison County, New York, named for Asa Munn, the first storekeeper in the place.

Murder; creek in Genesee County, New York, so named because the body of a man who was supposed to have been murdered was found in the stream.

Murfreesboro; city in Rutherford County, Tennessee, and town in Hertford County, North Carolina, named for Col. Hardy Murfree, an officer of the Revolution.

Murphy; town in Calaveras County, California, named for a pioneer miner.

Murphy; town in Cherokee County, North Dakota, named for A. D. Murphy, a judge of the superior court.

Murray; county in Georgia, named for Thomas W. Murray, former member of the legislature.

Murray; city in Callaway County, Kentucky, named for Hon. John L. Murray, member of Congress.

Murray; county in Minnesota, named for Hon. W. P. Murray, prominent State politician.

Murrieta; town in Riverside County, California, named for a former proprietor of a large tract of land, J. Murrieta.

Muscackituck; river in Indiana. An Indian word, meaning "pond river," and so named because of the many stagnant ponds upon its banks.

Muscatine; county and city in same county in Iowa, probably derived from the Indian and meaning "dweller in the prairie," but according to another theory derived from the French and Indian, Musquota, " prairie," and tine, a diminutive.

Muscle Shoals; series of rapids in the Tennessee River in northern Alabama, so named because of the great number of mussels found there.

Muscoda; village in (J rand County, Kansas. An Indian word, meaning "a prairie" or "grassy plain."

Muscogee; county in Georgia and town in Creek Nation, Indian Territory, named for a tribe of Indians of the Creek confederacy, whose name means "wanderer."

Musconetcong; river in New Jersey. Indian word, meaning "rapid stream."

Muscotah; city in Atchison County, Kansas. An Indian word, meaning "beautiful prairie" or "prairie of fire." Music; peak in the Rocky Mountains in Arizona, so named because of its resemblance to a big piece of music.

Muskeego; lake, river, and township in Waukesha County, Wisconsin. An Indian word, meaning "place of cranberries."

Muskegon; county, and city in same county in Michigan. An Indian word, meaning "marshy waters."

Muskingum; river and county in Ohio. An Indian word, meaning "moose-eye river," so called because of the number of moose and elk which inhabited the country.

Musquacook; chain of lakes in Maine. An Indian word, meaning "birch bark place." Mustang; stream in Texas. A Spanish word, meaning "wild horse of the prairie." Herds of wild horses having been abundant in Texas at an early date.

Muttonville; village in Ontario County, New York, so named because of the establishment of a tallow chandlery there.

Myerstown; village in Lebanon County, Pennsylvania, named for its founder, Isaac Myers.

Myrtle; village in Union County, Mississippi, so called because of the abundance of myrtle trees in the vicinity.

Mystic; river and village in New London County, Connecticut, and river in Massachusetts. From the Indian, missi, "great," and tuk, "tidal river;" hence "the great river."

N

Nacooche; town and valley in White County, Georgia. An Indian name, meaning "evening star."

Nahant; town and watering place in Essex County, Massachusetts. According to different authorities an Indian word, meaning "at the point," or "two things united," the latter meaning given because the town is formed of two islands connected by a beach.

Nahma; town in Delta County, Michigan, on Sturgeon River. The Indian name for sturgeon.

Naiwa; tributary of the Mississippi. An Indian word, meaning "copper snake river."

Namekagon; lake in Wisconsin. Derived from the Indian, nama, "sturgeon," signifying "a place where sturgeons are plenty."

Nameoki; town in Madison County, Illinois. An Indian word, meaning "fishing place," or "place of fish."

Nance; county in Nebraska, named for Albinus Nance.

Nansemond; river and county in Virginia. Said to be derived from the Indian, Neunschimend, "whence we fled," or " whence we were driven off."

Nantahala; rivers in Georgia, and Macon County, North Carolina. An Indian word, meaning "maiden's bosom."

Nanticoke; town in Broome County, New York, borough in Luzerne County, Pennsylvania, and mountain in the same State, and river in Delaware, named for the Indian tribe, the word meaning "tidewater people."

Nantucket; island and county in Massachusetts. This name appeared upon the maps in 1630 as Natocko, and some authorities state that it is derived from an Indian word, meaning "faraway;" others say that its present form is a direct derivation of the Indian, Nantuck, which means that the sandy, sterile soil tempted no one.

Napa; county, and city in same county, in California. Said to be an Indian word, meaning "city," or "house."

Narka; city in Republican County, Kansas, named for the daughter of a railroad official; the name of Indian derivation.

Narragansett; summer resort in Washington County, Rhode Island. An anglicization of the Indian name of a tribe, which in their language means, "people of the point."

Nash; county in North Carolina, named for General Francis Nash.

Nashota; town in Waukesha County, Wisconsin. An Indian word which, in the Algonquin and Dakota languages, means, respectively, "the twins," or "kicks up smoke."

Nashua; city in Hillsboro County, New Hampshire, and town in Chickasaw County, Iowa. An Indian word, meaning "the land between."

Nashville; town in Nash County, North Carolina, a number of towns and a city in Davidson County, Tennessee, named for (Jen. Francis Nash.

Nashville; town in Holmes County, Ohio, probably named for Judge Simon Nash.

Nassau; counties in Florida and New York and several towns in different States named for the Duchy of Nassau in Germany.

Natchaug; river in Connecticut. Derived from an Indian word, meaning "land between," or "in the middle."

Natchez; city in Adams County, Mississippi, named for the Indian tribe, the word meaning "hurrying men," or "one running to war."

Natick; town in Middlesex County, Massachusetts. An Indian word, meaning "the place of hills."

Natrona; county in Wyoming. Derived from the Spanish, natron, meaning "native carbonate of soda," and given this county because of the spring within its limits.

Naubuc; town in Hartford County, Connecticut. Said to be a corruption of the Indian, upauk, "flooded," or "overflowed."

Naugatuck; river and borough in New Haven County, Connecticut. Authorities differ as to the meaning of its Indian origin, giving both "one tree," and "fork of the river."

Nauvoo; city in Hancock County, Illinois, named in obedience to a "revelation" made to Joseph Smith, one of its Mormon founders.

Navajo; county, and town in Apache County, Arizona, named for the Indian tribe, who are said to have been so named by the Spaniards, the word meaning a kind of clasp knife, and as applied to the tribe signifying "a knife-whetting people."

Navarre; village in Stark County, Ohio, named for the province in Spain.

Navarro; county in Texas, named for Jose Antonio Navarro, a Mexican by birth, but a prominent Texas citizen.

Navesink; village in Monmouth County, New Jersey. An Indian word, meaning " high land between waters." Navidad; village in Jackson County, Texas. Spanish word, meaning "Christmas Day."

Nayattpoint; village in Bristol County, Rhode Island. Probably a corruption of the Indian, nayaug, meaning a "point" or "corner."

Nazareth; borough in Northampton County, Pennsylvania, named for the birthplace of Jesus Christ.

Nebo; several towns and villages in the United States and a mountain in the Wasatch Range, Utah, named for the mount in Palestine.

Nebo; town in Hopkins County, Kentucky. An Indian word, meaning "dead."

Nebraska; State and river in the United States. An Indian word, meaning "shallow, or broad water."

Necedah; village in Juneau County, Wisconsin. A corruption of the Chippewa Indian, nissida, "let there be three of us."

Needham; town in Norfolk County, Massachusetts, named for the town in England.

Needles; peaks of the Mojave Mountains in California, so named on account of their peculiarly sharp and slender outlines. A station on the Atchison, Topeka and Santa Fe Railroad in California.

Negaunee; city in Marquette County, Michigan. An Indian word, meaning "first," "ahead," "he goes before;" an effort to translate the English word "pioneer."

Neillsville; city in Clark County, Wisconsin, named for a family of early settlers.

Neligh; city in Antelope County, Nebraska, named for Hon. John D. Neligh.

Nelson; counties in Kentucky and Virginia, named for Thomas Nelson, governor of Virginia in 1781.

Nelson; village in Nuckolls County, Nebraska, named for C. Nelson Wheeler, who owned the town site.

Nelson; county in North Dakota, named for Hon. N. E. Nelson, a prominent pioneer settler.

Nelsonville; town in Putnam County, New York, named for Elisha Nelson, who built the first house in the village.

Nennescah; river in Kansas. An Indian word, meaning "good river."

Neodesha; city in Wilson County, Kansas, at the junction of the Fall and Verdigris rivers, and for this reason given the Indian name, which means "meeting of the waters."

Neoga; village in Cumberland County, Illinois. An Indian word, meaning "the place of the Deity."

Neosho; river and county in Kansas and city in Newton County, Missouri; Neosho Falls; city in Woodson County, Kansas. An Indian word, meaning "clear cold water."

Nepaug; small stream in Connecticut. An Indian word, meaning " waters," or "fresh pond."

Nephi; city in Juab County, Utah, named for the youngest son of Lehi, a character of the Book of Mormon.

Neponset; village in Bureau County, Illinois. An Indian word, meaning " he walks in his sleep."

Neptune City; borough in Monmouth County, New Jersey, so named because of its location on the seaside.

Nesbitt; town in De Soto County, Mississippi, named for early settlers.

Nescopeck; creek and borough in Luzerne County, Pennsylvania. An Indian word, meaning "deep and still water."

Neshaminy; stream in Bucks County, Pennsylvania. An Indian word, meaning "a stream formed by the confluence of two branches."

Neshannock; stream and a village in Mercer County, Pennsylvania; Neshannock Falls; village in Lawrence County, Pennsylvania. An Indian word, meaning " both streams," or "the streams making one by flowing together."

Neshoba; county in Mississippi. An Indian word, meaning "grey wolf."

Nesowadnehunk; stream and mountains in Maine. An Indian name, meaning "stream among the mountains."

Nesquehoning; stream and village in Carbon County, Pennsylvania. An Indian word, meaning "black lick."

Ness; county, and city in same county, in Kansas, named for Corpl. Noah V. Ness, of the Seventh Kansas Cavalry.

Nesselroad; village in Jackson County, West Virginia, named for the first postmaster.

Nettle Carrier; creek and village in Overton County, Tennessee, named for a Cherokee Indian of local note.

Nettleton; towns in Caldwell County, Missouri, and Lee County, Mississippi, named for a former vice-president of the Kansas City, Memphis and Birmingham Railroad.

Nevada; State of the Union, counties in Arkansas and California and mountains of the western coast. A Spanish word, meaning "snow clad, snowy land," originally applied to the snow-capped mountains.

New; village in Oconto County, Wisconsin, named for Hon. John C. New, of Indianapolis.

New Almaden; the most productive quicksilver mine in the United States, named for the mine in Spain.

Newark; cities in Essex County, New Jersey, and Licking County, Ohio, and town in Newcastle County, Delaware, named for the town in England.

Newaygo; county and village in same county in Michigan, named for an Indian chief. The name said to mean "much water."

New Bedford; city in Bristol County, Massachusetts. The name of the owner of the town site being Russell, the family name of the Duke of Bedford.

Newbern; city in Craven County, North Carolina, named for the town in Switzerland.

Newberry; mountain in California, named for Captain Newberry.

Newberry; village in Luce County, Michigan, named for John A. Newberry, stockholder in the Detroit, Mackinac and Marquette Railroad.

Newberry; county and town in same county in South Carolina, said to have been named for a prominent resident family, or, according to another authority, for a captain in Sumter's State troops.

New Braunfels; city in Comal County, Texas, named for the town in Prussia.

New Bremen; village in Auglaize County, Ohio, named for the Duchy in Germany.

New Brunswick; city in Middlesex County, New Jersey, incorporated in the time of and named for King George the Second, of the House of Brunswick.

Newburg; city in Orange County, New York, named for the town in Scotland.

(Newbury; town in Essex County, Massachusetts; Newburyport; city in Essex County, Massachusetts, originally a part of Newbury. Named for the town in England.

Newcastle; several places in the United States, among them a town in Lincoln County, Maine, named for the town in England or for the Duke of Newcastle.

New Egypt; village in Ocean County, New Jersey. The place so named because a great deal of corn was raised and ground at the mill there.

Newfane; town in Windham County, Vermont, said to have been named for Thomas Fane, one of the "men of Kent."

New Florence; city in Montgomery County, Missouri, named for the daughter of E. A. Lewis, an early settler, and given the prefix to distinguish it from another town of the same name in the State.

New Geneva; village in Fayette County, Pennsylvania, named for the principal city of Switzerland.

New Hamburg; village in Scott County, Missouri, named for the city in Germany.

New Hampshire; one of the States of the Union, named for the county in England.

New Hanover; county in North Carolina, named for the Duchy of Germany.

New Harmony; town in Posey County, Indiana, settled by the "Harmonists," and named for their sect.

New Haven; county, and town in same county, in Connecticut, settled by parties from Boston, who called it a "new haven."

New Haven; town in Addison County, Vermont, named for town in Connecticut.

New Iberia; town in Iberia Parish, Louisiana, given the ancient name of Spain Newicargut; river in Alaska. An Indian word, meaning "frog river."

New Jersey; one of the States of the Union; originally a grant to Sir George Carteret, who named it for his home on the Isle of Jersey, off the coast of England.

New Kent; county in Virginia, and island in Chesapeake Bay, named for the county in England.

New London; city and county in Connecticut, and town in Stanly County, North Carolina, named for the city in England.

New Madrid; county and city in same county in Missouri, the land originally a grant to Gen. George Morgan from Spain and named by him for its principal city.

New Marlboro; town in Berkshire County, Massachusetts, named for the town in Massachusetts, which in turn was named for the county in England.

New Mexico; Territory in the Union, named for the country of Mexico.

Newman; city in Coweta County, Georgia; Newmanville; village in Alachua County, Florida. Named for Gen. Daniel Newman, an officer in the Seminole war.

New Orleans; city in Orleans Parish, Louisiana, named for the city in France.

Newport; county in Rhode Island, and towns in Carteret County, North Carolina, and Herkimer County, New York, named for the city of Newport, Rhode Island.

Newport; city in Newport County, Rhode Island, so named by a party of settlers from Portsmouth, who called it "a new port."

Newport News; city in Warwick County, Virginia, named for Capt. Christopher Newport and Captain (or Sir William) Newce.

New Rochelle; city in Westchester County, New York, named for the city in France.

Newry; several places in the United States, among them the town in Oxford County, Maine, named for the town in Ireland.

New Smyrna; town in Orange County, Florida, named for the native place of the wife of Dr. Andrew Turnbull, a colonist.

Newton; county in Arkansas, named for Isaac Newton, who spoke in opposition to secession at the meeting in Little Rock, in 1861.

Newton; counties in Georgia, Indiana, Missouri, and Texas, and town in Baker County, Georgia, named for Sergt. John Newton, a Revolutionary officer.

Newton; city in Middlesex County, Massachusetts, originally a part of Cambridge, and when separated called "new town," afterward contracted to "Newton."

Newton; county in Mississippi, named for Sir Isaac Newton.

New York; one of the States of the Union and a county in same State, named for the Duke of York, who was the original grantee.

Nez Perce; county in Idaho, town in same county, and river in Yellowstone Park, named for a tribe of Indians, who were so named by the French settlers, the phrase meaning "pierced-nose."

Niagara; county in New York and river between Lake Erie and Lake Ontario. An Indian word, meaning " across the neck or strait," or "at the neck."

Niagara Falls; city in Niagara County, New York, named for the celebrated falls on the Niagara River.

Niantic; river, village, and bay in New London County, Connecticut. An Indian word, meaning "at the point of land on a tidal river."

Nicholas; county in Kentucky, named for Col. George Nicholas, a Revolutionary officer.

Nicholas; county in West Virginia, named for an early governor, W. C. Nicholas.

Nicholasville; city in Jessamine County, Kentucky, named for Col. George Nicholas, a Revolutionary officer.

Nicholai; village in Wasco County, Oregon, named for an early settler.

Nicholville; village in St. Lawrence County, New York, named for E. S. Nichols, an agent of the proprietor.

Nickajack; a cave in Alabama, said to have been the headquarters of the leader of a band of negroes, who was called "Nigger Jack," of which the present name is a corruption.

Nickerson; city in Nickerson County, Kansas, named for Thomas Nickerson, an officer of the Atchison, Topeka and Santa Fe Railroad.

Nicollet; county and village in same county in Minnesota, named for Jean Nicholas Nicollet, a French explorer.

Nicomanchee; very dark stream in Washington. An Indian word, meaning "shadowy water."

Nigger Baby Hill; mining camp in Dolores County, Colorado, so named because of the large amount of black oxide of manganese found in the outcrop.

Nilaks; mountain in Oregon. Derived from the Indian word, nilakshi, meaning "daybreak."

Ninety-six; town in Greenwood County, South Carolina, so named because it was 96 miles from the Cherokee Indian trading town of Keowee.

Nineveh; several towns and villages in the United States, named for the ancient Assyrian capital.

Niobrara; river and a village in Knox County, Nebraska. An Indian word, meaning " broad or large water," or " running water."

Nippenose; creek and valley in Pennsylvania. An Indian word, meaning "like summer," or "where cold does not penetrate."

Nishnabotna; river in Iowa, and village in Atchison County, Missouri. An Indian word, meaning "canoe making river."

Niskayuna; town in Schenectady County, New York. An Indian word, meaning "extensive corn flats."

Niwot; village in Boulder County, Colorado. The Indian name for Left Hand Creek.

Noank; village. in New London County, Connecticut. Derived from the Indian word, nayang, "point of land."

Noble; county in Indiana, named for Noah Noble, an early governor.

Noble; county in Ohio, named for James Noble, an early settler.

Noble; county in Oklahoma, named for Secretary of Interior John Noble.

Nobles; county in Minnesota, named for a prominent politician, William H. Nobles.

Noblesboro; town in Lincoln County, Maine, named for James Noble, an early settler.

Noblesville; city in Noble County, Indiana, named for Noah Noble, an early governor.

Nockamixon; village and township in Bucks County, Pennsylvania, an Indian word, meaning "where there are three houses."

Nodaway; county and river in Missouri. An Indian word with a much-disputed meaning, the following versions being among those given: "jump over river," "a kind of adder," or "a very venomous reptile."

Nogales; town in Santa Cruz County, New Mexico. Derived from the Spanish word, nogal, meaning "common walnut tree."

Nokomis; city in Montgomery County, Illinois, named for the mother of Wenonah in Longfellow's " Hiawatha," the Indian word meaning "grandmother."

Nolan; county in Texas, named for Philip Nolan, a trader and Indian tighter in the early days of Texas.

Nordhoff; town in Ventura County, California, named for Charles Nordhoff.

Norfolk; counties in Massachusetts and Virginia, and cities in Madison County, Nebraska, and Norfolk County, Virginia, named for the county in England.

Normal; town in McLean County, Illinois, so named because it is the seat of the State Normal School.

Normans Kill; stream in New York, named for Albert Andriessen Bradt de Norman, an early settler.

Norridgewock; town in Somerset County, Maine. An Indian word, meaning "place of deer," or, according to another authority, "smooth water between falls." * Norris; town within the corporate limits of Detroit, settled by and named for Col. P. W. Norris.

Norris; mountain in Yellowstone Park, named for Philetus W. Norris, the second superintendent of the park.

Norristown; borough in Montgomery County, Pennsylvania, named for Isaac Norris, who purchased the land from William Penn.

North; town in Orangeburg County, South Carolina, named for John F. North, its founder.

Northampton; counties in Pennsylvania and Virginia, and town in Hampshire county, Massachusetts, named for the county in England.

Northampton; county in North Carolina, named for the Earl of Northampton.

North Anna; river in Virginia, named for Anne, Queen of England.

North Bend; city in Dodge County, Nebraska, so called because it is situated in the north bend of the Platte River.

North Bend; village in Ohio, named for the bend in the Ohio River at this point.

North Carolina; one of the States of the Union, named for King Charles II. of England.

North Dansville; town in Livingston County, New York, named for Daniel P. Faulkner, an early settler.

Northeast; town in Dutchess County, New York, so name because of its geographical position in the county.

Northfield; town in Franklin County, Massachusetts, so called because of its northern situation in the county.

North Hero; town in Grand Isle County, Vermont, named for one of the two islands which were called "Two Heroes" and granted to Ethan Allen, the intention being that they should be owned by only brave men warmly disposed toward the Revolution.

Northport; characteristic name given to many places in the United States.

Northumberland; many places in the United States named for the county in England, among them being the counties in Pennsylvania and Virginia.

North Webster; village in Kosciusko County, Indiana, named for Daniel Webster.

Norton; county and city in same county in Kansas, named for Capt. Orloff Norton, of the Fifteenth Kansas Cavalry.

Norton; town in Bristol County, Massachusetts, named for the town in England.

Norton Sound; an inlet of Bering Sea on the coast of Alaska. named for Sir Fletcher Norton.

Nortonville; city in Jefferson County, Kansas, named for L. Norton, jr., of the Atchison, Topeka and Santa Fe Railroad Company.

Norwalk; city in Fairfield County, Connecticut, said to have been so named because when purchased from the Indians the northern boundary was to extend northward from the sea one day's walk, according to the Indian marking of the distance. According to another authority it is derived from nayang, "a point of land."

Norwalk; town in Warren County, Iowa, and city in Huron County, Ohio, named from the above.

Norway; towns in Herkimer County, New York, and Orangeburg County, South Carolina, named for the country in Europe.

Norwich; city in New London County, Connecticut, and village in Chenango County, New York, named for the city in England.

Norwich; village in Kingman County, Kansas, and town in Hampshire County, Massachusetts, named for the above.

Norwood; several places in the United States, named for the town in England.

Nottoway; river and county in Virginia, named for the Indian tribe, the word meaning "snake"—that is, an enemy.

Novato; village and township in Marin County, California. A Spanish word, meaning "new," "commencing in anything."

Novo-Arkhangelsk; seaport of Alaska, named for the city in Russia.

Noxubee; county in Mississippi. An Indian word, meaning "stinking water."

Nuckolls; county in Nebraska, named for an early settler.

Nueces; river and county in Texas. Derived from the Spanish word nuez, meaning "walnut."

Nunda; town in Livingston County, New York, and village in McHenry County, Illinois. Said by some authorities to be derived from the Indian word nundao, "hilly," and by others to mean "potato ground."

Nyack; village in Rockland County, New York, originally written Niack. An Indian word, meaning "a corner or point."

Nye; county in Nevada, named for James W. Nye, the first governor of the Territory.

O

Oahe; village in Hughes County, South Dakota. An Indian word, meaning "foundation.

Oak; a prefix much used in combination with lodge, mont, park, point, ridge, summit, ton, town, vale, and valley, and generally so given on account of the preponderance of this species of tree.

Oakham; town in Worcester County, Massachusetts, named for the town in England.

Oakland; city in Burt County, Nebraska, named for the man who purchased the town site from the original settler.

Oakley; city in Logan County, Kansas, named for Mrs. Eliza Oakley Gardner.

Oakley; village in Saginaw County, Michigan, named for an early pioneer.

Oatmans Flat; place in Arizona, so named because it was the scene of the massacre of Royce Oatman and his family by the Apaches.

Oberlin; village in Lorain County, Ohio, named for Jean Frederick Oberlin, a philanthropist.

O'Brien; county in Iowa, named for the Irish patriot, William Smith O'Brien.

Ocala; city in Marion County, Florida, named for the Indian village, the word meaning "green," or "fertile land."

Occoquan; river and a village in Prince William County, Virginia. An Indian word, meaning "hook shaped," or "a hook."

Ocean; county in New Jersey; Oceana; county in Michigan; Ocean City; village in Cape May County, New Jersey; Ocean Springs; town in Jackson County, Mississippi. So named because of their situation on the seashore, or some large body of water, or, as in the case of Ocean Springs, because of the presence of mineral springs.

Ocheyedan; town in Osceola County, Iowa. An Indian word, meaning "place of mourning."

Ochiltree; county in Texas, named for W. B. Ochiltree, a prominent politician of the State.

Ochlockonee; river in Georgia and Florida. An Indian word, meaning "yellow water." Ocklawaha; branch of the St. Johns River, Florida. An Indian word, meaning "muddy water."

Oconee; counties in Georgia and South Carolina, river in Georgia, town in Washington County, Georgia, and village in Shelby County, Illinois. An Indian word, meaning "great, large water," "water course, "small river," or, according to another authority, in the Shawnee language, a "bone."

O'Connor; town in Greeley County, Nebraska, named for Bishop O'Connor.

Oconomowoc; city in Waukesha County, Wisconsin. An Indian word, meaning "home of the beaver."

Oconto; county and city in Wisconsin. An Indian word, meaning "red ground," or, in the Menominee dialect, "tile place of the pickerel."

Ocopson; creek in Pennsylvania. An Indian name, meaning "brawling stream."

Ocou; river and village in Tennessee. An Indian word, meaning "a cow."

Odanah; town in Ashland County, Wisconsin. An Indian word, meaning "a town" or "village."

Odessa; town in Newcastle County, Delaware, named for the town in Russia.

Odin; several places in the United States, among them being a village in Marion County, Illinois. The name is one given to the Supreme Being by the ancient northern nations.

O'Fallon; village in St. Clair County, Illinois, named for Col. John O'Fallon, of St. Louis.

Offutt; village in Anderson County, Tennessee, named for the owner of the land upon which the post-office was built.

Ogalalla; village in Keith County, Nebraska, named for a tribe of Indians, who were so named because when they quarreled threw ashes in the faces of each other; the word meaning "scattering," "throwing at."

Ogden; city in Riley County, Kansas, named for Maj. E. A. Ogden, United States Army.

Ogden; town in Monroe County, New York, named for William Ogden, the son-in-law of the proprietor.

Ogden; city in Weber County, river, canyon, and valley in Utah, named for an old mountaineer of the Hudson Bay Company, Peter Skeen Ogden.

Ogdensburg; city in St. Lawrence County, New York, named for its original proprietor.

Ogema; town in Price County, Wisconsin; Ogemaw; county in Michigan. Derived from the Indian word meaning "great chief."

Ogle; county in Illinois, named for Joseph Ogle.

Oglesby; town in Lasalle County, Illinois, named for Richard J. Oglesby, former governor of the State.

Oglethorpe; county and a town in Macon County, Georgia, named for Gen. James E. Oglethorpe, the founder of the colony of Georgia.

Ogletown; village in Newcastle County, Delaware, named for Thomas Ogle, the former owner of the land.

Ogontz; river in Michigan. A derivation of the Indian word Ogsiasibi, meaning "little pickerel river."

Ogontz; towns in Montgomery County, Pennsylvania; Erie County, Ohio, and Delta County, Michigan, named for the Indian chief Ogontz, who was a missionary among his own people.

Ogreeta; village in Cherokee County, North Carolina. An Indian word, meaning "beautiful wild flower."

Ohio; State in the Union, river and counties in Indiana, Kentucky, and West Virginia. An Indian word, meaning "the beautiful river."

Ohiopyle; falls on the Youghiogheny River and town in Fayette County, Pennsylvania. An Indian word, meaning "white froth upon the water."

Ojai; valley in California, enclosed by a rim of mountains. An Indian word, meaning "the nest."

Ojo Caliente; village in Taos County, New Mexico. A Spanish word, meaning "spring and hot," and given this place on account of its numerous hot springs.

Okabena; lake in Minnesota. An Indian word, meaning "heron rookery."

Okahumka; town in Lake County, Florida. Derived from the Indian word okihumkee, meaning "bad water."

Okauchee; town in Waukesha County, Wisconsin. An Indian word, meaning "very long."

Okauvillee; village in Washington County, Illinois. From an Indian word, kaug, meaning " porcupine."

Okechobee; lake in Southern Florida. An Indian word, meaning "big river," or "large water."

Okee; town in Columbia County, Wisconsin. An Indian word, meaning "evil spirit," or if from anke, "earth," or "place."

Oketo; city in Marshall County, Kansas, named for an Indian chief, Arkatetah, the same being shortened by the settlers.

Oklahoma; a territory, county and city in same territory, in the United States. An Indian word, meaning "home for all Indians."

Oklokonee; river in Georgia. An Indian word, meaning "yellow water."

Okmulgee; river in Georgia. An Indian word, meaning "boiling water."

Okolona; town in Chickasaw County, Mississippi. An Indian word, meaning "much bent."

Okomi; river in Georgia. An Indian word, meaning "great, large water."

Oktibbeha; county in Mississippi. An Indian word, meaning "ice there in creek," or, according to another authority, "bloody water," because of the battles fought there between Chickasaws and Cboctaws.

Olathe; city in Johnson County, Kansas. An Indian word of the Shawnee dialect, meaning "beautiful."

Oldham; county in Texas, named for Williamson S. Oldham, a prominent lawyer and politician after the annexation.

Old Orchard Beach; town and beach in York County, Maine, so named because of the extensive orchard set out by its first settler.

Old Point Comfort; town in Elizabeth County, Virginia, so named by Capt. Christopher Newport, because he found it a safe haven after a severe storm; the "Old" added to distinguish it from New Point Comfort, a few miles away.

Oldtown; city in Penobscot County, Maine, so named because it has been a town site from aboriginal times.

Olean; city, town, and creek in Cattaraugus County, New York, the name given with reference to the oil springs in the region.

Oleona; village in Potter County, Pennsylvania, colonized by the violinist Ole Bull and taking its name from the first part of his.

Oliver; county in North Dakota, named for Hon. H. S. Oliver.

Olmsted; county in Minnesota, named for Hon. S. B. Olmstead.

Olokikana; lake in Florida. An Indian word, meaning "spotted lake," so named because dotted with green islands.

Olympia; city in Washington, named from the ancient mountain of Greece.

Omaha; city in Douglas County, Nebraska. An Indian word, meaning "upstream;" also the name of a tribe, designated as "upstream people."

Omar; village in Jefferson County, New York, named for a character in one of Johnson's allegories.

Onancock; town and bay in Accomac County, Virginia. An Indian name, meaning "foggy place."

O'Neals; village in Madera County, California, named for Charles O'Neal, an early settler.

Oneco; village in Windham County, Connecticut, named for the son of Uncas, the Mohegan sachem.

Oneida; counties in Idaho, New York, and Wisconsin, city in Knox County, Illinois, village and lake in New York; Oneida Castle; village in Oneida County, New York. Named for one of the tribes of the Six Nations, the word meaning "granite people," or "people of the beacon stone."

O'Neil; city in Holt County, Nebraska, named for Gen. John O'Neil, an early settler.

Onekama; village in Manistee County, Michigan. An Indian word, meaning "a portage."

Ong; village in Burlington County, New Jersey, named for an early settler.

Onida; town in Sully County, South Dakota. An Indian word, meaning "hunted, looked for."

Onion; creek in North Dakota, so named on account of the quantities of wild onions growing on its hanks.

Onondaga; county, and town in same county, and a lake in New York, named from the Indian tribe, the word meaning "people of the hills."

Onslow; county in North Carolina, named for Arthur Onslow, speaker in the British House of Commons.

Ontario; one of the Great Lakes, county in New York, and a village in Vernon County, Wisconsin. An Indian word, said by one authority to mean "beautiful lake;" by another, "beautiful prospect of rocks, hills, and water."

Onteora; village in the Catskills in Ulster County, New York. An Indian word, meaning "hills of the sky."

Ontonagon; county and river in Michigan. An Indian word, meaning "a fishing place," or, according to another authority, so named because an Indian maiden lost a-dish in the stream and exclaimed "nondonogan," which in her dialect meant "away goes my dish."

Oostanaula; river in Georgia. An Indian word, meaning "place of overtaking."

Opelika; city in Lee County, Alabama. An Indian word, meaning "great swamp."

Opelousas; town in St. Landry Parish, Louisiana, named from a tribe of Indians, the name signifying "black head," or "black leggins or moccasins."

Opequan; stream in Virginia. Derived from an Indian word, meaning "a froth-white stream," or perhaps from another, meaning "a rain-worn stream."

Orange; counties in California, Florida, and Texas, so named on account of the large orange groves.

Orange; county in Indiana, named for the county in North Carolina, the home of its settlers.

Orange; counties in New York, North Carolina, and Vermont, town in Orange County, Vermont, and New Haven County, Connecticut, named for William IV, Prince of Orange.

Orange; county, and town in same county in Virginia, so named because of the color of the surrounding highlands.

Orangeburg; county in South Carolina and town in same county, named for William IV, Prince of Orange.

Orbisonia; borough in Huntingdon County, Pennsylvania, named for William Orbison, an early settler.

Orchard; village in Morgan County, Colorado, originally called Fremont's "Orchard," because he halted his outfit here in a grove of cottonwoods and spent some time recruiting.

Orchard; village in Antelope County, Nebraska, so named because of the presence of a large orchard of apple trees.

Ord; city in Valley County, Nebraska, named for Gen. E. O. C. Ord.

Ordway; town in Otero County, Colorado, named for George N. Ordvvay, of the Denver board of supervisors.

Oreana; village in Humboldt County, Nevada. Latin word, meaning "town of gold."

Oregon; State of the Union, and a county in Missouri. The name said to have been derived from Origanum, a species of wild sage found along the coast in the State, but another authority states that it is derived from the Spanish Oregones, winch name was given the Indian tribes inhabiting that region, by a Jesuit priest, the word meaning " big-eared men."

Orejas Del Oso; mountain in Utah. A Spanish phrase, meaning "bears' ears."

Organ; mountains in New Mexico, so called because of their resemblance to the pipes of an organ.

Orion; village in Oakland County, Michigan, named for the constellation.

Oriskany; creek and village in Oneida County, New York; Oriskany Falls; village in Oneida County, New York. An Indian word, meaning "place of nettles."

Orland; town in Hancock County, Maine, said to have been so named because of the finding of an oar upon the shore by its first settler.

Orleans; town in Barnstable County, Massachusetts, named for the Duke of Orleans.

Orleans; comities in New York and Virginia, and a parish in Louisiana, named for the city in France.

Ormsby; county in Nevada, named for Major Ormsby.

Orneville; town in Piscataquis County, New York, named for the Hon. Henry Orne, of Boston.

Orofino; creek in Idaho, and towns in Siskiyou County, California, and Shoshone County, Idaho, so named by the Spanish because of their gold mines.

Orphans Island; island in Penobscot County, Maine; so named because it was an orphan's share of an estate of the Waldo Patent.

Orrick; town in Ray County, Missouri, named for John C. Orrick, of St. Louis.

Orrington; town in Penobscot County, Maine, the name being a misspelling of the original name of "Orangetown."

Orville; town in Hamilton County, Nebraska, named for Orville Westcott, a resident.

Orwigsburg; borough in Schuylkill County, Pennsylvania, named for Peter Orwig, its founder.

Osage; counties in Kansas and Missouri, an Indian reservation in Oklahoma, and many towns, cities, and rivers in the United States, named for the tribe of Indians whose name means "the strong."

Osakis; village in Douglas County, Minnesota. An Indian word, meaning "yellow earth."

Osawatomie; city in Miami County, Kansas, a combination of the names of the two rivers at whose junction the town is situated—Osage and Pottawattamie.

Osborne; county, and city in same county in Kansas, named for Vincent B. Osborne, of the Second Kansas Cavalry.

Osceola; counties in Florida, Iowa, and Michigan, city in St. Clair County, Missouri, towns in Mississippi County, Arkansas, and Lewis County, New York, villages in Polk counties, Nebraska and Wisconsin, and a mountain in New Hampshire, named for the Seminole Indian chief.

Oscoda; county, and village in Iosco County, Michigan. An Indian word, said by some to mean "fire," by others, "strong prairie."

Oshawa; village in Nicollet County, Minnesota. An Indian word, meaning "ferry him over," or "across the river."

Oskaloosa; cities in Mahaska County, Iowa, and Jefferson County, Kansas, named for the wife of the Indian chief Mahaska.

Oshkosh; city in Winnebago County, Wisconsin, named for an Indian chief, the name said to mean "the nail, claw, or horny part of the foot of beasts."

Oso; mountain in Colorado. A Spanish word, meaning "bear."

Ossineke; village in Alpena County, Michigan. An Indian word, meaning "stony land," or "place of a stone."

Ossining; town in Westchester County, New York, the name said to have been derived from that of the Indian tribe Scint Sinks, "stone upon stone," or from Osinsing, "place of stones."

Ossipee; river in Maine. Indian word, moaning " pine river."

Osso; town in King George County, Virginia. An Indian word, probably meaning "white waters."

Oswegatchie; river in New York. An Indian word, meaning "coming or going around a hill."

Oswego; county, city, town, and river in New York, city in Labette County, Kansas, and village in Kendall County, Illinois. Derived from the Indian On ti ahan toque, "where the valley widens," or, according to another authority, "flowing out."

Osweya; creek in McKean County, Pennsylvania. An Indian word, meaning "place of flies."

Otero; county in Colorado, named for Miguel Otero, of a prominent Mexican family.

Otero; county in New Mexico, named for Governor M. A. Otero.

Otis; town in Hancock County, Maine, named for James Otis, an early proprietor.

Otis; town in Berkshire County, Massachusetts, named for Harrison Cray Otis.

Otisfield; town in Cumberland County, Maine, named for James Otis, an early proprietor.

Otisville; village in Genesee County, Michigan, named for Byron Otis, an early settler.

Otisville; village in Orange County, New York, named for Isaac Otis, its first settler.

Otoe; county in Nebraska, named for the Indian tribe.

Otsego; counties in Michigan and New York, town and lake in New York, and village in Michigan. An Indian word, meaning "welcome water," or "place where meetings are held."

Otselic; town in Chenango and creek in Madison counties, New York. An Indian word, meaning "plum creek."

Otsquago; creek in Montgomery County, New York. An Indian word, signifying "under the bridge."

Ottawa; counties in Kansas, Michigan, and Ohio, a reservation in Indian Territory, city in Lasalle County, Illinois, and village in Lesueur County, Minnesota, named for the Indian tribe, the name meaning "traders."

Otter; creek in Missouri. The present name a translation of the original French name of "Loutre."

Otter Lake; village in the Lapeer County, Michigan, so named because of the abundance of otter in adjacent lakes.

Otter Tail; lake in Minnesota; Ottertail; county and town in Minnesota. So named because of a peninsula of the lake called by the Indians, Ptansinta, "otter tail."

Otto; town in Cattaraugus County, New York, named for Jacob S. Otto, of the Holland Land Company.

Ottumwa; city in Wapello County, Iowa. An Indian word said to mean "place of the lone chief," but more probably meaning, "rapids," or "tumbling water."

Ouachita; county and river in Arkansas, parish in Louisiana, named for a now extinct Indian tribe, the word meaning "male deer."

Ouray; county, city, and mountain in Colorado, named for a friendly chief of the Ute Indians.

Outagamie; county in Wisconsin, named for the Outagamies, or "Fox" Indians.

Ovid; village in Clinton County, Michigan, and town in Seneca County, New York, named for the Roman poet.

Owaneco; village in Christian County, Illinois. An Indian word, in some dialects meaning "God."

Owasco; lake, town, and creek in Cayuga County, New York. An Indian word meaning "the bridge," or "lake of the floating bridge."

Owassa; town in Hardin County, Iowa, derived from Owasse, Indian word for "bear."

Owatonna; river and city in Steele County, Minnesota. An Indian word meaning "straight river."

Owen; counties in Indiana and Kentucky; Owensboro; city in Daviess County, Kentucky. Named for Col. Abraham Owen of Kentucky, killed at Tippecanoe.

Owensburg; village in Greene County, Indiana, named for its founder.

Owingsville; city in Bath County, Kentucky, named for Col. T. D. Owings.

Owobopta; tributary of the Minnesota River. An Indian word meaning "where they dig roots."

Owosso; city in Shiawassee County, Michigan, named for the principal chief of the Chippewas in that country, the word meaning "he is afar off."

Owsley; county in Kentucky, named for Judge William Owsley, a former governor.

Oxbow; village in Jefferson County, New York, on the Oswegatchie River, so named because of a bend in the river at this point in the form of an ox bow.

Oxford; county and town in same county in Maine, town in Worcester County, Massachusetts, and borough in Pennsylvania, named for the university in England.

Oxford; city in Lafayette County, Mississippi, so named from the university city in England because it is the location of the State University.

Ozan; town and stream in Hempstead County, Arkansas. A corruption of the French, prairie d'ane, "prairie of the donkeys."

Ozark; county and city in Christian County, Missouri, and village in Dale County, Alabama. A corruption of the French name, aux arcs, meaning " with bows," a term descriptive of the Indians who inhabited the country.

Ozaukee; county in Wisconsin. An Indian word meaning "yellow clay."

P

Pacbeco; town in Contra Costa County, California, named for an early Spanish settler.

Pacbuta; town in Clarke County, Mississippi. A Choctaw Indian word meaning "possum creek."

Pacific; an ocean, the largest division of water on the globe, so named by Magellan, its discoverer, because of the fair weather encountered there after experiencing heavy gales in the straits.

Pacific; county in Washington; city in Franklin County, Missouri; and creek in Yellowstone Park, named for the ocean.

Pactolus; town in Pitt County, North Carolina, named for the ancient river in Asia Minor.

Paddock; village in Holt County, Nebraska, named for A. S. Paddock, United States Senator from that State.

Paducab; city in McCracken County, Kentucky, named for a celebrated Indian chief who formerly lived in the vicinity and was buried on the banks of Tennessee River, now within the city limits.

Page; county in Iowa, named for Colo lei Page, of Palo Alto fame.

Page; county in Virginia, named for James Page, an early governor of the State.

Pahaquarry; township in Warren County, New Jersey. An Indian word meaning "termination of two mountains."

Pahcupog; pond near Westerly, Connecticut. Name derived from the Indian word, Pahke-paug, meaning "pure water pond."

Painesville; village in Lake County Ohio, named for Gen. E. Paine, an early settler.

Paint; creek in Ohio. From the Indian word Olomon sepung, "paint stream."

Painted Post; village in Steuben County, New York, so named because of the erection of a painted monument by the Indians over the grave of their chief, Captain Montour.

Paint Rock; town in Concho County, Texas, so named because situated near a ledge of rock, profusely decorated with Indian hieroglyphics.

Pajaro; river in California, so named by the Spanish because of the number of wild geese or ducks found there, the word meaning "bird."

Palarm; town and stream in Faulkner County, Arkansas. A corruption of the French, "place des alarmes."

Palatine; several places in the United States, named from the division of Germany.

Palatka; city in Putnam County, Florida. An Indian word said by some to mean "spilled," and by others, "cow ford."

Palisades Park; borough in Bergen County, New Jersey, so named because of its location on the Palisades.

Palmer; town in Hampden County, Massachusetts, named for Chief Justice Thomas Palmer.

Palmer; village in Marquette County, Michigan, named for Waterman Palmer, of Pittsburg, its founder.

Palmer Lake; town and creek in El Paso County, Colorado, named for General Palmer, an official of the Denver and Rio Grande Railroad.

Palmers; creek in Chariton County, Missouri, named for Martin Palmer.

Palmyra; town in Wayne County, New York, named from the ancient Syrian town.

Palo; town in Linn County, Iowa, and village in Ionia County, Michigan. A Spanish word meaning "stick."

Palo Alto; town in Santa Clara County, California. A Spanish phrase meaning "high stick."

Palo Alto; county in Iowa and borough in Schuylkill County, Pennsylvania, named for the famous battlefield in Texas.

Palo Pinto; county and river in Texas. A Spanish phrase meaning "spotted stake, or timber."

Pamelia; town in Jefferson County, New York, named for the wife of Gen. Jacob Brown.

Pamlico; county, sound, and river in North Carolina. named for the ancient Indian village of Pomeick on the southern shores of the river.

Pamunkey; river and town in Orange County, Virginia. Said to have been derived from the Indian, Pihmunga, meaning "where he sweat."

Pana; city in Christian County, Illinois. Probably from the Indian word pena, "partridge."

Panasoffkee; town in Sumter County, Florida. From the Indian word panasofkee, "deep valley."

Panola; counties in Mississippi and Texas. An Indian word meaning "cotton."

Panton; town in Addison County, Vermont, named for Lord Panton, a British nobleman.

Paola; city in Miami County, Kansas, named for Baptiste Peoria, the town name being the Indian pronunciation.

Papillion; village and creek in Sarpy County, Nebraska, given the French name because many butterflies were seen upon the banks of the stream.

Papinsville; village in Bates County, Missouri, named for Pierre Melleeourt Papin.

Paragould; city in Greene County, Arkansas. A compound of the names of two railroad men, W. J. Paramore and Jay Gould.

Pardeeville; village in Columbia County, Wisconsin, named for John S. Pardee, the founder.

Paris; town in Oxford County, Maine, named for the city in France.

Paris; a town in Oneida County, New York, named for Isaac Paris, a merchant of Fort Plain.

Parish; town in Oswego and village in Erie County, New York; Parishville; town in St. Lawrence County, New York. Named for David Parish, an extensive landowner.

Parita; village in Bexar County, Texas. A Spanish word, meaning "grapevine."

Park; county in Colorado, so named because it includes a large area of South Park.

Park; county in Montana, so named because it is close to Yellowstone Park.

Parke; county in Indiana, named for Benjamin Parke, a prominent State politician.

Parker; city in Linn County, Kansas, named for J. W. Parker, former owner of the town site.

Parker; county in Texas, named for the family of Parker's Fort, who in 1836 were captured and killed by the Indians.

Parkerville; city in Morris County, named for C. G. Parker, former owner of the town site.

Parkersburg; town in Sampson County, North Carolina, named for a prominent citizen.

Parkersburg; city in Wood County, West Virginia, named for Alexander Parker, of Pennsylvania.

Parkers Landing; city in Armstrong County, Pennsylvania, named for the former proprietors.

Parkersville; village in Lyon County, Kentucky, named for Thomas Parker, a wealthy citizen.

Parkman; town in Piscataquis County, Maine, named for its early proprietor, Samuel Parkman, of Boston.

Parkman; town in Sheridan County, Wyoming, named for Francis Parkman.

Parkville; village in Platte County, Missouri, named for George S. Park, its founder.

Parksville; town in Edgefield County, South Carolina, named for a prominent family of the county.

Parmele; town in Martin County, North Carolina, named for a prominent resident.

Parmer; county in Texas, named for Martin Parmer, prominent politician in the early days of Texas.

Parramore; beach and island in Accomac County, Virginia, named for the family who were its former owners.

Parrott; town in La Plata County, Colorado, named for a California capitalist.

Parry; peak in the Front Range, Colorado, named for the botanist.

Parsons; city in Labette County, Kansas, named for Judge Levi Parsons, a prominent railroad official.

Parsons; town in Tucker County, West Virginia, named for a former resident.

Parsonsfield; town in York County, Maine, named for Thomas Parsons, an early proprietor.

Pasadena; city in Los Angeles County, California. An Indian word, meaning "crown of the valley."

Pascagoula; river and town in Jackson County, Mississippi, named for an Indian tribe, the name meaning "bread nation."

Pasco; county in Florida, named for Senator Pasco.

Pascoag; village in Providence County, Rhode Island. An Indian word, meaning "the dividing place," and so named because it is situated at the forks of the Blackstone River.

Paso Robles; city in San Luis Obispo County, California. A Spanish word, meaning "pass of the oak trees."

Pasquotank; county in North Carolina. An Indian word, meaning "divided tidal river," and given this county because a river forms one of its boundaries.

Passaconaway; mountain in New Hampshire, named for a sachem of the Merrimack tribe of Indians.

Passadumkeag; town in Penobscot County, Maine, situated at the mouth of a river of the same name, by reason of which it was given this Indian name, which means "falls running over a gravel bed."

Passaic; county, city, and river in New Jersey; derived either from the Indian word Passaic or Passajeek, "a valley," or from the Indian equivalent of "peace."

Passamaquoddy; bay on the coast of Maine. An Indian word, meaning "pollock ground," or "pollock-plenty place."

Passumpsic; river and village in Caledonia County, Vermont. An Indian word, meaning "much clear water."

Pastoro; mountain in Arizona, so named because of its high mountain pastures.

Patagumkis; tributary of the Penobscot River in Maine. An Indian word, meaning "sandy-ground cove."

Patapsco; river in Maryland. An Indian word, meaning "backwater."

Patchogue; village in Suffolk County, New York. An Indian word, meaning "turning place."

Paterson; city in Passaic County, New Jersey, named for William Paterson, an early governor.

Patkaskaden; tributary of James River. An Indian word, meaning "the tortoise" or "turtle." Patrick; county in Virginia, named for the orator, Patrick Henry.

Pattaquonk; hill near Saybrook, Connecticut. An Indian name, meaning "round place" or "round hill."

Patterson; town in Putnam County, New York, named for a family of early settlers.

Paulding; counties in Georgia and Ohio, a town in Jasper County, Mississippi, and a village in Paulding County, Ohio, named for John Paulding, who helped capture Major Andre.

Pauquepaug; brook in New Milford, Connecticut, name derived from the Indian word Papke-paug, meaning "pure-water pond."

Pautuck; river and a village in Suffolk County, New York. An Indian word, meaning "fall."

Pawling; town in Dutchess County, New York. Name derived from the Paulding, said originally to have been Pawling.

Pawnee; creek in Colorado, so named by the Indians because a party of 200 Pawnee Indians were here surrounded by a greatly outnumbering force of Sioux, who, when they found they could not capture the Pawnees, proceeded to starve them out; but the Pawnees refused to surrender to escape even this death, and the last man of them perished by starvation. The root of the word said to mean "a stone."

Pawnee; counties in Kansas, Nebraska, and Oklahoma, named for the Indian tribe mentioned above.

Pawpaw; creek and town in Morgan County, West Virginia; villages in Lee County, Illinois, and Van Buren County, Michigan, so named because of the presence of paw-paw fruit.

Pawtucket; river in New England and city in Providence County, Rhode Island. An Indian word, meaning "at the little falls."

Paxton; town in Ford County, Illinois. An Indian word, meaning "standing or dead water."

Paxton; town in Worcester County, Massachusetts, named for Charles Paxton, of Boston.

Paxton; town in Keith County, Nebraska, named for W. A. Paxton, of Omaha, Nebraska.

Payette; river and a village in Canyon County, Idaho, named for a member of the Hudson Bay Company.

Payne; village in Paulding County, Ohio, probably named for Henry B. Payne, United States Senator from that State.

Payne; county in Oklahoma, named for Captain Payne, "Oklahoma Boone."

Paynesville; town in Pike County, Missouri, named for a resident of St. Louis.

Peabody; city in Marion County, Kansas, named for F. H. Peabody, of Boston.

Peabody; town in Essex County, Massachusetts, named for George Peabody, the philanthropist.

Peace; creek in Florida, so named because it was the scene of a treaty of peace.

Peale; highest peak of the Sierra la Sal in Utah, named for Dr. A. C. Peale, the geologist.

Pearl; river in Mississippi; Pearlington; town in Hancock County, Mississippi; Pearl River; county in Mississippi. So named on account of the pearl fisheries which were early established by the French upon the above-mentioned river.

Pecan; village in Clay County, Georgia. An Indian word, meaning "nut."

Pecatonica; village in Winnebago County, Illinois. Probably derived from the Indian word Pickatolica, which was the name of a species of fish.

Peckamin; river in New Jersey. Derived from the Indian word pakihm, "cranberries."

Pecunktuk; stream in Vermont. An Indian word, meaning "crooked river."

Pedernales; rivers in North Carolina and Texas. A Spanish word, meaning "flints, rocks, or stones."

Peekskill; village in Westchester County, New York, named for Jan Peek, a Dutch mariner of the seventeenth century.

Pegumock; creek in New Jersey. An Indian word, meaning "dark stream."

Pelham; towns in Hampshire County, Massachusetts, and Hillsboro County, New Hampshire, named for Thomas Pelham Holies, Duke of Newcastle.

Pelham; village in Westchester County, New York, named for the original patentee, John Pell.

Pella; city in Marion County, Iowa, colonized by Dutch settlers, to whom the word meant "city of refuge."

Pemadumcook; lake in Piscataquis County, Maine. An Indian word, meaning "lake of the sloping mountain."

Pemaquid; point of land and village in Lincoln County, Maine. An Indian word, meaning "long point," or, according to another authority, "that runs into the water."

Pembina; county and city in same county in North Dakota, named from an Indian tribe, the name said to mean "high-bush cranberry."

Pembroke; town in Plymouth County, Massachusetts, named for the town in England.

Pembroke; town in Merrimack County, New Hampshire, probably named for the Earl of Pembroke.

Pemigewasset; river in New Hampshire. The word of Indian derivation, said to mean "crooked place of pines."

Pender; county in North Carolina, named for Gen. William D. Pender, an officer of the Confederate Army.

Pendleton; town in Madison County, Indiana, named for the former proprietor, Thomas M. Pendleton.

Pendleton; counties in Kentucky and West Virginia, named for Edmund Pendleton, a prominent politician of Virginia.

Pendleton; town in Niagara County, New York, named for Sylvester Pendleton Clarke, ex-governor of Grand Island.

Pendleton; town in Northampton County, North Carolina, named for a prominent resident.

Pendleton; town in Umatilla County, Oregon, named for George H. Pendleton.

Pendleton; town in Anderson County, South Carolina, named for Judge Henry Pendleton, a Revolutionary jurist.

Pend Oreille; lake in Idaho, named from a tribe of Indians who were given this name by the French because of their habit of wearing pendants in their ears, the word meaning "hanging ear."

Penfield; town in Green County, Georgia, named for Josiah Penfield.

Penfield; town in Monroe County, New York, named for Daniel Penfield, an early settler.

Penikese; one of the Elizabeth islands in Buzzards Bay, Massachusetts. An Indian word, meaning "sloping land."

Penn; the name of many townships, and the prefix to the name of many towns and villages in the United States, generally given them in honor of William Penn.

Pennington; borough in Mercer County, New Jersey, named for the Pennington family, two members of which were governors of the State.

Pennington; county in South Dakota, named for John L. Pennington, a former governor.

Pennsylvania; one of the States of the Union, named for William Penn, to whom the land comprised within the limits of this State was granted.

Penn Yan; village in Yates County, New York. The name is formed by a compound of the names of the two classes of settlers—Pennsylvanians and Yankees.

Pennypack; creek in Philadelphia County, Pennsylvania. An Indian word, meaning "body of water with no current."

Penobscot; county, bay, river, and town in Maine. Derived from the Indian word Penobskeag, meaning "rocky place," "river of rocks."

Penryn; village in Placer County, California, named for a borough in Cornwall, England.

Pensacola; bay and city in Escambia County, Florida. Said to be derived from the Indian word Pan-sha-okla, meaning "hair people."

Pentwater; river and lake in Michigan, from which a village also is named, being so named because of the supposition that the river had no outlet.

Peoria; county and city in Illinois and nation in Indian Territory. An Indian word, meaning "place where there are fat beasts."

Peosta; village in Dubuque County, Iowa. An Indian word, meaning "gorge in the rocks." Peotone; town in Will County, Illinois. Derived from the Indian word petone, meaning "bring," "bring here," or "bring to this place."

Pepin; lake between Wisconsin and Minnesota, and a county in Wisconsin, named for Pepin le Bref.

Pepperell; town in Middlesex County, Massachusetts, named for Sir William Pepperell, a member of the Massachusetts council.

Pepperville; township in Butler County, Nebraska, named for Hubbel Pepper, an early settler.

Pequabuck; river in Connecticut. An Indian word, meaning "clear or open pond."

Pequanac; village in Morris County, New Jersey. An Indian word, meaning "cleared land."

Pequannock; village in Hartford County, Connecticut. An Indian word, meaning "land naturally clear and open."

Pequots; town in Crow Wing County, Minnesota, named for a tribe of Indians, the word meaning "destroyers," "enemies," or "gray foxes," according to different authorities.

Perdido; rivers in Alabama and Florida, and a bay into which these empty, which was so named by the Spanish, the word meaning "lost," because a Spanish ship was destroyed there.

Pere Marquette; town in Mason County, Michigan, named for Father Marquette.

Perham; town in Aroostook County, Maine, named for Hon. Sidney Perham, a governor of the State.

Perham; town in Ottertail County, Minnesota, named for Josiah Perham, an official of the Northern Pacific Railroad,

Perkins; plantation in Franklin County, Maine, named for Dr. Perkins, of Farmington.

Perkins; county. in Nebraska, named for C. E. Perkins, an official of the Burlington and Missouri River Railroad.

Perkiomen; branch of the Schuylkill River in Montgomery County, Pennsylvania. An Indian word, meaning "where there are cranberries."

Perinton; town in Monroe County, New York, named for Glover Perrin, the first permanent settler.

Perry; counties in Alabama, Arkansas, Illinois, Indiana, Kentucky, Mississippi, Missouri, Ohio, Pennsylvania, and Tennessee; town in Wyoming County, New York, named for Commodore Oliver Hazard Perry.

Perry; city in Jefferson County, Kansas, named for John D. Perry, a railroad official.

Perrysburg; town in Cattaraugus County, New York, and village in Wood County, Ohio, named for Commodore Oliver Hazard Perry.

Perrys Mills; village in Clinton County, New York, named for George Perry, former proprietor.

Perryville; city in Perry County, Missouri, named for Commodore Oliver Hazard Perry.

Person; county in North Carolina, named for Gen. Thomas Person, an officer of the Revolution.

Perth; town in Fulton County, New York, named for the town in Scotland.

Perth Amboy; city in Middlesex County, New Jersey, the name a combination of the name of the Earl of Perth and a corruption of the original Indian name of the town, Ompage.

Peru; towns in Berkshire County, Massachusetts, and Clinton County, New York, named for the country in South America.

Pescadero; village in San Mateo County, California. A Spanish word, meaning "fishmonger."

Pescongamoc; lake in Maine near the Penobscot River. An Indian word, meaning "divided lake."

Peshtigo; river in Oconto County and town in Marinette County, Wisconsin. An Indian word, meaning "wild goose river."

Peterboro; town in Hillsboro County, New Hampshire, named for the city in England.

Peterboro; village in Madison County, New York, named for Peter Smith.

Petersburg; town in Arapahoe County, Colorado, named for Peter Magnes, its founder.

Petersburg; village in Kent County, Delaware, named for the descendants of Peter Fowler, who adopted his baptismal name as a surname.

Petersburg; town in Pike County, Indiana, named for Peter Brenton, an early settler.

Petersburg; town in Rensselaer County, Mew York, named for Peter Simmons, an early settler.

Petersburg; borough in Huntingdon County, Pennsylvania, named for Peter Fleck, an early settler.

Petersburg; city in Dinwiddie County, Virginia, founded by Col. William Byrd and Peter Jones, and named for the latter.

Petersham; town in Worcester County, Massachusetts, named for William Stanhope, Earl of Petersham.

Petersville; village in Bartholomew County, Indiana, named for Peter T. Blessing, its founder.

Petoskey; city in Emmett County, Michigan; an Indian word meaning "the sun, moon, or stars," or anything relating to the heavens.

Pettis; county in Missouri, named for Spencer Pettis, secretary of state of Missouri.

Pettit; island in Maine, named for the Pettit family.

Pewabic; town in Ontanagon County, Michigan, named from the river which bears the Indian name, Pewabik-seede, "iron river."

Pewakpa; tributary of the Dakota River; an Indian name meaning "elm river."

Pewamo; village in Ionia County, Michigan, named for the son of Shacoe, chief of the Chippewa Indians.

Pewaukee; village in Waukesha County, Wisconsin, named for the lake which bore the Indian name of Peewaukee-wee-ning, "lake of shells."

Peytona; village in Boone County, West Virginia, named for William M. Peyton.

Pheasant Branch; village in Dane County, Wisconsin, named for the stream which bears the Indian name of Peona, meaning "pheasant branch."

Pheba; village in Clay County, Mississippi, named for Mrs. Pheba Robinson.

Phelps; county in Missouri, and village in Atchison County, same State, named for Governor John S. Phelps.

Phelps; village in Ontario County, New York, named for Oliver Phelps, one of the original proprietors.

Philadelphia; county, and city in same county, in Pennsylvania, so named by William Penn in order that the principle of the Quakers—brotherly love—might be identified with their city, the name being that of the city in Asia.

Philadelphia; city in Jefferson County, New York, named for the above.

Philippi; town in Barbour County, West Virginia, both town and county being named for Philip Barbour.

Philipsburg; city in Granite County, Montana, named for the manager of the Granite mine.

Philipsburg; borough in Center County, Pennsylvania, named for its founders, two Englishmen, Henry and James Philips.

Philipstown; town in Putnam County, New York, named for Adolph Philipse, the original patentee.

Phillips; county in Arkansas, named for Sylvanus Phillips, a prominent resident.

Phillips; county in Colorado, named for R. O. Phillips, a prominent statesman.

Phillips; county, and city in same county, in Kansas, named for Col. William A. Phillips.

Phillips; lake in Maine, named for the man who has owned it for fifty years.

Phillips; town in Franklin County, Maine, named for a prominent resident family, by whom the townsite was formerly owned.

Phillips; city in Price County, Wisconsin, named for Elijah B. Phillips, a railroad constructor.

Phillipsburg; town in Warren County, New Jersey, named for a resident family.

Phillipsville; village in Humboldt County, California, named for a settler.

Phippsburg; town in Sagadahoc County, Maine, named for Sir William Phipps, governor of Massachusetts.

Phoenix; village in Oswego County, New York, named for Alexander Phoenix.

Phoenixville; borough in Chester County, Pennsylvania, named for the Phoenix Iron works.

Piasa; town in Macoupin County, Illinois. An Indian name for a huge bird which they chiseled in the ledge of rock on the banks of the Mississippi River, the word meaning " the man-devouring bird."

Piatt; county in Illinois. named for Col. John Piatt, an early settler.

Piccowaxen; creek in Maryland. An Indian word, meaning "torn shoes."

Pickaway; county in Ohio. A corruption of the name of a tribe of Indians originally known as Pickawillany.

Pickens; counties in Alabama, Georgia, and South Carolina, and town in Pickens County, South Carolina, named for Gen. Andrew Pickens, an officer of the Revolution.

Pickens; town in Holmes County, Mississippi, named for James Pickens, a landowner.

Pickensville; town in Pickens County, Alabama, named for Gen. Andrew Pickens, an officer of the Revolution.

Pickett; county in Tennessee, named for Col. George Edward C. A. Pickett, who "led the famous charge at the battle of Gettysburg."

Piedmont; city in Wayne County, Missouri, and town in Mineral County, West Virginia, situated at the foot of the Alleghenies. From the French pied, "foot," and mont, "mountain."

Piegan; village in Chouteau County, Montana, named for a tribe of Indians, the word meaning "pheasant."

Pierce; counties in Georgia, Nebraska, and Washington, and mountain in Humboldt County, California, named for Franklin Pierce.

Pierce; county in North Dakota, named for Hon. Gilbert A. Pierce, first United States Senator from North Dakota.

Pierce; village in Wharton County, Texas, named for Thomas W. Pierce, an early railroad man.

Pierceton; town in Kosciusko County, Indiana, named for Franklin Pierce, a former President of the United States.

Piermont; village in Rockland County, New York, so named because it is backed by high hills and facing the river, into which extends a long pier.

Pierrepont; town in St. Lawrence County, New York, named for Hezekiah B. Pierrepont, one of the original proprietors.

Pierrepont Manor; village in Jefferson County, New York, named for the Hon. William C. Pierrepont's residence.

Pierres Hole; valley in Idaho, named for an Iroquois chieftain in the employ of the Hudson Bay Company.

Pierson; village in Montcalm County, Michigan, named for O. A. Pierson, the first white settler.

Piffard; village in Livingston County, New York, named for David Piffard, a prominent settler.

Pigeon; one of the Apostle Islands, in Lake Superior, Wisconsin. A translation of the Indian name.

Pike; counties in Alabama, Arkansas, Georgia, Illinois, Indiana, Kentucky, Mississippi, Missouri, Ohio, and Pennsylvania, town in Wyoming County, New York, and the famous peak in Colorado, named for Gen. Zebulon M. Pike, the explorer.

Pikeville; town iii Wayne County, North Carolina, named for a prominent resident.

Pillsbury; village in Todd County, Minnesota, named for an early governor.

Pilot Grove; city in Cooper County, Missouri, so named because of the presence of a grove in a nearby prairie, which served as a landmark.

Pilot Knob; town in Iron County, Missouri, named from the hill which is a prominent feature of the landscape.

Pima; county, and a town in Graham County, Arizona, named for an Indian tribe.

Pinal; county in Arizona, named for a chief of the Apaches.

Pinckney; town in Lewis County, New York, named for Charles C. Pinckney, a prominent statesman of South Carolina.

Pinckney; town in Union County, South Carolina; Pinckneyville; towns in Clay County, Alabama, and Wilkinson County, Mississippi. Named for the celebrated Pinckney family of South Carolina.

Pinconning; village in Bay County, Michigan. An Indian word, meaning "potato place." Pine; creek in Indiana; the present name being a translation of the Indian name of Puck-gwun-nash-ga-muck.

Pine; county in Minnesota. so named because of its forests of coniferous trees.

Pine Log; town in Tuolumne County, California, so named because the crossing of the Stanislaus River at this point was originally formed by a large log.

Pinkham; grant in Coos County, New Hampshire, named for Daniel Pinkham, the grantee.

Pinole; town in Contra Costa County, California. A Spanish word, meaning "parched corn."

Pinon Blanco; peak and ridge in California. A Spanish phrase, meaning "mountain of white rock."

Pinos Altos; town in Grant County, New Mexico. A Spanish word, meaning "high pines."

Pintada; peak of the San Juan Mountains, California. A Spanish word, meaning "mottled or spotted."

Pipestone; county, and village in same county in Minnesota, so named because of its celebrated quarry of pipestone.

Pissacassick; river in New Hampshire; Piscasset; stream in Maine. Derived from an Indian word, meaning "white stone."

Piscataqua; river in New Hampshire, said to have been derived from the Indian word Pishgachtigok, meaning "the confluence of two streams."

Piscataquis; county, and a branch of the Penobscot River in Maine. An Indian word, meaning "divided tidal river."

Piscataway; village in Prince George County, Maryland. An Indian word, meaning "the place of white pines."

Pischelville; town in Knox County, Nebraska, named for the first postmaster, Anton Pischel.

Pisgah; town in Cooper County, Missouri, named indirectly for the mountain in Palestine.

Pishtaka; lake in northern Illinois. An Indian word, meaning "fox."

Pit; river in California, so named because the Indians dug pits upon its banks to catch men and animals.

Pitcairn; island in the Pacific, named for its discoverer, Major Pitcairn.

Pitcairn; town in St. Lawrence County, New York, named for Joseph Pitcairn, the original proprietor.

Pitcher; creek in Humboldt County, California, named for an early settler.

Pitcher; town in Chenango County, New York, named for Nathaniel Pitcher, lieutenant-governor of the State.

Pithole City; village in Venango County, Pennsylvania, named from a creek which had a deep hole in the rocks upon its banks.

Pitkin; county in Colorado and village in Gunnison County, Colorado, named for F. W. Pitkin, an early governor of the State.

Pitt; county in North Carolina, and mountain in Oregon, named for Sir William Pitt, Earl of Chatham.

Pittsboro; town in Calhoun County, Mississippi, named for an early settler.

Pittsboro; town in Chatham County, North Carolina; Pittsburg; city in Allegheny County, Pennsylvania. Named for Sir William Pitt, Earl of Chatham.

Pittsfield; town in Somerset County, Maine, named for William Pitts, of Boston.

Pittsfield; city in Berkshire County, Massachusetts; Pittston; town in Kennebec County, Maine; Pittsylvania; county in Virginia. Named for Sir William Pitt, Earl of Chatham, the celebrated English statesman.

Piute; county in Utah, named for an Indian tribe, the word meaning "true Utes."

Placer; county in California; Placerville; city in Eldorado County, California. A Spanish word, descriptive of the sand, pebbles, etc., found in the bottom of a river, and used when describing dirt with gold deposits.

Plainfield; city in Union County, New Jersey, so named because it is situated on a beautiful plain.

Plant City; town in Hillsboro County, Florida, named for H. C. Plant, who organized a railroad system in that State.

Plaquemines; parish, and a town in Iberville Parish, Louisiana, so named by Bienville on account of the quantities of persimmons which grew in the vicinity.

Plata; river in Colorado. A Spanish word, meaning "silver."

Platte; river in Nebraska, Colorado, and Wyoming. A French word, meaning "dull, flat, shallow," singularly applicable to this stream.

Platte; counties in Nebraska and Missouri, and city in Platte County, Missouri, named for the above.

Plattekill; town in Ulster County, New York. A Dutch word, meaning "flat brook."

Plattsburg; village in Clinton County, New York, named for Judge Zephaniah Piatt, its founder.

Plattville; village in Porter County, Indiana, named for Thomas Piatt, who laid it out.

Pleasanton; city in Linn County, Kansas, named for Gen. Alfred Pleasanton.

Pleasants; county in West Virginia, named for James Pleasants, an early governor.

Plessis; village in Jefferson County, New York, named for the town in France.

Plum; stream in Armstrong County, Pennsylvania, the name being a translation of the Indian name, Sipuas-hanne.

Plumas; county in California traversed by the Feather River. A Spanish word, meaning "feather."

Plymouth; counties in Iowa and Massachusetts, city in Sheboygan County, Wisconsin, and towns in Washington County, North Carolina, and Windsor County, Vermont, named for the above.

Plymouth; town in Plymouth County, Massachusetts, the landing place of the Pilgrims, which was named for the town in England where they were most hospitably entertained before sailing for America.

Plympton; town in Plymouth County, Massachusetts, doubtless named for one of the Plymptons of England.

Pocahontas; counties in Iowa and West Virginia, and villages in Bond County, Illinois, and Cape Girardeau County, Missouri, named for the celebrated Indian princess.

Pocantecs; stream running through "Sleepy Hollow," near Tarrytown, New York. An Indian word, meaning "a run between two hills."

Pocasset; village in Barnstable County, Massachusetts. An Indian word, meaning "at which a strait widens."

Pochaug; stream in Connecticut. An Indian word, meaning "where they divide in two."

Pockwocamus; lake on Penobscot River, Maine. An Indian word, meaning "mud pond."

Pocomoke; river in Maryland; Pocomoke City; town in Worcester County, Maryland. An Indian word, meaning "broken or diversified by knolls or hills."

Pocono; stream in Monroe County, Pennsylvania. An Indian word, meaning "stream between mountains."

Poconteco; river in Westchester County, New York, said to have been densely shaded by trees. An Indian word, meaning "dark river."

Pocosen; river in Virginia. Derived from the Indian word Pduck-assin, "place where balls, bullets, or lead was to be had."

Poe; township in Hancock County, West Virginia, named for a family of pioneers and Indian fighters.

Poestenkill; town in Rensselaer County, New York, named from its principal stream. A Dutch word, meaning "puffing or foaming creek."

Poge; cape at the north end of Chappaquidick Island, Massachusetts. Derived from an Indian word, which means "harbor" or "place of shelter."

Pogues; creek in Indiana, named for an early settler.

Pohopoco; stream in Pennsylvania. Derived from the Indian word Pochkapockla, "two mountains bearing down upon each other with a stream intervening."

Poinsett; county in Arkansas, named for Joel R. Poinsett, Secretary of War during the administration of Van Buren.

Point a la Hache; town in Plaquemines Parish, Louisiana. A French word, meaning "hatchet or ax, point."

Point Allerton; point near Boston, Massachusetts, named for a passenger on the Mayflower.

Point Arena; town in Mendocino County, California, on the coast. A French word, meaning "sandy point."

Point Bonita; southern extremity of Marin County, California. A French word, meaning "beautiful point."

Point Caswell; village in Pender County, North Carolina, named for Richard Caswell, a revolutionary governor and general.

Pointe Coupee; parish, and town in same parish in Louisiana, so named because of an extensive cut-off formed by the change in the course of the river. A French word, meaning "cut-off point."

Point Pleasant; town in Mason County, West Virginia, so named because it was once a place of great natural beauty.

Point Remove; stream in Conway County, Arkansas. A corruption of the French word remous, meaning "eddy."

Point Reyes; town in Marin County, California, named from the point on which a light-house is situated, called by the Spanish Punta des Reyes, "point of the kings."

Point Roberts; cape on the coast of Washington, named for its discoverer.

Point Saint Ignace; village in Mackinac County, Michigan, named for Saint Ignacius.

Point Shirley; point near Boston, Massachusetts, named for William Shirley, an early governor.

Pokagon; village in Cass County, Michigan, named for a Pottawattamie chief, the name meaning "woman butcher."

Pokomoka; river in Maryland. An Indian name, meaning "place of shellfish."

Poland; town in Androscoggin County, Maine, said to have been named for a noted Indian chief.

Poland; village in Mahoning County, Ohio, named for George Poland, its original proprietor.

Polk; counties in Arkansas, Florida, Georgia, Iowa, Missouri, Tennessee, Texas, and Wisconsin, and probably the counties of the same name in Minnesota, Nebraska, and Oregon, named for James K. Polk, a former President.

Polk; county in North Carolina, named for Col. William Polk, of the North Carolina Continental Line.

Polkton; town in Anson County, North Carolina, named for Leonidas Polk.

Pollepel; island on the Hudson River, New York. A Dutch word, meaning "ladle."

Polloksville; town in Jones County, North Carolina, named for a prominent citizen.

Polo; city in Ogle County, Illinois, named for the distinguished traveler Marco Polo.

Pomeroy; city in Meigs County, Ohio, named for its original proprietor, Samuel Wyllis Pomeroy.

Pomfret; towns in Connecticut, New York, and Vermont, named for the town in Yorkshire, England.

Pomme de Terre; river in Missouri. A French word, meaning "potato."

Pomona; city in Franklin County, Kansas, named for the goddess of fruit.

Pomperaug; river in Connecticut. An Indian word, probably meaning "place of offering."

Pompey; town in Onondaga County, New York, named for Pompey the Great.

Ponchartrain; lake in Louisiana, named for a French count who was an early explorer of the Mississippi Valley.

Ponkapog; town in Norfolk County, Massachusetts. An Indian word, meaning " sweet water." Pontiac; cities in Oakland County, Michigan, and Livingston County, Illinois, named for a chief of the Ottawa Indians.

Pontoosuc; villages in Hancock County, Illinois, and Berkshire County, Massachusetts, and hill in Glastonburg, Connecticut. An Indian word, meaning "falls on the brook."

Pontotoc; county and town in same county, in Mississippi, and town in Chickasaw Nation, Indian Territory, named for a Chickasaw Indian chief, the word meaning " weed prairie."

Pope; county in Arkansas, named for John Pope, a former governor.

Pope; county in Illinois, named for Nathaniel Pope, a former Congressional Delegate.

Pope; county in Minnesota, probably named for Gen. John Pope, who conducted the Minnesota exploring expedition.

Popham; fort at the mouth of the Kennebec River, Maine, named for Capt. George Popham, its builder, when governor of the first English colony in New England.

Poplarville; town in Pearl River County, Mississippi, named for "Popular" Jim Smith, owner of the store in which the first railroad depot at this point was located.

Poponoming; lake in Monroe County, Pennsylvania. An Indian name, meaning "where we are gazing."

Poquessing; stream in Pennsylvania. An Indian word, meaning "where there are mice."

Poquetanuck; stream and town in New London County, Connecticut. An Indian word, meaning " land open or broken up."

Poquonoc; river and hill in Connecticut. An Indian word, meaning "cleared land."

Porcupine; islands of Mount Desert, Maine, so called because at a distance they resemble a porcupine.

Portage; counties in Ohio and Wisconsin and town in Livingston County, New York, so named because they are situated between water courses.

Portage des Sioux; town in St. Charles County, Missouri, so named because at this point on the Mississippi the Indians carried their canoes across the peninsula to the Missouri.

Port Angeles; town in Clallam County, Washington, named by Don Francisco Elisa, a Mexican.

Port Austin; village in Huron County, Michigan, named for the first man to establish a business there.

Port Crane; village in Broome County, New York, named for one of the engineers of the Chenango Canal.

Port Deposit; town in Cecil County, Maryland, so named because it is one of the principal depots for the pine lumber rafted down the river.

Port Dickinson; town in Broome County, New York, named in honor of Daniel S. Dickinson, United States Senator, lieutenant governor, and attorney-general of New York.

Port Discovery; village in Jefferson County, Washington, named for a ship in the fleet of Vancouver, the explorer.

Porter; county in Indiana, named for Commodore David Porter.

Porter; town in Oxford County, Maine, named for Dr. Aaron Porter, an early proprietor.

Porter; town in Niagara County, New York, named for Judge Augustus Porter.

Port Gamble; village in Kitsap County, Washington, named for a United States naval officer.

Port Gibson; town in Claiborne County, Mississippi, named for David Gibson, the former owner of the town site.

Port Jervis; village in Orange County, New York, named for John B. Jervis, engineer of the Hudson and Delaware Canal.

Portland; cities in Cumberland County, Maine, and Multnomah County, Oregon, and borough in Northampton County, Pennsylvania, named, indirectly, for the town in England.

Port Leyden; town in Lewis County, New York, named after Leyden. Netherlands.

Port Morris; village in Westchester County, New York, named for Gouverneur Morris.

Port Orchard; town and harbor in Kitsap County, Washington, named for its discoverer.

Port Orford; cape and town in Curry County, Oregon, named for George, Earl of Orford.

Port Penn; town in Newcastle County, Delaware, named for William Penn.

Port Royal; river and a town in Beaufort County, South Carolina, so named "because of the fairness and bigness thereof."

Portsmouth; city in Rockingham County, New Hampshire, first named Strawberry Banke, but later changed to its present name because situated at the river mouth and a good harbor.

Portsmouth; city in Norfolk County, Virginia, named for the town in England.

Port Tobacco; town in Charles County, Maryland, and an inlet on the Potomac in the same State; the name having no connection with the plant, but being a corruption of the Indian word pautapang, meaning " a bulging out, a bay, or a cove." Port Townsend; harbor and village in Jefferson County, Washington, named for Marquis of Townsend.

Portville; town in Cattaraugus County, New York, so named because it was, at an early date, a prominent point for the shipment of lumber, shingles, etc.

Posey; county in Indiana; Poseyville; town in Posey County, Indiana. Named for Gen. Thomas Posey, an early governor of the State.

Possession; sound in Washington, so named by Vancouver because he landed there and took possession on the King's birthday.

Postboy; village in Tuscarawas County, Ohio, so named because a post boy was murdered near there.

Potaligo; village in Madison County, Georgia. An Indian word meaning "plenty of fat ducks."

Poteau; river in Arkansas. A French word meaning "post, stake, or pillar."

Potomac; river forming the boundary line between Maryland, Virginia, and West Virginia. According to different authorities, derived from the Indian word pethamook, "they are coming by water," or from the word potowanmeac, meaning "to make a fire in a place where fires are usually made;" still another authority gives its meaning as "the river of swans."

Potosi; town in Washington County, Missouri, a mining town, named from the South American mines.

Potsdam; village in St. Lawrence County, New York, named from the town in Prussia.

Pottawattomie; counties in Kansas and Oklahoma; Pottawattamie, county in Iowa, named for the Indian tribe. The word means "makers of fire," and was used to signify that this tribe assumed separate sovereignty by building a council fire for themselves.

Potter; town in Yates County, New York, named for Arnold Potter, the original proprietor.

Potter; county and township in Center County, Pennsylvania, named for Gen. James Potter, Revolutionary officer.

Potter; county in South Dakota, named for a prominent physician of the State.

Potter; county in Texas, named for Robert Potter, temporary secretary of the navy of Texas in 1836.

Potter Hollow; village in Albany County, New York, named for Samuel Potter.

Potterville; village in Eaton County, Michigan, named for George N. Potter.

Potts Camp; town in Marshall County, Mississippi, named for Col. E. F. Potts.

Pottstown; borough in Montgomery County, Pennsylvania; Pottsville; borough in Schuylkill County, Pennsylvania. Named for John Potts, a large landowner, who founded the town.

Poughkeepsie; city in Dutchess County, New York. Derived from the Delaware Indian word apokeepsingk, meaning "safe and pleasant harbor," or "shallow inlet, safe harbor for small boats."

Powder; stream in Wyoming, so named because of the dark powder-colored sand on its banks.

Powell; county in Kentucky, named for Lazerus W. Powell, a former governor.

Powell; county in Montana, named for the mountain in Colorado which was named for J. W. Powell, geologist and explorer.

Powellsville; town in Bertie County, North Carolina, named for a prominent resident.

Powellton; town in Fayette County, West Virginia, named for E. Powell, interested in a large coal and coke company there.

Powell Valley; village in Multnomah County, Oregon, named for an old settler.

Powelton; village in Hancock County, Georgia, named for a former resident.

Poweshiek; county in Iowa, named for an Indian chief.

Powhatan; county in Virginia and city in Brown County, Kansas, named for the celebrated Indian chief.

Pownal; towns in Cumberland County, Maine, and Bennington County, Vermont, named for Governor Thomas Pownal, of Massachusetts.

Poygan; village in Winnebago County, Wisconsin. An Indian word, meaning " pipe."
Poynette; village in Columbia County, Wisconsin, named for Peter Paquette; the present name a clerical error.

Poysippi; village in Waushara County, Wisconsin. Derived from the Indian word poygansippi, meaning "running into the lake."

Prairie; county in Arkansas, so named on account of its treeless plains.

Prairie; stream in Wisconsin. Derived from the Indian word musk-ko-day yaw se-be, "prairie river."

Prairie du Chien; city in Crawford County, Wisconsin. A French phrase, meaning "dog prairie."

Prairie du Rocher; village in Randolph County, Illinois, behind which is a rocky bluff. A French phrase, meaning "the meadow of the rock."

Prairie du Sac; village in Sauk County, Wisconsin, originally in the territory of the Sauk Indians. A French phrase, meaning "the meadow of the Sauks."

Prairie Home; village in Cooper County, Missouri, so named on account of the character of the land.

Pratt; county, and city in same county, in Kansas, named for Caleb Pratt, second lieutenant Company D, Second Kansas.

Prattsburg; town in Steuben County, New York, named for Capt. Joel Pratt, one of the first settlers.

Pratts Hollow; village in Madison County, New York, named for John and Matthew Pratt, early settlers.

Prattsville; town in Greene County, New York, named for Zadock Pratt.

Preble; county in Ohio and town in Cortland County, New York, named for Commodore Edward Preble.

Prentice; village in Price County, Wisconsin, named for Alexander Prentice, the first postmaster.

Prentiss; county in Mississippi, named for Sergt. Smith Prentiss, a gifted forensic orator.

Prescott; town in Yavapai County, Arizona, named for W. H. Prescott, the historian.

Prescott; city in Linn County, Kansas, named for C. H. Prescott, a railroad official.

Prescott; town in Hampshire County, Massachusetts, named for Col. William Prescott, commanding the Americans at the battle of Bunker Hill.

Prescott; city in Pierce County, Wisconsin, named for P. Prescott.

Presidio; county in Texas. A Spanish word, meaning "a garrison of soldiers."

Presque Isle; county in Michigan and town in Aroostook County, Maine. A French phrase, meaning "nearly an island."

Preston; township in Wayne County, Pennsylvania, named for Judge Samuel Preston, an early settler.

Preston; county in West Virginia; Prestonburg; town in Floyd County, Kentucky. Named for James P. Preston, an early governor of Virginia.

Preston Hollow; village in Albany County, New York, named for the first family of settlers.

Prestonville; town in Carroll County, Kentucky, named for James P. Preston, an early governor of Virginia.

Presumpscot; village in Cumberland County, Maine. Indian word, meaning "rough place in the river."

Preuss; mountain in Idaho, named for a topographer of the Fremont exploring party.

Pribilof; islands of Alaska, named for the Russian navigator who discovered them.

Price; creek in Humboldt County, California, named for an early settler.

Price; county in Wisconsin, named for Congressman William T. Price.

Primghar; town in O'Brien County, Iowa, named by combining the initials of the persons present at the laying of the corner stone.

Prince Edward; county in Virginia, named for Ed ward of England, son of Ferdinand.

Prince George; counties in Maryland and Virginia, named for Prince George of Denmark, afterwards King of England.

Princess Anne; county in Virginia, named for Princess, afterwards Queen, Anne of England.

Princeton; mountain in Colorado, named for Princeton University.

Princeton; city in Gibson county, Indiana, named for Hon. William Prince.

Princeton; town in Worcester County, Massachusetts, named for the Rev. Thomas Prince, pastor of Old South Church, Boston.

Princeton; town in Mercer County, West Virginia, named for the battlefield upon which Gen. Hugh Mercer fell.

Princetown; town in Schenectady County, New York, named for John Prince, a member of Albany County's assembly.

Prince William; county in Virginia, named for the Duke of Cumberland.

Proctor; town in Lee County, Kentucky, named for the Rev. Joseph Proctor.

Proctor; town in Rutland County, Vermont, named for Redfield Proctor, Senator from that State.

Proctor Knott; village in St. Louis County, Minnesota, named for Proctor Knott, of Kentucky.

Proctorsville; village in Windsor County, Vermont, named for the father of Senator Proctor.

Promised Land; village in Suffolk County, New York, so named because the land for factories was promised but never given.

Promontory; village in Boxelder County, Utah, so named because it is the highest point of the Promontory Range.

Prophetstown; village in Whiteside County, Illinois, named for the "Shawnee Prophet," the brother of the Indian chief Tecumseh.

Prospect; towns in New Haven County, Connecticut, and Waldo County, Maine, and peak in Yellowstone Park, so named because of the elevation.

Prosperity; town in Newberry County, South Carolina, named on optimistic hopes.

Providence; county and river in Rhode Island, named from the city in the same State, which was so called by Roger Williams, "for God's merciful providence to him in his distress."

Provincetown; town in Barnstable County, Massachusetts, incorporated as the Province Town, because the inhabitants were exempt from taxation.

Provo; river and town in Utah County, Utah, a contraction of the name—Provost—of the man for whom they were named.

Prowers; county in Colorado, named for John W. Prowers, a prominent stockman and trader in early days.

Psimmdse; several lakes in Minnesota, with wild rice growing on their banks. An Indian word, meaning "wild rice."

Ptansinta; peninsula on Lac Traverse and the Minnesota River. An Indian word, meaning "otter tail."

Puckaway; lake in Green Lake County, Wisconsin. An Indian word, meaning "cat-tail flag."

Puckety; stream in Allegheny County, Pennsylvania. An Indian word, meaning "throw it away."

Pueblo; county and city in same county in Colorado. A Spanish word, meaning "a collection of people, a town or village."

Puente; village in Los Angeles County, California. A Spanish word, meaning "bridge."

Puerco; river in New Mexico. A Spanish word, meaning "hog."

Puerto de Luna; village in San Miguel County, New Mexico. A Spanish word, meaning "port of the moon."

Puget; sound in Washington, named for Peter Puget, its discoverer.

Pulaski; counties in Arkansas, Georgia, Illinois, Indiana, Kentucky, Missouri, and Virginia; towns in Giles County, Tennessee, and Pulaski County, Virginia, and villages in Oswego County, New York, and Pulaski County, Illinois, named for the Polish patriot, Count Casimir Pulaski.

Pulteney; town in Steuben County, New York, named for Sir William Pulteney.

Pungoteague; stream and town in Accomac County, Virginia, supposed to be so named on account of the extremely sandy character of the county; the name, an Indian one, meaning "the place of powder."

Punta Gorda; town in De Soto County, Florida, so named on account of the point nearby. A Spanish word, meaning "large point."

Punxsutawaney; borough in Jefferson County, Pennsylvania. An Indian word, meaning "the habitation of the sand fly."

Purgatory; river in Colorado, tributary of the Arkansas. An anglicization of the French name "riviere Purgatoire."

Purvis; town in Marion County, Mississippi, named for the former owner of the railroad station site.

Put in Bay; bay in Ottawa County, Ohio, Lake Erie, and village in same county; so named because Commodore Perry put in there with his fleet.

Putnam; counties in Florida, Georgia, Illinois, Indiana, Missouri, New York, Ohio, Tennessee, and West Virginia; city in Windham County, Connecticut, and pond and creek in New York, named for Gen. Israel Putnam.

Pymatuning; tributary of the Chenango in Mercer County, Pennsylvania. An Indian word, meaning "the crooked mouthed man's dwelling place."

Pyramid; canyon of the Colorado River, so named because of the monument-like pinnacle of porphyritic rock which crowns the left bank near the entrance.

Pyramid; harbor in Alaska, so named because of the conical shape of one of its islands.

Pyramid; lake in Nevada, so named on account of the shape of an island in the lake.

Pyroxene; peak in the same range as the Old Bald in Montana; another name for the mineral augite.

Pysht; river in Washington. The Clallam Indian word for fish.

Q

Quakake; stream in Carbon County, Pennsylvania. An Indian word, meaning "pine lands."

Quantico; town in Wicomico County, Maryland. An Indian word, meaning "dancing, place of frolicking."

Quapaw; nation in Indian Territory, named from the Indian tribe; the word meaning "down-stream people."

Quasqueton; town in Buchanan County, Iowa, derived from an Indian word meaning "rapid water."

Quebec; village in Union County, Georgia. Said by some authorities to be derived from the Indian, meaning "being shut," "narrow," or, "fearful rocky cliff;" others say it is derived from the French word quelbec, "what a beak!"

Queen Anne; county in Maryland, named for Queen Anne of England, reigning at the time of its organization.

Queen Mahon; stream in Indiana County, Pennsylvania. Derived from the Indian word, Cuwei-mahoni, meaning "pine-tree lick."

Queens; county in New York, named for Catherine of Braganza, wife of Charles H, of England.

Quemahoning; stream in Somerset County, Pennsylvania. Derivation same as Queen Mahon.

Quenemo; village in Osage County, Kansas, named for an Ottawa Indian, who lived among the Sacs and Foxes, near Melvern.

Queponco; creek in Maryland. An Indian word, meaning "ashes of pine woods."

Quiccoane; branch of the Missouri River. An Indian word meaning "running river."

Quidnic; river and pond in Rhode Island and Connecticut. An Indian word, meaning "place at the end of the hill."

Quillayute; river in Washington, named for the Indian tribe Kwillehiut, of which the river's name is a corruption.

Quincy; city in Adams County, Illinois, and village in Branch County, Michigan, named for John Quincy Adams, a former President.

Quincy; city in Norfolk County, Massachusetts, named for Col. John Quincy.

Quindaro; town in Wyandotte County, Kansas, named for the Indian woman, former owner of the land. The Indian meaning, "a bundle of sticks."

Quinlan; village in Hunt County, Texas, named for G. A. Quinlan, former vice-president of the Houston and Texas Central Railroad.

Quinnebaug; river, and a village in Windham County, Connecticut. An Indian word, meaning "long pond."

Quinnesec; village in Dickinson County, Michigan. An Indian word, meaning "where the river forms smoke," and given this village on account of the falls in the Menominee River at this point.

Quinnipiac; river in Connecticut. An Indian word, meaning "long water pond," or, according to another authority, "the surrounding country."

Quinsigamond; lake in Worcester County, Massachusetts. An Indian word, meaning "the pickerel fishing place."

Quintana; town in Brazoria County, Texas, named for Andre Quintana, prominent in the early days of Texas.

Quitman; counties in Georgia and Mississippi, towns in Jackson County, Georgia, and Clarke County, Mississippi, and village in Nodaway County, Missouri, named for Gen. John A. Quitman, former governor of Mississippi and officer in the Mexican war.

Quitopahilla; branch of the Great Swatara in Lebanon County, Pennsylvania. An Indian word, meaning "a spring that flows from the ground among the pines."

Quogue; village in Suffolk County, New York. An Indian word, meaning "a clam."

R

Rabbit Ears; mountain of the Park Range, Colorado, so named on account of its resemblance to a rabbit ear.

Rabun; county in Georgia, named for William Rabun, an early governor of the State.

Raccoon; creek in Beaver County, Pennsylvania. Corruption of the Indian arrathkune, or arathcone, the procyon lotor of the naturalist.

Racine; county and a city in same county in Wisconsin, situated at the mouth of Root River. A French word meaning " root."

Radford; city in Montgomery County, Virginia, named for William Radford, a prominent citizen.

Radnor; village in Delaware County, Pennsylvania, named for the town in Wales.

Ragged; mountain in Knox County, Maine, so named on account of its ragged appearance.

Rahway; river in New Jersey. Said to be derived from the Indian word nawakwa, meaning " in the middle of the forest."

Rabway; city in Union County, New Jersey, named for the Indian sachem, Rahwack.

Rainier; town in Columbia County, Oregon, and mountain in Washington, named for Rear-Admiral Rainier.

Rains; county in Texas, named for Emory Rains, who was prominent in the politics of the Republic and later in those of the State.

Rainsville; town in Warren County, Indiana, named for the proprietor, Isaac Rains.

Rainy; lake in Minnesota. An anglicization of the original French name, lac de la Pluire.

Raisen; river in Michigan, so named on account of the abundance of grapes which formerly grew upon its banks.

Raleigb; county in West Virginia, city in North Carolina, and town in Smith County, Mississippi, and Shelby County, Tennessee, named for Sir Walter Raleigh.

Ralls; county in Missouri, named for Daniel Ralls.

Ralston; village in Lycoming County, Pennsylvania, named for Matthew C. Ralston.

Ramseur; town in Randolph County, North Carolina, named for Gen. Stephen Ramseur.

Ramsey; counties in Minnesota and in North Dakota, named for the war governor of Minnesota, Hon. Alexander Ramsey.

Randall; county in Texas, named for Horace Randall, a brigadier-general of the Confederacy.

Randalls; island in New York. named for Jonathan Randall, who owns it.

Randleman; town in Randolph County, North Carolina, named for a prominent citizen.

Randolph; counties in Alabama, Arkansas, Georgia, and Missouri, and towns in Coos County, New Hampshire; Orange County, Vermont, and Cattaraugus County, New York, named for John Randolph, of Roanoke, Virginia.

Randolph; county in Indiana, named for Thomas Randolph, killed at Tippecanoe.

Randolph; county in Illinois, named for Beverly Randolph.

Randolph; village in Dakota County, Nebraska, named for the first mail carrier between Sioux City and Elkhorn Valley—Jasper Randolph.

Randolph; county in North Carolina and town in Norfolk County, Massachusetts, named for Peyton Randolph, of Virginia.

Randolph; county in West Virginia, named for Edmund Randolph, an early governor.

Rangeley; town and plantation in Franklin County, Maine, and one of the Androscoggin lakes in the same State, named for an Englishman, an early settler and large landowner.

Rankin; county in Mississippi, named for Christopher Rankin, Congressman from that State.

Ransom; village in Hillsdale County, Michigan, named for Epaphroditus Ransom, former governor of the State.

Ransom; county in North Dakota, named for Fort Ransom.

Ransomville; village in Niagara County, New York, named for Clark Ransom, one of the first settlers.

Rapho; township in Lancaster County, Pennsylvania. A corruption of an Indian word meaning "a fort of tents."

Rapidan; river in Virginia, named for Anne, Queen of England, "rapid Anne."

Rapides; parish in Louisiana. A French word meaning "rapids" and given this parish on account of the rapids or falls in the Red River.

Rappahannock; river and county in Virginia. An Indian word meaning "a stream with an ebb and flow."

Raquette; river in Hamilton County, New York, from French word meaning "snowshoe."

Raritan; stream and a town in Somerset County, New Jersey. An Indian word meaning "forked river."

Raspberry; island, one of the Apostles, Wisconsin. Translation of an Indian word meaning "raspberries are plentiful here."

Rathbone; town in Steuben County, New York, named for Gen. Ransom Rathbone, an early settler.

Raton; village in Las Animas County, Colorado. A Spanish word meaning "mouse."

Raumaug; lake in Litchfield County, Connecticut. A corruption of the Indian word, Wonkemaug, meaning "crooked fishing place."

Ravalli; county in Montana, named for a Catholic priest.

Ravenna; village in Portage County, Ohio, named for the city in Italy.

Ravenswood; town in Jackson County, West Virginia, named for the Ravensworths, a family of England, but misspelled by the engravers in making the first maps and never corrected.

Rawhide; creek in Nebraska, said to be so named because a white man was flayed upon its banks by a party of Pawnee Indians.

Rawlins; county in Kansas and city in Carbon County, Wisconsin, named for John A. Rawlins, Secretary of War under President Grant.

Ray; creek in California, named for an early settler.

Ray; county in Missouri, named for John Ray, a member of the convention which formed the State constitution.

Raymond; village in Madera County, California, named for Raymond Whitcomb, who organized a party of tourists to make the trip to the Yosemite by stages from this point.

Raymond; town in Cumberland County, Maine, named for Capt. William Raymond.

Raymond; town in Rockingham County, New Hampshire, named for John Raymond, a grantee.

Raymondville; village in St. Lawrence County, New York, named for Benjamin Raymond, first agent.

Raynham; town in Bristol County, Massachusetts, named for the parish of Rainham, Essex County, England.

Raysville; village in Henry County, Indiana, named for Governor Ray.

Reading; town in Fairfield County, Connecticut, named for Col. John Read, an early settler.

Reading; town in Middlesex County, Massachusetts, and city in Berks County, Pennsylvania, named for the town in Berkshire, England.

Readsboro; town in Bennington County, Vermont, named for John Read, one of the original patentees.

Readstown; village in Vernon County, Wisconsin, named for its founder.

Rector; town in Clay County, Arkansas, named for Wharton or Elias Rector, distinguished in the early Indian affairs of the State.

Red; range of mountains in Alabama, so called on account of its hematite iron ores.

Red; river in Arkansas, so named on account of the color of the sediment with which it is freighted.

Red; group of mountains in Wyoming. so named because formed of porphyry, which becomes dark red when exposed to the sun.

Red Bank; towns in Marshall County, Mississippi, and Monmouth County, New Jersey, so named on account of the reddish appearance of the banks of the rivers upon which they are located.

Red Bud; several places in the United States bear this name, given them on account of the presence of a small ornamental North American tree; among them being a city in Randolph County, Illinois.

Red Cap; creek in California, named for a near-by mine.

Red Cedar; river in Iowa, so named on account of the abundance of this tree once found upon its banks.

Red Cloud; city in Webster County, Nebraska, named for the celebrated Indian chief.

Redden; village in Sussex County, Delaware, named for Col. William O. Redden.

Redfield; town in Dallas County, Iowa, named for Colonel Red field.

Redford; village in Wayne County, Michigan, so named because it was a fording place on the river Rouge.

Red Hook; town in Dutchess County, New York. A translation of the original Dutch name, Roode Hoeck, which they gave it on account of a near-by marsh covered with cranberries.

Red Jacket; village in Erie County, New York, named for a chief of the Seneca Indians, who derived his name from the brilliant red jacket which he wore, given him by a British officer.

Red Lake; county in Minnesota, named for a lake.

Red Oak; city in Montgomery County, Iowa, so named on account of a near-by grove of trees of this species.

Redondo Beach; city in Los Angeles County, California, named from a Spanish word meaning " round."

Red River; county in Texas and parish in Louisiana, named from Red River, which borders Texas on the north.

Red Bock; town in Douglas County, Minnesota, so named on account of a near-by granite boulder painted red by the Indians.

Red Rock; village in Columbia County, New York, named for a red rock, surmounted by a wooden column 10 feet high bearing the date 1825.

Redstone; branch of the Monongahela in Pennsylvania, derived from the Indian word, Machkachsen, meaning "red stone creek."

Redwillow; county in Nebraska, so named on account of the abundance of trees of this species.

Redwing; city in Goodhue County, Minnesota, named for an Indian chief.

Redwood; river in Indiana. Derived from the Indian word musqua me tig, meaning "redwood tree river."

Redwood; county in Minnesota, drained by a river of the same name, which was so named on account of the species of wood which grows upon its banks.

Reed; township in Butler County, Nebraska, named for David Reed, a pioneer.

Reedsburg; city in Sauk County, Wisconsin, named for D. C. Reed, an early settler.

Reedy; town in Roane County, West Virginia, named for a creek where reeds grow abundantly.

Reese; valley and river in Nevada, named for a guide.

Reese; stream in Lander County, Nevada, named for an early settler.

Reeseville; village in Dodge County, Wisconsin, named for Samuel Reese, the first settler.

Reeves; county in Texas, named for George H. Reeves.

Reevesville; town in Dorchester County, South Carolina, named for-a prominent family of the Aicinity.

Refugio; county and town in Texas, named for a Mexican missionary establishment on the Mission River. A Spanish word meaning "refuge."

Rehoboth; town in Sussex County, Delaware, given this scriptural name because it was first established as a place for yearly camp meetings.

Rehoboth; town in Bristol County, Massachusetts; a Hebrew word meaning "ample room." Said to have been founded by William Blackstone and so named by him as significant of his aim: "Room outside of the narrow confines of Puritan intolerance." Another authority ascribes the name to Rev. Samuel Newman, who established a church there and gave the town this name because "the Lord hath made room for us."

Reidsville; village in Knox County, Nebraska, named for Charles J. Reid, the first settler.

Reidsville; town in Rockingham County, North Carolina, named for David S. Reid, a former governor.

Remsen; town in Oneida County, New York, named for Henry Remsen, a patentee.

Rennert; town in Robeson County, North Carolina, named for a prominent resident.

Reno; county in Kansas, town in Washoe County, Nevada, and village in Venango County, Pennsylvania, named for Gen. Jesse L. Reno.

Rensselaer; county in New York; Rensselaerville; town in Albany County, New York. Named for Kilian van Rensselaer, who planted a colony on his lands to be known as Rensselaerwyck, now as above.

Renville; county in Minnesota, named for Joseph Renville, an Indian trader and prominent citizen.

Republic; county in Kansas, named for the Pawnee Republic, a principal division of the Pawnee Indians formerly located in this county.

Republican; village in Harlan County, Nebraska, named from the Republican River.

Revere; town in Suffolk County, Massachusetts, named for Paul Revere.

Revillagigedo; group of islands off the coast of Alaska, named for Conde Revila Gigedo, viceroy of New Spain.

Reynolds; county in Missouri, named for Thomas Reynolds, a former governor.

Reynoldsburg; village in Franklin County, Ohio, probably named for Jeremiah N. Reynolds.

Rhinebeck; town in Dutchess County, New York. A combination of the names of the man who founded the town—William Beekman—and his native town—Rhineland.

Rhode Island; one of the original thirteen States, said to have received its name from a small island in Narraganset Day named Roode Kylandt, "red island;" according to another authority, named for the island of Rhodes.

Rib; river in Wisconsin. A translation of an Indian word.

Rice; county in Kansas, named for Brig. Gen. Samuel A. Rice.

Rice; county in Minnesota, named for Senator Henry M. Rice, a pioneer.

Rice Lake; city in Barron County, Wisconsin, so called because situated on a lake where wild rice is abundant.

Riceville; town in Mitchell County, Iowa, named for three brothers.

Rich; county in Utah, named for Apostle Charles C. Rich, one of the members of the Church of Jesus Christ of the Latter Day Saints.

Richardson; county in Nebraska, named for William A. Richardson, former governor of the Territory.

Richburg; town in Allegany County, New York, named in honor of Alvan Richardson, the first settler, who went there from Otsego County in 1819.

Richburg; town in Chester County, South Carolina, named for a prominent family.

Richfield; city in Morton County, Kansas, so named because it was thought it would prove a "rich field."

Rich Hill; city in Bates County, Missouri, so named because of the fertile hill lands around it.

Richland; counties in Illinois, North Dakota, Ohio, South Carolina, and Wisconsin, and parish in Louisiana, so named on account of the rich character of the soil.

Richmond; counties in Georgia, New York, and North Carolina, and town in Berkshire County, Massachusetts, named for Lennox, the Duke of Richmond.

Richmond; town in Washington County, Rhode Island, thought to have been named for Edward Richmond, attorney-general of the colony.

Richmond; county in Virginia, and city in Henrico County of the same State, so named on account of its resemblance to Richmond, Surrey County, England.

Richthofen; mountain in Colorado, named for the geologist.

Richville; village in St. Lawrence County, New York, named for Salmon Rich, an early settler.

Rickreal; river and village in Polk County, Oregon. A corruption of the French, La Creole, meaning "the Creole."

Ridgefield; borough in Bergen County, New Jersey; Ridge Spring; town in Saluda County, South Carolina; Ridgeville; town in Dorchester County, South Carolina; Ridgeway; towns in Orleans County, New York, and Fairfield County. South Carolina. Named on account of the presence of ridges of some elevation nearby.

Ridgeway; borough in Elk County, Pennsylvania, named for John Jacob Ridgeway, of Philadelphia, a large landowner.

Ridley Park; borough in Delaware County, Pennsylvania, named for the native place of its settlers in Cheshire, England.

Rienzi; town in Alcorn County, Mississippi, named for the Roman tribune.

Riga; town in Lenawee County, Michigan, named for the city in Russia.

Riley; county in Kansas, named for Maj. Gen. Bennet Riley, United States Army.

Rimersburg; borough in Clarion County, Pennsylvania, named for John Rimer, its first settler.

Rincon; town in Donna Ana County, New Mexico. A Spanish word meaning "corner," or "inside corner."

Rindge; town in Cheshire County, New Hampshire, named for one of the original proprietors.

Ring-gold; county in Iowa, named for Maj. Samuel Ringgold, an officer of the Mexican war.

Ringwood; villages in Passaic County, New Jersey, and Halifax County, North Carolina, named for the town in England.

Rio Arriba; county in New Mexico intersected by the Rio Grande del Norte, "great river of the North." A Spanish name meaning "upper," or "high river."

Rio Blanco; county in Colorado, named from the White River, of which the county's name is the Spanish interpretation.

Rio de las Piedras; stream in New Mexico. A Spanish phrase meaning "the river of stones."

Rio de los Americanos; river in California. A Spanish phrase meaning "river of the Americans."

Rio de los Martires; river in California. A Spanish phrase meaning " river of the martyrs."

Rio de los Mimbres; river in New Mexico. A Spanish phrase meaning " river of the willows."

Rio de Mercede; river in California. A Spanish phrase meaning " river of mercy."

Rio Frio; river in Texas. A Spanish word meaning "cold river."

Rio Grande; river rising in the Rocky Mountains and emptying into the Gulf, which gives name to a county in Colorado. A Spanish phrase meaning "great river."

Rio Grande Pyramid; mountain of the San Juan Range, Colorado, so called because its form is that of a perfect pyramid.

Rio Llano; river in Texas. A Spanish phrase, meaning "river of the plain."

Rio Salinas; river in Arizona, having salty deposits upon its banks which caused it to be given this Spanish name, meaning "salt river."

Rio Seco; town in Butte County, California. A Spanish phrase, meaning "dry river."

Rio Verde; river in Arizona. A Spanish phrase, meaning "green river."

Rio Vista; town in Solano County, California, at the mouth of the Sacramento River. A Spanish phrase, meaning "river view."

Ripley; counties in Indiana and Missouri, and town in Chautauqua County, New York, named for Gen. Eleazer W. Ripley.

Ripley; town in Payne County, Oklahoma, named for a leading official of the Santa Fe Railroad.

Ripley; town in Jackson County, West Virginia, named for a resident.

Ripon; city in Fond du Lac County, Wisconsin, named for the town in England.

Rippey; town in Greene County, Iowa, named for Capt. C. M. Rippey, an old settler.

Rising City; village in Butler County, Nebraska, named for the owners of the town site, A. W. and S. W. Rising.

Rising Sun; village in Dearborn County, Indiana, so named by its founder, John James, when viewing the sunrise from that location.

Ritchie; county in West Virginia, named for Thomas Ritchie, editor of the Richmond Enquirer.

Rivanna, river and township in Virginia, named for Queen Anne, of England.

River Falls; city in Pierce County, Wisconsin, so named because of its situation near the falls of the Kinnikinnic River.

Riverside; many places in the United States, so named on account of their situation near some river, among these being a county in California and town in Washington County, Iowa.

Rivoli; town in Mercer County, Illinois, named for the town in Italy.

Roach; creek in Humboldt County, California, named for a man who was drowned in it.

Roan; plateau in Colorado, so named on account of the color of the cliffs rising from the Grand River Valley.

Roan; mountain in North Carolina, so named on account of the color of the laurel growing upon its summit.

Roane; county in Tennessee, named for Governor Archibald Roane.

Roane; county in West Virginia, named for Spencer Roane, judge of the supreme court of the State in its early days.

Roanoke; towns in Randolph County, Alabama, Howard County, Missouri, and Genesee County, New York, named for the home of John Randolph in Virginia.

Roanoke; county and city in same county in Virginia, river in Virginia and North Carolina, town in Huntington County, Indiana, and village in Woodford County, Illinois. An Indian word, designating a species of shell which they used for money.

Roaring; mountain in Yellowstone Park, so named on account of the shrill sound made by the steam escaping from a vent in its summit.

Roaring Fork; branch of the Grand River in Colorado, so named from its steep and rapid descent.

Robbinston; town in Washington County, Maine, named for its original owners, Edward H. and Nathaniel J. Robbins.

Roberts; county in South Dakota, named for Moses Robert (Robar) a fur trader.

Roberts; county in Texas, named for Oran M. Roberts, former governor of the State.

Robertson; county in Kentucky, named for ex-Chief Justice George Robertson, a leading pioneer.

Robertson; county in Tennessee, named for Gen. James Robertson, a pioneer.

Robertson; county in Texas, named for Sterling C. Robertson, who received a colonization grant from Mexico.

Robeson; county in North Carolina, named for Col. Thomas Robeson, of the North Carolina Revolutionary Militia.

Robinson; town in Summit County, Colorado, named for George B. Robinson, former lieutenant-governor of the State.

Robinson; city in Brown County, Kansas, named for Governor Charles Robinson.

Roche a Gris; river in Adams County, Wisconsin. A French phrase, meaning "gray rock."

Roche Moutonnee; branch of the Eagle River in Colorado, so named on account of the glacial rocks of its gorge.

Roche Percee; river in Boone County, Missouri. A French phrase, meaning "pierced rock."

Rochester; town in Plymouth County, Massachusetts, named for the town in England.

Rochester; city in Monroe County, New York, named for the senior proprietor, Col. Nathaniel Rochester.

Rochester; town in Ulster County, New York, named for the Earl of Rochester.

Rock; counties in Minnesota, Nebraska, and Wisconsin, and river in Wisconsin, so named on account of the rocky character of the soil.

Rockaway; river, and a borough in Morris County, New Jersey. Supposed to be derived from the Indian word Reckawackes, or Aehewek, meaning "bushy," or "difficult to cross."

Rockbridge; county in Virginia, so named on account of the natural bridge of rock over Cedar Creek.

Rockford; city in Winnebago County, Illinois, so named because of its situation on both sides of Rock River.

Rockford; village in Wells County, Indiana, so named because it is located at a ford on Rock Creek.

Rockingham; counties in New Hampshire, North Carolina, and Virginia, named for the Marquis of Rockingham, premier of England at the time of the repeal of the stamp act.

Rock Island; county, and city in same county in Illinois, so named on account of the island in the Mississippi which is formed of limestone.

Rockland; city in Knox County, Maine, so named because of its granite quarries.

Rockland; county in New York, so named on account of its extensive quarries of red sandstone.

Rockport; town in Spencer County, Indiana, so named because of the hanging rock, "Lady Washington Rock," on the Ohio River.

Rockport; town in Essex County, Massachusetts. so named on account of the granite quarries near the sea.

Rockville; village in Allegany County, New York, so named on account of a quarry in the vicinity.

Rockwall; county in Texas, so named on account of an underground wall.

Rodman; town in Jefferson County, New York, named for Daniel Rodman, of Hudson.

Rodney; town in Jefferson County, Mississippi, named for Judge Rodney, of the State.

Roger Mills; county in Oklahoma, named for Roger Q. Mills, Senator from Texas.

Rogers; mountain in Tennessee, named for William B. Rogers, the geologist.

Rogue; river in Oregon, named for the Tototins, an Indian tribe of nefarious habits, who were termed Coquins by the French and Rogues by the English.

Rohnerville; town in Humboldt County, California, named for Henry Rohner, an early settler.

Rolesville; town in Wake County, North Carolina, named for a prominent resident.

Rolette; county in North Dakota, named for the Hon. Joseph Rolette, an early settler of Red River Valley.

Rolfe; town in Pocahontas County, Iowa, said by some authorities to be named for the young Englishman who married Pocahontas, but by others for the man who previously owned the town site.

Rollinsford; town in Strafford County, New Hampshire, named for a resident family.

Rollinsville; town in Gilpin County, Colorado, named for John Q. A. Rollins.

Rome; many towns and villages in the United States, named for the city in Italy, among them the city in Oneida County, New York.

Romulus; towns in Wayne County, Michigan, and Seneca County, New York, named for the founder of Rome.

Rondout; creek in Ulster County, New York, the name being a corruption of "redoubt," a fortification built upon the stream by the early Dutch.

Roodhouse; city in Greene County, Illinois, named for John Roodhouse, its founder.

Rooks; county in Kansas, named for John C. Rooks, member of Company I, Eleventh Kansas.

Root, town in Montgomery County, New York, named for Erastus Root, of Delaware County.

Roscoe; town in Coshocton County, Ohio, named for William Roscoe, the English historian.

Roscommon; county in Michigan, named for the county in Ireland.

Rose; town in Wayne County, New York, named for Robert L. Rose, of Geneva.

Rosebroom; town in Otsego County, New York, named for Abraham Rosebroom, one of the earliest settlers.

Rosedale; city in Wyandotte County, Kansas, so named because when located the townsite was a mass of wild rose bushes.

Rosita; town in Custer County, Colorado, said to have been so named by the early miners because of the thickets of wild roses which surrounded the springs in the vicinity.

Ross; town in Kent County, Michigan, named for Daniel Ross.

Ross; county in Ohio, named for Hon. James Ross, of Pennsylvania.

Rossie; town in St. Lawrence County, New York, named for a sister of David Parish, the proprietor.

Rossville; city in Shawnee County, Kansas, named for W. W. Ross, agent of the Pottawatomie Indians.

Rossville; village in Richmond County, New York, now a part of New York City, named for the proprietor of a large tract of land.

Rossville; town in Fayette County, Tennessee, named for Jon Ross, a Cherokee chief.

Roswell; town in El Paso County, Colorado, named for Roswell P. Flower, of New York.

Roswell; town in Cobb County, Georgia, named for Roswell King.

Rothville; town in Chariton County, Missouri, named for John Roth, an early settler.

Rotterdam; town in Schenectady County, New York, named for the city in the Netherlands.

Roubedeau; river in Delta County, and pass in Scotts Bluff County, Nebraska, named for Antoine Roubedeau, a French trader.

Rouse Point; village in Clinton County, New York, named for a resident family.

Routt; county in Colorado, named for John L. Routt, last governor of the Territory.

Rowan; county in Kentucky, named for John Rowan, a distinguished lawyer of the State.

Rowan; county in North Carolina, named for Matthew Rowan, prominent in the early politics of the State.

Rowesville; town in Orangeburg County, South Carolina, named for Gen. William Rowe.

Rowletts; town in Hart County, Kentucky, named for John P. Rowlett.

Rowley; town in Essex County, Massachusetts, named for the town in England.

Royal; village in Antelope County, Nebraska, named for Royal Thayer.

Royal Oak; village in Talbot County, Maryland, so named because of a nearby oak into which the British shot a cannon ball in the war of 1812.

Royalston; town in Worcester County, Massachusetts, named for Col. Isaac Royal, one of its proprietors.

Rubicon; river in Wisconsin, named from the famous river in Italy.

Ruby; peak in Colorado, so named on account of its color.

Rulo; village in Richardson County, Nebraska, named for Charles Rouleau.

Rumford; town in Oxford County, Maine, said to have been named for Count Rumford.

Rumsey; town in McLean County, Kentucky, named for Edward Rumsey, a prominent resident of the State.

Runnels; county in Texas, named for Henry R. Runnels, former governor.

Runnelsville; town in Madison County, Mississippi, named for a prominent family of the State.

Rush; county in Indiana; Rushville; town in Rush County, Indiana, and city in Schuyler County, Illinois. Named for Dr. Benjamin Rush, of Philadelphia.

Rush; county in Kansas, named for Alexander Rush, captain Company H, Second Regiment Kansas Colored Volunteers.

Rusk; county in Texas, named for Gen. Thomas J. Rusk, United States Senator from that State.

Russell; county in Alabama, named for Col. Gilbert Russell, of that State.

Russell; county and city in same county in Kansas, named for Capt. Avra P. Russell, Company K, Second Kansas.

Russell; counties in Kentucky and Virginia, and city in Logan County, Kentucky, named for Gen. William Russell.

Russell; village in St. Lawrence County, New York, named for Russell Atwater, its original proprietor.

Russellville; village in Hampshire County, Massachusetts, named for the Russell family, prominent in the business interests of the vicinity.

Russian River; township in Sonoma County, California, on a river of the same name, so named because a Russian settlement was early located here.

Rutherford; counties in North Carolina and Tennessee; Rutherfordton; town in Rutherford County, North Carolina. Named for Gen. Griffith Rutherford, a noted Indian fighter.

Rutherford; borough in Bergen County, New Jersey, named for John Rutherford, an extensive landowner.

Rutland; town in Worcester County, Massachusetts, said to have been named for Rutland, near Leicestershire, England.

Rutland; county in Vermont, town in Jefferson County, New York, and village in Lasalle County, Illinois, named for the town in Vermont.

Ryans; Creek in Humboldt County, California, named for an early settler.

Rye; town in Rockingham County, New Hampshire, named for the home of its English settlers.

S

Sabatis; hill in Maine, named for an Indian who accompanied Arnold's expedition.

Sabeta: peak in Colorado, named for the wife of Ouray, the chief of the Ute Indians.

Sabetha; city in Nemaha County, Kansas, probably a corruption of the word Sabbath, which was the name of the temporary fort, established on Sunday, for which the town was named.

Sabine; county, lake, and town in Texas, and parish in Louisiana. A French word, meaning " cypress." Sable; cape, the southernmost point of the mainland in Florida, and stream in Michigan. A French word, meaning "sandy."

Sabotawan; mountain in Maine, the most easterly of the Spencer Range. An Indian word, meaning "the end of the pack," "where the strap is pulled together."

Sac; county in Iowa, named for the Indian tribe, the name said to mean " red bank."

Sacandaga; tributary of Hudson River, so named because of a great marsh lying along its banks. An Indian word, meaning "drowned lands."

Sachem Head; watering place in New Haven County, Connecticut, so named because an Indian chief was once captured there.

Sacketts Harbor; village in Jefferson County, New York, named for Augustus Sacket, its first settler.

Saco; river, and a city in York County, Maine. Derived from an Indian word, sohk or sauk, "pouring out;" hence the outlet or discharge of a river or lake.

Sacramento; river, city, and county in California, named by the Spaniards, the word meaning "the sacrament."

Sadlersville; town in Robertson County, Tennessee, named for W. R. Sadler, an early settler.

Safford; village in Pima County, Arizona, named for A. P. K. Safford, governor of the Territory.

Sagadahoc; county in Maine bordering on the Atlantic Ocean. An Indian word, meaning "land at the mouth," or the "mouth of the river."

Sageville; village in Hamilton County, New York, named for Hezekiah Sage.

Sag Harbor; village in Suffolk County, New York. Derived from the Indian word, saggaponack, "place where the ground nuts grow."

Saginaw; river, county, bay, and city in Michigan, said to derive its meaning from an Indian word, meaning " an outlet.

Sago; town in Muskingum County, Ohio. An Indian word, meaning "welcome."

Saguache; county, and town in same county, in Colorado. An Indian word, meaning "water at the blue earth."

Sahabe; peak in Cascade Mountains, Okanogan County, Washington, named by the Mazamas, a mountaineering club of Portland, Oregon, from the Chinook word sahabe, "high," "above."

Saint Anthony; town in Stearns County, Minnesota, located near the falls of the same name, which were named by a French missionary, because "of the many favors received through the intercession of that saint."

Saint Augustine; city in St. John County, Florida, so named because the first landing was made there on that day.

Saint Bernard; parish in Louisiana, named by the French for the saint.

Saint Charles; parish in Louisiana, named for the saint.

Saint Charles; county, and city in the same county, in Missouri, so named because it was the purpose of the vicar of Pontoiseto establish a seminary there in honor of that saint, where the Indians should be educated.

Saint Clair; county, lake, and city in Michigan, said to have been so named because the lake was discovered by the French upon that saint's day.

Saint Clair; counties in Alabama, Illinois, and Missouri; town in Antelope County, Nebraska; and borough in Schuylkill County, Pennsylvania; Saint Clairsville; village in Belmont County, Ohio. Named for Gen. Arthur St. Clair.

Saint Clement; town in Pike County, Missouri, named for the patron saint of Clement Grote, an early settler.

Saint Croix; river in Maine, probably so named because of its resemblance at Oak Bay to a cross.

Saint Croix; river of Minnesota and Wisconsin, from which the county in Wisconsin derived its name, itself being named for Monsieur St. Croix, who was drowned at its mouth.

Saint Derion; village in Nemaha County, Nebraska, named for Joseph Derion, an Indian chief of the Otoe tribe.

Saint Elias; mountain in Alaska, named for the saint upon whose day it was discovered.

Saint Francis; stream in Minnesota and county in Arkansas; Saint Francois; county in Missouri. Named for the founder of the Franciscan order.

Sainte Genevieve; county, and city in same county, in Missouri, named for the French saint.

Saint George; town in Knox County, Maine, named for the island which is now called Monhegan, but was originally named by its discoverer, Capt. George Weymouth, for his patron saint.

Saint George; town in Dorchester County, South Carolina, located in the defunct county of St. George, for which it is named.

Saint George; town in Chittenden County, Vermont, named for George III. of England.

Saint George; town in Tucker County, West Virginia, named for St. George Tucker, clerk of the house of delegates.

Saint Helena; parish in Louisiana, named for the French saint.

Saint Helens; mountain in Washington, named for Lord St. Helens, British ambassador to Madrid.

Saint Ignace; township in Mackinac County, Michigan, named for a Catholic church erected within its limits.

Saint James; parish in Louisiana, named for the French saint.

Saint James; city in Watonwan County, Minnesota, named for the first settler, James Purrington.

Saint James; town in Phelps County, Missouri, named for a large mine owner in the vicinity.

Saint John; county in Florida, named from St. Johns River.

Saint John; city in Stafford County, Kansas, named for Governor John P. St. John.

Saint Johns; river in Florida, called by the Spanish discoverers San Juan Bautista, because upon this saint's day it was discovered.

Saint Johns; village in Clinton County, Michigan, named for John Swegles.

Saint Johnsbury; town in Caledonia County, Vermont, named for St. John de Crevecoeur, French consul at New York, and a benefactor of Vermont.

Saint Johnsville; town in Montgomery County, New York, named for an old church established there in early days.

Saint John the Baptist; parish in Louisiana, named for the river.

Saint Joseph; counties in Indiana and Michigan, named for the river which flows through both States, it being named for the husband of the Virgin Mary by its early French Catholic explorers.

Saint Joseph; city in Buchanan County, Missouri, named for Joseph Robidoux, an early French settler.

Saint Lawrence; gulf, river, and county in New York, the name having been extended from the gulf—which was so named because discovered on the feast day of this saint—to the river and county.

Saint Louis; river and county in Minnesota, named for the river, said to have been named for Louis XIV, of France.

Saint Louis; county and city in Missouri, named for Louis XV, of France.

Saint Mary; county in Maryland, so named because the first landing in this State was made on the day of the annunciation.

Saint Marys; city in Pottawatomie County, Kansas, named for a Catholic mission.

Saint Matthews; town in Orangeburg County, South Carolina, named for the county, now defunct, in which it was formerly located.

Saint Paul; city in Ramsey County, Minnesota, named for a church which was built for M. Galtier, an early Catholic missionary.

Saint Paul; city in Howard County, Nebraska, named for J. N. and N. J. Paul, its first settlers.

Saint Peter; village in Cedar County, Nebraska, named for John Peter Abts, the first settler.

Saint Peters: town in Saint Charles County, Missouri, named for a Jesuit mission established there in early days.

Saint Regis Falls; village in Franklin County, river and falls in New York, named for a canonized Jesuit missionary.

Saint Stephens; town in Berkeley County, South Carolina, named for the now defunct parish in which it was formerly located.

Saint Tammany; parish in Louisiana, named for the chief of the Delaware Indians, the name meaning "beaver leader."

Saint Vrain; creek in Colorado, named for Ceran St. Vrain, an early explorer.

Salado; town in Bell County, Texas. A Spanish word, meaning "salted;" salt being abundant in the vicinity.

Salamanca; village in Cattaraugus County, New York, named for Senor Salamanca, a Spanish financier, interested in the Atlantic and Great Western Railroad.

Salem; city in Essex County, Massachusetts, so named by its early settlers because they hoped to enjoy peaceful security there. An Indian word, meaning "peace."

Salero; hill in Arizona, said to have been so named because a saltcellar of ore, from the hill, was made by the padres of St. Joseph for the table of their bishop. A Spanish word, meaning "saltcellar."

Salida; city in Chaffee County, Colorado, at the junction of the Arkansas River with its large branch from the south. A Spanish word, meaning "point of departure."

Salina; town in Onondaga County, New York; Salinas; river and city in Monterey, County, California; Saline, counties in Arkansas, Illinois, Kansas, Missouri, and Nebraska, and river in Arkansas. So named on account of salt springs or salt deposits within their limits.

Salisbury; town in Litchfield County, Connecticut, named for a resident.

Salisbury; town in Essex County, Massachusetts, named for the town in England.

Salisbury; city in Chariton County, Missouri, named for Lucius Salisbury, of the county.

Salisbury; town in Herkimer County, New York, named for the town in Connecticut.

Sallis; town in Attala County, Mississippi, named for Dr. James Sallis, the former owner of the land.

Sallisaw; stream and town in Cherokee Nation, Indian Territory. Supposed to have been derived from the French name, Bayou Salaison, "meat-eating bayou."

Sallys; town in Aiken County, South Carolina, named for the Salley family, prominent residents of the State.

Salmon; river in Washington, so named on account of the shoals of salmon that ascend the river in the summer.

Salmon Falls; river and village in Strafford County, New Hampshire, named for the falls in the river, where the salmon stop in their upward course.

Salt; creek in Colorado, so named on account of the character of the mineral deposits.

Saltillo; borough in Huntingdon County, Pennsylvania, named for the town in Mexico. A Spanish word, meaning "salted river."

Salt Lake; county, and city in same county, in Utah, named for the famous lake of that State.

Saluda; river, county, and town in same county, in South Carolina, and town in Polk County, North Carolina. An Indian word, meaning "corn river."

Salunga; village in Lancaster County, Pennsylvania, derived from the Indian word Chickiswalunga, meaning "the place of the crawfish."

Salyersville; town in Magoffin County, Kentucky, named for Samuel Salyer, a member of the State legislature.

Samoa; village in Humboldt County, California. named for an Indian chief.

Sampson; county in North Carolina, named for Col. John Sampson, officer of the Revolution.

Samsonville; village in Ulster County, New York, named for Gen. Henry A. Sampson.

Samuel Adams; mountain in New Hampshire, named for a revolutionary patriot.

San Antonio; city in Bexar County, Texas, named for the Roman Catholic mission, San Antonio de Velero, otherwise the Alamo.

San Bernardino; county, and city in same county, in California, named for an old Spanish mission.

Sanborn; county in South Dakota and town in O'Brien County, Iowa, named for George W. Sanborn, division superintendent of the Chicago, Milwaukee and St. Paul Railroad.

Sanbornton; town in Belknap County, New Hampshire, named for a family of early settlers.

Sanders; town in Carroll County, Kentucky, named for an old settler.

San Diego; county, and city in same county, in California. A corruption of St. Iago, the patron saint of Spain, for whom they were named.

Sandisfield; town in Berkshire County, Massachusetts, named for Lord Sandys, first lord of trade and the plantations.

Sand Lake; town in Kent County, Michigan, so named because a sand bar extends across the center of a near-by lake.

Sandusky; town in Illinois, county, river, and city in Ohio, whose name by some authorities is said to be derived from the Indian word Outsandouke, "there is pure water here;" or Sa-anduste, "large bodies or pools of water." Another authority states that it was named for Jonathan Sandousky, a Polish trader of the vicinity.

Sandwich; town in Barnstable County, Massachusetts, named for the town in England.

San Fernando; town in Los Angeles County, California, named for an old Spanish Catholic mission.

Sanford; city in Orange County, Florida, named for Gen. H. S. Sanford, United States minister to Belgium.

Sanford; town and township in York County, Maine, named for Peleg Sanford, an early proprietor.

Sanford; town in Moore County, North Carolina, named for Colonel Sanford, a civil engineer.

San Francisco; bay, county, and city in same county, in California, said by some to have been named for the old Spanish mission of San Francisco de Assisi, by others to have been named for the founder of the order to which Father Junipero, the discoverer of the bay, belonged.

San Gabriel; town in Los Angeles County, California, named for an old Spanish mission.

Sangamon; county and river in Illinois, named for an Indian chief.

Sangerfield; town and township in Oneida County, New York, named for Judge Jedediah Sanger.

Sangerville; town in Piscataquis County, Maine, named for Col. Calvin Sanger, its proprietor.

Sanilac; county in Michigan; Sanilac Center; town in Sanilac County, Michigan. Named for an Indian chief.

San Jacinto; county, river, and town in Texas, and village in Glenn County, California. A Spanish word, meaning "hyacinth."

San Joaquin; county and river in California. A Spanish phrase, meaning " whom Jehovah has appointed."

San Jose; city in Santa Clara County, California, named for the patron saint of Mexico.

San Juan; river and counties in Colorado and New Mexico, named for Saint John.

San Juan; county in Washington, named for the Greek navigator, Juan de Fuca.

San Luis Obispo; county, and city in same county, in California, named for an old Spanish mission.

San Luis Rey; town in San Diego County, California, named for Louis IX, of France.

San Mateo; county, and city in same county, in California. Spanish form for St. Matthew.

San Miguel; counties in Colorado and New Mexico, and town in San Luis Obispo County, California. The Spanish form of St. Michael.

Sanpete; county in Utah, named for an Indian chief.

San Quentin; town in Marin County, California, said to be named for a former resident.

Santa Barbara; county, and city in same county, in California, named for an old Spanish mission.

Santa Clara; county, and town in same county, in California, named for an old Spanish mission.

Santa Cruz; counties in Arizona and California, city and island in the latter State. A Spanish word, meaning "holy cross."

Santa Fe; county, and city in same county, in New Mexico; and city in Haskell County, Kansas, and town in Monroe County, Missouri. A Spanish phrase, meaning "holy faith."

Santa Ynez; town in Santa Barbara County, California, named for an old Spanish mission. The Spanish form of St. Agnes.

Sapinero; town in Gunnison County, Colorado, named for a subchief of the Ute Indians.

Saranac; river and lake in New York; Saranac Lake; village in Franklin County, New York. An Indian word, meaning "river that flows under a rock."

Saratoga; county, town, and lake in New York; Saratoga Springs; town and village in Saratoga County, New York. An Indian word, said to mean "place of the miraculous water in a rock."

Sarcoxie; city in Jasper County, Missouri, named for a friendly Indian chief Sardinia; town in Erie County, New York, named for the island in Italy.

Sardis; town in Panola County, Mississippi, named for the ruined city of Asia Minor.

Sargent; county in North Dakota, named for a former general manager of the Northern Pacific; Railroad.

Sarpy; county in Nebraska, named for Peter A. Sarpy.

Sassafras; stream in Maryland. The English form of the Indian word, Winakhanne.

Satartia; town in Yazoo County, Mississippi. Derived from an Indian word, meaning "pumpkin place."

Saucon; township and creek in Northampton County, Pennsylvania. An Indian word, meaning "the outlet of a smaller stream."

Saugatuck; river in Connecticut, and villages in Fairfield County, Connecticut, and Allegan County, Michigan. An Indian word, meaning "outlet of the tidal river."

Saugerties; town in Ulster County, New York. One authority states that it is an Indian word, meaning "at the outlet;" another gives it as from the Dutch, zaeger's kill, meaning "sawyer's creek," given it because a sawmill was erected on the town site.

Saugus; town in Essex County, Massachusetts. The Indian name of Lynn.

Sauk; county, and city in same county, in Wisconsin; Sauk Center; city in Stearns County, Minnesota; Sauk Rapids; village in Benton County, Minnesota. Named from an Indian tribe, the word meaning "people living at a river mouth."

Sault Sainte Marie; city in Chippewa County, Michigan, situated at the foot of the rapids of St. Mary's River. A French phrase, meaning " falls of St. Mary."

Saunders; tributary of the Yellowstone in Montana, named for a trapper who lived in the region.

Saunders; county in Nebraska, named for Governor Alvin Saunders.

Sauratown; town in Stokes County, North Carolina, named for an Indian tribe.

Sausalito; town in Marin County, California. A Spanish word, meaning "little willow."

Sauvie; island in the Columbia River, Oregon, named for Jean Baptiste Sauve, a French Canadian, who kept a dairy there.

Savanna; city in Carroll County, Illinois; Savannah; town in Wayne County, New York, and city and river in Georgia. The name derived from the Spanish word savanne, meaning "grassy plain."

Savoy; town in Berkshire County, Massachusetts, named for the town in Switzerland.

Sawadabscook; branch of the Penobscot River in Maine. An Indian word, meaning "place of large, smooth rocks."

Sawyer; county in Wisconsin, named for Philetus Sawyer, Senator from that State.

Saxapahaw; town in Alamance County, North Carolina. A corruption of the name of an Indian tribe, Sissipahaw.

Saybrook; town in Middlesex County, Connecticut, named for Lords Say and Brook.

Sayre; borough in Bradford County, Pennsylvania, probably named for R. S. Sayre, chief engineer of the Lehigh Valley Railroad.

Scammon; city in Cherokee County, Kansas, named for four brothers, early settlers from Illinois.

Scandia; city in Republic County, Kansas, named for the Scandinavian agricultural society, by whom it was colonized.

Scandinavia; village in Waupaca County, Wisconsin, named for the people by whom it was settled.

Scantic; river and village in Hartford County, Connecticut. Derived from the Indian word Peskatuk, meaning " branch of the river."

Scarboro; town in Cumberland County, Maine, named for the town in England.

Scarsdale; town in Westchester County, New York, named for the town in Derbyshire, England.

Scatacook; river in Connecticut. An Indian word, meaning "the confluence of two streams."

Schaghticoke; town in Rensselaer County, New York, situated at the confluence of the Hoosic and Hudson rivers. Derived from an Indian word, Pachgatgoch, "the place where a river branches or divides."

Schellsburg; borough in Bedford County, Pennsylvania, named for the man who laid it out.

Schenectady; county and city in same county in New York. Derived from an Indian word, meaning "over beyond the plains."

Schererville; village in Lake County, Indiana, named for Scherer Wright, its founder.

Schleicher; county in Texas, named for Gustav Schleicher, member of Congress from that State.

Schleisingerville; village in Washington County, Wisconsin, named for B. Schleisinger Weil, its founder.

Schley; county in Georgia, named for William Schley, a former governor.

Schodack; town in Rensselaer County, New York. An Indian word, meaning "meadow or fire plain," so called because it was in ancient times the seat of the council fires of the Mohegans.

Schoharie; creek, county, and town in same county in New York. An Indian word, meaning "flood wood or drift wood."

Schonbrunn; town in Tuscarawas County, Ohio. A German word, meaning "beautiful fountain."

Schoodic; river and chain of lakes in Maine. An Indian word to which many meanings are credited, among them, "trout place," "burnt lands," "a place where water rushes," and "where fish live all the year."

Schoolcraft; county and village in Kalamazoo County, Michigan, named for Henry R. Schoolcraft, distinguished for his Indian researches.

Schroeppel; town in Oswego County, New York, named for Henry W. Schroeppel, an early resident.

Schroon; lake, river, mountain, and town in Essex County, New York. Opinions differ as to the derivation of this name, some saying that it is derived from the Indian, Shaghnetaghrowahora, meaning "the largest lake," or from the Saranac Indian, "daughter of the mountains;" another authority stating that it was named for the Duchess Scharon, of the court of Louis XIV.

Schulenburg; town in Fayette County, Texas, named for a man prominent in the organization of a corporation that built the town.

Schuyler; counties in Illinois, Missouri, and New York, named for Gen. Philip Schuyler, early mayor of Albany, New York.

Schuyler; city in Colfax County, Nebraska, named for Schuyler Colfax.

Schuylerville; village in Saratoga County, New York, named for Gen. Philip Schuyler, prominent man, and early mayor of Albany.

Schuylkill; county and river in Pennsylvania; so named because the first explorers passed its mouth without seeing it, which caused them to give it this Dutch name meaning " hidden stream."

Scio; town in Allegany County, New York, named for the island in the Mediterranean.

Sciota; village in McDonough County, Illinois, river and county in Ohio. Derived from the Indian word Seeyotah, meaning "great legs," and applied to the river on account of its numerous and long branches.

Scipio; town in Cayuga County, New York, named for the Roman general.

Scitico; village in Hartford County, Connecticut. An Indian word, meaning "at the branch."

Scituate; town in Plymouth County, Massachusetts, named for the stream running into the harbor, which derived its name from the Indian word Satuit, "cold brook."

Scooba; town in Kemper County, Mississippi. An Indian word, meaning "reed brake."

Scotland; many places in the United States, among them the counties in Missouri and North Carolina, named for the country in Great Britain.

Scott; county in Arkansas, named for Judge Andrew Scott.

Scott; counties in Illinois, Indiana, and Kentucky, named for Gov. Charles Scott, of the latter State.

Scott; counties in Iowa, Kansas, Tennessee, and Virginia, and city in Scott County, Kansas, named for Gen. Winfield Scott.

Scott; counties in Minnesota and Mississippi, named for Gov. Abram M. Scott.

Scott; county in Missouri, named for John Scott.

Scottdale; borough in Westmoreland County, Pennsylvania, named for Thomas A. Scott, of the Pennsylvania Railroad.

Scotts Creek; township in Jackson County, North Carolina, named for John Scott, a trader among the Cherokees.

Scotts Bluff; county in Nebraska, named for the bluff where a man named Scott met his death by starvation.

Scottsboro; town in Baldwin County, Georgia, named for Gen. John Scott.

Scottsburg; village in Livingston County, New York, named for Matthew and William Scott, early settlers.

Scottsville; town in Allen County, Kentucky, named for Gen. Charles Scott, an early governor of the State.

Scottsville; village in Monroe County, New York, named for Isaac Scott, the first settler.

Scranton; town in Jackson County, Mississippi, named for city in Pennsylvania.

Scranton; city in Lackawanna County, Pennsylvania. named for Joseph H. Scranton, its founder.

Screven; county in Georgia, named for Gen. James Screven, a Revolutionary officer.

Scriba; town in Oswego County, New York, named for George Scriba, the resident proprietor.

Scurry; county in Texas, named for William B. Scurry, brigadier-general in the Army of the Confederacy.

Seaboard; town in Northampton County, North Carolina, named from the Seaboard Air Line.

Seabright; borough in Monmouth County, New Jersey, named for the town in England.

Sea Cliff; village in Nassau County, New York, where camp meetings were formerly held upon a cliff by the salt water, from which circumstance the village was named.

Sea Isle City; borough in Cape May County, New Jersey, so named because it is situated near the seashore.

Searcy; county in Arkansas, named for Judge Richard Searcy.

Searsmont; town in Waldo County, Maine; Searsport; town in Waldo County, Maine. Named for David Sears, of Boston, Massachusetts.

Seattle; city in King County, Washington, named for the chief of the Duwamish tribe of Indians, See-aa-thl.

Sebago; lake in York County, and lake, pond, and town in Cumberland County, Maine. An Indian word, meaning "a stretch of water," or "place or region of river lake."

Sebamook; lake in Maine. An Indian word, given two different meanings, "large bay lake" and "bright water."

Sebastian; county in Arkansas, named for Senator William K. Sebastian.

Sebethe; river in Connecticut. Supposed to be derived from the Indian word sepoese, "small river."

Sebewa; village in Ionia County, Michigan. Derived from the Indian word sibiwe, "a rivulet, a brook."

Sebewaing; village in Huron County, Michigan. Derived from the Indian word sibiweng, "at the creek."

Seboeis; lake, stream, and plantation in Penobscot County, Maine. Supposed to be derived from an Indian word, meaning "little river."

Secaucus; town in Hudson County, New York. Thought to be derived from the Indian word sekakes, used in reference to snakes.

Seco; village in Boxelder County, Utah, and creek in Texas. A Spanish word, meaning "dry."

Sedalia; city in Pettis County, Missouri. A modification of the original name, Sadieville, having been named for the daughter of a settler.

Sedan; city in Chautauqua County, Kansas, named for the town in France.

Sedgwick; fort in Colorado, counties in Colorado and Kansas, city in the latter State, and mountain in Idaho, named for Gen. John Sedgwick.

Sedgwick; town in Hancock County, Maine, named for Maj. Robert Sedgwick.

Seekonk; town in Bristol County, Massachusetts. Said to be derived from an Indian word, meaning " black, or wild goose."

Seguin; town in Guadalupe County, Texas, named for Col. Juan Seguin, a Mexican who joined fortunes with the Texans in 1836.

Seiglingville; town in Barnwell County, South Carolina, named for Gen. Randolph Seigling, prominent capitalist of Charleston.

Selinsgrove; borough in Snyder County, Pennsylvania, named for a family of early settlers.

Sellersville; borough in Bucks County, Pennsylvania. The anglicized form of the original name, Zoellers, a family of early residents for whom it was named.

Sellwood; town in Multnomah County, Oregon, named for Governor Sellwood.

Selma; city in Dallas County, Alabama, named for the "Songs of Selma," in Ossian.

Seminole; town in Hillsboro County, Florida, and nation in Indian Territory, named for the Indian tribe, the word said to mean " wild men."

Sempronius; town in Cayuga County, New York; named for the celebrated Roman tribune, father of the Graccii.

Senath; village in Dunklin County, Missouri, named for the wife of A. W. Douglass, an early settler.

Senatobia; creek and town in Tate County, Mississippi. A Choctaw Indian word, meaning "white sycamore."

Seneca; counties in New York and Ohio and nation in Indian Territory, cities in Nemaha County, Kansas, and Newton County, Missouri, and town in Ocowee County, South Carolina; Seneca Falls; village in Seneca County, New York. Named for an Indian tribe, said to be a corruption of Sinnekaas, a name given them by the Dutch.

Senegar; creek in Maryland. Derived from the Indian word, Sinne-hanne, "a strong stream."

Sequatchie; county and river in Tennessee. An Indian word, meaning " hog river." Sequoia; town in Tuolumne County, California, named for a famous Cherokee Indian who invented an alphabet for his tribe.

Severance; city in Doniphan County, Kansas, named for one of the three proprietors.

Severy; city in Greenwood County, Kansas, named for L. Severy, of Emporia, a director of the Santa Fe.

Sevier; county in Arkansas, named for Ambrose H. Sevier, a Congressional Delegate.

Sevier; county in Tennessee, named for John Sevier, first governor of the State.

Seward; counties in Kansas and Nebraska, city in county of same name in latter State, town in Schoharie County, and mountain in New York, named for William H. Seward, the American statesman.

Sewickley; borough in Allegheny County, Pennsylvania. An Indian word, meaning "sweet water."

Seymour; city in Jackson County, Indiana, named for a civil engineer.

Shackelford; county in Texas, named for a surgeon, captain of a band called the "Red Rovers," who helped the Texans in their revolution.

Shakopee; city in Scott County, Minnesota, named for an Indian chief who formerly lived there; the name meaning "six."

Shamokin; borough in Northumberland County, Pennsylvania. Derived from the Indian word, Schahamoki, meaning "a place of eels."

Shamong; town in Burlington County, New Jersey. An Indian word, meaning "place of the big horn."

Shandaken; town in Ulster County, New York. An Indian word, meaning "rapid waters."

Shannock; river in Connecticut. An Indian word, meaning "place where two streams meet."

Shannon; county in Missouri, named for George F. Shannon, of Marion County.

Shannon; county in South Dakota, named for Peter C. Shannon, former chief justice.

Shapleigh; town in York County, Maine, named for Nicholas Shapleigh, one of the earliest proprietors".

Sharkey; county in Mississippi, named for William L. Sharkey, provisional governor during Governor Clark's absence at Fort Pulaski in 1805-66.

Sharon; city in Barber County, Kansas, and town in Schoharie County, New York; the name is of biblical derivation.

Sharon; town in Madison County, Mississippi, so named because the Sharon seminary for girls was situated there at an early day.

Sharon Springs; city in Wallace County, Kansas, and village in Schoharie County, New York; the name is of biblical derivation.

Sharp; county in Arkansas, named for Ephraim Sharp, representative from Lawrence County.

Sharpsburg; town in Bath County, Kentucky, named for Moses Sharp.

Sharpsburg; borough in Allegheny County, Pennsylvania, named for James Sharp, the original proprietor.

Shasta; county in California named from the Indian tribe, Saste or Shastika.

Shaume; river in Massachusetts. An Indian word, meaning "a fountain or spring."

Shavano; peak of the Sawateh Range in Colorado. named for a Ute Indian.

Shaw; town in Bolivar County, Mississippi, named for the owner of the lands through which the railroad passes.

Shawan; town in Baltimore County, Maryland. An Indian word, meaning "south."

Shawangunk; river, town in Ulster County, and mountain in New York. Said to be an Indian word, meaning "white stone" or " white salt rocks."

Shawano; county and city in same county in Wisconsin. Derived from the Chippewa Indian word jawanong, meaning "on the south."

Shawnee; county in Kansas and nation in Indian Territory; Shawneetown; city in Gallatin County, Illinois. Named for the Indian tribe, the word meaning "southerners," and given them because they emigrated northward from the Savannah River.

Sheboygan; county and city in same county in Wisconsin. Derived from the Chippewa Indian word jibaigan, meaning a perforated object, such as a pipe stem.

Sheepeater; cliffs in the Yellowstone Park, named for a tribe of Indians, the only known aboriginal occupants of the park.

Sheepscot; river and bay in Maine. Derived from the Indian word sipsa-couta, meaning "bird-flocking river" or "little bird place," because the Indians resorted there for young ducks.

Sheffield; town in Franklin County, Iowa, named for James Sheffield, a railroad contractor.

Sheffield; town in Berkshire County, Massachusetts, named for the city in England.

Shelburne; towns in Franklin County, Massachusetts, and Chittenden County, Vermont, named for William Fitz Maurice, second Earl of Shelburne.

Shelby; counties in Alabama, Illinois, Indiana, Iowa, Kentucky, Missouri, Ohio, Tennessee, and Texas, and town in Orleans County, New York.

Shelbyville; cities in Shelby counties, Illinois, Indiana, and Missouri. Named for Gen. Isaac Shelby, former governor of Kentucky.

Sheldon; town in Franklin County, Vermont, named for a resident family.

Shell Rock; town in Butler County, Iowa, so named on account of the rocks near the river.

Shelter; island off Long Island, New York. Probably the translation of the original Indian name of Manhanset-aha-cusha-wommuck, meaning "an island sheltered by islands."

Shelton; town in Mason County, Washington, named for an early settler.

Shenandoah; county and river in Virginia, city in Page County, Iowa, borough in Schuylkill County, Pennsylvania, and town in Page County, Virginia. An Indian word said by some to mean "the sprucy stream," by others, "a river flowing alongside of high hills and mountains;" and still another authority states that it means "daughter of the stars."

Shepaug; river in Connecticut. Derived from the Indian word, Mashapaug, meaning "large pond."

Shepherd; village in Isabella County, Michigan, named for I. N. Shepherd, its founder.

Shepherdstown; town in Jefferson County, West Virginia, named for Capt. Thomas Shepherd.

Sherborn; town in Middlesex County, Massachusetts, named for the town of Sherborne, England.

Sherburne; county in Minnesota, named for Moses Sherburne, associate justice of the Supreme Court.

Sheridan; counties in Kansas, Nebraska, and Wyoming, town in Madison County, Montana, and mountain in Yellowstone Park, named for Gen. Philip H. Sheridan.

Sherlock; township in Finney County, Kansas, named for a capitalist connected with the Santa Fe Railroad.

Sherman; counties in Kansas, Nebraska, and Oregon, village in Wexford County, Michigan, and mountain in Idaho, named for Gen. W. T. Sherman.

Sherman; county, and city in Grayson County, Texas, named for Sidney Sherman, general of the Texas army, and the one who raised the cry of "Remember the Alamo" at the battle of San Jacinto.

Sherman; village in Chautauqua County, New York, named for Koger Sherman, a signer of the Declaration of Independence.

Sherwood; village in Branch County, Michigan, named for the forest in England.

Sheshequin; village in Bradford County, Pennsylvania. An Indian word, meaning "mysterious rattle."

Shetucket; river in Connecticut. An Indian word, meaning "land between the rivers," or, according to another authority, "confluence of rivers."

Shiawassee; county and river in Michigan. An Indian word, meaning "straight-running river." Shickshinny; borough in Luzerne County, Pennsylvania, protected by a cordon of hills of five summits. An Indian word, meaning "five mountains."

Shields; river in Montana, named for a member of the Lewis and Clarke expedition.

Shinnecock; village in Suffolk County, New York, named for an Indian tribe.

Shinnston; town in Harrison County, West Virginia, named for the owners of the land upon which it was built.

Shintaka; several marshes in Minnesota. An Indian word, meaning "tamarack."

Shippensburg; borough in Cumberland County, Pennsylvania, named for an early proprietor.

Shippenville; borough in Clarion County, Pennsylvania, named for Judge Shippen, of Meadville.

Shirley; town in Piscataquis County, Maine, named for the town in England.

Shirley; town in Middlesex County, Massachusetts; Shirleysburg; borough in Huntingdon County, Pennsylvania. Named for Gen. William Shirley, an early governor of Massachusetts.

Shivwits; plateau in Arizona. An Indian word, meaning "people of the springs."

Shobonier; town in Fayette County, Illinois, named for an Indian chief.

Shocco; creek in North Carolina, named for the Indian tribe Shoccoree.

Shohokin; stream in Wayne County, Pennsylvania. An Indian word, meaning "where there is glue."

Shohola; stream in Pike County, Pennsylvania; Shohola Falls; village in Pike County, Pennsylvania. An Indian word, meaning "weak, faint, distressed."

Shope; lake in Wisconsin. An Indian word, meaning "a shoulder."

Shoreham; town in* Addison County, Vermont, so named because located on the shores of Lake Champlain.

Shoshone; county, and town in Lincoln County, Idaho, named for a tribe of Indians, the name meaning "inland Indians." or, according to another authority, "snake Indians."

Shoup; village in Lemhi County, Idaho, named for G. L. Shoup, United States Senator.

Showers; creek in Humboldt County, California, named for an early settler.

Shreveport; city in Caddo County, Louisiana, named for Henry M. Shreve.

Shrewsbury; many places in the United States, named for the town in England.

Shrewsbury; town in Worcester County, Massachusetts, named for George Talbot, Earl of Shrewsbury.

Shubrick; peak in Humboldt County, California, so named because the steamer Shubrick went aground in the vicinity.

Shullsburg; city in Lafayette County, Wisconsin, named for Jesse W. Shull, the first settler.

Shurz; mountain in Wyoming, named for Carl Shurz, Secretary of the Interior under President Hayes.

Shushan; village in Washington County, New York, named for the ruined city in Persia.

Shutesburg; town in Franklin County, Massachusetts, named for Governor Samuel Shute, a relative of Governor Bernard.

Sibley; county in Minnesota, named for Henry H. Sibley, an early pioneer of the Territory.

Sidney; town in Delaware County, New York, named for Admiral Sir Sidney Smith.

Sidney; cities in Shelby County, Ohio, and Kennebec County, Maine, named for Sir Philip Sidney.

Sidon; town in Leflore County, Mississippi, named for the ancient city of Palestine.

Sierra; counties in California and New Mexico. Derived from the Spanish, Sierra Madre, "Main Range," Rocky Mountains.

Sierra La Sal; mountains in eastern Utah, so named from salt springs near their base.

Sigel; village in Shelby County, Illinois, named for Gen. Franz Sigel, an officer of the rebellion.

Sigourney; city in Keokuk County, Iowa, named for the poetess, Mrs. Lydia H. Sigourney.

Sikeston; city in Scott County, Missouri, named for John Sikes.

Siler City; town in Chatham County, North Carolina, named for a prominent family of the neighborhood.

Silliman; mountains in California and Nevada, named for Benjaman Silliman, the chemist.

Silverbow; county in Montana, so named because of its shape, and on account of the presence of this precious metal.

Silver Cliff; town in Custer County, Colorado, so named because silver was found in a cliff near the present town site.

Silver Lake; city in Shawnee County, Kansas, so named because the Kansas River forms a lake at this point.

Simpson; county in Kentucky, named for Capt. John Simpson, member of Congress.

Simpson; county in Mississippi, named for Judge Josiah Simpson.

Simpsonville; village in Shelby County, Kentucky, named for Capt. John Simpson, member of Congress from that State.

Simpsonville; town in Greenville County, South Carolina, named for a prominent family of the State.

Sincarte; town in Mason County, Illinois, corrupted name of the passage which was originally named by the French, Chenal Ecarte, "a remote channel."

Sinclairville; village in Chautauqua County, New York, named for Maj. Samuel Sinclair, the first settler, who located there in 1810.

Singleys; town in Humboldt County, California, named for an early settler.

Sing Sing; creek in Chemung County, New York, named for John Sing Sing, a friendly Indian.

Sinking; creek in Breckinridge County, Kentucky, so named because it sinks beneath the surface of the ground for a space of 6 miles.

Sinnemaboning; stream in Pennsylvania. An Indian word, meaning "stony lick."

Sinsinawa Mound; village in Grand County, Wisconsin. A combination of the Indian word, Sinsiawe, meaning "rattlesnake," and mound, because situated near a truncated cone several hundred feet high.

Sioux; many places in the United States bear the name of this Indian tribe, among them the counties in Iowa and Nebraska. The word meaning a "species of snake," the appellation of the tribe being "enemies."

Sir Johns; run; small stream in Morgan County, West Virginia, named for an officer of Braddock's army.

Siskiyou; county in California and mountains in Oregon. By some authorities said to be a corruption of the original name given the district in California by the French—Six Cailloux, meaning "six bowlders;" others state that it is an Indian word meaning "bob-tailed horse," the mountains between California and Oregon having been so named because a famous bob-tailed race horse was lost on the trail.

Siskowit; lake in Wisconsin. An Indian word, meaning "a kind of fish resembling a trout."

Sisladobsis; lake in eastern Maine. An Indian word, meaning "rock lake."

Sisseton; town in Roberts County, South Dakota. An Indian word, meaning "fish scale mound village."

Sisson; village in Siskiyou County, California, named for a former hotel keeper.

Sissowkissink; creek on the west side of Delaware River, Pennsylvania. Derived from the Indian word, Shihuwen, "place of black ducks."

Sitgreaves; pass in Arizona, named for Captain Sitgreaves, United States Army.

Sitkum; village in Coos County, Oregon. An Indian word, meaning "half," or "a part."

Skagit; county in AVashington, named for an Indian tribe.

Skanawono-Weshance; tributary of Wisconsin River. An Indian word, meaning "the creek that runs through bluffs."

Skaneateles; lake, town, and village in Onondaga County, New York. An Indian word, meaning "long lake."

Skilesville; town in Muhlenburg County, Kentucky, named for James R. Skiles.

Skippack; stream and a village in Montgomery County, Pennsylvania. Derived from the Indian word Schki-peek, "pool of stagnant, offensive water."

Skitticook; branch of the Mattawamkeag River, Maine. An Indian word, meaning " dead-water stream."

Skokowish; river in Washington, named for an Indian tribe, the word said to mean "a portage."

Skookumchuck; village in Lewis County, Washington. An Indian word, meaning "strong water."

Skowhegan; town in Somerset County, Maine. An Indian word, said to mean "spearing," or "place of watch."

Skull; valleys in Utah and Yavapai County, Arizona; Skull Valley; village in Yavapai County, Arizona. So named on account of the many skulls of Indians found there.

Skunk; stream in Iowa. Translation of the Indian name Checauqua.

Skunkscut; range of hills in Glastonbury, Connecticut. An Indian word, meaning "at the high place."

Slateford; village in Northampton County, Pennsylvania, so named because it is the center of manufacture of school slates.

Slatersville; village in Providence County, Rhode Island, named for Samuel Slater, its founder.

Slatington; borough in Lehigh County, Pennsylvania; so named on account of its extensive slate quarries.

Slaughtersville; town in Webster County, Kentucky, named for G. G. Slaughter, an old settler.

Sleepy Eye; lake and village in Brown County, Minnesota, named for the Indian chief Ishanumbak, "man whose eyes have the appearance of sleep."

Slidell; town in St. Tammany Parish, Louisiana, named for the celebrity of that name.

Sligo; many places in the United States, named for the town in Ireland.

Slipperyrock; stream and borough in Butler County, Pennsylvania. Derived from the Indian word "Wesch-ach-ach-apochka, meaning "slippery rock."

Sloansville; village in Schoharie County, New York, named for John R. Sloan, an early settler.

Slocums; island in Michigan, named for its owner.

Slough; creek in Yellowstone Park, which was erroneously so described by its discoverer; it being, in fact, a swift running stream.

Smackover; stream in Union County Arkansas. Derived from the French chemin couvert, "covered road."

Smethport; borough in McKean County. Pennsylvania, named for Theodore Smethe, a friend of the original proprietor.

Smith; county in Kansas, named for J. Nelson Smith.

Smith; county in Mississippi, named for Maj. David Smith.

Smith; river in Montana, named for Robert Smith, former Secretary of the Navy.

Smith; river in Nevada, named for Lieut. Kirby Smith.

Smith; county in Tennessee, named for Gen. Daniel Smith, a patriot and early settler of the State.

Smith.; county in Texas named for John W. Smith, killed at the Alamo.

Smith Center; city in center of Smith County, Kansas. named for J. Nelson Smith, of the Second Colorado Regiment.

Smithfield; town in Dutchess County, New York, named for Peter Smith.

Smithfield; town in Johnson County, North Carolina, named for John Smith, State senator.

Smiths Ferry; village in Beaver County, Pennsylvania, named for Jesse Smith, the man who established the ferry.

Smithtown; town in Suffolk County, New York, named for Richard Smith, an early proprietor.

Smithville; village in Jefferson County, New York, named for Jesse Smith, a lumber dealer.

Smithville; village in Ritchie County, West Virginia, named for the former owner of the land.

Smithville; town in Clay County, Missouri, named for Humphrey Smith, the first settler.

Smokes; creek in Erie County, New York, named for an Indian who resided near its mouth.

Smyrna; many places in the United States, named for the ancient city of Syria, among them the village in Chenango County, New York.

Smyth; county in Virginia, named for Gen. Alexander Smyth, member of Congress from that State.

Snake; river in Idaho and Washington and Yellowstone park. The name is said to be a translation of the name of an Indian tribe, the Shoshones.

Snapeene; stream in Montana. An Indian word, meaning "crooked mouth."

Snelling; military post in Hennepin County, Minnesota, named for Colonel Josiah Snelling, under whose direction it was built.

Snohomish; river and town in Washington, named for an Indian tribe.

Snoqualmie; river in Washington, named for an Indian tribe.

Snowden; township in Allegheny County, Pennsylvania, named for Judge Snowden, of Pittsburg.

Snowmass; mountain in Colorado, so named because of the snow field under its summit.

Snyder; county in Pennsylvania; Snydertown; borough in Northumberland County, Pennsylvania. Named for Governor Simon Snyder of the State.

Socatean; stream in Maine, named for Standing Atean, a warrior of an Indian tribe, or from an Indian word, meaning "half burned land, and half standing lumber."

Socorro; county in New Mexico, named for "Our Lady of Succor."

Sodus; bay, and town in Wayne County, New York. Derived from the Indian word, assorodus, meaning, "silvery water."

Solano; county in California, named for a chief of the Suisun Indians.

Solon; towns in Somerset County, Maine, and Cortland County, New York, named for one of the seven wise men of Greece.

Solution; creek in Yellowstone Park, so named because it is the outlet to Riddle Lake.

Solvay; village in Onondaga County, New York, so named because the Solvay Process works are situated there.

Somers; town in Tollard County, Connecticut, named for Lord Somers.

isomers; town in Westchester County, New York; Somerville; city in Middlesex County, Massachusetts. Named for Capt. Richard Somers, naval officer in the Tripolitan war.

Somerset; county in Maryland, named for Lady Mary Somerset.

Somerset; counties in Maine, New Jersey, and Pennsylvania, named for the county in England.

Somers Point; borough in Atlantic County, New Jersey, named for a family of residents.

Somervell; county in Texas, named for Alexander Somerville, a brigadier-general of the Texas militia.

Somerville; town in Somerset County, New Jersey, probably named for an English nobleman.

Somonauk; village in Dekalb County, Illinois, derived from the Indian word essemiauk, meaning "paw paw tree."

Sonoma; town and county in California, said to have been named for the chief of the Chocuyens, the word meaning "valley of the moon."'

Sonora; city in Tuolumne County, California. The name said to be the Indian pronunciation of the Spanish word " senora."

Sopris; peak of the Elk Mountains in western Colorado, named for Capt. Dick Sopris, one of the early settlers of the State.

Souderton; borough in Montgomery County, Pennsylvania, named for a family of early settlers.

Souhegan; river in New Hampshire. An Indian word meaning "worn-out lands."

Souneunk; stream in Maine. An Indian word meaning "that runs between mountains."

Southampton; county in Virginia, and towns in Hampshire County, Massachusetts, and Suffolk County, New York, named for the town in England.

South Anna; river in Virginia, said to have been named for Anne, Queen of England.

Southboro; town in Worcester County, Massachusetts, so named because formed of the south part of Marlboro.

South Carolina; one of the thirteen original States, first named for Charles IX of France, and later for Charles II. of England.

South Hero; town in Grand Isle County, Vermont, named for one of the two islands which were called Two Heroes, granted to Ethan Allen. It was intended that they should be owned by only brave men warmly disposed toward the Revolution.

Southport; city in Brunswick County, North Carolina, so named because it is situated in the southern part of the State.

South River; borough in Middlesex County, New Jersey, so named to distinguish it from the North River district.

Southwick; town in Hampden County, Massachusetts, named for its first settler.

Spafford; town in Onondaga County, New York, named for Horatio Gates Spafford, author of the first gazetteer of that State.

Spalding; county in Georgia, named for the Hon. Thomas Spaulding.

Spartanburg; county, and town in same county, in South Carolina, so named because it was settled just after the Revolution by hunters from Virginia.

Spearville; town in Ford County, Kansas, named for Alden Speare, of Boston.

Spencer; counties in Kentucky and Indiana, and city in Owen County of the latter State, named for Capt. Spier Spencer, killed at Tippecanoe.

Spencer; town in Worcester County, Massachusetts, said to have been named for Spencer Phips, former governor; or for Charles Spencer, second Duke of Marlborough.

Spencerport; village in Monroe County, New York, named for William H. Spencer, a pioneer settler.

Sphinx; mountain in Montana, so named on account of its resemblance in shape to the Sphinx of Egypt.

Spink; county in South Dakota, named for S. L. Spink. a former Congressman.

Spirit Lake; town in Dickinson County, Iowa, named from the lake which the Indians called "spirit water."

Spivey; city in Kingman County, Kansas, named for R. M. Spivey, president of the Arkansas Valley Town and Land Company.

Split Rock; village in Essex County, New York, so named because situated near a curiously formed rock.

Spokane; county, city, river, and falls in Washington, named for an Indian tribe, the name meaning "children of the sun."

Spottsylvania; county in Virginia, named for Alexander Spotswood, early lieutenant-governor.

Sprague; town in Lincoln County, Washington, named for General Sprague, interested in the Northern Pacific Railroad.

Springfield; city in Hampden County, Massachusetts, named for the town in Essex County, England.

Springfield; village in Sarpy County, Nebraska; so named because of the abundance of springs.

Springfield; village in Orangeburg County, South Carolina, so named by its founder because he "expected to see a town spring up in the old fields."

Spring Valley; village in Pierce County, Wisconsin; Springville; village in Laporte County, Indiana. So named because of the abundance of springs.

Sproul; creek in Humboldt County, California, named for a settler.

Spuyten Duyvil; channel connecting the Hudson and Harlem rivers. So named on account of the oath sworn by a Dutch shipmaster that he would pass the mouth of the creek "in spite of the devil."

Squam; lake in New Hampshire. Derived from the Indian word nesquamsauke, meaning "the pleasant water place."

Squaw; mountain, and a township in Piscataquis County, Maine. Abridged version of the translation of its Indian name, meaning "the mountain which belongs to a woman."

Stafford; county and town in Kansas, named for Lewis Stafford, captain Company E, First Kansas Regiment.

Stafford; village in Fort Bend County, Texas, named for a prominent citizen.

Stafford; county in Virginia, named for a county in England.

Stair; falls on the east branch of the Penobscot River, Maine. A translation of the Indian name.

Stambaugh; village in Iron County, Michigan, named for the man who opened the Iron River mine.

Stamping Ground; village in Scott County, Kentucky, so named because the buffalo herds tramped down the underbrush in early days.

Standish; town in Cumberland County, Maine, named for Miles Standish.

Stanford; mountain in California, named for Governor Leland Stanford.

Stanley; town in Gaston County, North Carolina, named for Elwood Stanley, member of Congress.

Stanley; town in South Dakota, named for Henry M. Stanley.

Stanly; county in North Carolina, named for John Stanly, member of Congress.

Stanton; counties in Kansas and Nebraska and city in Montcalm County, Michigan, named for Edwin M. Stanton, Secretary of War under Lincoln.

Stanton; town in Powell County, Kentucky, named for Hon. Richard H. Stanton, of Maysville.

Stark; counties in Illinois, North Dakota, and Ohio, towns in Coos County, New Hampshire, and Herkimer County, New York; Starke; county in Indiana. Named for Gen. John Stark.

Starkey; town in Yates County, New York. Named for John Starkey, one of the first settlers.

Starks; town in Somerset County, Maine; Starksboro; town in Addison County, Vermont; Starkville; town in Oktibbeha County, Mississippi. Named for Gen. John Stark, of Revolutionary fame.

Starr; county in Texas, named for James H. Starr, secretary of the treasury of the republic of Texas.

Starr King; lake and mountains in California and New Hampshire, named for the Rev. Starr King.

State Center; town in Marshall County, Iowa, so named because it is thought to be a geographical center.

State College; borough in Center County, Pennsylvania, so named because it is the seat of the Pennsylvania State College of Agriculture.

State Line; town in Wayne County, Mississippi, near the boundary line between that State and Alabama.

Staten; island, part of Richmond County, New York, named by the Dutch for the Staaten general.

Staunton; river, and a city in Augusta County, Virginia, named for the parish in England.

Steamboat Rock; town in Hardin County, Iowa, so named because there is a large rock in the river near which resembles a steamboat in form.

Steamboat Springs; town in Routt County, Colorado, so named because of the sound which issues from an opening in the rocks.

Stearns; county in Minnesota, named for C. T. Stearns.

Steel; mountain in Washington, named for William G. Steel, of Portland, Oregon.

Steele; counties in Minnesota and North Dakota, named for a resident of Minneapolis, a town-site promoter.

Steele; village in Jefferson County, Nebraska, named for D. M. Steele, railroad man.

Steelton; borough in Dauphin County, Pennsylvania, so named on account of the shops and works near there.

Steelville; city in Crawford County, Missouri, so named on account of the mines nearby.

Steen; mountain in Oregon, named for Col. Enoch Steen.

Steilacoom; town in Pierce County, Washington, named for an Indian tribe, the name said to have been derived from stolukwhamish, "river people."

Stephens; county in Texas, named for Alexander H. Stephens, the American statesman.

Stephenson; county in Illinois, named for Col. Benjamin Stephenson.

Stephenson; village in Menominee County, Michigan, named for Robert Stephenson.

Stephentown; town in Rensselaer County, New York, named for Stephen van Rensselaer.

Steptoe; town in Whitman County, Washington, named for Colonel Steptoe, United States Army.

Sterling; city in Rice County, Kansas, named for Sterling Rosan, father of C. W. and J. H. D. Rosan, early settlers.

Sterling; town in Worcester County, Massachusetts, named for Lord Sterling, an American general.

Sterlingburg; village in Jefferson County, New York, named for James Sterling, the builder of an iron furnace there.

Stetson; town in Penobscot County, Maine, named for the original proprietor, Amasa Stetson.

Steuben; counties in Indiana and New York; towns in Washington County, Maine, and Oneida County, New York; Steubenville; city in Jefferson County, Ohio. Named for Baron von Steuben, a Prussian soldier who fought in the American Revolution.

Stevens; county in Kansas, named for Thaddeus Stevens.

Stevens; county in Minnesota, named for Colonel Stevens, of Minneapolis, prominent pioneer.

Stevens; stream in Caledonia County, Vermont, named for Capt. Phineas Stevens.

Stevens; county in Washington, named for Isaac I. Stevens, first governor of Washington.

Stevenson; mountain, and island in Yellowstone Lake, named for James Stevenson, of the U. S. Geological Survey.

Stevens Point; city in Portage County, Wisconsin, named for the Rev. J. D. Stevens, missionary to the Indians.

Stevensville; village in Berrien County, Michigan, named for Thomas L. Stevens, who laid out the town.

Stevensville; town in Ravalli County, Montana, named for Isaac I. Stevens, the first governor of Washington.

Stewart; county iii Georgia, named for Gen. Daniel Stewart.

Stewart; county in Tennessee, named for Duncan Stewart.

Stewartstown; town in Coos County, New Hampshire, named for John Stewart, one of the original proprietors.

Stewartsville; city in Dekalb County, Missouri, named for Robert M. Stewart, a former governor.

Stilesville; village in Hendricks County, Indiana, named for Jeremiah Stiles, the proprietor.

Stillwater; city in Washington County, Minnesota, named for a lumber company which selected this site for its mill.

Stillwater; town in Saratoga County, New York, so named because of the "still water" in the Hudson River near the town.

Stockbridge; town in Berkshire County, Massachusetts, named for the town in England.

Stockport; town in Columbia County, New York, and Wayne County, Pennsylvania, named for the town in England.

Stockton; cities in California and Missouri and town in Chautauqua County, New York, named for Commodore R. F. Stockton, who took part in the conquest of California.

Stockton; borough in Hunterdon County, New Jersey, named for a resident family.

Stockville; village in Frontier County, Nebraska, so named because stock raising was an important industry.

Stoddard; county in Missouri," named for Amos Stoddard, military officer and author.

Stoddard; town in Cheshire County, New Hampshire, named for Col. Samson Stoddard, one of the original proprietors.

Stokes; county in North Carolina, named for Col. John Stokes, a Revolutionary officer.

Stone; county in Arkansas, named for Gen. T. J. (Stonewall) Jackson.

Stone; county in Missouri; Stoneham; town in Middlesex County, Massachusetts. So named because of the sterile soil.

Stonewall; county in Texas and town in Pamlico County, North Carolina, named for Gen. T. J. (Stonewall) Jackson.

Storey; county in Nevada, named for Colonel Storey, killed in battle with the Pyramid Lake Indians.

Story; county in Iowa, named for Judge Joseph Story, of the Supreme Court.

Stoughton; town in Norfolk County, Massachusetts, named for William Stoughton, lieutenant-governor and chief justice of the province.

Stoughton; city in Dane County, Wisconsin, named for Luke Stoughton, who platted the village.

Stoutsville; village in Monroe County, Missouri, named for Robert P. Stout, of Kentucky.

Stow; town in Middlesex County, Massachusetts, named for the town in England.

Stoystown; borough in Somerset County, Pennsylvania, named for an early settler and Revolutionary soldier, John Stoy.

Strafford; county in New Hampshire, named for a town in England.

Strasburg; town in Tuscarawas County, Ohio, and borough in Lancaster County, Pennsylvania, named for the city in Germany.

Stratton; town in Windham County, Vermont, named for Samuel Stratton, an early settler of Vernon.

Strawberry Point; town in Clayton County, Iowa, so named because of an abundance of these berries.

Streeter; creek in Nansemond County, Virginia, named for a resident family.

Strong; creek in Humboldt County, California, named for an early settler.

Strong; city in Chase County, Kansas, named for W. B. Strong, president Atchison, Topeka and Santa Fe Railroad Company.

Strong; town in Franklin County, Maine, named for Caleb Strong, former United States Senator.

Strother; town in Monroe County, Missouri, named for Prof. French Strother.

Stroudsburg; borough in Monroe County, Pennsylvania, named for Col. Jacob Stroud, its first settler.

Stuart; village in Holt County, Nebraska, named for Peter Stuart, an early settler.

Sturbridge; town in Worcester County, Massachusetts, named for Stourbridge, England.

Sturgeon; town in Boone County, Missouri, named for Isaac H. Sturgeon, of St. Louis.

Sturgeon Bay; city in Door County, Wisconsin, named for the bay which abounds with this fish.

Sturgis; town in St. Joseph County, Michigan, named from the prairie which was named for Judge John Sturgis, first settler.

Stutsman; county in North Dakota, named for Hon. Enoch Stutzman, a pioneer settler prominent in the State's history.

Stuyvesant; town in Columbia County, New York, named for Governor Peter Stuyvesant.

Suamico; river in Wisconsin. An Indian word, meaning "the yellow sand."

Sublett; town in Cassia County, Idaho, named for Captain Sublette, a partner in the Rocky Mountain Fur Company. Succasunna; town in Morris County, New Jersey, in a locality famous for its iron ore. Derived from the Indian sukeu, "black," and achsun, "stone;" hence "place where the black stone is found."

Sudbury; town in Middlesex County, Massachusetts, named for the town in England.

Suffern; town in Rockland County, New York, named from the Suffern family, which owned considerable property in the county.

Suffield; town in Hartford County, Connecticut, originally called Southfield, and situated in Massachusetts; so named because "being the southernmost towne that either at present or is like to be in that county."

Suffolk; counties in Massachusetts and New York, and many places in the United States, named for the county in England.

Sugar; creek in North and South Carolina, named for the Indian tribe Sugaree.

Suisun; town in Solano County, California, named for an Indian tribe.

Sullivan; county and town in Indiana, named for Daniel Sullivan, killed by the Indians when bearing messages from Captain Clark, after the capture of Vincennes.

Sullivan; county and town in Franklin County, Missouri, named for the county in Tennessee.

Sullivan; town in Hancock County, Maine, named for an original proprietor.

Sullivan; counties in New Hampshire, New York, Pennsylvania, and Tennessee; towns in Cheshire County, New Hampshire, and Madison County, New York, named for Maj. Gen. John Sullivan, a Revolutionary officer.

Sully; county in South Dakota, named for Alfred Sully, who commanded a brigade in Dakota.

Sulphur Springs; town in Hopkins County, Texas, so named because of its local features.

Summer; lake in Oregon, so called because of the warm weather which was experienced there by the Fremont party.

Summerfield; city in Marshall County, Kansas, named for E. Summerfield, of Lawrence, Kansas.

Summers; county in West Virginia, named for George W. Summers, Congressman from Virginia.

Summerville; town in Dorchester County, South Carolina, so named because it is a summer resort for residents.

Summit; counties in Colorado and Ohio; city in Union County, New Jersey, and town in Pike County, Mississippi, so named because of their elevation.

Summit; county in Utah, so named because of its mountains.

Summit Hill; borough in Carbon County, Pennsylvania, so named because of the elevation.

Sumner; county in Kansas, named for Charles Sumner, an American statesman.

Sumner; town in Oxford County, Maine, named for Governor Increase Sumner.

Sumner; county in Tennessee, named for Col. Jethro Sumner.

Sumter; counties in Alabama, Florida, Georgia; county and town in South Carolina, and fort in Charleston Harbor, named for Gen. Thomas Sumter, of South Carolina, an officer of the Revolution.

Sunapee; lake in New Hampshire, for which a town in Sullivan County and mountain in the same State are named. From an Indian word, shehunk-nippe, "wild goose pond."

Sunbury; borough in Northumberland County, Pennsylvania, named for a village on the Thames.

Suncook; river in New Hampshire. From an Indian word, schunk-auke, meaning "goose place."

Sunderland; town in Franklin County, Massachusetts, named for Charles Spencer, Earl of Sunderland.

Sunflower; river and county in Mississippi, no doubt descriptively named.

Sun Prairie; town in Dane County, Wisconsin, so named because a party of pioneers, after a nine days' tramp over the prairies in the rain, came to this spot as the sun came out.

Superior; lake in Michigan. Translation of the original French name Lac Superieur aux Outaouacs, "the upper lake of the Ottawas."

Surprise; creek in Yellowstone Park, so named because recent explorations rind its course different than was formerly supposed.

Surry; county in North Carolina, named for Lord Surry, an advocate of American independence.

Surry; county in Virginia, and town in Cheshire County, New Hampshire, named for the county in England.

Survey; peak in the Yellowstone Park, so named because a signaling point for the Indians.

Suspecaugh; stream in New Jersey. An Indian word, meaning "muddy or standing water."

Susquehanna; river, county, and borough in Pennsylvania. From an Indian word, suckahanne, "water."

Sussex; counties in Delaware, New Jersey, and Virginia, named for the county in England.

Sutro; village in Lyon County, Nevada, named for Adolph Sutro.

Sutter; county and several small towns in California, named for Col. John Sutter.

Sutton; town in Merrimack County, New Hampshire, named for town of the same name in Worcester County, Massachusetts, said to be named for the town in England.

Sutton; county in Texas, named for Lieutenant-Colonel Sutton, of the army of the Confederacy.

Suwanee; county, town, and river in Florida, creek and town in Gwinnett County, Georgia. Interpretations of this Indian word are various, some stating that it is from Shawnee, the tribe, while others give its derivation as from sawani, meaning "echo" or "echo river."

Swain; county in North Carolina, named for David L. Swain, an early governor.

Swainsboro; town in Emanuel County, Georgia, named for Col. Stephen Swain, of the State legislature.

Swampscott; town in Essex County, Massachusetts. Various derivations are given this word—from the Indian word wonnesquamsauke, "the pleasant water place;" from m'sqm-ompsk, "red rock," or "at the red rock;" or from another Indian word, meaning "broken waters."

Swannanoa; stream and town in Buncombe County, North Carolina. An Indian word, meaning "beautiful."

Swansboro; town in Onslow County, North Carolina, probably so named on account of the swans frequenting the neighborhood.

Swansea; town in Bristol County, Massachusetts, named for the town in "Wales.

Swanville; village in Erie County, Pennsylvania, named for John L. Swan, its first settler.

Swarthmore; borough in Delaware County, Pennsylvania, named for the district in England.

Swedesboro; town in Gloucester County, New Jersey, so named because settled by Swedes.

Sweet Grass; county in Montana, named from the sweet-grass hills.

Sweet Springs; city in Saline County, Missouri, so named because of its neighboring springs.

Sweetwater; river in Wyoming, giving name to a county, the river having been so named because its waters have a sweet taste.

Swepsonville; village in Alamance County, North Carolina, named for George W. Swepson, a capitalist.

Swift; county in Minnesota, named for an early governor.

Swisher; county in Texas, named for James G. Swisher, a signer of the Texas declaration of independence.

Switzerland; county in Indiana, named for the country in Europe.

Sylva; town in Jackson County, North Carolina, named for a prominent resident.

Sylvan Grove; city in Lincoln County, Kansas, so named because situated near the Twin Groves, on the north bank of the Saline River.

Symmes; town in Hamilton County, Ohio, named for John Cleves Symmes, judge in the Northwest Territory.

Syracuse; city in Onondaga County, New York, named for the ancient city of Sicily.

T

Tabery; village in Oneida County, New York, named for the iron-mining town in Sweden.

Table Rock; village in Pawnee County, Nebraska, so named because situated near a large, flat-topped rock.

Tacoma; city in Washington. From the Indian word Tahoma, meaning "the highest," "near heaven."

Taconic; range of hills in Massachusetts and village in Fairfield County, Connecticut. An Indian word, meaning "forest," or "wilderness."

Taghkanick; creek and village in Columbia County, New York. An Indian word, said to mean "there is water enough."

Tahoe; lake in California and Nevada. An Indian word, meaning "big water."

Talbot; county in Georgia, named for Matthew Talbot, acting governor of the State in 1819.

Talbot; county in Maryland, probably named for Sir Robert Talbot, of Ireland, who married Grace, the daughter of Sir George Calvert, the first Lord Baltimore, though some authorities state that it was named for the uncle of Lady Talbot

Talbott; village in Jefferson County, Tennessee, named for Col. John Talbott.

Talbotton; town in Talbot County, Georgia, named for Matthew Talbot, acting governor of the State in 1819.

Taliaferro; county in Georgia, named for Col. Benjamin Taliaferro.

Talladega; city and county in Alabama. An Indian name, meaning "at the end," "on the border," hence a town on the frontier.

Tallahassee; city in Florida, so named because it is supposed to have been the site of Indian cornfields in remote times. An Indian word, meaning "old town." Tallahatchie; county in Mississippi, named from the principal branch of the Yazoo River in the same State. An Indian word, meaning "river of the rock."

Tallapoosa; river in Georgia and Alabama, giving name to a county in Alabama and a city in Haralson County, Georgia. An Indian word, meaning "swift current," or, according to some authorities, "stranger," "newcomer."

Talleyville; village in Newcastle County, Delaware, named for the Talley family, early residents.

Tallula; village in Menard County, Illinois; Tallulah Falls; town in Rabun County, Georgia. From an Indian word, meaning "leaping waters."

Tama; county in Iowa. An Indian word, meaning "beautiful," "pleasant," "lovely," or the name of the wife of the Indian chief Poweshiek. Still another authority states that it is named for a chief whose name meant "bear whose voice makes the rocks tremble."

Tamalpais; village in Marin County, California. A Spanish word, meaning "region of the Tamal Indians."

Tamanend; village in Schuylkill County, Pennsylvania, named for an Indian chief, the word meaning " beaver-like," or "amiable."

Tamaqua; borough in Schuylkill County, Pennsylvania. From an Indian word, meaning "beaver stream."

Tampa; bay and city on the West coast of Florida. From the Indian word Itimpi, " close to it, near it."

Taney; county in Missouri, named for Roger B. Taney, Chief Justice of the United States.

Tangipahoa; river, town, and parish in Louisiana, named for an Indian tribe, the word meaning "those who gather maize stalks."

Tankhanna; creek in Pennsylvania. An Indian word, meaning "the smaller stream."

Taopi; village in Mower County, Minnesota, said to be named for an Indian chief who befriended the whites in the Minnesota massacre, the word meaning "wounded."

Tappan; town in Harrison County, Ohio; Tappantown; village in Rockland County, New York. From the Indian word Thuphane, meaning "cold stream."

Tar; river in North Carolina; Tarboro; town in Edgecombe County, North Carolina. Named from the above, which received its name on account of the tar made upon its banks by early colonial settlers. Wheeler gives the origin of the name of the river as from the Indian word Tau, "river of health."

Tarrant; county in Texas, named for an early settler prominent in politics after the annexation.

Tarrant; creek in Virginia, named for the family who owned much land along its Western border.

Tarryall; peak and stream in Colorado, so named because of the rich placers found along the latter.

Tarrytown; village in Westchester County, New York. Modification of its former name of Terwen, "wheat town," given on account of its large crops of that cereal.

Tatamy; borough in Northampton County, Pennsylvania, named for a chief of the Delaware Indians who was prominent in the colonial history of the State.

Tate; county in Mississippi, named for a prominent family of which T. S. Tate was a member.

Tatonka; village in Ellsworth County, Kansas. An Indian word, meaning "buffalo."

Tattnall; county in Georgia, named for Josiah Tattnall, an early governor.

Tatum; town in Marlboro County, South Carolina, named for a resident family.

Taunton; river and city in Bristol County, Massachusetts, named for the town in England.

Tawas; city in Iosco County, Michigan, a contraction of Tawawa.

Tawawa; town in Shelby County, Ohio. Indian word meaning "trader."

Taycheedah; village in Fond du Lac County, Wisconsin, so named because of the Indian camp made upon Lake Winnebago. An Indian word, meaning "lake camp."

Taylor; peak in Humboldt County, California, named for an early settler.

Taylor; counties in Florida, Georgia, Iowa, and Kentucky, and town in Cortland County, New York, named for Gen. Zachary Taylor.

Taylor; town in Lafayette County, Mississippi, named for an early settler.

Taylor; county in Texas, named for a family of early settlers.

Taylor; county in West Virginia, named for John Taylor, of Caroline County, Virginia.

Taylor; county in Wisconsin, named for David Taylor, justice of the supreme court.

Taylor Center; village in Wayne County, Michigan, named for Gen. Zachary Taylor.

Taylor Ridge; mountains in Floyd County, Georgia, named for Richard Taylor, a Cherokee chief, who lived near their bass.

Taylors Falls; village in Chisago County, Minnesota, named for one of the first settlers, member of the Northwest Lumber Company.

Taylorsville; village in Bartholomew County, Indiana, named for Gen. Zachary Taylor.

Taylorsville; town in Spencer County, Kentucky, named for Richard Taylor, the former proprietor of the land.

Taylorsville; town in Alexander County, North Carolina, named for John L. Taylor, former judge of the State.

Tazewell; county in Illinois, named for Governor Littleton W. Tazewell, of Virginia.

Tazewell; town and county in Virginia, and village in Marion County, Georgia, named for Senator Henry Tazewell, of Virginia.

Tchemanah.aut; stream in Hot Springs County, Arkansas. A corruption of the French chemin en haut, "high road."

Tecumseh; village in Lenawee County, Michigan, city in Pottawatomie County, Oklahoma, and city in Nebraska, named for the Shawnee Indian chief, the generally accepted meaning of the word being "a panther crouching."

Tehachapi; town and pass in Kern County, California, named for the Indian tribe Ta hi cha pa han na.

Tekonsha; village in Calhoun County, Michigan, named for the Indian (thief of the tribe who formerly occupied the town site.

Telfair; county in Georgia, named for Edward Telfair, one of the early governors of the State.

Tell; city in Indiana, named by its Swiss colonists for William Tell.

Teller; town in Colorado, named for Senator Teller of the State.

Temescal; town in Riverside County, California. From a Spanish word, meaning "sweat house."

Temple; town in Hillsboro County, New Hampshire, named for John Temple, a relative of Earl Temple, of England.

Templeton; town in Worcester County, Massachusetts, said to have been named for Earl Temple.

Tenafly; borough in Bergen County, New Jersey. A Dutch word, meaning "at the meadow."

Tenasillihee; island in the Columbia River, Oregon. An Indian word, meaning "little land."

Tenino; town in Thurston County, Washington, named for an Indian tribe.

Tennessee; tributary of the Ohio River which gives name to a State of the Union. Three different derivations are given the name: From Tanase, the name of the most important village of the Cherokee Indians; from an Indian word meaning "a curved spoon;" or from Taensa, an Indian tribe of the Watchesan family.

Tensas; parish in Louisiana, named for a now extinct tribe of Indians.

Teocalli; mountain in Colorado, so named because shaped like a Mexican pyramid.

Terrebonne; parish in Louisiana, named for a place in Canada. A French word, meaning "good land."

Terre Haute; city in Indiana, built upon a bank 60 feet above the river. A French word, meaning " high land." Terrell; county in Georgia, named for Dr. William Terrell, an early member of Congress from that State.

Terre Noir; creek in Arkansas. A French word, meaning "black land."

Terrill; mountain in Utah, named for the wife of J. H. Renshawe, of the United States Geological Survey.

Terry; town in Hinds County, Mississippi, named for Bill Terry, a resident.

Terry; county in Texas, named for Frank Terry, commander of the Texas Rangers in the civil war.

Terryville; village in Litchfield County, Connecticut, named for a manufacturer of wooden clocks there.

Teton; county, river, and mountain in Montana; range of mountains in Wyoming; and town in Fremont County, Idaho, named for an Indian tribe whose name was variously written Teton, Titon, or Titowan.

Teutopolis; village in Effingham County, Illinois, originally settled by a colony of Germans from Cincinnati.

Tewksbury; town in Middlesex County, Massachusetts, probably named for the town in England.

Texarkana; city in Miller County, Arkansas, near the border between Arkansas and Texas. The name formed of a combination of these two names.

Texas; largest of the United States. Said by some to be a Spanish word applied to the republic, but the generally accepted version of the name is that it is an Indian word, used as a token of friendship. A county in Missouri, named for that republic.

Thames; river in Connecticut, named for the one in England.

Thatchers; island in Massachusetts, named for Anthony Thacher, who was shipwrecked there in 1635.

Thayer; city in Neosho County, Kansas, named for Nathaniel Thayer, of Boston.

Thayer; county in Nebraska, named for Governor John M. Thayer.

Theresa; county in Jefferson County, New York, named for the daughter of James Le Ray de Chaumont.

Thibodaux; town in Lafourche Parish, Louisiana, named for H. S. Thibodeaux.

Thielsen; mountain in Oregon, named for Hans Thielsen, chief engineer of the Oregon and California Railroad.

Thomas; county in Georgia, named for Gen. Jett Thomas.

Thomas; county in Kansas, named for Maj. Gen. George H. Thomas.

Thomas; mountains in Utah, named for Col. L. Thomas.

Thomaston; town in Upson county, Georgia, named for Gen. Jett Thomas.

Thomaston; town in Knox County, Maine, named for Gen. John Thomas, of Massachusetts.

Thomasville; town in Thomas County, Georgia, named for Gen. Jett Thomas.

Thomasville; town in Davidson County, North Carolina, named for State Senator Thomas.

Thorndike; town in Waldo County, Maine, named for Thomas Thorndike, one of the original proprietors.

Thornton; town in Holmes County, Mississippi, named for Dr. C. C. Thornton, a large land owner.

Thornton; town in Grafton County, New Hampshire, probably named for three brothers, Thornton, early settlers, but by some credited to Hon. Mathew Thornton.

Three Oaks; village in Berrien County, Michigan; so named on account of three large oaks near the village.

Three River; peak in Yellowstone Park; so named because the three rivers, Gallatin, Madison, and Gardiner, take their rise on its slopes.

Three Rivers; city in Michigan; so named because situated at the junction of the St. Joseph, Portage, and Rocky rivers.

Throckmorton; county in Texas, named for Dr. William E. Throckmorton, one of the first pioneers of northern Texas.

Throgs Neck; cape in Westchester County, New York, named for John Throckmorton, an original patentee.

Throop; town in Cayuga County, New York, named for Hon. Enos T. Throop, governor.

Thurman; town in Warren County, New York, named for John Thurman.

Thurston; county in Nebraska, named for Senator John M. Thurston.

Thurston; town in Steuben County, New York, named for William R. Thurston, a landholder.

Thurston; county in Washington, named for Samuel R. Thurston, delegate to Congress from Oregon Territory.

Tibbetts; creek in Westchester County, New York, named for the family who have owned the adjoining land for one hundred and thirty years.

Tibee; creek in Mississippi. For derivation see Oktibbeha.

Ticonderoga; town in Essex County, New York. Said to be a modification of the Indian word, Chiderogo, "sounding waters;" other meanings given are "brawling water," or "noisy."

Tiffin; city in Ohio, named for Edward Tiffin, the first governor.

Tillery; town in Halifax County, North Carolina, named for a prominent citizen.

Tilton; town in Belknap County, New Hampshire, named for Charles E. Tilton, of New York.

Tiltonsville; town in Jefferson County, Ohio, named for a family of early proprietors.

Timmonsville; town in Florence County, South Carolina, named for the Timmons family.

Tin Cup; town in Gunnison County, Colorado, so named because in its early days when a mining camp, gold was so plentiful that it was measured in a tin cup.

Tintah; town in Traverse County, Minnesota. From an Indian word, meaning "prairie."

Tinton Falls; town in Monmouth County, New Jersey. Corruption of Tintern, Monmouthshire, England.

Tioga; counties in New York and Pennsylvania, river traversing both States, and a borough in Pennsylvania. An Indian word given various interpretations: "at the forks," "swift current," or "a gate," place of entrance.

Tioinati; tributary of the St. Lawrence in New York. An Indian word meaning "beyond the point."

Tioughnioga; river in central New York. An Indian word meaning "meeting of the waters."

Tippah; county in Mississippi, named for the wife of Pontotoc, Chickasaw Indian chief, the word meaning " cut off."

Tippecanoe; river and county in Indiana, and village in Harrison County, Ohio.

An Indian word given the various meanings of "at the great clearing," "the long-lipped pike," and "buffalo fish."

Tipton; county and city in Indiana, named for Gen. John Tipton, Senator from that State.

Tipton; county in Tennessee, named for Capt. Jacob Tipton, father of Gen. Jacob Tipton.

Tisbury; town in Dukes Comity, Massachusetts, named for the town in England.

Tishomingo; county in Mississippi, named for the king of the Chickasaw Indians, the name meaning "warrior chief."

Tishtang; creek in Humboldt County, California, fancifully named to suggest the sound of the water.

Tiskilwa; village in Bureau County, Illinois. Said to be derived from various Indian words with the meanings "a kind of bird," "a plover," or "an old boy," meaning a bachelor.

Tissaack; mountain in Yosemite Valley, California. An Indian word meaning "goddess of the valley."

Titonka; village in Kossuth County, Iowa. An Indian word meaning "big house."

Titus; county in Texas, named for James Titus, a prominent citizen.

Titusville; town in Brevard County, Florida, named for its founder, Colonel Titus, who was a leader in the Kansas crusade.

Titusville; city in Crawford County, Pennsylvania, named for Jonathan Titus, former owner of the town site.

Tivoli; village in Dutchess County, New York, named for the town in Italy.

Tobesofka; creek in Georgia, go named because an Indian lout a dish of meal while crossing it. Sofskee, meaning "dish of meal," and tobe, "I have lost."

Tobyhanna; stream in Lehigh County, Pennsylvania, thickly banked with alder hushes. Indian, meaning "alder stream."

Tocomo; river in Florida, named for a tribe of Indians, the name meaning "lord, ruler, master."

Todd; county in Kentucky, named for Col. John Todd.

Todd; county in Minnesota, named for Captain Todd, of the Regular Army.

Tohickon; stream in Bucks County, Pennsylvania. Indian, meaning "driftwood stream."

Tolly; point at the junction of Severn River and Chesapeake Bay, Maryland, where Captain Tolly was wrecked.

Tomah; city and township in Wisconsin, named for the chief of the Menominee Indians.

Tomahawk; city in Lincoln County, Wisconsin, and town in Searcy County, Arkansas. An Indian word, meaning "beating thing," "a savage implement," or, according to another authority using a different derivation, "strike them," or "he is stricken."

Tomasaki; mountain in Utah, named for a Ute Indian.

Tombicon; stream in Bucks County, Pennsylvania. An Indian word, meaning "place of crab apples."

Tombigbee; river in Mississippi. Derived from the Indian Itumbi-bikpe, "coffin makers."

Tombstone; town in Pima County, Arizona, so named by its founder, because when starting out on his prospecting tour he was assured he would "find his tombstone."

Tome; village in Valencia County, New Mexico. A contraction of Santo Tomas, Spanish for St. Thomas.

Tom Green; county in Texas, named for Gen. Tom Green, distinguished in the early history of the State, and later in the civil war.

Tomoka; river in Florida, named for an Indian tribe.

Tompkins; county and town in Delaware County, New York; Tompkinsville; village in Richmond County, New York, and Monroe County, Kentucky. Named for Daniel D. Tompkins, governor of New York in 1807.

Toms; river in Ocean County, New Jersey, said to have been named for Capt. William Tom, an early English settler.

Tonawanda; stream, and town in Erie County, New York. An Indian word meaning, "swift water."

Tonganoxie; town in Leavenworth County, Kansas, named for a Delaware Indian who kept a stopping place near the present town site.

Tonica; village in Lasalle County, Illinois, probably named from the Indian, the word said to mean "a place or country inhabited." Tooele; county in Utah, so named on account of a species of rush which grows in the mountains.

Topeka; city in Kansas and village in Mason County, Illinois. Indian, meaning "a good place to dig potatoes."

Topsfield; town in Essex County, Massachusetts, named from the parish in England.

Topsham; town in Sagadahoc County, Maine, named for the seaport in England.

Toronto; many towns and cities in the United States bear this Indian name, meaning "oak tree rising from the lake," which has been transferred to them from the city in Canada.

Torowcap; valley in Arizona. Indian, meaning "a clayey locality."

Torrey; peak in Colorado, named for the botanist.

Torrey; town in Yates County, New York, named for Henry Torrey.

Torrington; town in Litchfield County, Connecticut, named for the town in England.

Totowa; borough in Passaic County, New Jersey. From the Indian word tosawei, meaning "to sink, dive, or go under water," as timbers do when carried over a waterfall.

Totoganic; river in Wisconsin. Indian, meaning "place of floating logs."

Totoket; hill in New Bedford, Connecticut. Probably an Indian word, meaning "on the great tidal river."

Tottenville; village in Richmond County, New York, named for the Tottens, family of early residents.

Toulbah; mountain in Maine, in shape resembling a turtle. Indian, meaning "turtle."

Towaliga; river in Georgia, so named because the Indians roasted the scalps of the whites upon its banks. Towelaggie, "roasted scalps."

Towanda; village in McLean County, Illinois, and borough in Bradford County, Pennsylvania. Indian, meaning "where we bury the dead."

Tower City; borough in Schuylkill County, Pennsylvania, and town in Cass County, North Dakota, named for Charlemagne Tower, father of the present United States ambassador to Russia.

Towner; county in North Dakota, named for O. M. Towner, a member of the Territorial council.

Towns; county in Georgia, named for George W. B. Towns, former governor of the State.

Townsend; town in Newcastle County, Delaware, named for Samuel Townsend, a large land owner.

Townsend; town in Middlesex County, Massachusetts; Townshend; town in Windham County, Vermont. Named for Charles Townshend, who was a member of the ministry during Governor Wentworth's term of office.

Towson; town in Baltimore County, Maryland, named for the family of which Gen. Nathan Towson was a member.

Tracy; village in Piatt County, Missouri, named for an official of the Chicago, Rock Island and Pacific Railroad.

Traill; county in North Dakota, named for W. J. S. Trail, a representative of the Hudson Bay Company.

Transylvania; county in North Carolina, so named on account of its geographical position—" beyond the forest."

Trappe; borough in Montgomery County, Pennsylvania, so named on account of the high steps which led up to one of the early taverns, designated by the German settlers as " treppe."

Travellers Rest; town in Greenville County, South Carolina, named for an inn situated there in early days.

Traverse; county hi. Minnesota, situated on a lake of the same name. French word, meaning "crossing."

Travis; county in Texas, named for Col. William B. Travis, one of Texas' most prominent men during its early days, who fell at the Alamo.

Treadwell; bay in New York, named for Thomas Treadwell, an old resident.

Treasury; mountain in Colorado, so named on account of the mines which it contains.

Trego; county in Kansas, named for Edward P. Trego, captain Company H, Eighth Kansas, killed during the civil war.

Trempealeau; county and village in same county in Wisconsin, deriving their name from the island in the Mississippi, which was designated by the early French voyageurs Mont qui trempe a l'eau, "mountain which stands in the water."

Trenton; city in New Jersey, named for Col. William Trent, speaker of the assembly.

Trexlertown; town in Lehigh County, Pennsylvania, named for John Trexler.

Tribune; city in Greeley County, Kansas, named for the Tribune (New York), Greeley's newspaper.

Trident; mesa in Colorado, so named because of the three spurs which rise from it.

Trigg; county in Kentucky, named for Col. Stephen Trigg, slain by the Indians at the battle of Blue Licks.

Trimble; county in Kentucky, named for the lion. Robert Trimble.

Trinchera; creek in Colorado. Spanish word, meaning "cut-bank river."

Trinity; county in California, named from the river, so named from the supposition of its first American explorers that it emptied into the Bay of Trinidad, which was entered by its Spanish discoverers on Trinity Sunday.

Trinity; town in Randolph County, North Carolina, named from Trinity College, formerly located there.

Trinity; river and county in Texas, named for the river, named for the Triune God.

Tripp; county in South Dakota, named for Bartlett Tripp, United States minister to Austria in 1893.

Troup; county in Georgia, named for Hon. George M. Troup, Senator from that State.

Trousdale; county in Tennessee, named for Governor William Trousdale.

Troy; cities in Kansas, Mississippi, and New York, named for the ancient Troy of Asia Minor.

Troy; town in Montgomery County, North Carolina, named for Matthew Troy, a prominent lawyer.

Truckee; river in California, named for the old Indian guide of General Fremont.

Truesdale; town in Warren County, Missouri, named for William Truesdale, former owner of the townsite.

Trumansburg, village in Tompkins County, New York, named for the Tremaines, family of early settlers.

Trumbull; county in Ohio, named for Johnathan Trumbull, first governor of Connecticut, the land formerly being within Connecticut's Western Reserve.

Truro; town in Barnstable County, Massachusetts, named for the town in England.

Truxton; town in Courtland County, New York, named for Commodore Thomas Truxton.

Tryon; town in Polk County, North Carolina, named for William Tryon, colonial governor.

Tuckahoe; creek in New Jersey. Indian, "where deer are shy."

Tucker; county in West Virginia, named for St. George Tucker, an eminent Virginia jurist.

Tuftonboro; town in Carroll County, New Hampshire, named for J. Tufton Mason, to whom the grant was made.

Tukuhnikavats; peak of the Sierra la Sal in Utah, named for a Ute Indian. The word means "Dirt Seer."

Tulare; county and city in California. Indian, "place of tules, or reeds."

Tuleys; creek in Humboldt County, California, named for an early settler.

Tully; town in Onondaga County, New York, named for Marcus Tullius Cicero, the Roman orator.

Tulpehocken; stream in Pennsylvania. Indian, "land of turtles."

Tumwater; town in Thurston County, Washington. An Indian word, meaning "waterfall." Another authority interprets it as "the beating of the heart."

Tunica; county and town in Mississippi, named for the Indian tribe, the word meaning "the people."

Tunkhannock; borough in Wyoming County, Pennsylvania. An Indian word, meaning " the small stream." Tuppeckhanna; stream in Pennsylvania. An Indian word, meaning "the stream which flows from a large spring."

Turbutville; borough in Northumberland County, Pennsylvania, named for a family who had large land holdings in the State.

Turin; town in Lewis County, New York, named from the city in Italy.

Turkey; river in Iowa, so named because much frequented by wild turkeys.

Turmans; creek in Sullivan County, Indiana, named for Benjamin Turman, first settler on the west side of the county.

Turner; town in Androscoggin County, Maine, named for the Rev. Charles Turner, of Scituate, Massachusetts.

Turner; county in South Dakota, named for J. W. Turner, legislator.

Turnersville; town in Robertson County, Tennessee, named for Major Turner.

Turnwall; creek in Clark County, Arkansas, corruption of the French, terre noir, "black land."

Turret; mountain in Yellowstone Park, so named from its shape.

Tuscaloosa; county and city in Alabama named for an Indian chief, the name meaning " black warrior." Tuscarawas; river and county in Ohio, and several townships. An Indian word which authorities-give the two different meanings, "old town," because the oldest Indian town in that part of the State was situated on the banks of the river; and "open mouth."

Tuscarora; village in Livingston County, New York, and river in Pennsylvania, named for the Dusgaoweh Indians, a tribe of the Six Nations, whose name signifies "shirt-wearing people."

Tuscola; county in Michigan and city in Douglas County, Illinois, probably named for an Indian chief, Tusco, who formerly lived in the vicinity. The name meaning " warrior." Tuscumbia; city in Colbert County, Alabama, and village in Miller County, Missouri, named for a Chickasaw Indian chief, although another authority favors the derivation of the Cherokee, "grand battle ground."

Tuskegee; town in Macon County, Alabama. Probably derived from the Indian word, taskialgi, "-warriors."

Tusquitee; village in Clay County, North Carolina. Indian, "high valley."

Tusten; town in Sullivan County, New York, named for Col. Benjamin Tusten.

Tuttle; lake in "Wisconsin, named for an early settler.

Tuxedo; a few places in the United States bear this Indian name, which undoubtedly is derived from P'tauk-seet-tough, meaning "the place of bears."

Twiggs; county in Georgia, named for Gen. John Twiggs.

Twin Rivers; two small streams, so named because entering Lake Michigan, from Wisconsin, at the same point. Town in Manitowoc County, named for the above.

Two Hearted; river in Michigan. An erroneous translation of the Indian name Nizhodesibi, "twin river."

Two Licks; branch of the Conemaugh in Indiana County, Pennsylvania. Translation of the Indian name, Nischahoni.

Twowater; branch of the White River in eastern Utah, so named because having two main sources—Bitterwater and Sweetwater forks.

Tygart; valley and river in West Virginia, named for David Tygart, an early settler.

Tyler; county in Texas, named for John Tyler, President of the United States.

Tyler; county in West Virginia, named for John Tyler, governor of Virginia.

Tylerville; village in Jefferson County, New York, named for Josiah and Frederick Tyler, early settlers.

Tymochtee; stream and town in Wyandot County, Ohio, the former flowing around a large plain. An Indian word, meaning "around the plain."

Tyndall; mountain in California, named for the English physicist.

Tyngsboro; town in Middlesex County, Massachusetts, named for Ebenezer Tyng, but according to Mason received its name from Mrs. Sarah Tyng Winslow.

Tyringham; town in Berkshire County, Massachusetts, named for the family of Tyringham, of which Governor Bernard was a descendant and representative.

Tyrone; borough in Blair County, Pennsylvania, named for the county in Ireland.

Tyrrel; county in North Carolina, named for Sir John Tyrrel, a lord proprietor.

U

Uchee; village in Russell County, Alabama. An Indian word, meaning "corn."

Udall; city in Cowley County, Kansas, named for Cornelius Udall.

Uhrichsville; city in Tuscarawas County, Ohio, named for a family of early settlers.

Uinkaret; group of volcanic mountains in Grand Canyon, Colorado, and plateau in Arizona. An Indian word, meaning "pine mountain."

Uinta; counties in Utah and Wyoming and mountain range in Utah, named for a branch of the Ute Indians, the word meaning "pine land."

Uiukufki; stream in Indian Territory. Indian, "muddy water."

Ukiah; city in California, named for the Indian tribe, of whose name, Yokaia, it is a corruption, the word meaning "lower valley."

Ulmers; town in Barnwell County, South Carolina, named for the Ulmer family.

Ulster; county in New York, named for the province in Ireland.

Ulysses; city in Grant County, Kansas, and village in Butler County, Nebraska, named for Gen. Ulysses S. Grant.

Umatilla; river and county in Oregon, said by some to be named for a tribe of Indians. Others state that it is derived from U-a-tal-la, meaning "the sand blew bare in heaps," this part of the country having ridges of sand alternating with bare ground.

Umbagog; lake lying partly in New Hampshire and partly in Maine. An Indian word, said to mean "doubled up." Other authorities favor "clear lake, shallow," or "great waters near another."

Umcolcus; lake and stream in Maine. An Indian word, meaning "whistling duck."

Ummo; mountain in Mariposa County, California. An Indian word, meaning "lost arrow."

Unalaska; island in the Aleutian Archipelago. Indian, meaning "the land near Alayeska, or Alakshak."

Unadilla; village in Dooly County, Georgia; river, town, and village in Otsego County, New York. Indian, "place of meeting."

Unaweep; canyon in Colorado, so named because of the color of its sandstone. Indian, "red rock."

Uncasville; village in New London County, Connecticut, named for a war chief of the Mohegan Indians.

Uncompahgre; river and mountain in Colorado. Derived from the Indian, Unca, "hot;" pah, "water;" gre, "spring;" "hot water spring."

Underhill; town in Chittenden County, Vermont, named for two brothers, shareholders under the original charter.

Union; counties in Georgia, Illinois, Iowa, Mississippi, New Mexico, North Carolina, Pennsylvania, South Dakota, and Tennessee, and parish in Louisiana, named to express the sentiment which now actuates the American people.

Union; county and town in New Jersey, founded during the civil war, so named to express the patriotic sentiment of that section.

Union; county in Kentucky, believed to be so named because of the unanimity of the people when the division of the county from which this was taken was made.

Union; county in Indiana, formed by the union of parts of Wayne and Fayette counties.

Union; county in South Carolina, named from the Union Church on Brown Creek.

Union; mountain in Nevada, so named because it appears to be made up of many peaks.

Unionville; town in Orange County, New York, named to commemorate the friendly adjustment of the matter of the questioned ownership of the locality of the present town site.

Upotog; stream in Muscogee County, Alabama. Indian, meaning " covering, spreading out." Upshur; counties in Texas and West Virginia, named for Abel P. Upshur, Secretary of State under President Tyler.

Upson; county in Georgia, named for Stephen Upson, an eminent lawyer of the State.

Upton; county in Texas, named for John and W. F. Upton, prominent citizens oi the State, the former an officer of the civil war.

Ursina; borough in Somerset County, Pennsylvania, named for Mr. Bear, one of its founders. The Latin form.

Utah; State in the Union, county and lake in same State, named for the Ute Indians, the word meaning "home, or location, on the mountain top."

Utica; city in New York, named for the ancient city in Africa; towns in Livingston County, Missouri, and Hinds County, Mississippi, and village in Macomb County, Michigan, named for the above.

Utuhu; lake in Michigan. Indian, "oak."

Uvalde; county and town in Texas, named for Jose Uvalde.

Uxbridge; town in Worcester County, Massachusetts, named for Henry Paget, Earl of Uxbridge.

V

Vacaville; town in Solano County, California. Spanish word, meaning "cow," "beef."

Vaiden; town in Carroll County, Mississippi, said to be named for Dr. Vaiden, a resident planter.

Vailsburg; borough in Essex County, New Jersey, named for the Vail family, residents of the neighborhood.

Valatie; village in Columbia County, New York, situated near a small falls. Derived from a Dutch word, meaning "little falls."

Valentia; county in New Mexico, named for the city in Spain.

Vallejo; city in California, named for Gen. M. G. Vallejo.

Valley; counties in Montana and Nebraska, so named on account of the topography oi the county.

Valley; town in Douglas County, Nebraska, so named because situated at the junction of the Republican Valley branch of the Union Pacific and the main line.

Valley Forge; village in Chester County, Pennsylvania, so named because situated at the mouth of Valley Creek, where a forge was erected in the days antedating the Revolution, by Isaac Potts.

Valley Junction; town in Polk County, Iowa, so named because situated at the junction of the Chicago, Rock Island and Pacific and Des Moines Valley railroads.

Valley Ridge; town in Dunklin County, Missouri, so named because of the peculiarity of the land.

Van Buren; counties in Arkansas, Iowa, Michigan, and Tennessee, named for Martin Van Buren, the eighth President of the United States.

Vance; county in North Carolina; Vanceboro; town in Craven County, same State. Named for Z. B. Vance, governor and Senator.

Vances; town in Orangeburg County, South Carolina, named for the Vance family, who formerly kept the ferry at this place.

Vancouver; town and military fort in Clarke County, Washington, named for Capt. George Vancouver, royal navy, who explored that part of the country in 1791.

Vandalia; city in Fayette County, Illinois, giving name to city in Missouri and village in Cass County, Michigan, the town in Illinois having been so named at the suggestion of a wag, who told the story of the Goths and Vandals to the commissioners, jokingly giving them to understand that the selected town site was the scene of their encounters.

Vandemere; town in Pamlico County, North Carolina, named from a resident family.

Vanderburg; county in Indiana, named for Henry Vanderburgh, judge of the first court formed in the State.

Van Etten; village in Chemung County, New York, named for James B. Van Etten, member of the assembly in 1852.

Van Leuvens Corners; village in Albany County, New York, named for Isaac Van Leuven.

Van Wert; county in Ohio, named for Isaac Van Wert, one of the militiamen who assisted in the capture of Major Andre.

Varinagrove; town in Henrico County, Virginia, named for the town in Spain, because the same kind of tobacco is raised in both places.

Varnville; town in Hampton County, South Carolina, named for a resident family.

Van Zandt; county in Texas, named for Isaac Van Zandt, member of Texas congress, prominent politician.

Varysburg; village in Wyoming County, New York, named for William Vary, one of the first settlers.

Vashon; island in Washington, named for a captain in the British navy.

Vassalboro; town in Kennebec County, Maine, named for Florentins Vassall, a proprietor of the Plymouth patent.

Vaughns; creek in Simpson County, Mississippi, named for an early settler.

Veazie; town in Penobscot County, Maine, named for Gen. Samuel Veazie, large property owner.

Venable; creek in Fluvanna County, Virginia, named for Lewis Venable.

Venango; county and borough in Crawford County, Pennsylvania. From the Indian Innungah, in reference to a figure found on a tree, carved by the Fries.

Ventura; river, county, town, and city in California. Spanish, meaning "luck, fortune, favorable chance." Vera Cruz; town in Wells County, Indiana, named for the old city of Mexico.

Verde; river in Arizona with water of a greenish cast. Spanish word, meaning "green."

Verdery; town in Greenwood County, South Carolina, named for a resident family.

Vergennes; city in Addison County, Vermont, named for Charles Granvier, Count de Vergennes.

Vermilion; counties in Indiana and Illinois, parish in Louisiana, villages in Erie County, Ohio, and Edgar County, Illinois, named from the river in South Dakota, said to have been so named because of the red earth produced by the burning of the shale overlying the outcrop of coal, by ignition from autumnal fires.

Vermont; State of the Union, so named because of the appearance of its mountains. Derived from the French, Vert Mont, "green mountains."

Vermontville; village in Eaton County, Michigan, named for the State.

Vernal Fall; waterfall in Yosemite Valley, California, so named because of the beautiful greenish tints which it displays.

Vernon; many places in the United States, named for the home of Washington—Mount Vernon—among them the parish in Louisiana.

Vernon; county in Missouri, named for Miles Vernon, of Laclede County.

Vernon; county in Wisconsin, given this name to suggest the greenery of the surrounding country.

Verona; many places in the United States, named for the city in Italy, among them the town in Hancock County, Maine.

Verplanck; village in Westchester County, New York, named for Philip Verplanck.

Versailles; many places in the United States bear the name of the palace in Paris.

Vershire; town in Orange County, Vermont; name formed by a combination of the first syllable of the State name and "shire," the English suffix designating county.

Vevay; city in Switzerland County, Indiana, named for the town in Switzerland.

Vicksburg; city in Mississippi, named for Neivitt Vick, its founder.

Victor; village in Ontario County, New York, so named because the French commander in a battle fought there thought he had captured the Iroquois Indians for the French.

Victor; town in Montana, named for a noted Flathead chief.

Victoria; county in Texas, indirectly named for D. Felix Victoria, first president of Mexico, known as "Guadalupe" Victoria.

Vidalia; town in Concordia Parish, Louisiana, named for Vidal, the Spanish governor of the district in which the town is situated.

Vienna; many places in the United States have been named for the city in Austria.

Vigo; county in Indiana, named for Col. Francis Vigo.

Vigo; town in Concho County, Texas, named for a place in Spain.

Vilas; county in Wisconsin, named for Senator William F. Vilas.

Villa Rica; town in Carroll County, Georgia, having gold mines. Spanish words, meaning "rich city."

Villenova; town in Chautauqua County, New York. Spanish, meaning "new town."

Vinalhaven; island and town in Knox County, Maine, named for John Vinal, of Boston.

Vincennes; city in Knox County, Indiana, named from the fort built by Sieur de Vincennes.

Vineland; borough in Cumberland County, New Jersey, so named because it was the intention of its founder to raise grapes on an extensive scale, which was realized to a considerable extent.

Vining; city in Clay County, Kansas, named for E. P. Vining, an officer of the Union Pacific Railroad.

Vinton; county in Ohio, named for S. F. Vinton, member of Congress from that State.

Viola; village in Richland County, Wisconsin, named for Viola Buck.

Virgil; town in Cortland County, New York, named for the poet, Publius Vergilius Maro.

Virgin; river in Utah. Derived from the original Spanish name, Rio Virgen, "river of the virgin."

Virginia; one of the original thirteen States, named for Elizabeth, Queen of England.

Virginia; city in Storey County, Nevada, named for the State.

Virginia; cascade in Yellowstone Park, named for the wife of Hon. Charles Gibson, president of the Yellowstone Park Association.

Visalia; city in Tulare County, California, named for Vise, a hunter.

Volney; villages in Allamakee County, Iowa, and Oswego County, New York, named for Count Volney, the French writer.

Voluntown; village in New London County, Connecticut, so named because the greater part of the town was granted to the volunteers of the Narragansett war.

Volusia; county in Florida, named for a town within its limits supposed to have been named for Volus, an English settler.

Voorheesville; village in Albany County, New York, named for Theodore Voorhees, director of the Delaware and Lackawanna Railroad.

W

Waas; mountain in Utah, named for a Ute Indian chief.

Wabash; counties in Indiana and Illinois, river flowing through both States, and city in Indiana. From the Indian word Uuabache, "cloud borne by an equinoctial wind," or, according to another authority, "white water."

Wabasha; county, and city in same county, in Minnesota, named for an Indian chief of the Sioux Nation. According to another authority, it is derived from wapahasa, "a standard of battle."

Wabaunsee; county and town in Kansas, named for a Potawatomi Indian chief, the name signifying "dim daylight," or "causer of paleness," given because he captured an enemy's camp just at the break of day.

Wabeno; town in Forest County, Wisconsin. Indian word, meaning "men of the dawn," or "eastern men."

Wacasassee; river and bay in Florida, so named because of the herds of cattle frequenting it. Indian, "cow range."

Waccamaw; town in Georgetown County, South Carolina, and river, lake, and township in North Carolina, named for the Indian tribe.

Wachusett; mountain in Massachusetts. An Indian word, meaning "the mountain" or "near the mountain."

Waco; town in Smith County, Mississippi, village in Cleveland County, North Carolina, and city in McLennan County, Texas, named for an Indian tribe, the name meaning " heron."

Waconia; village in Carver County, Minnesota. Indian, meaning "living spring."

Waconda; village in Mitchell County, Kansas. An Indian word, meaning "the great spirit," "the creator of all things," "the god of war."

Wacouta; village in Goodhue County, Minnesota. Indian, meaning "shooter," the name of an Indian chief who lived at Red Wing.

Waddington; town in Humboldt County, California, named for an early settler.

Waddington; village in St. Lawrence County, New York, named for Joshua Waddington, proprietor.

Wadena; county, and village in same county, in Minnesota, and town in Fayette County, Iowa. Probably from the Indian word odana, "town."

Wadesboro; town in Anson County, North Carolina, named for Col. Thomas Wade.

Wading River; village in Suffolk County, New York, named for the river, which was so called because the Indians waded into it for the shellfish to be found there.

Waga; tributary to the Minnesota River. Indian, "cottonwood."

Wagara; stream in New Jersey. Derived from the Indian word woakeu, "crooked" or "bent," and aki, "a place."

Wagener; town in Aiken County, South Carolina, named for F. W. Wagener, capitalist, of Charleston.

Wahkiakum; county in Washington, named for a tribe of Indians.

Wahoo; village in Lumpkin County, Georgia, and town in Saunders County, Nebraska. Indian, meaning a species of elm, but in the Miami dialect meaning "egg."

Wahpeton; city in Richland County, North Dakota. Indian word, meaning "leaf village."

Waitsfield; town in Washington County, Vermont, named for Gen. Benjamin Waite, the first settler.

Wakarusa; town in Elkhart County, Indiana, and stream in Kansas. Indian word, meaning "thigh deep."

Wakatomika; village in Coshocton County, Ohio. Indian word, meaning "other-side town."

Wake; county in North Carolina, named for wife of Governor Tryon, it being her maiden name.

Wakeeney; city in Trego County, Kansas, named for its founders, A. E. Warren and J. F. Keeney.

Wakefield; city in Clay County, Kansas, named for the Rev. Richard Wake, one of its founders.

Wakefield; town in Middlesex County, Massachusetts, named for Cyrus Wakefield.

Wakefield; village in Wake County; Wake Forest; town in Wake County. Named for the wife of Governor Tryon, it being her maiden name.

Wakenda; town in Carroll County, Missouri. Indian word, meaning "worshiped."

Wakulla; county in Florida, named for the famous spring, near the Gulf coast. Indian word, meaning "mystery."

Walden; town in Orange County, New York, named for Jacob T. Walden, a prominent citizen.

Walden; town in Caledonia County, Vermont, named for commanding officer of the military forces present during the building of a road in the vicinity.

Waldo; county in Maine; Waldoboro; town in Lincoln County, Maine. Named for Brig. Gen. Samuel Waldo, I of Boston.

Waldron; island in Washington, named for W. T. Waldron, of the ship Porpoise.

Wales; town in Hampden County, Massachusetts, named for James Lawrence Wales.

Walesboro; village in Bartholomew County, Indiana, named for John P. Wales, its founder.

Walhalla; towns in Pembina County, North Dakota, and Oconee County, South Carolina. Scandinavian name, meaning "palace of immortality."

Walhonding; river in Ohio. Indian word, meaning "white woman."

Walke; point in North Landing River, Virginia, named for the family which are the oldest residents of Princess Anne County.

Walker; county in Alabama, named for Senator J. W. Walker, of the State.

Walker; county in Georgia, named for Freeman Walker.

Walker; lake and river in Esmeralda County, Nevada, and pass in California, named for Joseph Reddeford Walker, guide of Fremont's Second Expedition.

Walker; county in Texas, named for Robert J. Walker, Secretary of the Treasury during the Polk administration.

Walkerville; city in Silverbow County, Montana, named for the owner of the "Alice" mine.

Wallace; county in Kansas, named for Gen. William H. L. Wallace, veteran of the Mexican war.

Wallace; town in Duplin County, North Carolina, named for a prominent resident.

Wallawalla; county and city in Washington. Indian word, meaning "a small, rapid river," or "rushing water." Wallenpaupack; stream in Pennsylvania. Indian word, meaning "deep and dead water."

Waller; county in Texas, named for Edwin Waller, former postmaster-general under the republic.

Wall Hill; town in Marshall County, Mississippi, named for William Wall.

Wallington; borough in Bergen County, New Jersey, named for Walling Van Winkle, the former owner.

Walloostook; river in Maine. Indian word, meaning "stream where you get boughs," or "fine, beautiful river."

Walpack; township in Sussex County, New Jersey. Indian word, meaning "a sudden bend of a stream around the base of a rock."

Walpole; town in Norfolk County, Massachusetts, named for Sir Robert Walpole.

Walpole; town in Cheshire County, New Hampshire, named for the town in England.

Walsenburg; town in Huerfano County, Colorado, named for Fred Walsen, a banker and old settler.

Walterboro; town in Colleton County, South Carolina, named for the Walter family, prominent residents of the State.

Walthall; town in Webster County, Mississippi, named for Gen. Edward Walthall.

Waltham; city in Middlesex County, Massachusetts, from which the town in Addison County, Vermont, is named, the former supposedly receiving its name from Waltham Abbey, England.

Walton; county in Georgia, named for George Walton, one of the signers of the Declaration of Independence.

Walton; city in Harvey County, Kansas, named for a stockholder of the Atchison, Topeka and Santa Fe Railroad.

Walton; town in Delaware County, New York, named for William Walton, a large land proprietor.

Walworth; county in Wisconsin, and town in Wayne County, New York, named for Chancellor Reuben H. Walworth. The county in South Dakota named for the above.

Wamego; city in Pottawatomie County, Kansas, said to be so named because formerly there was no water in the village. Indian word, meaning "clear of springs." Other authorities say that it was named for an Indian chief whose name meant "running waters."

Wamesit; village in Middlesex County, Massachusetts. From the Indian word wame, "all," or " whole," and auke, "a place."

Wampum; borough in Lawrence County, Pennsylvania. The name of the Indian shell money.

Wanaque; river and valley in New Jersey. An Indian word, meaning "sassafras place."

Wanatah; town in Laporte County, Indiana, named from an Indian chief, whose name signified "he that charges on his enemies."

Wangunbog; pond in Connecticut. Indian word, meaning "bent pond."

Wapakoneta; village in Auglaize County, Ohio. Indian word, meaning "clay river."

Wapanucka; town in Choctaw Nation, Indian Territory. Derived from Wappanocca, the name given the Delawares by other Indians, it signifying "Eastlanders."

Wapato; village in Washington County, Oregon. The Indian designation of a bulbous root, resembling a potato.

Wapella; village in Dewitt County, Illinois, named for a chief of the Fox tribe, the name meaning "he who is painted white."

Wapello; county and city in Iowa. Indian word given the two meanings, "the pioneer" and "the little prince."

Wapiti; village in Summit County, Colorado. An Indian word, meaning "elk."

Wappinger; creek and town in Dutchess County, New York; Wappingers Falls; village in Dutchess County, New York. Named for an Indian tribe.

Wapsipincon; river in Iowa, so named because of the root which is found in great abundance upon its banks. Indian word, meaning "white potatoes."

Wapwallopen; stream and village in Luzerne County, Pennsylvania. Indian name, said by some to mean "the place where the messengers were murdered;" by others, "where the white hemp grows."

Waquapaug; stream in Rhode Island. Indian word, meaning "at the end of the pond."

Ward; town in Boulder County, Colorado, named for the Ward lode, discovered in 1860.

Ward; village in Boone County, Indiana, named for Thomas Ward, Congressman from that State.

Ward; peak in Montana, named for Artemus Ward.

Ward; point on Staten Island, New York, named for the man who formerly owned that part of the island.

Ward; county in North Dakota, named for Hon. Mark Ward, of South Dakota.

Ward; county in Texas, named for Thomas W. Ward, the commissioner of the general land office under the first State governor of Texas.

Wards; island in New York, named for Jasper and Bartholomew Ward, former proprietors.

Wards; town in Saluda County, South Carolina, named for the Ward family, prominent residents of the State.

Wardsboro; town in Windham County, Vermont, named for William Ward, of Newfane, the principal proprietor.

Ware; county in Georgia, named for Nicholas Ware, an early Senator from Georgia.

Ware; town in Hampshire County, Massachusetts, so named on account of the weirs, or weirers, formerly constructed in the river to catch salmon.

Wareham; town in Plymouth County, Massachusetts, named for the town in England.

Waresboro; town in Ware County, Georgia, named for Nicholas Ware, an early Senator from that State.

Warner; town in Merrimack County, New Hampshire, named for Col. Jonathan Warner, of Portsmouth.

Warnerville; village in Schoharie County, New York, named for Capt. George Warner, the first settler.

Warramaug; pond in Litchfield County, Connecticut. An Indian word, meaning "good fishing place."

Warren; creek in Humboldt County, California, named for a settler.

Warren; counties in Georgia, Illinois, Iowa, Kentucky, Mississippi, Missouri, New York, New Jersey, North Carolina, Ohio, Pennsylvania, and Virginia; borough in Warren County, Pennsylvania; towns in Knox County, Maine; Worcester County, Massachusetts; and Herkimer County, New York; and a fortification in Boston Harbor; named for Joseph Warren, who fell in the battle of Bunker Hill.

Warren; county in Indiana, named for Gen. Francis Warren.

Warren; city in Trumbull County, Ohio, named for Gen. Moses Warren, of Lyme, Connecticut.

Warren; towns in Grafton County, New Hampshire, and Bristol County, Rhode Island, named for Admiral Sir Peter Warren of the royal navy.

Warrenton; town in Warren County, North Carolina, named for Gen. Joseph Warren, officer of the Revolution, who fell in the battle of Bunker Hill.

Warrick; county in Indiana, named for Capt. Jacob Warrick, killed in the battle of Tippecanoe.

Warsaw; city in Kosciusko County, Indiana, and town in Benton County, Missouri, named for the capital of Poland.

Warwick; towns in Franklin County, Massachusetts, and Kent County, Rhode Island, named for the Earl of Warwick.

Warwick; county in Virginia, named for the town in England.

Wasatch; range of mountains and county in Utah. Indian word, meaning " lake of many waters."

Wasco; county in Oregon, said to be named for an Indian tribe, though it may have been derived from wasko, "grass, or grass people." It is also the name of an Indian dish.

Waseca; several small streams in Minnesota and Dakota, probably giving name to the town and county in Minnesota. Indian word, meaning "red earth or paint," or, according to another authority, "a pine tree."

Washabaugh; county in South Dakota, named for Frank Washabaugh, prominent State politician.

Washburn; town in Aroostook County, Maine, named for Israel Washburn, jr., governor of the State during the civil war.

Washburn; mountain in Yellowstone Park, named for Gen. Henry Dane Washburn.

Washburn; county in Wisconsin, named for Cadwallader C. Washburn, former governor.

Washington; State of the Union, counties in Arkansas, Georgia, Idaho, Illinois, Indiana, Iowa, Kansas, Kentucky, Maine, Maryland, Mississippi, Missouri, New York, North Carolina, Ohio, Pennsylvania, South Dakota, Tennessee, Vermont, Virginia, Wisconsin; parish in Louisiana; town in Berkshire County, Massachusetts; highest peak of the White Mountains in New Hampshire; and doubtless the counties in Alabama, Colorado, Florida, Minnesota, Nebraska, Oregon , Rhode Island, Texas, and Utah, and many other towns; Washington; city, capital of the United States; Washingtonville; town in Orange County, New York. Named for Gen. George Washington.

Washita; county in Oklahoma and village in Montgomery County, Arkansas. An Indian word, said to mean either "male deer" or "the country of large buffaloes."

Washoe; county and city in Nevada, named for a tribe of Indians who formerly lived in the vicinity.

Washta; town in Cherokee County, Iowa. Indian word, meaning "good."

Washtenaw; county in Michigan, named for the east branch of Grand River; the name said to be derived from the Indian word, washtenong, "river that is far off."

Wasioja; town in Dodge County, Minnesota, so named because of the pine trees growing near. An Indian word meaning "pine grove."

Wassaic; village in Dutchess County, New York. Indian word, meaning "difficult, or hard work."

Wastedo; town in Goodhue County, Minnesota. An Indian word, meaning "good."

Watab; village in Benton County, Minnesota. Indian word meaning "root of pine, or fir, to sew a canoe."

Wataga; village in Knox County, Illinois. From the Potawatomi Indian word, meaning, "I heard;" or, if derived from ahweataga, "he has gone to ramble."

Watauga; river in Tennessee and county in North Carolina. Indian word, meaning "river of islands."

Wateree; river and town in Richland County, South Carolina, named for the Indian tribe—the word meaning "to float on the water."

Waterford; town in Marshall County, Mississippi, so named on account of the great volume of water contained in Spring Creek at this point.

Waterford; village in Saratoga County, New York, so named on account of a ford over to Haven Island.

Waterford; town in Caledonia County, Vermont, so named because of its situation on the Connecticut River.

Waterloo; many places in the United States named for the famous battlefield.

Watertown; town in Middlesex County, Massachusetts, so called because it was "a well-watered place," and the first means of communication between this place and Boston was by water.

Watertown; town in Jefferson County, New York, so named on account of the extraordinary amount of water power there.

Water Valley; city in Yalobusha County, Mississippi, so named on account of the perpetual stream passing there.

Waterville; city in Maine, so named because situated at Ticonic Falls on the Kennebec River, which furnishes the motive power for its factories.

Watervliet; city on the Hudson, in Albany County, New York. From the Dutch, meaning "flowing stream."

Wathena; city in Doniphan County, Kansas, named for a chief of the Kickapoo Indians.

Watkins; village in Schuyler County, New York, named for Dr. Samuel Watkins, of London, one of the first proprietors.

Watkinsville; town in Oconee County, Georgia, named for Col. Robert Watkins, of Augusta, member of the State legislature.

Watonwan; county in Minnesota. Indian word, meaning "see."

Watrous; town in Mora County, New Mexico, named for Samuel B. Watrous, an early settler.

Watson; town in Lewis County, New York, named for James Watson, former proprietor.

Watson; town in Hampshire County, West Virginia, named for Joseph Watson, the former owner of the land.

Wattsburg; borough in Erie County, Pennsylvania, named for David Watts, an early settler.

Waubay; village in Day County, South Dakota. Indian word, meaning "place of hatching."

Waubeek; towns in Linn County, Iowa, and Dunn County, Wisconsin. Indian word, meaning "metal," or "metallic substance."

Waubesa; lake in Wisconsin. Indian word, meaning "swan."

Wauconda; village in Lake County, Illinois. Indian word, meaning "the good spirit," or "master of life."

Waukarusa; stream in Kansas. Indian word, meaning "hip deep."

Waukau; town in Winnebago County, Wisconsin. Indian word, meaning "habitually," or "often."

Waukegan; city in Lake County, Illinois. Indian word, meaning "house or fort," "white man's dwelling."

Waukesha; city and county in Wisconsin. Indian word, meaning "fox."

Waukon; town in Allamakee County, Iowa. Indian word, meaning "moss on trees that is eatable." Waunakee; village in Dane County, Wisconsin. From the Indian word, wanaki, "he lies," or "he lives in peace."

Wauneta; village in Chase County, Nebraska. Indian word, meaning "winter camp."

Waupaca; county in Wisconsin, named for the Menominee Indians, the meaning being " pale water." Wauponsee; town in Grundy County, Illinois. For derivation see Wabaunsee.

Waupun; town in Fond du lac County, Wisconsin. Indian word, meaning "early, or early day," or, according to another authority, from waba, meaning "east."

Wauregan; village in Windham County, Connecticut. Indian word, meaning "a good thing."

Wausau; city in Wisconsin. Corruption of wassa, meaning "faraway."

Wausaukee; river in Wisconsin. Indian word, meaning "distant land."

Wauseon; village in Fulton County, Ohio, named for an Indian chief.

Wauwatosa; city in Wisconsin. Corruption of wewatessi, meaning "firefly."

Wauzeka; village in Crawford County, Wisconsin, named for an Indian chief, the name said to mean "pine."

Waverly; village in Pike County, Ohio, named for Scott's novels.

Wawarsing; town in Ulster County, New York. Indian word, meaning " blackbird's nest."

Wawayanda; town in Orange County, New York. Said to be the Indian corruption of the English phrase "away over yonder."

Waxhaw; creek in North and South Carolina, towns in Union County, North Carolina, and Lancaster County, South Carolina, named for an Indian tribe.

Wayland; town in Middlesex County, Massachusetts, named for Francis Wayland.

"Wayland; village in Steuben County, New York, named for Rey. Francis Wayland, of Rhode Island.

Waymansville; village in Bartholomew County, Indiana, named for Charles L. Wayman, its founder.

Wayne; counties in Georgia, Illinois, Indiana, Iowa, Kentucky, Michigan, Mississippi, Missouri, New York, North Carolina, Ohio, Pennsylvania, Tennessee, and West Virginia, and probably the counties of the same name in Nebraska and Utah;

Waynesboro; borough in Franklin County, Pennsylvania, and towns in Wayne County, Mississippi, and Burke County, Georgia; Waynesburg; borough in Greene County, Pennsylvania, and town in Stark County, Ohio; Waynesfield; town in Auglaize County, Ohio; Waynesville; towns in Haywood County, North Carolina, and Warren County, Ohio. Named for Gen. Anthony Wayne, hero of the Revolution.

Wayzata; village in Hennepin County, Minnesota. Indian word, meaning " at the mouth."

Weakley; county in Tennessee, named for Robert Weakley, member of the House of Representatives and the reviser of the constitution of Tennessee.

Weare; town in Hillsboro County, New Hampshire, named for Meshech Weare, chief justice of the province of New Hampshire.

Weatherford; city in Parker County, Texas, said to be named for Jefferson Weatherford, one of its early settlers.

Weatogue; village in Hartford County, Connecticut. Indian word, meaning "wigwam place."

Weauatucket; river in Connecticut. Indian, "land at the end of tide water."

Weaverville; town in Trinity County, California, named for a pioneer.

Weaverville; town in Buncombe County, North Carolina, named for a family numerous in the State.

Webb; county in Texas, named for Judge James Webb, politician in the early days of the State.

Webberville; village in Ingham County, Michigan, named for Herbert Webber, an early settler. .

Weber; county and river in Utah, named for a well-known trapper and guide.

Webster; counties in Georgia, Iowa, Kentucky, Mississippi, Missouri, and West Virginia, parish in Louisiana, and probably the county of the same name in Nebraska, towns in Merrimack County, New Hampshire, and Worcester County, Massachusetts, and mountain in New Hampshire; Webster Groves; city in St. Louis County, Missouri. Named for Daniel Webster, the statesman.

Wecuppemee; river in Connecticut. Indian word, meaning "the linden or basswood."

Wedge; mountain in Montana, so named on account of its shape.

Weedsport; village in Cayuga County, New York, named for Elisha and Edward Weed, first settlers.

Weehawken; town in Hudson County, New Jersey. Indian word, meaning "maize land."

Weeping Water; river in Nebraska. Translation of the Indian word "Nehaga."

Weir; city in Cherokee County, Kansas, named for T. M. Weir, its founder.

Weisner; mountain in Idaho, named for a topographer with the Mullan expedition.

Weissport; borough in Carbon County, Pennsylvania, named for Col. Jacob Weiss, officer of the Revolution, who early settled in the Lehigh Valley.

Weitchpec; town in Humboldt County, California, named for an Indian tribe, the word said to mean "the junction of rivers."

Welaka; town in Putnam County, Florida. Indian word, meaning " river of lakes."

Welch; town in McDowell County, West Virginia, named for Capt. J. A. Welch, of the county.

Weld; county in Colorado, named for Lewis Ledyard Weld, first secretary of Colorado Territory.

Weld; town in Franklin County, Maine, named for Benjamin Weld, one of the original owners.

Weldon; town in Halifax County, North Carolina, named for a resident family.

Wellfleet; town in Barnstable County, Massachusetts. The name doubtless a corruption of "whale fleet."

Wellington; city in Sumner County, Kansas, named for the Duke of Wellington.

Wells; county in Indiana, named for Capt. William Wells, killed at the Fort Dearborn massacre.

Wells; town in York County, Maine, supposed to be named for the town in England.

Wells; town in Hamilton County, New York, named for Joshua Wells, the first settler.

Wells; county in North Dakota, named for the Hon. E. P. Wells, of Jamestown, an old settler.

Wellsboro; borough in Tioga County, Pennsylvania, named for Mrs. Henry Wells Morris, an early resident.

Wellsburg; town in Chemung County, New York, named for a family who formerly owned most of the town site.

Wellsburg; city in Brooke County, West Virginia, named for Alexander Wells.

Wells River; village in Orange County, Vermont, named for the stream which received its named from Captain Wells, who was drowned in it.

Wellsville; city in Franklin County, Kansas, named for D. L. Wells, a railroad contractor.

Wellsville; city in Columbiana County, Ohio, named for William Wells, who laid it out.

Wendell; town in Franklin County, Massachusetts, named for Oliver Wendell, a Boston banker.

Wenham; town in Essex County, Massachusetts, named for the town in England.

Wenona; city in Marshall County, Illinois; Wenonah; borough in Gloucester County, New Jersey. Derived from the Indian, meaning "first-born daughter."

Wentworth; town in Grafton County, New Hampshire, named for Benning Wentworth, former governor of the State.

Wentzville; town in St. Charles County, Missouri, named for the man who laid it out.

Wepatuck; mountain in Connecticut. Indian word, meaning "place at the narrow pass or strait." Wesaw; river in Miami County, Indiana, named for an Indian chief.

Wesley; towns and township in Washington counties, Ohio and Maine, named for John Wesley, the founder of Methodism.

Wesson; town in Copiah County, Michigan, named for Col. J. M. Wesson, its founder.

West Baton Rouge; parish in Louisiana. See Baton Rouge.

West Bend; city in Washington County, Wisconsin, so named because of the bend in Milwaukee River at this point.

Westboro; town in Worcester County, Massachusetts, formerly a part of Marlboro, hence its name.

Westby; village in Vernon County, Wisconsin, named for O. T. Westby, an early settler.

West Carroll; parish in Louisiana, named for Charles Carroll of Carrollton.

Westchester; county in New York, named for the town in England.

West Creek; town in Ocean County, New Jersey. Derived from an Indian word, meaning "place to get meat or eatables."

Westerlo; town in Albany County, New York, named for Rev. Eilardus Westerlo, of Albany.

West Feliciana; parish in Louisiana. See East Feliciana.

Westfield; town in Hampden County, Massachusetts, so named because situated on the west boundary of an early survey.

Westhampton; town in Hampshire County, Massachusetts, so named because, until its incorporation, it was the west parish of Northampton.

West Haverstraw; town in Rockland County, New York, named from haverstraw, a Dutch word originally written haverstroo and meaning "oat straw." Believed to have been suggested by wild oats growing there.

Westminster; town in Worcester County, Massachusetts, named from the borough of London.

Westmoreland; counties in Pennsylvania and Virginia, named for the county in England. Town in Pottawatomie County, Kansas, named for the county in Pennsylvania.

Weston; town in Middlesex County, Massachusetts, and city in Platte County, Missouri, so named because situated at the western edge of their respective counties.

Westphalia; village in Clinton County, Michigan, named for the province in Germany.

Westport; town in Clatsop County, Oregon, named for John West.

West Station; town in Holmes County, Mississippi, named for A. M. West, prominent citizen and president of Mississippi Central Railroad.

Westville; town in Simpson County, Mississippi, named for Col. Cato West.

Westville; town in Chariton County, Missouri, named for Dr. William S. West, the first postmaster.

Westville; town in Kershaw County, South Carolina, named for a prominent family.

Wet; mountains in Colorado, so named because of the heavy rains upon them in the summer season.

Wetmore; city in Nemaha County, Kansas, named for W. T. Wetmore, vice-president of the Central Branch Union Pacific.

Wetumka; city in Elmore County, Alabama, near the falls of the Coosa River. Indian word, meaning "waterfall," "tumbling water."

Wetzel; county in West Virginia, named for Lewis Wetzel, a noted pioneer and Indian fighter.

Wewoka; stream and village in Seminole Nation, Indian Territory. Indian word, meaning "barking water."

Wexford; county and town in Michigan, probably named for the county in Ireland.

Weyauwega; village in Waupaca County, Wisconsin. Probably a corruption of the Indian word ouiawikan, "he embodies it," but according to another authority the name of a trusted Indian guide in the employ of Governor Doty, the name meaning "whirling wind."

Weyers Cave; town and cavern in Augusta County, Virginia, named for Bernard Weyer.

Weymouth; town in Norfolk County, Massachusetts, named for the town in England.

Wharton; county and town in Texas, named for William H. and John A. Wharton, of a family prominent in the State.

Whatcom; county and town in Washington. Indian word, meaning "noisy water."

Whately; town in Franklin County, Massachusetts, named for Thomas Whately, member of the board of trade.

Wheatland; borough in Mercer County, Pennsylvania, named for the estate of the Hon. James Buchanan.

Wheeler; mountain in Nevada, named for Capt. George M. Wheeler.

Wheeler; town in Steuben County, New York, named for Capt. Silas Wheeler, the first settler.

Wheeler; county in Oregon, named for H. H. Wheeler, first mail carrier between The Dalles and Canyon City.

Wheeler; county in Texas, named for Royal T. Wheeler, former chief justice of the State supreme court.

Wheeling; city in West Virginia, so named because the Indians placed the head of a white victim on a pole and gave the place the name weal-ink, "a place of a human head." The present name of the place is a corruption of the Indian name.

Wheeling; village in Livingston County, Missouri, named for the above.

Wheelock; town in Caledonia County, Vermont, named for Eleazer Wheelock, president of an Indian charity school situated there, but another authority states that it was named for John Wheelock.

Whippany; river in Morris County, New Jersey. Indian word, meaning "arrow stream."

Whipple; peak in the Monument range, California, named for Lieutenant Whipple of the Pacific railroad explorations.

Whiskah; river of Gray's harbor, Washington. Indian word, meaning "stinking water."

Whitakers; town in Edgecombe County, North Carolina, named for a family numerous in the State.

White; county in Arkansas, named for the river which forms the eastern boundary.

White; branch of the Green River in Colorado and eastern Utah, so named because of the white cliffs of its canyon.

White; county in Georgia, named for the Rev. George White.

White; county in Illinois, named for Leonard White, an early settler.

White; county in Indiana, named for Isaac White, of Illinois.

White; rivers in Indiana and South Dakota. Translation of the name originally given them by the French, Riviere la Blanche.

White; city in Morris County, Kansas, named for F. C. White, superintendent of the Union Pacific Southern branch.

White; river in Minnesota, so named because of the color of the water.

White; river in Nebraska, so named because the soil near its head is white clay.

White; county in Tennessee, named for Hugh L. White, a pioneer settler of Knoxville.

307

White Bluffs; town in Dickson County, Tennessee, named for the White Bluff Iron Forge, which was formerly in operation near the present town site.

White Castle; town in Iberville Parish, Louisiana, named for the large white plantation house, visible from the river.

White Cloud; towns in Mills County, Iowa, and Doniphan County, Kansas, named for the Indian chief Ma-hush-kah.

White Creek; town in Washington County, New York, named for the creek whose bed is formed of white quartzy pebbles.

White Deer; creek in Union County, Pennsylvania. Translation of its Indian name, Woaptuchanne.

Whitefield; towns in Coos County, New Hampshire, and Lincoln County, Maine, named for the Rev. George Whitefield.

Whitehall; town in Bladen County, North Carolina, named for an old resident.

White Haven; borough in Luzerne County, Pennsylvania, named for Josiah White.

White Pigeon; village in St. Joseph County, Michigan, named for an Indian chief.

White Pine; county in Nevada, so named because of the trees of this species growing there.

White Plains; village in Westchester County, New York, so named because located near the limestone debris of the valley of the Bronx.

Whitesboro; village in Oneida County, New York, named for Judge Hugh White, the pioneer settler of the county.

Whitesburg; town in Letcher County, Kentucky, named for C. White, member of the State legislature at the time of the formation of the town.

Whiteside; county in Illinois, named for Capt. Samuel Whitesides, captain in the war of 1812.

Whitestown; town in Oneida County, New York, named for Judge Hugh White, pioneer settler of the county.

White Sulphur Springs; town in Meagher County, Montana, named for the medicinal springs located in the vicinity.

Whitesville; village in Jefferson County, New York, named for Thomas White, one of the first settlers.

Whiteville; town in Columbus County, North Carolina, named for James B. White, first member of the State assembly.

Whitewater; river and town in Wayne County, Indiana, so named because of the whitish cast of the waters of the river.

Whitfield; county in Georgia, named for George Whitfield, a missionary.

Whiting; town in Monona County, Iowa, named for Senator Whiting.

Whiting; town in Jackson County, Kansas, named for Mrs. Whiting, wife of Senator C. S. Pomeroy.

Whiting; town in Addison County, Vermont, so named because 3 of the 48 proprietors bore that name; another authority states that it is named for John Whitney, of Massachusetts.

Whitingham; town in Windham County, Vermont, named for Nathan Whiting, one of the grantees.

Whitley; counties in Kentucky and Indiana, named for Col. William Whitley.

Whitman; county, town, and college in Washington, named for Dr. Marcus Whitman, an early missionary.

Whitmires; town in Newberry County, South Carolina, named for the Whitmire family.

Whitney; loftiest peak of the Sierra Nevadas, named for Prof. J. D. Whitney, State geologist of California.

Whitney; peak in Colorado, named for W. D. Whitney, the philologist.

Whitney Point; town in Broome County, New York, named in 1824 for Thomas Whitney, first postmaster.

Whitneyville; village in New Haven County, Connecticut, named for Eli Whitney, its founder.

Wichita; counties in Kansas and Kentucky; city in Sedgwick County, Kansas; river in Texas; Wichita Falls; town in Wichita County, Texas. Named for an Indian tribe, the name meaning "white man."

Wickenburg; town in Maricopa County, Arizona, named for Henry Wickenburg, a pioneer.

Wickliffe; town in Ballard County, Kentucky, named for a prominent family of the State.

Wicomico; county and river in Maryland. Indian word, meaning "where houses are building." Wiconisco; stream and a village in Dauphin County, Pennsylvania. Indian word, meaning "wet and muddy."

Wicopee; mountain in New York. Indian word, meaning "long hill."

Wilbarger; county in Texas, named for Josiah and Mathias Wilbarger, early settlers.

Wilber; village in Saline County, Nebraska, named for C. D. Wilber, who laid it out.

Wilbraham; town in Hampden County, Massachusetts, supposed to have been named for a family of that name from England.

Wilcox; county in Alabama, named for Lieut. Joseph M. Wilcox.

Wilcox; county in Georgia, named for Capt. John Wilcox.

Wilcox; township in Newaygo County, Michigan, named for S. N. Wilcox.

Wilcox; village in Elk County, Pennsylvania, named for A. I. Wilcox.

Wild Rice; stream in Minnesota, so named because this plant grows abundantly upon its banks.

Wilkes; counties in Georgia and North Carolina, named for John Wilkes, member of British Parliament.

Wilkes-Barre; city in Luzerne County, Pennsylvania, named for two members of the British Parliament, American sympathizers, John Wilkes and Colonel Barre.

Wilkesboro; town in Wilkes County, North Carolina, named for John Wilkes member of the British Parliament and American sympathizer.

Wilkin; county in Minnesota, named for Alexander Wilkin, second secretary of the Territory.

Wilkinsburg; town in Allegheny County, Pennsylvania, named for William Wilkins, Secretary of War under President Tyler.

Wilkinson; counties in Georgia and Mississippi, named for Gen. James Wilkinson, of Maryland.

Will; county in Illinois, named for Dr. Conrad Will, many years member of the State legislature.

Willamette; river in Oregon. Indian word said to have originally been Wallamet, derived from the same root as Walla Walla and Wallula; when applied to water, meaning "running." Another authority gives its definition as "the long and beautiful river."

Willey; peak in the White Mountains, New Hampshire, named for the Willey family, who were killed in an avalanche in 1826.

Williams; river and mountain in Arizona, named for one of the guides of the Fremont expedition.

Williams; creek in Humboldt County, California, named for an early settler.

Williams; town in Colusa County, California, named for its founder.

Williams; county in North Dakota, named for Hon. E. A. Williams, one of the Territorial pioneers and prominent in the political life of the State.

Williams; county in Ohio, named for David Williams, one of the captors of Major Andre.

Williams; river in Vermont, named for the Rev. John Williams.

Williamsburg; town in Iowa County, Iowa, named for an early settler.

Williamsburg; town in Piscataquis County, Maine, named for William Dood, of Boston, an early settler.

Williamsburg; town in Hampshire County, Massachusetts, named for a family resident of the neighborhood.

Williamsburg; village in Clermont County, Ohio, named for Gen. William Lytle, its founder.

Williamsburg; county in South Carolina and city in James City County, Virginia, named for William III., of England.

Williamson; counties in Illinois and Tennessee, named for General Williamson.

Williamson; town in Wayne County, New York, named for Charles Williamson, first agent of the Pulteney estate.

Williamson; river in Oregon, named for Lieut. R. S. Williamson, an early explorer of that part of the country.

Williamson; county in Texas, named for Judge Robert Williamson, last of the alcaldes of Texas.

Williamsport; city in Indiana, said to be named for James D. Williams, former governor.

Williamsport; city in Pennsylvania, named for William Hepburn, one of the first associate judges of the county of Lycoming.

Williamston; town in Martin County, North Carolina, named for a family numerous in the State.

Williamston; town in Anderson County, South Carolina, named for the family of Col. James Williams, officer of the Revolution.

Williamstown; town in Grant County, Kentucky, named for William Arnold, probably the first settler.

Williamstown; town in Orange County, Vermont, named for the town of the same name in Berkshire County, Massachusetts, which was named for Col. Ephraim Williams, the founder of Williams College.

Williamsville; city in Wayne County, Missouri, named for Asa E. Williams, who laid it out.

Williamsville; village in Erie County, New York, named for Jonas Williams, early settler.

Willimantic; river, and a city in Windham County, Connecticut. Indian word, meaning a "good lookout," or, according to another authority, "good cedar swamps."

Willis; city in Brown County, Kansas, named for Martin Cleveland Willis, an early settler.

Williston; town in Williams County, North Dakota, named for Associate Justice Lorenzo P. Williston.

Williston; town in Barnwell County, South Carolina, named for the Willis family, prominent residents of the vicinity.

Williston; town in Chittenden County, Vermont, named for Samuel Willis, one of the grantees.

Willoughby; village in Lake County, Ohio, named for Professor Willoughby of New York.

Wilmette; village in Cook County, Illinois, named for Quilmette Indian half-breed.

Wilmington; city in Delaware, the present name a corruption of the name Willington, given it in honor of Thomas Willing.

Wilmington; towns in Middlesex County, Massachusetts; New Hanover County, North Carolina, and Windham County, Vermont, named for Spencer Compton, Earl of Wilmington.

Wilmot; town in Merrimack County, New Hampshire, named for Dr. Wilmot, an Englishman.

Wilna; town in Jefferson County, New York, named for the town in Russia.

Wilpiquin; stream in Maryland, so called because the Nanticokes carried the skulls and bones of the dead and buried them in the caverns. Indian word, meaning "the place of interring skulls."

Wilson; mountains in Colorado and Utah, named for A. D. Wilson, topographer.

Wilson; county and town in Ellsworth County, Kansas, named for Hiero T. Wilson, merchant of Fort Scott.

Wilson; village in Niagara County, New York, named for Reuben Wilson, an early settler.

Wilson; county and town in same county in North Carolina, named for Louis D. Wilson, State senator and officer of Mexican war.

Wilson; county in Tennessee, named for Maj. David Wilson.

Wilson; county in Texas, named for James C. Wilson.

Wilson; point in Washington, named for Capt. George Wilson of the British navy.

Wilton; town in Hillsboro County, New Hampshire, named for the town in England.

Winamac; town in Pulaski County, Indiana. Indian word, meaning "catfish."

Winchendon; town in Worcester County, Massachusetts, named for the estate in England to which Governor Francis Bernard was heir.

Winchester; city in Frederick County, Virginia, named for the town in England.

Wind Gap; borough in Northampton County, Pennsylvania, which takes its name from the gap in the Blue Mountains, the first below the Delaware water gap.

Windham; town and county in Connecticut, for which the county of the same name in Vermont and the village in Portage County, Ohio, were named, itself being named for a town in England.

Windham Center; town in Cumberland County, Maine, named for the earls of Egremont.

Windom; village in Cottonwood County, Minnesota, and town in McPherson County, Kansas, named for the Hon. William Windom, member of the cabinet during the Harrison Administration.

Windsor; many places in the United States have been named, directly or indirectly, for the town in England, among them being a county in Vermont, towns in Berkshire County, Massachusetts, Broome County, New York, and Kennebec County, Maine.

Winfield; town in Cowley County, Kansas, named for the Rev. Winfield Scott, of Leavenworth.

Winfield; town in Herkimer County, New York, named for Gen. Winfield Scott.

Wingohocking; south branch of Frankford Creek, Pennsylvania. Indian word, meaning " a favorite spot for planting.

Winhall; town in Bennington County, Vermont, named for its two proprietors, Winn and Hall.

Winkler; county in Texas, named for C. M. Winkler, judge of the State court of appeals.

Winn; parish in Louisiana, named for Gen. Richard Winn, noted lawyer of the State.

Winnebago; counties in Illinois, Iowa, and Wisconsin, and village in Faribault County, Minnesota, named for a tribe of Indians, the name meaning "people of the dirty waters."

Winnebeegosish; lake in Minnesota. Indian word, meaning "very dirty or roily water."

Winneconne; village in Winnebago County, Wisconsin. From an Indian word, winikaning, "dirty place."

Winnegance; village in Sagadahoc County, Maine, named from a near-by river. Indian word, meaning "beautiful water."

Winnemucca; town in Humboldt County, Nevada, mountain peak, lake, and town in same State, named for a chief of the Shoshone Indians.

Winnepe; lake in Minnesota. Indian word, meaning "place of dirty water."

Winnepesaukee; lake in New Hampshire. Indian word, meaning "good water discharge."

Winneshiek; county in Iowa, named for an Indian chief.

Winnetka; village in Cook County, Illinois. Indian word, meaning "beautiful place." Winnsboro; city in Fairfield County, South Carolina, named for Gen. Richard Winn, its founder.

Winona; city and county in Minnesota, and town in Montgomery County, Mississippi. Indian word, meaning "first-born daughter."

Winslow; town in Kennebec County, Maine, named for Gen. John Winslow.

Winston; county in Alabama, named for John A. Winston, former governor of the State.

Winston; county in Mississippi, named for Col. Louis Winston.

Winston; city in Forsyth County, North Carolina, named for Joseph Winston, soldier of the Revolution.

Winthrop; towns in Kennebec County, Maine, and Suffolk County, Massachusetts, named for the Winthrop family, whose founder in America was John Winthrop, governor of the Massachusetts colony in 1629.

Winton; town in Hertford County, North Carolina, named for a member of Congress.

Winyah; bay in Georgetown County, South Carolina. Corrupted name of the tribe of Wiriyaw Indians.

Wirt; county in West Virginia, named for William Wirt, Attorney-General of the United States during the Monroe Administration.

Wisacky; town in Sumter County, South Carolina. Corruption of the name of the Waxhaw Indians.

Wiscasset; town in Lincoln County, Maine. Indian word, meaning "place of the yellow pine."

Wisconk; river in New Jersey. Indian word, meaning "the elbow."

Wisconsin; State of the Union, and important river. Indian word, meaning "wild, rushing river."

Wiscoy; village in Allegany County, and stream in Wyoming County, New York. Indian word, meaning "under the banks," or, according to another authority, "many fall creek."

Wise; counties in Virginia and Texas, named for Henry A. Wise, prominent politician of the former State.

Wissahickon; creek in Montgomery County, Pennsylvania. Indian word, meaning "catfish stream."

Wissinoming; north branch of Frankford Creek, Pennsylvania. Indian word, meaning "where we were frightened."

Witakantu; lake in Minnesota. Indian word, meaning "high islands."

Withlacoochee; river and town in Hernando County, Florida. Indian word, meaning "little river," or, according to another authority, "long, narrow river."

Wiwoka; tributary of the Coosa River, Alabama. Indian word, meaning "roaring water."

Woburn; city in Middlesex County, Massachusetts, named for the town in England.

Wolcott; town in New Haven County, Connecticut, named for Frederick Wolcott.

Wolcott; town in Wayne County, New York; Wolcottville; village in Litchfield County, Connecticut. Named for Oliver Wolcott, Secretary of the Treasury during the administrations of Washington and Adams.

Wolf; river in Kansas. Translation of the French name, riviere de Loup.

Wolf; rapids in the Yellowstone, Montana, so named by Clarke because a wolf was seen there.

Wolf; stream in Pennsylvania. From the Indian word, Tummeink, "where there is a wolf."

Wolfe; county in Kentucky, named for Nathaniel Wolfe, member of the State legislature.

Wolfeboro; town in Carroll County, New Hampshire, named for General Wolfe, the hero of Quebec.

Wolhurst; station in Arapahoe County, Colorado, named for Senator Wolcott, who owns real estate there.

Wolverton; creek in California, named for a settler.

Womelsdorf; borough in Burks County, Pennsylvania, named for John Wommelsdorf, its founder.

Wonakaketuk; stream in Vermont. Indian word, meaning "river of otters."

Wonewoc; village in Juneau County, Wisconsin. Corruption of the Indian word, wonowag, "they howl," meaning the wolves.

Wononsco; lake in Litchfield County, Connecticut. From an Indian word, meaning "bend of the pond land."

Wood; county in Ohio, named for Col. Eleazer D. Wood, distinguished at the battle of Niagara.

Wood; county in Texas, named for George T. Wood, former governor.

Wood; county in West Virginia, named for James Wood, an early governor of Virginia.

Wood; county in Wisconsin, named for Joseph Wood, member of the legislature creating the county.

Woodbridge; village in Hillsdale County, Michigan, named for William Woodbridge, secretary of Michigan Territory.

Woodbridge; town in Bergen County, New Jersey, so named because of the wooded ridge rising from the Hackensack meadows.

Woodbury; county in Iowa, named for Levi Woodbury, of New Hampshire.

Woodbury; city in Gloucester County, New Jersey, named for an English town.

Woodbury; town in Washington County, Vermont, named for Col. Ebenezer Wood, first grantee.

Woodford; counties in Illinois and Kentucky, named for Gen. William Woodford.

Woodbull; town in Steuben County, New York, named for Gen. Nathaniel Woodhull, Revolutionary officer.

Wood River; village in Hall County, Nebraska, so named because situated on the banks of the river of that name.

Woodruff; county in Arkansas, named for William E. Woodruff, sr., a pioneer.

Woodruff; valley in Nevada, named for Capt. I. C. Woodruff.

Woodruff; town in Spartanburg County, South Carolina, named for a prominent family.

Woods; county in Oklahoma, named for Samuel Wood, of Kansas, the "s" added through a mistake of the printer.

Woodsfield; village in Monroe County, Ohio, named for Archibald Woods, of Wheeling, West Virginia.

Woodson; county in Kansas, named for Daniel Woodson, former secretary of the Territory of Kansas.

Woodsonville; village in Hart County, Kentucky, named for Senator Thomas Woodson.

Woodstock; town in Windham County, Connecticut, originally in Massachusetts, named for the town in England.

Woodstown; borough in Salem County, New Jersey, named for a resident family.

Woodville; village in Jefferson County, New York, named for Ebenezer, Ephraim, and Jacob Wood, first settlers.

Woolwich; town in Sagadahoc County, Maine, named for the military depot in England.

Woonsocket; cities in Providence County, Rhode Island, and Sanborn County, South Dakota. From the Indian word, meaning "at the place of mist."

Wooster; city in Wayne County, Ohio, named for Gen. David Wooster, officer of the Revolution.

Worcester; county in Maryland, named for the Earl of Worcester, who married a Calvert of Maryland.

Worcester; county and city in Massachusetts, named for the county in England.

Worth; counties in Georgia, Missouri, and Iowa, and town in Jefferson County, New York, named for Gen. W. J. Worth, an office in the Mexican war.

Worthington; town in Hampshire County, Massachusetts, named for Col. John Worthington, proprietor.

Worthington; village in Nobles County, Minnesota, for which the tow n in Greene County, Indiana, was named, the former named for the Worthington family of Ohio.

Worthville; town in Jefferson County, New York, named for Gen. William J. Worth, an officer of the Mexican war.

Worthville; town in Randolph County, North Carolina, named for Governor Jonathan Worth and State Treasurer J. M. Worth.

Wray; town in Yuma County, Colorado, named for John Wray, foreman for I. P. Olive.

Wrentham; town in Norfolk County, Massachusetts, named for a town in England.

Wright; counties in Iowa, Minnesota, and Missouri, and town in Schoharie County, New York, named for the Hon. Silas Wright.

Wright City; village in Warren County, Missouri, named for Dr. H. C. Wright, an early settler.

Wrightsboro; town in McDuffie County, Georgia, named for Judge Augustus R. Wright.

Wrightson; mountain in Arizona, named for the manager of the Salero Company.

Wrightstown; village in Brown County, Wisconsin, named for H. 8. Wright, who early established a ferry there.

Wrightsville; borough in York County, Pennsylvania, named for Samuel Wright, an early settler.

Wrightsville Beach; town in New Hanover County, North Carolina, named for a family of Wilmington.

Wrightville; town in Dunklin County, Missouri, named for the Wright brothers, its founders.

Wurtsboro; village in Sullivan County, New York, named for Maurice Wurtz.

Wyalusing; borough and stream in Bradford County, Pennsylvania. From the Indian, meaning either "the place of the hoary veteran," or "the beautiful hunting grounds."

Wyandot; county in Ohio; Wyandotte; city in Wayne County, Michigan; county in Kansas, and nation in Indian Territory. Named for the Wyandot Indian tribe.

Wyanet; village in Bureau County, Illinois. Indian word, meaning "beautiful."

Wyncoops; town in Chemung County, New York, named for William Wyncoop, an early settler.

Wynooche; river in Washington, so named because of the sudden changing of its bed; Indian word, meaning "shifting."

Wyoming; State of the Union. Indian word, meaning "large plain."

Wyoming; counties in New York and West Virginia, named for the valley in Pennsylvania, whose name was corrupted from an Indian word, meaning "large or extensive plains or meadows;" another authority favors "within a habitation," referring to the enclosure effected by the valley.

Wysox; tributary of the Susquehanna. Indian word, meaning "the place of grapes."

Wythe; county in Virginia; Wytheville; town in Wythe County, Virginia. Named for George Wythe, one of the signers of the Declaration of Independence.

X

Xenia; city in Green County, Ohio; Greek word, meaning "friendly hospitality."

Y

Yadkin; county in North Carolina, said to be named for a tribe of Indians, though some authorities favor the idea that it was named for an early settler.

Yager; creek in Humboldt County, California; Yagerville; town in Humboldt County, California. Named for an early settler.

Yahara; tributary of Rock River, Wisconsin. Indian word, meaning "catfish river."

Yakima; county, city, and river in Washington, said to have been named for a tribe of Indians, the name meaning "black bear," or, according to other authorities, "coward."

Yale; university in New Haven, Connecticut, named for Elisha Yale, of London, which gives name to many places in the United States, among them the village in St. Clair County, Michigan, and the mountain in Colorado.

Yalobusha; county in Mississippi. Indian word, meaning "tadpole place."

Yamhill; county, and river in Oregon, named for the Yamil Indians, a tribe of the Kalapooian family.

Yancey; county in North Carolina, named for Bartlett Yancey, prominent politician of the State.

Yankee; this name, with various suffixes, forms the name of many places in the United States. The name is said to be the Indian pronunciation of the word "English," and bestowed upon the inhabitants of New England by the people of Virginia when they refused to aid them in a war with the Cherokees, it meaning to them "cowards." After the battle of Bunker Hill, the people of New England having established a reputation for bravery, accepted the name and gloried in it.

Yankton; county and city in South Dakota. Corruption of Yanktonnais, the name of an Indian tribe.

Yantic; river in Connecticut. Indian word, meaning "extending to the tidal river." Yaquina; bay and town in Lincoln County, Oregon, probably named for Yaquina, a female Indian chief.

Yardley; borough in Bucks County, Pennsylvania, named for a family of early settlers.

Yarmouth; town in Barnstable County, Massachusetts, named for a seaport town of England.

Yates; county in New York, named for Joseph C. Yates, early governor of the State.

Yates Center; town in Woodson County, Kansas, named for Abner Yates, former owner.

Yazoo; county and river in Mississippi, named for a tribe of Indians, the name said to mean "to blow on an instrument."

Yell; county in Arkansas, named for Col. Archibald Yell, former governor of the State.

Yellow Jacket; pass in Colorado, so named because infested with these insects.

Yellow Medicine; county and river in Minnesota. From the Indian word, Pajutazee, "yellow root," probably meaning a root used by them medicinally.

Yellowstone; river in Montana and Wyoming. Name derived from its original French name, Roche jaune, meaning "yellow rock or stone," though by some said to be from the Indian, mi-tsi-a-da-zi, "rock yellow river."

Yellville; town in Marion County, Arkansas, named for Col. Archibald Yell, former governor of the State.

Yemassee; village in Hampton County, South Carolina, named for a tribe of the Shawnee Indians, the word meaning "mild, gentle, peaceable."

Yoakum; town in Dewitt County, Texas, named for a man who was instrumental in building up the town.

Yolo; county in California. From the Indian, meaning "place abounding with rushes," or, according to another authority, "possession of royal blood."

Yonkers; city in New York, named for a manor house built by the Dutch, the word meaning" young lord," and first applied in this country to Adrien Van der Douck, a patentee.

York; county and town in Maine, named for the Duke of York, James H, of England.

York; counties in Pennsylvania, South Carolina, and Virginia; Yorktown; town in York County, Virginia. Named for the county in England.

Yosemite; valley in California, probably named for a small tribe of Indians formerly living in the vicinity, the name meaning "grizzly bear."

Youghiogheny; river in Maryland and Pennsylvania. Indian word, meaning "stream flowing in an opposite direction."

Young; county in Texas, named for William Cooke Young.

Youngs; bay and river in Washington, named for Sir Charles Young, of the royal navy.

Youngstown; village in Niagara County, New York, named for John Young, a merchant of the place.

Youngstown; city in Ohio, named for John Young, an early resident.

Youngsville; town in Franklin County, North Carolina, named for a prominent family.

Yount; peak in the Yellowstone Park, named for Harry Yount, early hunter and guide.

Ypsilanti; city in Michigan, named for a Greek prince.

Yreka; town in Siskiyou County, California, named for an Indian tribe. Also said to be a corruption of Weikah, "whiteness," the Indian name for Mount Shasta.

Yuba; river and county in California. Derived from the original Spanish name of the river, el Rio de las Uvas, "the river of the grapes."

Yuma; counties in Arizona and Colorado, city in Arizona and town in Colorado, named for an Indian tribe, the name meaning "sons of the river."

Z

Zanesfield; village in Logan County, Ohio, named for Col. Isaac Zane.

Zanesville; city in Ohio, named for Ebenezer Zane, who, with John McIntire, founded the city.

Zapata; county in Texas, named for a Mexican colonel who led a force of Mexicans and Texans against Mexico in 1839.

Zavalla; county in Texas, named for. Gen. Lorenzo de Zavala, a Mexican who espoused the cause of Texas's independence and was vice-president of the Republic.

Zebulon; town in Pike County, Georgia, named for Col. Zebulon M. Pike.

Zionsville; town in Boone County, Indiana, named for William Zion, a pioneer.

Zuni; river in New Mexico, named for an Indian tribe, the name said to mean "they live in mud houses;" another authority favors " the people of the long nails."

Zwingle; village in Jackson County, Iowa, named for Ulrich Zwingle, a Swiss reformer.

www.ingramcontent.com/pod-product-compliance
Lightning Source LLC
Chambersburg PA
CBHW081406270326
41931CB00016B/3392